At Home Abroad

A book in the series
Cornell Studies in Political Economy

A series edited by
Peter J. Katzenstein

A full list of titles may be found after the index.

ALSO BY HENRY R. NAU

Trade and Security: U.S. Policies at Cross-Purposes. Washington: American
Enterprise Institute Press, 1995.

The Myth of America's Decline: Leading the World Economy into the 1990s.
New York: Oxford University Press, 1990.

Domestic Trade Politics and the Uruguay Round. New York: Columbia
University Press, 1989. Editor and Contributor.

Technology Transfer and U.S. Foreign Policy. New York: Praeger, 1976.

*National Politics and International Technology: Nuclear Reactor Development
in Western Europe.* Baltimore: Johns Hopkins University Press, 1974.

At Home Abroad

*Identity and Power
in American
Foreign Policy*

HENRY R. NAU

A Century Foundation Book
Cornell University Press
ITHACA AND LONDON

Copyright © 2002 by The Century Foundation, Inc.

First published 2002 by Cornell University Press

Printed in the United States of America

Nau, Henry R.
    At home abroad : identity and power in American foreign policy / Henry R. Nau.
        p. cm. – (Cornell studies in political economy)
    Includes bibliographical references (p.) and index.
    ISBN 0-8014-3931-0 (cloth : alk. paper)
    1. United States–Foreign relations–1989- . 2. United States–Foreign relations–1989- .–Philosophy. 3. National characteristics, American–Political aspects. 4. Balance of power. 5. United States–Foreign relations–1989—Forecasting. I. Title. II. Series.
  E840 .N38 2002
  327.73–dc21

2001005555

For
My Parents, John and Johanna

Contents

Foreword

The American experience in international affairs, especially by comparative standards, has generally been a happy one. Beginning with an astonishingly successful eighteenth-century alliance with the French (who did not have much luck against the British on their own) during the War of Independence, the United States has come to view success as a routine outcome of differences and conflicts with other nations. America also has achieved a continuous increase in its importance and influence in world affairs, and it has more or less done so on its own terms. Its early dominance of the North American continent provided a large measure of insulation from the sorts of pressures generated by threatening neighbors or scarce resources. Its consistent success in terms of economic progress provided an underpinning of material well-being and war-making potential that made it both an enormously important market and extremely valuable ally. In other words, if it seems that the United States has been able, as it were, to be unusually "true to itself" in matters international, it may well be because the nation simply has had a number of advantages that made such a course possible. All this may seem obvious, but, surprisingly, it is often overlooked when explaining what are undoubtedly the exceptional characteristics of American foreign policy.

In *At Home Abroad*, Henry Nau provides an analysis of American foreign policy that is theoretically innovative and intellectually provocative, emphasizing the role of American identity in the practice of diplomacy and statecraft in the post–Cold War era. In positing national identity as a necessary part, along with power, of a cohesive model of state behavior, Nau transcends the narrow and increasingly tedious debates between realists and idealists over the role of power or ideas as determinants of global order. Interests and norms are both essential, Nau argues, as the demise of the militarily powerful but politically bankrupt Soviet Union has demonstrated so compellingly.

Henry R. Nau is professor of political science and international affairs at the Elliott School of International Affairs at the George Washington University. His previous works, including *The Myth of America's Decline* (1990) and, most recently, *Trade and Security: U.S. Policies at Cross-Purposes* (1995), reflect his deep understanding of the issues faced by the United States since the end of the Cold War. His book is part of The Century Foundation's focus on the changing character of global affairs since the Soviet decline and demise, which already has resulted in the publication of, among others, Richard Ullman's *Securing Europe,* Michael Mandelbaum's *The Dawn of Peace in Europe,* Jonathan Dean's *Ending Europe's Wars,* and David Calleo's *Rethinking Europe's Future.*

In this work, Nau offers a fresh perspective on the theory and practice of conflict, alliance politics, the promotion of democracy, and the management of economic globalization in the twenty-first century. He stresses that traditional models fail to advance the national interest with allies in Europe and Japan, among potential adversaries in Russia and Asia, and among the diverse states of Latin America, the Middle East, and Africa. He describes how a lasting partnership with mature democracies in Europe and Japan can evolve into a sense of shared destiny, which is the basis for the kind of democratic security community that makes for enduring and stable peace. He argues that states that share commitments to open markets, legal institutions, and protecting the rights of citizens will not resort to force to settle their disputes, however much their lesser interests may diverge. In this sense, the give and take of national democracy—divided powers, active debate, and the kind of freedom that allows new ideas to be tested—is replicated internationally.

Looking to the future, Nau argues that it is not enough for America to have a preponderance of traditional military and economic power in the world. The United States also must project a more comfortable self-image that recognizes the spread of American core values and the unprecedented opportunity to assist suffering and democratizing countries around the globe. His caution, however, is that a cyclical predisposition to isolationism, to the false hopes of technical supremacy, or to noble values of international cooperation that lack practicality may not allow this to happen.

Overall, *At Home Abroad* provides the basis for fresh and important ways to think about America's role in the world. On behalf of the Trustees of The Century Foundation, I welcome Nau's contribution to our understanding of American foreign policy.

RICHARD C. LEONE, President

The Century Foundation
August 2001

Preface

I began this book in 1993–94 with generous support from The Century Foundation (formerly the Twentieth Century Fund) and the Lynde and Harry Bradley Foundation. My hope was to write a study that systematically integrated the influence of values and power in American foreign policy. I had published a book in 1990, *The Myth of America's Decline,* that focused on policy purposes and ideas, not just relative power, to explain the rise and fall of great powers. That book anticipated subsequent events rather well. The demise of the Soviet Union without a sudden loss of relative military power and the revival of the United States, reversing its economic decline, reinforced the focus on national ideas that motivate the generation and use of military and economic power. As great power conflicts waned, scholars struggled to understand the influence of ideas, cultures, norms, law, and identity on state behavior.

This study benefits enormously from the resulting constructivist turn in the study of international relations. At the same time, it draws deeply from the classical and structural realist traditions. I deliberately seek to bridge the two intellectual cultures: one seeking to understand the meaning that states (human beings) ascribe to the generation and use of military and economic power, and the other defining the constraints and consequences of power for state behavior whatever meaning we attach to power. We may consider stormy weather to be good or bad. But whatever meaning we give it, stormy weather has consequences, such as causing pneumonia, that are independent of our interpretation. The same is true of relative power in international affairs. Its significance depends on whether nations see one another as friends or foes. But its consequences, such as the stronger nation having more options to act unilaterally than the weaker, do not depend on these interpretations.

The book covers the entire world, and it has been an enormous challenge to write. I had to go to school on many countries and topics that I knew only fleetingly or not at all. If I have learned something and this book succeeds, I owe it all to the many colleagues who have tutored me along the way. I begin with my George Washington University colleagues, an unusually energetic and talented group of scholars: Gordon Adams, Deborah Avant, Nathan Brown, Bruce Dickson, Robert Dunn, Maurice East, Amitai Etzioni, Harvey Feigenbaum, Martha Finnemore, Harry Harding, Jim Goldgeier, Dalia Dassa Kaye, Carl Linden, Kristin Lord, Ed McCord, Cynthia McClintock, Constantine

Menges (now at the Hudson Institute), Jim Millar, Mike Mochizuki, Ronald Palmer, Peter Reddaway, Bernie Reich, Jim Rosenau, Susan Sell, David Shambaugh, Jay Smith, Mike Sodaro, Richard Thornton, and Sharon Wolchik. Each of them either read parts of the manuscript or provided invaluable guidance to sources and ideas. Another university colleague who deserves special mention is Deborah Morse. She typed countless drafts (because she uses ten fingers; I only one) not only of this book, but also of previous books over the many years she has taken care of me.

I also drew help from numerous colleagues at other universities and institutions: Peter Andreas, Doug Bandow, Claude Barfield, Tim Borstelmann, Michael Calingaert, David Callahan, Dale Copeland, Michael Cox, Dan Deudney, Klaus Deutsch, Brewster Denny, Matt Evangelista, Aaron Friedberg, Alton Frye, Roy Ginsberg, Ernie Haas, Kim Holmes, Robert Hormats, John Ikenberry, Bruce Jentleson, Iain Johnston, Bob Keohane, Elizabeth Kier, Jun Kurihara, Hal Malmgren, Mike Mastanduno, Jonathan Mercer, Andy Moravscik, Janne Nolan, John Odell, John Owen, Lou Pauly, Robert Pastor, Dan Philpott, Robert Powell, Peter Rodman, John Ruggie, James Scott, Simon Serfaty, Randy Schweller, Anne-Marie Slaughter, Jack Snyder, Alan Tonelson, Alex Wendt, Bill Wohlforth, and Robert Zoellick.

I am grateful to individuals at The Century and Bradley Foundations who not only provided intellectual counsel and supported me financially, but showed unusual patience when medical problems delayed my work: Beverly Goldberg, Steven Greenfield, Michael Joyce, Richard C. Leone, Michelle Miller Adams, Jason Renker, and Diane Monroe Sehler. I also owe a special debt to Timothy Murray, a retinal surgeon and friend at the Bascom Palmer Eye Institute, University of Miami. He operated successfully on my left eye in 1995 when I feared I might lose my sight, a particularly frightening prospect for someone who works almost exclusively with his eyes.

I single out two colleagues who meant more to me in this enterprise than they can fully understand: Peter Katzenstein and Rob Paarlberg. They not only encouraged me at crucial moments, but shared an intellectual bond that validated my efforts to explore ideas and approaches that were sometimes out of the mainstream. At Cornell University Press, Roger Haydon taught me something I wish I had learned much earlier: how to say more with fewer words. And I have never worked with more meticulous and congenial editors than Teresa Jesionowski and Julia Nemer.

Finally, my wife, Micki (Marion), and daughter, Kimberly, suffered gamely through yet another book. I took valuable time away from them, including a leave in Florida during my daughter's senior year in high school, which I can never give back. I know they understand why I had to do it, even if my purposes were not always noble but often selfish.

I dedicate the book to my parents, John Fredrick Nau and Johanna Leonora Hasenkampf Nau. As I write this, they are alive in their ninety-first and eighty-seventh year, respectively, celebrating their sixty-third year of marriage. They are more than an inspiration. They have lived and loved in ways that will linger long after them, not just in the family but among the many individuals they touched through six decades of service in the ministry and in the university community.

HENRY R. NAU

Potomac, Maryland
August 2001

At Home Abroad

At Home Abroad

Overcoming America's Separatist Self-Image

America has never felt at home abroad. The reason is not primarily external threats to U.S. security or prosperity. Even after taking into account the terrorist attacks on September 11, 2001, America has been relatively immune throughout its history from direct attack. The reason is America's self-image— a self-image that sharply divides America from the rest of the world and portrays America as an exceptional New World society that remains suspicious and uncomfortable in the Old World society of multilateral diplomacy, entangling alliances, economic globalization, and frequent war.

This exceptional, or separatist, self-image creates intolerable tension in American foreign policy. Nationalists and neoisolationists try to limit America's involvement in the Old World. They are profoundly skeptical of the United Nations; arms control agreements; humanitarian interventions; continuing Cold War alliances with Europe and Japan; and cross-border efforts to liberalize global trade, finance, and immigration flows. They prefer to rely on national strength to defend America, including antiballistic missile defenses, and to act unilaterally or in ad hoc coalitions to battle terrorism, sanction rogue states, uphold U.S. trade laws, and protect U.S. borders and citizens abroad. Internationalists pull America in the opposite direction. They seek to engage the Old World and remake it in the image of the New. They promote strategies of democratic enlargement and economic engagement, cooperative security to control nuclear weapons and limit missile defense systems, and multilateral institutions to attack global problems of poverty, pollution, drugs, and AIDS. Realists are caught in between. They engage the Old World, like the internationalists, but do not seek to reform it, just to defend the New World, like the nationalists. They are happy to play the Old World game of balancing power. Except when a major threat exists, however, the realists generally lose out. In the short run, nationalists can always defend America more robustly without the constraints of alliances, and internationalists can always offer a more appealing rationale for the New World to be involved in the Old World, namely to transform the Old World, not just to balance and perpetuate it indefinitely. As a result, America wins wars when threats intrude, but loses the peace when threats recede. It balances in a crisis, but

1

after the crisis it goes home or designs a New World order that quickly exceeds its resources.

Given the tension created by America's self-image, U.S. foreign policy cycles between realist, internationalist, and nationalist phases. Major global threats, such as World Wars I and II and the Cold War, trigger a realist phase. The end of these threats then invites an internationalist phase. After World War I, Woodrow Wilson tried to launch the League of Nations. Toward the end of World War II, Franklin Roosevelt set up the United Nations. And after the Cold War, George H. W. Bush and Bill Clinton adopted ambitious internationalist agendas to promote the "New World Order" and "Enlargement of Democracy." Just as quickly, however, the internationalist phase exhausts America's patience and resources and brings about a nationalist phase. America retreated in the 1920s, demobilized rapidly from 1945–47, and before the events of September 11 appeared to be entering a more nationalist phase. In contrast to Bill Clinton (and to a lesser extent, his own father), George W. Bush called for a major review of American military commitments around the world, pushed a broader missile defense shield, and raised questions about existing arms control agreements, United Nations peacekeeping missions, and the division of labor with Europe and Japan in hot spots such as Kosovo and the Korean peninsula. The terrorist attacks of 2001 triggered a new realist phase.

Have the terrorist attacks now changed everything? Bush, it is argued, has abandoned nationalism in favor of internationalism. The United States has put together a global coalition to fight terrorism, including unprecedented cooperation with Russia in central Asia. Not only the Cold War but also the post–Cold War era have apparently ended. Perhaps. This book, however, sounds a note of caution. The patterns of American behavior are deeply rooted. Threat has always provoked unusual exertions and unexpected coalitions. But, just as surely, success in suppressing the threat brings ambitious goals (e.g., nation-building in Afghanistan or extended terrorist wars against Iraq, Somalia, etc.) followed by prickly impatience (e.g., with a long war or with reluctant allies). America overreaches and then retreats, committed to remake the world but unable to share the task, especially with other democratic nations.

Is America doomed to this perpetual agitation in foreign affairs? I argue that it is not. America's separatist self-image is long out of date. Much of the Old World that America shuns or seeks to reform is no longer Old. It is now New. The great industrial powers of today are all free societies, not very different fundamentally from the United States. The rich nations of Canada and western Europe have strong and mature democratic institutions, and Japan is the first Asian society in history to approach the standards of a mature industrial democracy. These nations fought each other for five hundred years and created the Old World of war and balance of power that made America so uncomfortable. Today, these nations no longer fight or even threaten one another militarily. They apply similar political values and institutions to motivate and control the use of coercive force at home and abroad. This similarity or convergence of political standards enables them to reduce, if not eliminate, the use of military power in their relations with one another and to resolve economic and other disputes by peaceful and legal means. Mature democratic states almost never go to war against one another.

This democratic community of the richest, most powerful nations in the world is totally unprecedented. It is much more novel than globalization. In fact, it is the reason globalization exists on such a massive scale. The major democratic powers promote competitive markets and the rule of law within their own societies. They pursue these same features with one another and create the hallmarks of contemporary globalization—open markets, activist nongovernmental organizations, and international institutions to resolve disputes peacefully. Democratic markets and societies then radiate outward to impact relations with democratizing and nondemocratic countries around the world. The democratic core of great power relations is just as important for understanding globalization today as the technology of the Internet and information revolution. Without this core, global markets would not have embraced the information revolution as quickly or enthusiastically as they did. Think how globalization might have developed if the Soviet Union had won the Cold War and dominated world markets.

The democratic community of major great powers is novel, to be sure, and it may not last. As power can change, so can self-image. Democracy may not be the end of history. Democratic societies can weaken, and, when they drift apart, they too may fight and shatter global markets. Nevertheless, today's community of strong (mature) democracies constitutes the safest and most hospitable space America has ever occupied in world affairs. If America were to identify more with the other mature democracies, recognizing that these countries share the same New World goals of freedom and equal rights that motivated the founding of America, America might finally sustain a presence in the world that matches its responsibilities to its resources—this country might come to feel more at home abroad.

Why is the reality of a democracy of industrial great powers discounted or trivialized in contemporary studies of American foreign policy? Traditional foreign policy perspectives do not develop this idea of national self-image and therefore cannot account for how it changes and influences national interests. Either they subordinate this idea and focus primarily on the relationship of the military and economic power of separate nations (neoisolationists and realists), or they deal with the domestic values of only one nation, such as the United States, and assume that its values apply to all nations (internationalists). None considers explicitly the national self-image of other countries and how U.S. foreign policy behavior may depend not only on the distribution of

3

relative national power among these countries, but also on the relative similarity or dissimilarity among national self-images.

In this book, I seek to close this gap. I do so by developing the idea of national self-image, or what I formally call national identity, as a separate and independent factor, along with national power, defining national interests and influencing foreign policy behavior. I then juxtapose the national identity and power of the United States and other countries to establish a structure of relative power and relative identity that constrains U.S. foreign policy. By considering identity and power simultaneously and equally, I go beyond traditional realist or national interest studies, which either treat national identity as a by-product of national power or examine relative national power as if national identities always diverge. And, by including the national identities of other countries, I add perspective to traditional internationalist studies, which too often treat national identities as universalist or collectivist rather than relative and contested. Although this book applies the identity and power approach to the analysis of U.S. foreign policy, the approach can be used to study the foreign policy of any country.

✓ What do I mean by national identity? Power and interest are concrete, but national self-image is more abstract. Does it really matter, or is it simply a rationalization of national power? It actually matters more than material power, I believe, because without a unified and healthy self-image, a nation has no incentive to accumulate or use material power. It cannot defend its national interests; indeed, it may disintegrate. Consider what happened to the Soviet Union. At one time, the communist self-image motivated the Soviet people to work and sacrifice to accumulate national power. Over later decades, however, the Soviet people lost this motivation. Soviet military power remained formidable, but the Soviet economy stagnated. Then, in December 1991, Soviet leaders and citizens decided not to use Soviet military power to preserve the Soviet state. They no longer believed that the Soviet Union was a legitimate institution to use deadly force, and the legitimacy to use military force devolved to fifteen separate republics.

The capacity to use military force *legitimately* (not just the capacity to use force) lies at the heart of national identity. In the contemporary world, the nation, through the state or central government, is the only institution that possesses this capacity. It can arrest its citizens and deprive them of their liberty and even their lives if they violate the laws of the nation. It can call on its men and women to fight and die in wars against other nations. Citizens concede this right to nations through a combination of processes, some voluntary and some coercive, some rational (ideological consensus) and some historical (ethnic, cultural, and religious affinities). However constructed, the belief that the nation may use force legitimately unites the country and creates the motivation to defend its national interests.

4

Is national identity then just another name for domestic politics? No. National identity is more than simply the sum of domestic interest group politics. To be sure, each citizen or group has its own view of the national identity, just as it has its own view of the national interest. But inside a nation, citizens do not pursue these differing views with military force. If they did, the country would not exist, and national life would be indistinguishable from international life. The disintegration of national life is exactly what happened in the United States in 1861. The country dissolved and, for four years, civil war (indistinguishable except in name from interstate war) raged across the territory of a once-united nation.

National identity goes beyond domestic politics or special interests. It is the common belief that causes all domestic groups to aggregate their views around a specific institution (e.g., the Confederacy instead of the Union, or Russia instead of the Soviet Union) and to grant that institution the capacity to use force legitimately against or on behalf of its citizens. Domestic groups care, of course, about much more than safety and whether governments can use force against them or not. They also care about prosperity, social justice, the environment, and so on. These concerns too are part of national identity. But domestic groups do not seek these other goals inside the nation through the use of force. They do not contest the national government's monopoly on the legitimate use of police or military force. This agreement, itself a part of domestic politics, precedes or underlies all the rest of domestic politics. It is not morally superior to other domestic concerns but practically superior because, without it, no other domestic concerns could be pursued peacefully.

Accordingly, national identity is the principal idea on which a nation accumulates and legitimates the use of lethal force. This idea may be a creed or ideology, as in the case of the identity of the United States. Or it may be a religious bond, as in the case of the contemporary Muslim state of Iran. We can measure the similarity or dissimilarity of these ideas, and so track relative national identities just as we track relative national power.

Defined in this way, the identities of separate nations may conflict or converge. The United States and the Soviet Union fought the Cold War as much because they pursued different national ideas to legitimate the use of force as because they pursued relative national power. Each side tried to persuade its citizens that the principles on which it based the legitimate use of force were worthy of support and sacrifice. In the end, national identities, not just the balance of power, decided the Cold War. After 1970, relative military power between the United States and the Soviet Union changed little and so explains little about the events of 1991. What changed was the relative political strength of the two countries. U.S. citizens, after troubling times in the late 1960s and 1970s, regained political confidence in their society and launched a powerful economic and military recovery. Soviet citizens, meanwhile, became increasingly disillusioned with their society, stopped sacrificing to increase military and economic power, and eventually abandoned the institutions of the Soviet Union. The competition between national identities was at least as important as the competition for national power and was probably decisive in motivating the power competition.

National identities may also converge. When they do, they create the basis of community in international affairs. As countries come to agree on the terms that legitimate the use of force, they can anticipate better when other countries are likely to use force and thus are not immediately surprised or threatened by such use. This convergence facilitates the management of the balance of power. In the first half of the nineteenth century, monarchies in Russia, Prussia, and Austria shared similar aristocratic national identities and managed a relatively peaceful balance of power known as the Concert of Europe. Today, the world's great industrial powers share similar democratic national identities and appear to eliminate the balancing of military power from their relationships altogether.

Conflict or convergence of national identities is therefore a powerful regulator of military competition among independent nations. Relative national identities can harden or soften the consequences of relative national power. And identity changes can reduce or increase threats even if there are no power changes. Military capabilities by themselves are not the threat. Who (i.e., the identity of the nation) possesses the capabilities defines the threat. France with hundreds of nuclear weapons is not a military threat to the United States; North Korea with a few nuclear weapons is.

If we compare national power to a strong wind, national identity is the weather vane that tells us in which direction this wind is blowing. National identity positions national power and thus defines threat and national interests. If national identities converge—if the weather vanes line up in the same direction—military power blows outward and military competition is not a significant factor among the converging nations. This is the case today among the major democratic powers. If national identities diverge—the weather vanes oppose one another—military competition becomes a significant factor in interstate relations. This may be the case today in U.S.-Chinese relations. In such a situation, one task of diplomacy is to balance or stabilize the military competition, as traditional national interest studies emphasize. But another task of diplomacy is to reposition the weather vanes so that the countries oppose one another at a less direct or threatening angle. In this effort, diplomacy cannot ignore or downplay the role of national identities (i.e., domestic ideologies) in order to moderate the balance of power, as national interest studies urge. Rather, diplomacy has to balance power in order to moderate opposing national identities. Balancing power is not an end in itself but a way to affect the external incentives that states face and thereby nudge their internal identities toward configurations that are less confrontational.

When we consider both identity and power, we can define four distinct spaces or contexts in which America relates to other countries (see fig. 1.2 in chap. 1 for a visual representation). The first is *hierarchy*, in which America shares similar national identities with other nations but possesses an unequal amount of power. This space defines U.S. military relations with the principal democratic allies of NATO (Canada, France, Germany, Italy, and the United Kingdom) and Japan. The second space is a confederated or republican *security community*, in which nations share similar national identities and possess roughly equal power. This space defines U.S. economic relations with the mature democracies in the Group of Seven (G-7) countries: Canada, France, Germany, Italy, the United Kingdom, and Japan. The third space is *hegemony*, in which national identities diverge and one country has disproportionate power. This space defines U.S. relations with emerging nations in Africa, the Middle East, and, to a lesser extent, Asia and Latin America (lesser because democratization and a narrowing of identity differences are further along with some countries in these regions). Finally, the fourth space is the traditional arena of *anarchy*, in which national identities diverge and nations possess roughly equal power. This space defines U.S. relations with Russia, at least in the military area, and potentially with China if China continues to grow and remain authoritarian.

In each of these spaces, the structure of power and identity imposes different constraints and opportunities on American foreign policy. There is no one set of national interests. Ideally, the United States (or any country) promotes its national interests both by pursuing power and by drawing other states toward its national identity. Converging identities safeguard national security just as surely as dominant military power. But structural pressures differ in each space and suggest different kinds of U.S. foreign policy behavior and different prospects for international institutions to achieve the national interest.

When U.S. national identity converges with that of other democracies, there are more options than traditional studies allow. Realists, who emphasize primarily the structure of power, predict a return to balance-of-power rivalries among the rich democracies, first through intensified trade competition and eventually through weakening security ties and traditional military rivalries. On the other hand, internationalists and constructivists, who emphasize primarily common institutions and collective identities, predict growing hierarchy through centralized organizations, such as NATO and a more institutionalized G-7 summit process.

In this book, which considers power and identity equally, I predict neither anarchy nor hierarchy. Rather I suggest the possibility that converging nations, especially if their identities reflect the substantive content of liberal democracies, may relate to one another through a loosely confederated, or republican, security community. In such a community, the United States increasingly coordinates its policies with other democracies, but not through centralized international institutions that may threaten democratic accountability. Rather republican configurations rely heavily on decentralized or nationally centered institutions and policy initiatives. National alternatives then compete through international processes of open markets, noninstitutionalized but vigorous multilateral diplomacy, converging regulatory standards, overlapping civil societies, complementary court systems, and intensified interparliamentary exchanges. This middle ground between the balance of power and centralized institutions manages economic competition among democratic states without triggering either renewed balance-of-power rivalries or threats to democratic control from centralized international institutions. Over time, republican configurations may evolve toward a more centralized system, as the republican system in the United States did in 1787 and then after the Civil War. But, as the U.S. Civil War and the EU's recent experience with the democratic deficit suggest, this process of centralizing institutions is neither inevitable nor easy. Today, between the United States and other rich democracies, it may also be unnecessary, as I argue in chapter 4.

In the spaces of hegemony and anarchy, where American identity diverges from that of other nations, the constraints of power and identity again act differently than predicted by conventional perspectives. In these spaces, realists predict power moving always toward a more equal distribution or equilibrium. Nations resist any one nation's monopolizing power. The United States may be dominant now, but this will not last. Other states are already clashing with the United States and, eventually, they will beat back the American empire. The world will return to a multipolar or anarchic structure. According to realists, the United States should anticipate this development and prepare for new power struggles with Russia, China, and other emerging nations. Internationalists see a different set of constraints and opportunities. They anticipate a globalizing society tied together by common problems—proliferation, pandemics, and pollution—and revolutionary information technologies. They see an opportunity to transcend traditional interstate politics and to organize global action around nongovernmental organizations (NGOs), transnational institutions, and universal principles of human rights, essentially the values and institutions of liberal democratic societies. Internationalists urge the United States to lead this global effort and bring China, Russia, and developing nations into regional and world institutions to eradicate war, oppression, ignorance, poverty, and disease.

The power and identity perspective predicts a different dynamic. Competition under hegemony and anarchy is double-tracked. It involves a tendency toward counterbalancing (under hegemony) and balancing (under anarchy), as realists predict, but it also involves interaction to influence and reposition national identities, as institutionalists and constructivists predict. Both tracks are evident in contemporary U.S. relations with weak democracies and authoritarian states, where U.S. power dominates. As the world's only military and economic superpower, the United States faces traditional resentment and counterbalancing against the dominant power, particularly from Russia, China, and nonwestern developing nations. But it also faces no immediate military rival, and the military balance under hegemony is more stable than it is under anarchy. In addition, the United States projects a national identity of democratic freedom and market opportunities, which is as much admired and envied around the world as it is resented. This identity, in contrast to a military or nondemocratic self-image, softens American dominance and encourages trade and nongovernmental interactions with weaker democratizing or nondemocratic societies, such as Russia and China. Economic engagement, it is believed, can facilitate growth and a more equitable balance of power, and this redistribution of power, in turn, may contribute to a mellowing of authoritarian ideologies and eventually an enlargement of the world's democratic community.

The question in these structural circumstances is whether power or identity dynamics dominates. If power shifts toward greater equality but identities continue to diverge, the relationships between the United States and countries such as China and Russia may slide into anarchy. The international system will become more contentious and unstable. If, on the other hand, power shifts but identities converge (Russia and China become more, not less, politically open and accessible), the relationships may drift toward the security community space and a widening at the margins of the democratic peace.

Whichever dynamics prevails, structural changes take a long time. Democracies do not emerge overnight, and they cannot be imposed. In the meantime, the United States will have to deal with both aspects of double-tracked anarchy—balancing power and influencing the positioning of national identities. It will need insurance policies, such as NATO expansion, the broadening of the U.S.-Japan Security Treaty, and missile defenses. And it will need engagement policies, such as the liberalization of trade with China and Russia and financial assistance for emerging nations to encourage domestic reforms. In hegemony and anarchy, balancing power and economic engagement are not alternatives; they are complements. Economic engagement and the possibility of repositioning national identities sustain the American motivation to balance power, and balancing power safeguards against the possibility that economic engagement empowers new adversaries who choose not to narrow their identity differences with democracies.

The power and identity perspective is so new, it warrants careful development. Chapter 1 explores the theoretical roots of this perspective. In the political science literature, realism and neorealism have dominated foreign policy studies, predicting that countries, especially great powers such as the United States, will balance power to protect their national interests. But empirical research by realist scholars since the 1980s has found that states do not balance against power; instead, they balance against threat. And threat is often a function of nonmaterial factors, such as intentions, perceptions, military strategies, elite politics, political regimes, and domestic cultural factors. Nonrealist studies pay more attention to these nonmaterial factors. Liberal studies focus directly on intentions, how preferences are chosen domestically and relate to one another internationally. Neoliberal studies focus on international institutions and the way they gather information, lower transaction costs, and bind states to improve mutual outcomes beyond the possibilities predicted by realism. More recently, constructivist research argues that interactions not only improve outcomes but also constitute or reconstitute the interests and identities of the states involved. Not just behavior and outcomes but interests and identities change in ways that are not predicted by purely materialist considerations.

This book builds on these developments. It stays close to realist concerns about the use of force, but reaches out to constructivist concerns about nonmaterial factors, such as norms, cultures, and identities, that interpret and motivate the use of force. Whereas constructivists focus primarily on social identity, I define national identities in terms of both a liberal (autonomous or internal) and a social (interrelated or external) dimension. The liberal or internal dimension captures the relative priority citizens assign to ideological, cultural, ethnic, religious, and other factors in establishing the rules for the use of legitimate force at home. The external dimension captures the history and experience of associations among countries that influence their inclination to use force against one another. I then juxtapose these two dimensions of national identity across countries within a global or regional system to define a contructivist distribution or structure of relative national identities. This structure predicts levels of threat between countries based on nonmaterial factors, before we consider material disparities, and exists alongside the realist structure of relative national power. These two structures interact to create different types of international communities or cultures. These communities then impose varying constraints on the foreign policy of individual nations. Not all of these communities dictate a struggle for power or a centralization of institutions.

Chapters 2 and 3 differentiate this approach from existing foreign policy debates and from traditional understandings of domestic politics. Chapter 2 reviews the debates among the various traditions of U.S. foreign policy. Since the end of the Cold War, these debates have followed predictable historical lines. Advocates of downsizing America's role (neoisolationists such as Pat Buchanan), of continuing a policy to contain rival states (realists such as Henry Kissinger), of preserving American hegemony (primacists such as Charles Krauthammer), or of reinventing American foreign policy in terms of global issues and multilateral institutions (internationalists such as Tony Lake) threaten to perpetuate the cycle of engagement, exhaustion, and exit that keeps America from feeling at home abroad. All of these positions fail to consider the limits imposed by America's national identity. A liberal society is not likely to flourish in a closed or isolated environment, nor is it likely to pursue power indefinitely just for the sake of world order or American primacy. Least of all is it likely to impose and dilute its values, both at the same time, in a flurry of global initiatives and organizations.

Chapter 3 explores the historical evolution of U.S. liberal national identity and its consequences for American foreign policy. The chapter demonstrates that changes in U.S. national identity, both autonomous and relational (especially with Europe), correlate with historic watersheds in American foreign policy as much as changes in U.S. national power. U.S. isolation from Europe and expansion across the continent prior to 1860 was a consequence of a conflicted national identity as well as of weak national power. The country's ascent thereafter to the world stage to make the world safe for democracy derived from its new unity and democratic convictions forged in the Civil War, not just from its rising industrial and administrative capabilities. And its passionate engagement in the Cold War followed the further deepening of national unity through the New Deal, which added a social and economic (as well as political) dimension to democracy and sharpened the contrast with other social systems, such as communism in Europe. Today, U.S. foreign policy commitments to universal human rights derive from a still deeper revolution going on in American society, a multicultural emancipation of minorities through the civil rights and gender movements of the 1960s and 1970s. Chapter 3 not only establishes the independent influence of national identity on foreign policy, but shows as well that national identity is far more than merely the sum of domestic politics.

Chapter 4 begins the review of U.S. foreign relations under differing configurations of identity and power. It addresses U.S. relations with other strong democracies and demonstrates how structural constraints of converging identities and competing capabilities call for a permanent partnership with Europe and Japan. Such a partnership does not sacrifice formal American sovereignty but recognizes that the United States is not likely to use significant military force successfully without the cooperation of Europe and Japan or in the face of their active opposition (the case, for example, in the Balkan, Persian Gulf, and now terrorist wars). This partnership also recognizes shared, albeit not identical, liberal commitments to promote open markets and societies and to resolve disputes peacefully through similar regulatory, legal, and nongovernmental institutions. Permanent partnership does not end differences among the democracies. The United States, Europe, and Japan continue to disagree over how to relate to third countries, such as Russia, China, Iraq, and Cuba; over various defense options, such as antiballistic missile defenses and a European rapid reaction force separable from NATO; over trade disputes; and over the role that governments should play to soften economic competition in domestic and global markets. But permanent partnership does reinforce the existing reality that the advanced democracies do not settle these differences by resorting to the use of military threat or force against one another. In this sense, the strong democracies already have a common international identity, which like domestic identity proscribes the pursuit of other objectives among them by the threat or use of military force. In the republican, nationally centered partnership advocated in this book, the United States (or another ally) may still act unilaterally to pursue a particular interest, just as domestic groups do in a democratic nation, but the United States is not likely to pursue that interest by using force against its fellow democracies and expect to succeed.

Chapters 5, 6, and 7 treat the details of U.S. relations with countries whose identities diverge. Chapter 5 examines U.S. relations with Russia and the formerly communist states of Europe. These relations take place under the structural conditions of double-tracked anarchy. But because Russia is relatively weaker and relatively less authoritarian than it was earlier, threat derives more from domestic developments and potentially shifting national identities than it does from military competition. Structural pressures in these circumstances call for NATO expansion, but not as a traditional alliance to defend countries against cross-border aggression, such as Russian intervention in Belarus or Ukraine. NATO is not facing confrontation with Russia. Rather NATO expands to preempt political instability and provide confidence for economic development in countries that are farthest along in stabilizing democratic identities, such as Poland, Hungary, and the Czech Republic. Further NATO expansion, therefore, depends on domestic political developments in prospective members and follow-up initiatives by the EU to expand its membership and spur growth. By this logic, NATO cannot expand to include persistently nondemocratic states, especially an authoritarian Russia. This converts NATO into a collective security institution (the internationalist solution) long before the domestic prerequisites exist in Russia or the other formerly communist countries to participate in a viable all-European security architecture. Russia is not threatened by meddling neighbors, and its presence in NATO (through the NATO-Russia Permanent Joint Council) and the G-7 (through the G-8— the G-7 countries plus Russia) unnecessarily complicates security and economic initiatives in Europe (as happened when Russia opposed NATO actions in Kosovo and walked out of the Joint Council). A better venue for cooperation with Russia is the United Nations, where Russia already has great power veto status. The UN affiliate in Europe, the Organization for Security and Cooperation in Europe (OSCE), monitors peacekeeping operations, elections, and arms control agreements in central and eastern Europe and operates in the Caucasus and Muslim republics of the former Soviet Union, where NATO forces could not intervene in any case without Russian consent or, failing that, without provoking a serious crisis with Russia.

Chapter 6 reviews U.S. relations in Asia through the structural lens of both a republican security community with Japan and a hegemonic relationship with China. These structural configurations argue against realist prescriptions that the United States treat Japan and China evenhandedly and play these countries off against one another by making each of them feel closer to the United States than they do to one another. Such prescriptions ignore the fact that Japan is a democracy and China is not. Structural logic also rejects internationalist prescriptions that trade and economic growth in China will necessarily lead to a more liberal Chinese political system. Economic engagement may only strengthen an authoritarian adversary. Alignments of power and identity in Asia argue instead for a strategy of concentric multilateralism. This strategy addresses all three aspects of contemporary structural reality in Asia— the political affinity between Japan and the United States, the potential military competition with China, and the economic engagement that may reposition and narrow identity differences with China and other nondemocracies in the Asian region. The core multilateral circle is a democratic security community and military alliance among the United States, Japan, and an emerging democracy in South Korea. A second wider and looser multilateral circle extends to the budding democracy in Taiwan, the democratizing countries of the Association of Southeast Asian Nations (ASEAN), the mature South Pacific democracies of Australia and New Zealand, and the poor but enduring democracy of India. And a third pan-regional structure of trade and confidence-building relations builds bridges to China, Vietnam, Myanmar and eventually to North Korea, using the ASEAN Regional Forum (ARF) and the Asian Pacific Economic Cooperation (APEC) forum to increase transparency and trust. This multilateralization of U.S. relations in Asia will not be as easy or go as far as multilateralism in Europe. Political identities fragment and diverge more in Asia than in Europe. But without some incremental movement toward greater multilateralization in Asia, America's traditional bilateral position in the region is untenable. This position is based more on a balance-of-power than security community logic. And, traditionally, given the influence of its democratic identity, America has not been able to sustain a pure balance-of-power role in the world except in the face of immediate threat.

Chapter 7 covers U.S. relations with Latin America, the Middle East, and Africa. Realists pay little attention to developing countries unless these countries figure in the larger balance of power, as they did during the Cold War. Internationalists, on the other hand, advocate frequent interventions in these regions to protect human rights and resolve global problems of poverty and disease. Structural logic based on power and identity, by contrast, advocates U.S. interventions only when U.S. material (power) and moral (identity) stakes are balanced. When both trade and political (i.e., democratic) affinities are growing in tandem, as in Latin America, the logic suggests a deepening involvement, widening the North American Free Trade Agreement (NAFTA) into a Free Trade Area for the Americas (FTAA). In the Middle East and Africa, however, the United States faces more limited options. Muslim and western identities stubbornly diverge, as do local ethnic and regional identities in most of Africa. Trade and economic relationships, except for oil in the Middle East, are too small to warrant frequent or sustained U.S. interventions, even though moral claims have increased as American citizens identify more with Israel and sub-Saharan Africa. Structural realities thus dictate that the United States resist the temptation to do something for moral reasons simply because it has the overwhelming material power to do so (as it did in Somalia). In this situation, the United States needs greater moral legitimacy from the participation of local, regional, and global partners—more public-spirited African leaders to end civil wars and reconcile ethnic differences, coalitions of moderate Arab states in the Persian Gulf to defend oil interests and reduce terrorism against Israel and the West, constructive European leaders to balance and revitalize the peace talks between Arabs and Israelis, and UN financial institutions to reform statist economies and open markets across the developing world.

* * *

The U.S. national identity is now widely shared among the great industrial powers of the world. This fact, more than globalization and the information revolution, distinguishes the modern world. It is a world that has moved closer to America; but if America is going to feel more at home in this world, it will have to shed its bifurcated New World–Old World mentality. How to think about this task is the subject of the next chapter.

CHAPTER ONE

Identity and Power

The Sources of National Interest

What motivates the behavior of individuals and states? Ideas and images are just as important as the mere possession of power.[1] Indeed, without mental images, power remains inert, and countries have no motivation to use it. After World War I, the United States was the most powerful country in the world. But its self-image did not motivate the use of that power in world affairs. Had it seen itself differently, America might have stopped Hitler sooner—inadequate mental images in the 1930s cost American lives in the 1940s.

Today, two big ideas dominate the way Americans think about themselves and the use of national power. Neither of these ideas is wrong, but neither is complete. Unless we correct and expand these ideas, this country may misuse its military and economic power in world affairs—or decide not use it at all, as a dispirited Soviet Union did when it disappeared in 1991.

The first idea is the *national interest*. This idea holds that the United States has a set of concrete material interests that must be pursued to protect American security and promote American prosperity. These interests can be calculated objectively from America's physical or geopolitical circumstances. They include the protection of our borders and sea-lanes, access to vital raw materials and markets, and prevention of dominance of the Western Hemisphere, Europe, or Asia by any other single power. But do U.S. interests oppose the European Union (EU), a single emerging power of democratic states that dominates Europe? Are nuclear weapons in the hands of France and Great Britain the same threat to American interests as nuclear weapons in the hands of Beijing or North Korea? The national interest is not objective. America is not just a piece of geography; it is a liberal democracy. And liberal nations, such as the United States and member states of the EU, do not behave like despotic ones, even under identical physical circumstances. Right after World War II, the armies of the United States and the Soviet Union confronted one another in the center of Europe. Both occupied conquered lands, and both faced similar external uncertainties. The United States, a liberal society, rapidly demobilized its military forces and launched the Marshall Plan to rebuild western Europe. The Soviet Union, a totalitarian society, used its military forces to impose communist regimes in eastern Europe and extract industrial materials to rebuild the Soviet Union. National identities dictated these responses, not the objective power circumstances. The national interest begins with what kind of society the nation is, not just what its geopolitical circumstances are.

The second idea is the *balance of power*. This idea captures the unending struggle among nations to preserve independence. The United States exploited the balance of power to win its own independence, by aligning with France and other countries against England, and maneuvered thereafter to keep European great powers out of the Western Hemisphere. But, while using power to forge and protect the New World, the United States rejected the balance of power in the Old World as the sport of despotic governments. It overlooked the fact that all nations, New World and Old, balance power, although for different purposes. New World countries seek a balance of power that favors democracy. Old World nations seek a balance of power that favors autocracy. The resulting global balance of power always reflects a moral order.

The Cold War balance of power between the United States and the Soviet Union maintained the nuclear peace and blunted nuclear proliferation. But it also protected a despotic Soviet Union and created moral equivalency between liberal and communist societies. Today's balance of power is less conflicted. The great industrial powers are all liberal democracies. Liberal democracies protect individual rights and resolve trade and other disputes with one another amicably through international institutions and the rule of law. They create world organizations to promote universal human rights and encourage corporate and nongovernmental institutions to interact across national boundaries and establish world markets. Globalization today is a product of these liberal societies, not a threat to them—global markets would look very different if the Soviet Union had won the Cold War. The balance of power is also always a community of power, and this community of power reflects the relative convergence or divergence of the political identities of great powers.

The rest of this chapter explores these ideas, which affect U.S. identity and its conduct in world affairs. It develops the concept of national identity, which, along with national power, influences the national interest. And it develops the idea of international community (or culture), which, along with the balance of power, constitutes the structure of the international system.

National Identity and National Interests

The holy grail in traditional thinking about American foreign policy is the national interest. George Washington referred to it in 1795 as "the substantial and permanent interest of our country."[2] Lord Palmerston, a British prime minister in the nineteenth century, immortalized the concept when he said that Britain had no permanent friends or enemies, only permanent interests.[3]

Every modern study of American foreign policy begins with an incantation of the national interest.

OLD NATIONAL INTEREST

The guru of thinking about the national interest in postwar American foreign policy is Hans J. Morgenthau. In a seminal textbook, Morgenthau authors the doctrine of national interest: "The main signpost that helps political realism to find its way through the landscape of international politics is the concept of interest defined in terms of power."[4] By "interest defined in terms of power," Morgenthau means that states act mainly to acquire economic and military power to ensure their national survival. As Morgenthau hastens to add, nations do not always or only pursue national interest and power—states also act on moral or ideological grounds. "Political realism," Morgenthau insists, "is aware of the moral significance of political action." But, he adds, "political realism refuses to identify the moral aspirations of a particular nation with the moral laws that govern the universe."[5] States aspire to different moral ends, but they all need power to achieve those ends. Hence, the tendency of states to pursue interests defined in terms of power is more nearly universal than their tendency to pursue interests defined in terms of common moral purposes. This law of power, Morgenthau believes, creates the basis for a science of international politics, much like the law of gravity created the basis for a science of physics.

In these terms, the science of national interest has exercised a firm grip on American thinking about foreign policy. It taps into a predilection in American thinking to check moral pretense with power and to construct a system of checks and balances in both domestic and international politics that effectively prevents any one moral point of view from achieving superiority over another. Within such a framework, "prudence" becomes the "supreme virtue in politics."[6] To believe in the superiority of one's moral claims is imprudent, if not immoral. Thus, Morgenthau can conclude not only that power is a more objective standard for assessing state behavior, but also that "a foreign policy derived from the national interest is in fact morally superior to a foreign policy inspired by universal moral principles."[7]

But to treat the interests of all states as morally equivalent to one another does not avoid universal pretensions; it becomes one. For it elevates what states value above what individuals value or the international community values. States that oppress or eliminate some of their citizens (genocide) can claim the same moral status as other states. This idea came from European politics in the fifteenth through seventeenth centuries, when princes and monarchs seized power from local barons (individuals) and the Catholic Church (which then constituted the international community).[8] Before the French Revolution, most states in Europe looked alike. Absolute monarchs exercised power in the interests of a small hereditary aristocracy and its emerging culture.

Often closer to one another than their own people, the elites of monarchic states interacted largely on the basis of external factors—geographic features, proximity, relative power, and so on. The doctrine of "interests defined in terms of power" made sense.

After the French Revolution, however, states began to differ internally. Monarchs gradually disappeared (partly perhaps because, under the influence of realist advisers, they ignored internal affairs). State power came to reside in nations (nation-states), in individual citizens (liberal states), in religious authorities (fundamentalist states), or in elite and military institutions (communist, fascist, and other one-party states). Now it made less sense to assume that states were alike internally and that state interests were solely or primarily a function of external interests defined in terms of relative power.

External factors do not disappear, of course. National interests and relative power remain important. Indeed, we can imperil liberty by ignoring power. When Morgenthau wrote, realism had just guided the liberal western states to victory in World War II. The coming conflict between the United States and the Soviet Union would vindicate once again the important role of power in defending western liberties. This experience gave birth to an even more stylized version of realist thinking, known as neorealism. Neorealism places together in a black box all the internal characteristics of individual states and examines international outcomes exclusively in terms of the external distribution of relative power. Working at a structural level of analysis, neorealists do not pretend to explain how individual states might behave, but they issue a stern warning to individual states: if you do not take into account the distribution of relative power and balance against greater power, you will certainly suffer and may fail to survive in an anarchic world.

Realism's warning is still valid. Relative power protects individual states against threats to their internal values. But relative power is only part of the story. States defend themselves by other means. They also express domestic concepts of justice that discipline the use of coercive force at home and seek to persuade other states to accept international concepts of justice that are consistent with their domestic concepts and can discipline the use of coercive force abroad. If they succeed, other states threaten them less, and states survive by persuasion and consent as much as by power and coercion. Such persuasion may be difficult if states differ markedly in their internal affairs and in what they consider to be just and fair. But if these internal assessments converge, states may be able to accommodate their respective needs and aspirations and thus moderate the balance of power.

NEW CONCEPTS

Realist scholarship itself suggests that, in influencing foreign policy, more is at work than the external imperative to balance power. States judge threat in terms of power factors, such as proximity of adversaries (geopolitics), power differentials and trends, relative administrative capabilities to extract domestic resources, and whether offensive or defensive weapon systems dominate.[9] But states also judge threat in terms of what states intend to do with their power.[10] Intentions are a function of nonmaterial and often domestic factors. They derive from perceptions or misperceptions of what other states believe.[11] They reflect elite politics in which different domestic groups intend different things.[12] Intentions also arise from more deeply seated military strategies and cultures, which often determine whether weapons are used for offensive or defensive purposes;[13] and intentions mirror the attributes of states themselves, such as whether these states are revolutionary or status quo states.[14] In the end, as some realists conclude, the "national interest derives from national identity..., the nature of the country whose interests are being defined."[15]

Thus realist research itself unpacks the black box of internal factors affecting the motivation to use and balance power. But in so doing, this research opens a Pandora's box. How many of these internal factors do we have to consider and which factors should take priority over others? One solution adopted in recent scholarship is simply to turn full attention to the study of domestic factors. Domestic politics or, at best, foreign policy making becomes the focus of international politics.[16] This solution, however, risks abandoning the focus on external structural factors, such as the balance of power, and exposes the analysis of American foreign policy to the perils of a world in which other countries advocate opposing domestic values and gain power to advance them against the United States.

A second solution in recent scholarship is to sweep up all these nonmaterial factors at the domestic and international levels and aggregate them at the systemic level into a structure of social relationships (as opposed to power relationships). Through this structure, it is argued, countries share interpretations of relative power by assigning roles to one another as friends or foes.[17] This sociological or constructivist turn in international studies, however, risks substituting a lock box for a Pandora's box and excluding foreign policy studies altogether. If a state's foreign policy acquires meaning only in the context of an external social relationship, is a state's individual foreign policy relevant any longer? It is not, unless the state possesses an autonomous domestic capacity to criticize and potentially alter the prevailing international social structure.[18] If, as some scholars conclude, Mikhail Gorbachev ended the Cold War by reconceiving the Soviet Union as a partner rather than an adversary of the West, he did so only because he was able to draw on some independent capacity in the Soviet Union to reinterpret Soviet purposes and argue against the prevailing definition of the Soviet Union as adversary.[19]

Thus, both domestic politics and constructivist approaches face significant weaknesses in dealing with nonmaterial influences on foreign policy. In this book, I develop twin concepts to compensate for these weaknesses: national identity at the domestic level, and the structure of relative national identity at the international level. I deal with the concept of national identity next and with the structure of national identities in the following section of this chapter.

The concept of national identity surmounts the problem of Pandora's box. It does this by identifying at the domestic level the most important consensus that makes domestic politics possible. Citizens, especially in a democracy, disagree about many things—foreign policy, taxes, court appointments, health care, social security, education, the environment, and a host of other issues. What defines domestic politics and distinguishes it from international politics is the agreement among all these citizens that they will not pursue their disagreements with the use of physical force (or that if they do they are subject to the legitimate laws of the land and their relevant penalties). Citizens may have the capacity to use force, but they do not have the legitimacy to use it. Domestic parties agree that only national institutions have such legitimacy. If citizens decide that ethnic or local groups can use force legitimately, civil war breaks out. The United States emerged when British subjects in America no longer accepted the right of King George III to levy taxes and use physical imprisonment to collect them. The South seceded when it no longer accepted the right of the federal government to decide the issue of slavery. And the Soviet Union broke up when its leaders and citizens no longer accepted the right of the Soviet government to use military power to defend itself.[20]

How do we define and measure national identity? *National interest* has the advantage of measuring a nation in material terms—numbers of soldiers, weapons, and missiles; gross national output; population; and so on. National identity measures the nation in nonmaterial terms. It addresses the key factor that motivates national power, namely the consensus by which the citizens of a nation agree that only the state can use force legitimately. This consensus has two dimensions in the study of foreign policy—an internal one that defines the rules by which the state can use force legitimately against members of its own society, and an external one that defines the rules by which the state can use force legitimately against other societies. The two dimensions are independent, but they also interact. They correspond to the two aspects of personal identity formation. A person's identity is shaped both by external, physical and social, factors (family, class, community, etc.) and by internal, biological and rational, factors (genetics and self-consciousness). No person exists in an external vacuum, but no person is incapable of challenging and changing his or her external environment. Similarly, a nation's identity is shaped by its internal preferences and its external relationships.[21]

Most nations define their identity in one of two ways. They legitimate the use of force on the basis of protecting and serving an *ethnic* or *traditional community* that shares common linguistic, cultural, racial, or religious characteristics; or they legitimate the use of force on the basis of protecting and serving an *ideological community* composed of a variety of ethnic groups that unite around a set of common beliefs.[22] Japan and Germany exemplify countries with relatively homogeneous ethnic or cultural identities; the United States, Switzerland, Belgium, and the former Soviet Union are examples of multi-ethnic societies with primarily ideological identities. When nations are weak—many post-colonial countries in Africa come to mind—ethnic or ideological affinities may not suffice to hold the nation together; charismatic leaders and autocratic central institutions become the defining features of nationhood.[23]

INTERNAL IDENTITY

The internal dimension of identity defines the rules for the legitimate use of force at home.[24] Do governments define citizenship, base legislation, and enforce laws primarily on the basis of a common culture, as traditional nation-states in Europe did? Do they base these actions primarily on religion, as Iran and other fundamentalist states do, or on race, as apartheid South Africa did? Or do they base such actions principally on a set of ideas or an ideology, as the formerly communist countries did and liberal democracies do today?

Obviously, these internal sources of identity overlap and conflict. The United States initially had both an ethnic and an ideological identity. Its population was predominantly Anglo-Saxon, and this ethnic group justified the use of force to enslave a black population. At the same time, the nation was founded on a new set of constitutional ideas that held that all men were created equal. These two sources of national identity were in conflict from the very beginning. Through the Civil War, women's suffrage movement, and civil rights revolution, America had to sort out which factor was more important in legitimating the use of power against its own citizens. Today, Europe is sorting out similar issues. Germany debates the status of longtime-resident Turkish immigrants and whether Germany is a cultural community defined primarily by blood or a democratic community that includes individuals irrespective of culture, and the EU is accumulating laws based on common democratic values that supersede traditional national authorities (although the EU still lacks independent police powers to enforce these laws). In the Middle East, Iran and Israel wrestle to determine whether they are primarily religious or secular states.

Internal identity is, foremost, about how a country perceives itself. Although states, like individuals, also define themselves by how others perceive them, the self is always more than just the sum of others' perceptions.[25] This autonomous aspect of national identity exists even in realist studies. Kenneth Waltz, the founder of neorealism, defines anarchy as the absence of "a monopoly on the legitimate use of force." Notice that anarchy is not just the absence of a monopoly of physical power—a single power may exist, as in the case of hegemony, but anarchy means that its use of power is not considered legitimate. Legitimate, Waltz writes, means that "public agents are organized to prevent and to counter the private use of force."[26] No such public agents exist at the international level, but they do exist in every nation. These national agents may not monopolize the *capacity* to use force; private groups often retain the right to bear arms. But national agents do monopolize the *legitimacy* to use force. If a nation is to exist, private groups cannot use their arms legitimately against the state.

Thus, even for neorealists, it is not just the capacity but the legitimacy to use force that defines the identity of the state. And legitimacy is not derivative of power—they vary independently. Legitimacy may be centralized and power decentralized, as in the case of a federal or confederal community. Power may be centralized and legitimacy decentralized, as in the case of empire or hegemony. Waltz subsequently conflates the legitimacy and power dimensions of state identity. He reasoned that, because all states performed this function of organizing public agents to counter the private use of force, states were functionally similar and hence undifferentiated. But he overlooked the fact that states were also separate by virtue of the principle of sovereignty and that this separateness derived from the different substantive standards of sovereignty (e.g., Catholicism vs. Protestantism in seventeenth-century Europe) by which states legitimated the use of force to rule and defend their own citizens.[27]

These standards, like capabilities, vary. Take the case of Canada and the United States. They exist as separate centers of power, but not as significantly different liberal democratic states legitimating that power. When they use force internally, they create little fear or uncertainty in the other country. The same is not true in the case of China and the United States. When China cracks down on dissidents, the United States wonders what motivates the use of Chinese power internally and fears that, if China treats its own citizens in this manner, it may also use force for similar purposes against outside states.

These differences among countries in the internal dimension of identity are real and should be investigated and measured in international studies, just as we investigate and measure differences among countries in terms of power capabilities. Measures of internal identity are imperfect, to be sure, but so are measures of power capabilities. Here I draw on measures of identity that classify countries as democratic or nondemocratic (the polity IV data set and the Freedom House Index of political freedom),[28] but other measures are possible. Scholars debate whether culture, geography, class, or politics (e.g., democracy) matters most in shaping identity and motivating states.[29] Democracy measures, however, have an advantage. They weigh, in effect, how countries set priorities among several features of their society—ideas, culture, religion, race, and so on—when these countries decide and enforce laws against their own citizens. On a democracy spectrum, countries that give priority to race, religion, or culture are likely to be found at the nondemocratic end because a democracy by definition makes laws and enforces them on grounds other than a citizen's race, religion, or cultural origin. Democracy measures have a further advantage. They change, albeit not quickly, whereas cultural, geographic, and even class distinctions tend to be more frozen in time.

A democracy, as defined by the measures used in this study, has three basic features.[30]

1. Free, fair, and broadly participatory elections in which opposing political parties compete and rotate periodically in government, transferring power back and forth peacefully over a long period of time.
2. Separation of powers among governmental institutions, all of which, including in particular the military, are under the control of and accountable to elected officials.
3. Fundamental protection of civil liberties, including, among other rights, freedom of speech, assembly, association, and religion; protection of private property; due process of law; trial by jury; independent judiciaries; and the right to vote.

This definition incorporates both thin and thick dimensions of democracy. A country may be classified as a democracy if it has a wide franchise and holds periodic elections that are broadly considered to be free and fair, but this country will not rank as high, based on our definition, as a country that not only holds broadly based free and fair elections but regularly rotates power in government between opposing parties. Similarly, the latter country will not rank as high as one that not only rotates opposing parties in power but brings all bureaucracies, especially military ones, under the direction of elected officials and institutions. The most advanced or mature democracies not only rotate parties in power and subordinate bureaucracies to elected officials, but also provide constitutional protection of basic individual political and civil rights.

EXTERNAL IDENTITY
The external dimension of national identity deals with how states evaluate ethnic, ideological, and other sources of identity in their relations with other states. No state follows exactly the same rules for the use of force abroad that it does at home. Obviously, it is operating in a different environment in which no single state has a monopoly over the legitimate use of force, as each state does at home. On the other hand, no state is completely schizophrenic, its behavior abroad consistently deviating from its behavior at home. As Thomas Risse-Kappen, a political scientist, notes, "actors infer external behavior from the values and norms governing the domestic political practices that shape the identities of their partners in the international system."[31] Thus, internal identities inform external behavior, but external behavior is also a function of separate and independent identity factors.[32] Although a country might prefer to

follow the same rules governing the legitimate use of force abroad as it does at home, whether it will be able to do so depends on the rules that other countries follow at home and on how wide or narrow a gap exists between the rules and procedures followed by one country and those pursued by another. The relative difference between internal national identities is one factor affecting the way states behave toward one another in the external environment.

Another factor is the way countries have traditionally or historically interacted. Countries gain or lose trust in one another through ongoing interactions and communications. They develop a shared understanding of who they are and what their intentions may be. This is the social (as opposed to autonomous or internal) dimension of national identity. In some cases, countries develop adversarial relations; at different periods, England and France were enemies, as were France and Germany. In other cases, countries develop cooperative relations; in 2001, the relationship between France and Germany, the special relationship between Great Britain and the United States, and the close ties between Russia and the Serbian people of Yugoslavia are all examples. This process of socialization is a function of many factors—previous wars, alliances, regularity of contacts through trade and diplomatic activities, membership in common institutions, and so on. All of these factors can be measured, and nations compared, in terms of the external dimension of national identity.[33]

I adopt here a very general measure of external identity: I differentiate countries in terms of their inclination to use force against other countries. This inclination may range from no use of force, to an inclination to use force for defensive purposes only, to a willingness to use force for limited offensive purposes, and finally to the use of force for aggressive purposes. Some states show no inclination to use force against one another, such as democratic states or simply friendly states. Other states use force for defensive purposes only; they are called defensive positionalists and seek to minimize the difference between their gains and those of other states in order to defend themselves.[34] Revisionist or aggressive states, by contrast, seek to maximize the difference between their gains and those of others so that they may expand and potentially dominate other states. Accommodationist states fall somewhere between defensive and aggressive uses of force. These states consider the use of offensive force legitimate for certain purposes (e.g., Britain's acceptance of Hitler's occupation of the Rhineland), but not ultimately to challenge a multipolar balance of power (e.g., Britain's perception of Hitler's conquest of the rest of Czechoslovakia beyond the Sudetenland in March 1939).[35]

NEW NATIONAL INTEREST

National identity and national power both define the national interest. Figure 1.1 illustrates this dual calculus graphically for the United States (but fig. 1.1 could be drawn for any country by simply changing the substance of

Figure 1.1. Power and Identity Incentives Defining National Interest

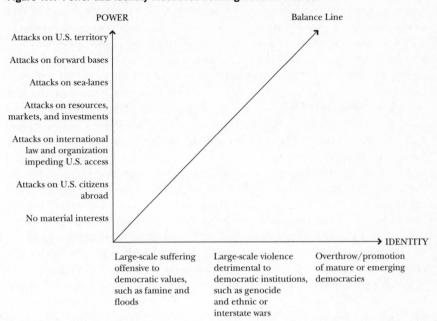

POWER   Balance Line

Attacks on U.S. territory
Attacks on forward bases
Attacks on sea-lanes
Attacks on resources,
markets, and investments
Attacks on international
law and organization
impeding U.S. access
Attacks on U.S. citizens
abroad
No material interests

→ IDENTITY

| Large-scale suffering offensive to democratic values, such as famine and floods | Large-scale violence detrimental to democratic institutions, such as genocide and ethnic or interstate wars | Overthrow/promotion of mature or emerging democracies |

the identity dimension). The vertical arrow traces a path of increasing incentives for the United States to act or intervene in international affairs based on its power (material) interests. The horizontal arrow traces increasing U.S. incentives to intervene based on its identity (moral) interests. Realist studies counsel the United States to adhere closely to the vertical arrow. Internationalist studies counsel it to follow the horizontal arrow. Neither approach balances U.S. material and moral interests. The identity and power approach, by contrast, counsels American foreign policy to track along the diagonal arrow in figure 1.1. This path traces external situations in which America's material and moral interests are likely to be balanced. Along this path, American foreign policy action has a greater chance to succeed because it matches external material imperatives with proportionate internal moral commitments.

Balances and Communities of Power

Nations have reasons to trust or distrust one another before they consider the balance of power. Countries evaluate one another by differences in internal and external identity, as well as by differences in power. The structure of relative national identity captures this nonmaterial aspect of international relations. It juxtaposes separate national identities across the international system and creates three levels of nonmaterial relations in international affairs. The first level is how states independently perceive themselves and others (autonomous identity). The second level is how the other states perceive them and how the first states, in turn, respond to the others' perceptions (social identity). And the third level is a distillation of interactions among separate national identities that constitutes the culture of the international community. This culture reflects international and transnational organizations and norms that grow out of the configuration of identities, but is not reducible to the separate identities of states or their specific interactions. It is a structural level of nonmaterial reality to go along with the more familiar, material structure of the balance of power.[36]

Classical realists recognize these three levels of nonmaterial reality but do not make them explicit in their theories. Regarding autonomous identity, for example, Zbigniew Brzezinski talks about how "Russia's longer term role in Europe will depend largely on its self-definition," and Henry Kissinger remarks that "once a nation's image of itself is destroyed, so is its willingness to play a major international role."[37] Regarding social identity, John Lewis Gaddis points out how the Cold War would have been different if the relationship between the Soviet and American *domestic* systems had been different: "If the Soviet Union had been the superpower that it actually was but with a system of checks and balances that could have constrained Stalin's authoritarian tendencies, a Cold War might have happened, but it could hardly have been as dangerous or as protracted a conflict."[38]

Classical realists, such as Morgenthau and Kissinger, also talk openly about the cultural level of international communities. Morgenthau characterizes seventeenth- and eighteenth-century Europe as a "community of Christian princes" and remarks how their "common awareness of . . . common standards restrained their ambitions . . . , imposed 'moderation' upon their actions, and instilled in all of them 'some sense of honor and justice' [i.e., common culture]."[39] Kissinger notes that the Concert of Europe, the balance among the great powers in the nineteenth century, "relied the least on power to maintain itself" and constituted "not only a physical equilibrium but a moral one" because "the Continental countries were knit together by a sense of shared values." "In this manner," Kissinger concludes, "legitimacy became the cement by which the international order was held together."[40] Samuel Huntington explicitly addresses issues of identity and the structure of identity when he argues that civilizations, the highest form of culture, may divide nations in the future because civilizational differences "are far more fundamental than differences among political ideologies or political regimes."[41]

If realist arguments depend so heavily on observations about domestic images, international communities, shared values, and identity, why not incorporate these ideas explicitly into a more complete theory of international relations? This step would take nothing away from realism. The structure of relative national power is still an important and independent influence on state behavior. But now it operates alongside the structure of relative national identity, which interprets and influences how the balance of power operates. If identities in this structure diverge, hostile nations create a dangerous balance of power. On the other hand, if identities converge, communities of nations may moderate the balance of power.

STRUCTURES OF IDENTITY AND POWER

Figure 1.2 depicts graphically the possible structures of relative national identity and relative national power. The vertical axis registers the distribution of power. At the bottom of the axis, power is decentralized and relatively equally distributed. Toward the top, it is unequally distributed and eventually centralized. The horizontal axis depicts the distribution of national identities. Toward the left side of the axis, identities converge. Toward the right side, identities diverge. The two structures define four spaces: hierarchy, security community, hegemony, and anarchy. (Anarchy as used in fig. 1.2 and throughout this book refers to double-track anarchy, involving competition for legitimacy as well as power.) These spaces are continuous, not dichotomous, allowing for a rich variety of international systems and possible changes between them.[42]

In each space, structural pressures of relative power and relative identity lead to different outcomes and hence constraints on foreign policy. These constraints do not determine specific state behaviors. States may act outside these constraints because other, more proximate factors at the level of strategic interactions, domestic politics, and ideas also influence behavior. But structures impose a high cost on some behaviors and exclude other behaviors altogether. For example, a small power is not likely to consider, let alone take, military action against a dominant power. And, as historical experience suggests, one mature democracy is not likely to use military force against another mature democracy.

Structural analysis is not suitable for every purpose, but it is appropriate for foreign policy analysis at the level of grand strategy. And it complements studies of more specific foreign policy behavior from a strategic choice, comparative case study, or domestic politics perspective. The latter perspectives can look only at what structures permit.[43] As a consequence, these perspectives may attribute causal significance to proximate factors when structural factors are primary. Behavior between states, for example, may be traced to the influence of international institutions, strategic choices, domestic political and cultural factors, or even specific individuals. But these influences may be derivative of broader structural factors, such as converging identities or unipolar power configurations, and hence may be intervening, not independent, variables. In 2001, the United Nations and its secretary-general, Kofi Annan, might be seen as a primary cause of the importance of human rights in international

Figure 1.2. Identity and Power Approach to American Foreign Policy

DISTRIBUTION OF IDENTITY

		Converge	Diverge
DISTRIBUTION OF POWER	Unequal	U.S. relations in NATO U.S.-Japan security treaty HIERARCHY	U.S. relations with nondemocratic nations in Asia, Africa, Middle East, and Latin America HEGEMONY
	Equal	SECURITY COMMUNITY European economic and monetary union (EU) U.S. relations in G-7	DOUBLE-TRACK ANARCHY U.S. relations with Russia and, in the future perhaps, China

affairs. An equally and perhaps more important cause, however, may be the unipolar power of the United States and other liberal democracies that place a high value on human rights.

In this book, I first measure empirically the structure of relative power and relative identity in U.S. relations with various foreign countries—this could be done for any country, not just the United States. I locate the resulting structural configurations of identity and power in the spaces in figure 1.2 and then reason deductively from these structural circumstances to extrapolate the broad constraints on U.S. foreign policy options. Using this approach, I derive a grand strategy for the United States or the range of U.S. policies in various structural settings that are likely to be successful because they match both material and moral constraints. Along the way, I contrast the grand strategy suggested by a structure of both relative identity and relative power with the broad policies recommended by realism, which considers primarily the structure of relative power, and by internationalist (institutionalist) and constructivist accounts, which give priority to the structure of relative information (ideas) and identities.

Previous research offers plenty of evidence that structural constraints matter in foreign policy behavior. For example, in figure 1.2, we can hold the distribution of power constant across the top two cells (power remains unequally distributed) and ask if it makes a difference for broad foreign policy behavior. Studies of alliances dominated by a hegemonic power suggest that it does. Foreign policy behavior in NATO, where national identities more closely converge, is norm-centered and consensual, whereas such behavior in the former Warsaw Pact, where national identities more noticeably diverged, was authority-centered and constitutive.[44] Similarly, we can hold the distribution of identity constant across the two right-hand cells of figure 1.2 (identities remain diverging) and ask if behavior differs in hegemony as opposed to anarchy. Again, studies show it does—behavior is less violent under hegemony.[45] Finally, across the two bottom cells of figure 1.2, where the distribution of power remains constant (roughly equal distribution), we observe behavioral differences between countries living together in a security community and those living together under anarchy.[46] All these differences are well documented, and I draw on this literature to deduce the broad directions of American foreign policy that are likely to meet the structural constraints of identity and power and thus be successful.

Traditional thinking confines international relations to only one of the spaces in figure 1.2, the lower right-hand box. This is the realist world of anarchy in which there is no dominant nation and national identities permanently diverge. Specific identities may change (Russia replaces Turkey among the great powers, or Russia replaces the Soviet Union), but identities never converge among the great powers as a whole. Such a move would equal hierarchy, the upper left-hand box, which, according to traditional studies, is the opposite of international politics. Thus, identities drop out of the struggle among competing great powers, and anarchy becomes the single-track pursuit of relative power. But, in fact, modest hierarchies do exist in international (as opposed to domestic) affairs, such as the integrated command structure of NATO and the EU. And anarchies operate differently than traditional thinking envisions because states struggle not only for power but also for legitimacy—to persuade other states to accept the balance of power as fair and just.

HIERARCHY

Hierarchical structures are not all the same. By confining such structures to domestic affairs and by ignoring the fact that domestic hierarchies (states) differ in terms of the rules by which they legitimate power, traditional thinking misses a crucial aspect of centralizing power in international affairs. As states pool power at the international level, they raise the question of the rules by which that power will be legitimated. In short, they raise the question of the identity of the new hierarchy. The European Union is centralizing power. In so doing, it has raised the question at the international level of whether that power will be democratic or nondemocratic. Will power in the European Union be divided and balanced among executive, parliamentary, and judicial institutions (the European Council, Parliament, and Court of Justice)? Or will it remain solely in the hands of unchecked executive institutions (the European Council and Commission)? The United States faces similar, although less acute, issues of whether to centralize power and, if so, how to democratize it, in relations within international organizations such as NATO, the G-7, and the World Trade Organization (WTO). This question of democratic deficit is a central aspect of international politics, particularly among democratic countries, yet it is almost completely ignored by traditional studies, which either minimize the significance of international institutions (realists) or advocate more international institution–building without often considering the issues of democratic accountability (internationalists).

SECURITY COMMUNITY

Traditional thinking also misses the possibility of security communities, the lower left-hand box of figure 1.2. As the name implies, these communities moderate the traditional security dilemma created by anarchy. Countries that legitimate the use of force on similar grounds threaten one another less and do not engage as aggressively in competitive arms races and military rivalries. Such communities do not automatically bring peace, for peace depends on the degree of convergence among national identities and on the substance of the rules by which converging states legitimate power. But such communities reduce the chances of war.

Figure 1.3 shows a variety of security communities. The horizontal axis measures the internal dimension of national identity in terms of the substance of the rules, democratic or nondemocratic, by which converging states legitimate the use of force at home. The vertical axis measures the external dimension of national identity in terms of the inclination of converging states to use force defensively or offensively against one another based on historical experiences.

The strongest security communities appear in box A. Here mature democracies, in which institutional checks and balances and constitutional due process make it difficult to use force internally and externally, achieve high levels of peaceful relations. For all practical purposes, they eliminate the need to balance military power in relations with one another. Liberal democracies compete economically, sometimes fiercely. But a firewall of robust civil societies and pluralist political institutions separates economic competition from military rivalries. Most disagreements are sorted out in courts and private negotiations. Despite significant disagreements over trade and political issues, such as sanctions against Cuba or Iran, the major industrial democracies do not acquire, threaten, or use military force to settle these issues.

The reality of this democratic peace is incontrovertible, but the reasons for it are not well understood.[47] Some scholars believe it has to do with traditional alliance behavior and the lingering effects of the Cold War alliance—the major democracies had converging external identities in that conflict and came closer together on internal dimensions of identity by containing a common adversary for over forty years. The longer the democratic peace persists beyond the end of the Cold War, however, the less persuasive this explanation becomes. Other explanations point to features of internal identity within and among democracies. These features include institutional checks and balances, normative preferences for legal and peaceful resolution of disputes, a large civil sector that counterbalances government and diversifies private interests,

Figure 1.3. Convergence of Identity in Security Communities

INTERNAL DIMENSION

	Democracy	Nondemocracy
Defensive	Democratic peace A	Holy Alliance B
Offensive	C Democratizing vs. Democratic states	D Alliance of totalitarian states

EXTERNAL DIMENSION

and finally a propensity to trade and create transnational markets and international legal institutions, which discourage resorting to war.[48]

The strongest democracies, exhibiting all three salient features used in this book to define a mature democratic society, do not fight one another. But how strong do democracies have to be to enjoy the democratic peace? Some democracies may be or may become weaker internally and develop more competitive external rivalries with mature democracies. Weaker democracies are more unstable and may be more inclined to use force offensively (box C of fig. 1.3). Initially democratizing states, such as Russia, might fear more powerful neighboring democracies, such as NATO members, and resume competitive military armaments.[49] Or two strong democracies, such as the United States and Japan, might grow cynical and frustrated over economic disputes and gradually weaken their security ties. Moreover, democratic states continue to disagree about the use of military and economic force toward third countries, and these disagreements might spill back and eventually alienate democratic states from one another. In short, the democratic peace may unravel. It is not permanent, and there may be persisting perils as states struggle to become democratic and cope with stronger democracies on their borders.[50]

Security communities are also possible among nondemocratic states (right-hand side of fig. 1.3). But because nondemocracies discipline the use of force less stringently in their own societies, these communities may be less peaceful and enduring. The Holy Alliance brought together conservative monarchies in Russia, Prussia, and Austria and managed a relatively peaceful balance of power during the first half of the nineteenth century (box B). Totalitarian states formed fascist security communities before World War II (e.g., Germany and Italy) and communist security communities after World War II (e.g., Soviet Union and China) (box D). But, again, these totalitarian security communities were short-lived, perhaps because they require a pyramid of power rather than pluralistic institutions and members struggle to decide which state will be top dog. Such communities may not differ significantly from traditional alliances, which are always temporary.

HEGEMONY

Traditional studies also miss the possibility of hegemony or empire. They consider hegemony to be unstable and fleeting. Under anarchy, states always balance against greater power. Thus, smaller powers, threatened by a rising hegemon, would swiftly move against such a power, and hegemony would not last very long.[51]

In fact, however, hegemony may be a highly stable system. After all, empires have lasted for long periods of time, especially in non-European parts of the world.[52] For all practical purposes, a hegemon's military power is uncontested—other powers are too small and scattered to generate military challenges, and open military conflicts are rare or limited to ad hoc terrorist activities. Challenges take place instead in the form of political and economic clashes. Thus, more depends on the distribution of relative identities, which defines political relations, than on the distribution of relative power, which defines military relations.

The hegemon's identity is particularly important. Smaller nations face two choices: isolate themselves from the dominant power or engage the dominant power economically in order to gain power over the longer run. If the hegemon is not willing to engage in open economic relations from which smaller nations might gain, smaller nations will isolate themselves, if they are able, or submit only grudgingly, if they are not. The former was the case of the nonaligned nations during the Cold War, which sought to distance themselves from both the Soviet Union and the United States; the latter was the experience of satellite countries in eastern Europe under the Soviet empire. If the hegemon is more open and accommodating, smaller states may climb on the bandwagon with, rather than withdraw from, the hegemonic state. Through trade and economic advance, smaller states strengthen their material capabilities, and some may go on to challenge the hegemon politically. The Asian tigers joined the bandwagon with the U.S. and free-world economic system during the Cold War, and some of them—Singapore and Malaysia, for example—have gone on to challenge the United States and other western countries politically by advocating Asian or Confucian identities (emphasizing authority and communitarian values) as alternatives to western values (emphasizing individualism and consumerism).

ANARCHY

Relations among countries whose identities diverge and whose power is roughly equal, such as Cold War relations between the United States and the former Soviet Union, take place under anarchy. But anarchy now has two tracks.[53] It involves countries balancing power to ensure that military force does not disrupt markets and that market outcomes are not used to gain military advantage. But it also involves countries engaging to develop markets, soften external rivalries, and persuade other states that their power is legitimate. Economic engagement, all but excluded in traditional and especially neorealist thinking, is a particularly important tool for American foreign policy. It offers a hopeful rationale for continuing to balance power—something that a liberal society is unlikely to do for its own sake. And, if it works, it creates essential external conditions, such as prosperity, to encourage liberal change in other countries in the only way that such change can be authentic, namely through indigenous choice.

The end of the Cold War confirmed that anarchy is not just a struggle for power but also a process of recognizing and repositioning relative national identities. In this sense, the ideological differences between the United States and the Soviet Union during the Cold War were not a perverse aspect of the balance of power, as realists have traditionally argued.[54] The political competition was not only necessary; it was actually helpful. At the beginning of the Cold War, competition identified the need to establish and stabilize a military balance. It is conceivable that the United States and the Soviet Union might have avoided military confrontation at the outset of the Cold War. George Kennan and Henry Kissinger have long argued that the United States missed repeated opportunities to negotiate with Stalin and his immediate successors,[55] but the argument is not convincing. Even great statesmen were unlikely to overcome the enormous and justified suspicions that divided Stalinist and American societies. If President Harry Truman exaggerated the political differences between the two countries, he did not exaggerate them very much. The devastation found in eastern Europe and the former Soviet Union at the end of the Cold War is evidence enough of what was at stake. Deep differences necessitated mutual armament. As long as one side felt weaker than the other—the United States in the 1950s, the Soviet Union in the 1960s—neither side could risk reconciliation. Détente emerged in the 1970s only after the military balance stabilized. Once it did, political competition was the decisive factor that led to the termination of the Cold War.[56] Without the renewed confidence of the United States under President Ronald Reagan, the Cold War might have gone on forever. That is exactly what realists expected, the same realists who counseled against drawing clear ideological contrasts between the two societies.[57] Of course, the political and military competition entailed dangers. But the dangers would have been greater if the United States had ignored the political differences or if it had tried to balance military power without a clear sense of its political purposes.

INSTITUTIONS AND MARKETS
Traditional studies assume that structures of diverging identity never change and that structures of decentralized power (or polarity) change, usually by

war, but never escape anarchy. Over long periods of time, however, structures do change and anarchy may be mitigated. Relationships between countries move from one space in figure 1.2 to another. The remarkable event of the post–World War II period is how relationships among the world's great industrial powers evolved peacefully from anarchy to a security community. The critical event for the next fifty years is whether relations between a dominant United States and potential new powers, such as Russia and China, will evolve from hegemony to anarchy or from hegemony to a relatively peaceful security community.

Altering structural relationships is a task for grand strategy. It is not a task for one nation's grand strategy, however, or even the grand strategy of several nations. Structures do not change quickly and are not the direct product of intentional policies. Nevertheless, great powers can act in ways that take into account both existing and potentially desired structural constraints. Presumably, all nations prefer moving other nations toward their identity and toward a compatible organization of power (e.g., toward the left and top of fig. 1.2). To implement this preference, states use two instruments: institutions and markets.

Earlier studies of international institutions and regimes, known as neoliberal institutionalism, suggest that states can use institutions to achieve better material outcomes under anarchy, but that institutions cannot change the structure of anarchy itself.[58] More recent studies suggest that institutions may do more; they may bind states and alter their identities and interests, not just enhance their material benefits.[59] Institutions have this effect, however, among states that are of similar types, that is, that have converging identities. Institutions therefore, may be the effect rather than the cause of structural identity changes. Indeed, the structural opportunity for institutions is greatest in the security community and, ultimately, the hierarchy spaces of figure 1.2, where identities have already converged. States are more willing to bind themselves when they trust one another.

The bigger question is how states arrive in these spaces from hegemony or anarchy. Clearly, the debate among diverging identities is critical—a major source of identity change is ideas.[60] Traditional studies discount ideological competition and focus on military (for realists) and economic (for internationalists) initiatives. But bringing in the structure of identity puts a lot more emphasis on political competition. Autonomous political struggles inside countries as well as political competition between countries supply the changes in relative motivation, which precipitate shifts in relative economic and military power. Such political developments, in turn, alter the prospects and functioning of international institutions as much as international institutions constitute and change state interests and identities. (Chap. 3 suggests how domestic identity changes in the United States coincided with and perhaps caused the historical changes in U.S. power and role in international institutions.)

As an instrument of change, institutions also have a major drawback, especially when power is unequally distributed. They consolidate existing structures of identity and power and give a disproportionate advantage to great powers. Smaller countries sense this inequality. During the Cold War, developing nations spurned institutions established by the great powers, such as the General Agreement on Tariffs and Trade (GATT), International Monetary Fund (IMF), and World Bank, and advocated alternative institutions under the New International Economic Order (NIEO), such as the United Nation Conference on Trade and Development (UNCTAD). Government institutions, which are often thought to be the friends of the poor in domestic systems, are too weak at the international level to provide significant opportunities for greater equality.

Markets may be more powerful instruments of international economic redistribution and structural change, but traditional perspectives insist on treating markets as autonomous and exogenous. As such, markets are outside the control of governments and cannot serve as instruments of state policy to bring about structural change. Indeed, markets threaten state sovereignty and democratic societies.[61]

For example, neorealism equates markets with anarchy, putting them outside the control of any one state. But markets and anarchy are not structurally similar.[62] In markets of any consequence, no one shoots anyone—legitimate public agents exist to prevent and counter the use of force by private agents. By neorealism's own definition, this situation is the exact opposite of anarchy. Classical realist and Marxist studies consider markets to be exogenous— capitalism concentrates and spreads wealth and undermines the political power of dominant states or classes, whatever those states or classes might try to do to stop it.[63] For libertarians too, markets function autonomously without the need for government policies or regulations. This tendency to see markets as disembedded or outside the control of governments lies behind perceptions today that globalization threatens national sovereignty and is driving the international community headlong toward the lowest common denominator in workers' wages, communal solidarity, and environmental protection.

This traditional view of markets is misguided. Markets, whether capitalist or socialist, do not exist apart from governments. Instead, markets reflect the inherent values of the societies in which they operate. Adam Smith, the intellectual father of capitalist markets, understood this basic point from the outset. He wrote *The Theory of Moral Sentiments* before he wrote *The Wealth of Nations*. In the first book, he explores what holds society together to make markets possible, concluding that moral factors matter more than material ones. "The most exquisite sensibility both to the original and sympathetic feelings of others" is a more important virtue, he writes, than one's own "original selfish feelings."[64] Assuming that such sentiments (in his day, Christian sentiments) hold the society together, he goes on to explore the practical basis of markets and material exchanges. In the second book, he concludes that as society becomes more complex and interdependent (the industrial revolution had just begun) human beings cannot arrange to provide for their daily needs by appealing only to the handful of people they may know sentimentally or personally. They have to enter into a division of labor and appeal to the "great multitudes," whose assistance they need but whom they do not know, on the basis of self-interest. But this appeal to self-interest is not an abandonment of social solidarity or sympathetic feelings. Indeed, it is possible only on the basis of such solidarity. For if the butcher, brewer, and baker (Smith's famous trio reflecting the division of labor) do not already live in a society in which they share a sympathetic feeling for the well-being of others, they will not trust one another in the impersonal marketplace to supply their daily needs in exchange for their daily production.[65]

Markets, properly understood, require trust.[66] They do not destroy trust, as radical socialists claim, or operate without it, as libertarian capitalists claim. The issue, therefore, is not how markets undermine society but how societies create markets. What kind of moral values do societies impose on markets? On this issue, democratic and nondemocratic societies disagree profoundly. Nondemocratic societies sanction a community in which the individual takes no active part in government and accepts government control in most, if not all, aspects of civil society, including the marketplace. Liberal democratic societies, on the other hand, advocate a community in which individuals take an active role in government and possess certain inalienable rights to property, privacy, and protection against physical abuses. Democratic markets enfranchise many participants and promote competition. Nondemocratic markets privilege central management and promote control. Liberal markets create inequalities, but government-dominated markets do so even more (witness the privileges of party elites in the formerly communist countries). What is more, government-dominated markets freeze inequalities, whereas liberal markets create a vast middle class and the opportunity for the majority of citizens to ascend or descend the ladder of wealth.

GLOBALIZATION

From this perspective, global markets today are neither operating outside the control of liberal governments nor spawning international institutions that threaten freedom and national sovereignty.[67] Global markets reflect the broad values and institutions of liberal societies. These values and institutions include the growth of a large private sector of trade and investment activities and the emergence of quasi-judicial processes for resolving trade conflicts, such as the dispute settlement mechanisms of the WTO and the North American Free Trade Agreement (NAFTA). Indeed, because liberal democracies dominate global markets, the global economic system is an embryo of an emerging global democracy—I say embryo because it is still fragile and underdeveloped and because, beyond its core of liberal societies, it involves relations with nondemocratic countries, such as China, or early democratizing countries, such as Mexico. These countries do not yet practice fully the rule of law or embrace the standards of political and civil rights that exist in strong democracies. In addition, international organizations today are largely intergovernmental organizations, accessible primarily to government leaders and bureaucrats in member countries but not directly accountable to private citizens and groups. Except in the EU, which has a weak European Parliament, international organizations, even among liberal democracies, are not subject to scrutiny by elected international parliaments and do not elect their leaders by popular vote.

It helps, therefore, to think about the politics of global markets in two stages.[68] The first stage involves relations among the mature democracies, the G-7. Among these countries, markets reflect a common belief in individual freedom, open information, and entrepreneurial and institutional competition. The issue is no longer whether individuals should be free and equal but the degree to which they should be free and equal. The United States has a more individualistic political culture; continental Europe and Japan a more communitarian one. Such differences are healthy among mature democracies. The precise mix of liberty and equality in any society is unknowable in any definitive sense. Indeed, there may be only two great social injustices: when we treat equal people unequally, and when we treat unequal people equally.

Markets among democracies, however, have to be subject to the same democratic accountability as markets within democracies. Within G-7 markets in 2001, executive power is much stronger than legislative or judicial power. The G-7 annual summit, which brings together the heads of state and government of the liberal democracies, has grown in recent decades to include a set of ongoing bureaucratic relationships among trade, finance, foreign ministry, defense, and other officials. As these relationships become more important for setting national policies, parliaments need to become more involved to check directly the exercise of power by international executive institutions. The United States, in particular, with its more individualistic democracy, has an interest in avoiding a situation in which international bureaucracy grows faster than international accountability. Europe provides an example of the political trouble this can cause. The rapid growth of EU authority and institutions outpaced the powers of the European Parliament and created the democratic deficit. EU and national bureaucrats made laws in Brussels without the kind of direct and immediate scrutiny from a weak European Parliament that national parliaments provide at home. The resulting democratic deficit alienated many European citizens (and rightly so) and set back the process of European integration. Developing powerful executive institutions removed from direct parliamentary controls may only heighten the perception that globalization is racing ahead, outside the control of democratically elected governments, and that international institutions threaten national sovereignty and values.[69]

The second stage of the politics of globalization concerns relations with emerging nations. Some of these nations may be democratizing, but others remain nondemocratic. Nondemocratic and even some democratizing countries do not reserve a large space in their political systems for civil society and competitive markets. The government's tentacles reach deeply into the enterprise and judicial life of the country and preclude, or at least seriously obstruct, the noncoercive and nonarbitrary (impartial) management of disputes. China's entry into the WTO and Mexico's membership in NAFTA raise these issues acutely—strong labor unions do not exist to protect workers' rights, courts are not independent and are often corrupt, and no or only weak parliaments scrutinize the daily process of lawmaking among the insulated political elites. In G-7 relations with these countries, global markets do not express a common belief in the freedom and autonomy of private individuals and nongovernmental groups. And participation by these countries in international institutions, which on its face seems to increase democracy, may actually retard the opening of international institutions to greater parliamentary and public scrutiny. Indeed, the secrecy under which some international institutions operate, for example, the IMF and the World Bank, is often due to the insistence of the nondemocratic and democratizing countries themselves. These countries oppose the release of sensitive information about their government's policies and budgets because they do not release such information inside their own countries.

Thus, the case for globalization with emerging nations rests on different grounds. It rests on the argument that economic engagement with these countries will eventually lead to greater political liberalization, creating opportunities for more private-sector activity and encouraging a civil society that is protected from arbitrary government intervention. Global markets, in short, are a way to bring about a different type of state—markets change identities.

The evidence for this argument draws from the experiences of countries such as Spain, Greece, South Korea, Taiwan, and Chile. Through their inclusion in western security and economic relations, these countries evolved from authoritarian societies to emerging democracies. But the evidence is not totally persuasive. Capitalist economies have existed in some countries that were not democratic (e.g., interwar Germany and Japan, and Chile under Pinochet) and exist now in others (e.g., Singapore, Malaysia, and perhaps Hong Kong under mainland Chinese rule). And democracy may weaken or conceivably be lost in a capitalist economy, as some fear may happen in newly democratizing countries.

Capitalist markets, therefore, do not guarantee liberal governments. Economic engagement may affect the *external* identity of nondemocratic countries, but there is no evidence that it alters their *internal* identity. Democratic peace studies find that commerce restrains the use of force within and among democracies. But these studies do not find that commerce plays the leading role in maintaining peace or that commerce is directly associated with bringing about democratic practices.

On the other hand, liberal capitalist markets are clearly associated with democratic government. As Robert Heilbroner, an economic historian, points out, it is a "powerful fact that no non-capitalist country has attained the levels of political, civil, religious, and intellectual freedom found in all advanced capitalism," and "democracy has so far appeared only in nations in which capitalism is the mode of economic organization."[70]

Thus, democratic countries face both an opportunity and a risk in market relations with nondemocracies. The opportunity lies in the fact that capitalist development may be a prerequisite, although not a guarantee, of democracy. The risk lies in the possibility that by fostering market ties democratic countries may simply build up a potential nondemocratic adversary. Democracies and nondemocracies do not have to become adversaries, but the historical record shows that such countries tend to fight one another more often than democracies fight among themselves. In these situations, therefore, the democratic countries will have to both open markets and balance power.

U.S. Foreign Policy

Using measures of relative identity and power that I develop in chapters 4–7, we can map current U.S. foreign relations with various countries in the spaces identified in figure 1.2. This map suggests that the United States does not have one set of national interests determined by relative power. It has several sets because U.S. identity converges with some countries and diverges with others.

The most important U.S. relationships are with the other rich, industrial great powers. These relations, however, do not take place under anarchy. They constitute instead a security community. Where America possesses preponderant power, as it does in the military area, relationships move toward hierarchy. In NATO, for example, the unequal distribution of power has facilitated an unprecedented level of integration of military command and control systems. It is not clear whether this level of integration will be sustained. As the European nations acquire more equal military capabilities over time, America will face tough choices, as chapter 4 details. But U.S. relations with other democracies in economic areas, where power is more equally distributed, suggest that integrated military institutions may not be necessary to preserve the distinguishing feature of a security community, namely that members do not use military force against other members.

The hegemonic space in figure 1.2 clearly characterizes contemporary U.S. relations with emerging nations throughout the world. In this space, U.S.

power dominates, but national identities diverge. Internal identities split between a liberal America, on the one hand, and a communist China or fundamentalist Muslim states, on the other. In addition, external identities reflect a century or more of colonial and hostile relations between the United States (and other western powers) and these countries. Unequal power, on the other hand, helps to stabilize these relationships. In the short and near term, the United States faces no direct or serious threat from China. Hegemony creates a more stable military environment than might be expected under anarchy.

Under hegemony, as noted earlier, emerging states have a choice. They can balance against the United States, or they can assimilate. In Latin America and parts of Asia, emerging nations are integrating with the world economy and moving, however slightly in some cases, toward more liberal democratic societies. In the Middle East (except for Israel and moderate Arab states) and among rogue states in north Africa, northeast Asia, and south Asia, emerging nations are challenging the United States, albeit indirectly through terrorist and asymmetric warfare.

China is perhaps the most important potential challenger to American and western hegemony. China is pursuing an aggressive arms buildup to achieve a better balance of power with the United States (not unlike what the Soviet Union did after the Cuban missile crisis to close the strategic missile gap with the United States). The United States may do all it can do to reassure China that America will not use its superior power aggressively, but it is unlikely that American assurances alone will satisfy Beijing. Given the distrust between the two countries regarding the legitimate use of force, China will probably not feel safe or self-confident until it achieves a more equitable balance in military armaments.

The United States will have to strengthen its security community with Japan and emerging democracies in South Korea and Taiwan to balance power with China. But the purpose of balancing power is not just to stabilize military expectations but to reposition national identities, especially external identities. The United States has to ease China's revisionist aims and convince China that it can achieve its goals within the existing and evolving international system. The best way to do this, of course, is to include China in the broad and growing markets of the world economy. From an identity and power perspective, however, economic engagement is not an alternative to balancing power—the United States has to do both. It must balance power without provoking China to full-scale anarchic rivalry, and it must expand trade to temper China's external feeling of alienation without expecting that trade will do much to spread the rule of law or alter China's internal identity. The power and identity approach counsels intermediate strategies somewhere between the realist balance-of-power approach and the internationalist economic-engagement-leads-to-political-liberalization approach. Chapters 6 and 7 provide the details of U.S. strategies toward China and emerging nations.

Russia is the only country that rivals the United States in nuclear capabilities and in some categories of conventional arms, such as sea and air power. Hence, military power is more evenly distributed between the United States and Russia than between the United States and China. And although Russia's internal identity has shifted away from totalitarian communism, this identity, by any objective measure (as I discuss in chap. 5), still diverges sharply from that of the United States and other mature democracies. The external dimension of Soviet/Russian identity has changed more. Russia no longer stations military forces in the heart of central Europe, it is negotiating with the United States to reduce nuclear arms further, its conventional forces are significantly weakened, and it is cooperating with the United States in the war against terrorism in southwest Asia. Nevertheless, Russia has used brute military force to suppress rebels in Chechnya, part of the Russian Federation. It still pursues imperialist pretensions in Belarus, perhaps in Ukraine, and in the Muslim republics of the former Soviet Union, albeit often with the complicity of repressive rulers in these countries. It continues to compete diplomatically with the United States in the Balkans, the Caucasus, the Baltic states, Iran, the Middle East, and China. And its new president Vladimir Putin is clearly a more assertive leader than Boris Yeltsin. What is more, Russia, western Europe, and the United States continue to share an external history of military intervention and imperialism, conditioning them to be wary of one another when it comes to deciding when the use of force is legitimate in interstate relations.

Ignoring these dimensions of relative national identity, conventional analysis continues to squeeze U.S.-Russian relations into one of two boxes, either anarchy and conflict or hierarchy and cooperation. If Russia is no longer an adversary, it must be an ally. If NATO was formerly an alliance against the Soviet Union, it must now become a collective security arrangement that includes Russia and the former Soviet republics.[71] Conversely, if Russia is still an adversary, it cannot be an ally and NATO must expand to contain Russian imperialism.

The fact is that, at the moment, Russia is neither adversary nor ally. The Russian leaders and people have not yet decided where they are going; Russia's identity is in flux. America will have to continue to balance power with Moscow for some time to come, but, because external identities have converged, it can do so now with greater prospects of peaceful management of military force. And, potentially, America can also influence the repositioning of internal Russian identity, not only to preserve the improved status quo but also to expand shared values and ultimately create an all-European democratic security architecture that includes Russia.

* * *

Old thinking reifies notions of the national interest and the balance of power. New thinking adds critical missing elements to these mental constructs. It does not replace but completes them. National identity organizes and motivates national economic and military power and tells us for what political purposes nations legitimate and use their wealth and power. Relative identity and power then determine the type of international community in which countries exist; national interests differ in different types of community. U.S. foreign relations with most countries today have less to do with balancing military power and more to do with managing political and economic ties.

Historically, the United States needed a military threat to stay engaged in the world. That may be the case again unless America changes its mental images. If it looks for direct military threats, it will find none, retreat, and stand by idly until such threats eventually reemerge. If it looks instead for the sources of military threat in the alignment and shifts of domestic political identities, the United States may find a more congenial world and stay in that world to influence it at manageable cost.

This understanding of the nature and circumstances of American foreign policy is a far cry from the traditional understandings that guided American foreign policy in the past and continue to dominate the post–Cold War debate. As we examine in the next chapter, these traditions perpetuate old thinking and offer us little help as we try to escape the cycles of withdrawal and messianism that have plagued American foreign policy.

CHAPTER TWO

Trade-Offs

America's Foreign Policy Traditions

Since the end of the Cold War, the debate about American foreign policy has followed predictable patterns. Neoisolationists and nationalists summon America to come home, to end Cold War entanglements in Europe and Asia, and to husband U.S. resources behind the natural geographic barriers of two oceans and friendly borders with Mexico and Canada. Realists foresee new threats that need to be contained—threats of economic supremacy from Europe and Japan, of renewed great power conflicts with Russia and China, and of failed and rogue nations that fuel ethnic hatred and international terrorism. Internationalists herald the dawn of a new global age of innovation and information, spreading democratic and nongovernmental institutions, reining in the power of military and industrial establishments, and universalizing labor, human, and environmental rights.

These arguments reflect the main traditions in American foreign policy, perpetuating the cycle of engagement, exhaustion, and exit that historically plagues it. None can sustain an American presence in the world, even the relatively friendly democratizing world of the early twenty-first century. The reason is simple. They all incorporate the same separatist self-image that divides America sharply from the rest of the world and makes it difficult to integrate what America is at home and what the world is like abroad.

Neoisolationists and nationalists reject dependable ties with foreign countries, even with other democracies, and in the process not only diminish the significance of American values, but ultimately vitiate them with policies of unilateralism, protectionism, and nativism (anti-immigration). Internationalists go to the opposite extreme. They empathize so thoroughly with other countries that they dilute American values and, in the process of reforming and building other nations, exhaust the physical and ultimately the psychic resources of the United States. Realists accept the world the way it is (or as they perceive it), actively balancing and manipulating power with other countries; but in the process they lose contact with what motivates American power. By constantly maneuvering, they disparage the American belief that there is more to politics, domestic and foreign, than the perpetual pursuit of power.

Each tradition fails to integrate U.S. domestic values and foreign policy behavior. Isolationism turns inward and becomes narcissistic. Internationalism turns outward and becomes strident. Realism straddles the divide between values and power and becomes cynical. As a result, America is constantly agitated—it never feels at home abroad.

This chapter explores the contradictions in the traditional debate over U.S. foreign policy. My purpose is not to support one tradition or the other but to show that they all share the same separatist self-image, which creates a tradeoff between American values at home and American power abroad. Nationalists and realists often see American values as a domestic obstacle to the use of American power. Internationalists often view American values as an international substitute for American power. But American values and power are not in conflict; they change independently in U.S. foreign relations. If American identity converges with that of other democratic nations, the relevance of both American power and American values changes. The realist prescription to balance military power against these nations makes no sense, nor does the internationalist formula to reform nations that are already democratic. And, in such circumstances, the nationalist appeal to protect America's sovereignty is not an assertion of American values but a rejection—a rejection that casts off democratic allies abroad and undercuts democratic self-confidence at home. U.S. foreign policy traditions do not seem very helpful at a time when all of the industrial great powers are mature democracies.

In what follows, I examine four traditional perspectives on American foreign policy—neoisolationism or nationalism; two versions of realism, one premised on equilibrium and stability (which I label realist) and a second, more ambitious one based on primacy and American hegemony (which I label primacist); and, finally, internationalism.[1]

Neoisolationist or Nationalist America

At the beginning of the twenty-first century, the nationalist approach to American foreign policy seeks to undo the ambitious foreign policy legacies of the Cold War and its aftermath. Weary of working with allies and frustrated by UN humanitarian interventions, this approach seeks to bring America back to more modest goals, to root American foreign policy in the natural separateness of American geography, and to create maximum flexibility for American diplomacy to defend military and economic interests within and beyond this hemisphere. By trimming American commitments in Europe and Asia, staying away from chronic instability in developing nations, and emphasizing American unilateralism, the nationalist school embraces independence and autonomy. Neoisolationists favor few, if any, commitments abroad; nationalists accept some commitments as long as the United States retains maximum discretion to implement them.[2]

Nationalists assume that American politics is relatively immune from foreign quarrels. America can wait safely in its geographic sanctuary and still be ready to act decisively if overseas quarrels eventually provoke attacks on American soil. Yet, despite their confidence in America's situation, nationalists see the country as weaker and more vulnerable than do realists. Hence, they insist that America stay closer to home and husband its resources. They fear that UN diplomats or corporate elites may conspire to squander American might and flexibility in premature adventures around the world.

For strict nationalists, the Old World of anarchy persists. Differences and conflicts outside America abound, and these differences are insurmountable. Neither the spread of democracy advocated by internationalists nor the world order and stability pursued by realists are likely to mitigate these differences. As Alan Tonelson, a nationalist-oriented commentator, wryly argues, "A more orderly, more democratic world would of course be wonderful. But both goals seem fanciful." What is more, neither goal is necessary for American security. "We have thrived even though we have been surrounded by dictators for most of our national life."[3] Hence, wherever disorder threatens abroad, America should get as far away as possible. Nationalists advocate a "rope-a-dope" national security strategy: hang back and let other countries punch each other out. America can always step in later, after the belligerents are weaker and America is stronger. Just as Britain in the nineteenth century stayed out of the continent's quarrels and balanced power from offshore, so America, with even greater geostrategic advantages, can stay out of the quarrels of both Europe and Asia and intervene, if at all, only when it is absolutely necessary.[4]

Neoisolationists, the most ardent advocates of minimal American commitments abroad, believe that America's major advantage is strategic immunity. The United States is unique not just ideologically but geographically. It is the only great power in history to be surrounded by two vast oceans with no great power challenging it in its hemisphere. (By contrast, England always had some great power on the European continent challenging its power, Europe always had Russia, and Japan always had China.) What is more, the United States has unchallenged sea and air power in the oceans, its ships and planes dominating the skies and sea-lanes and serving as an early warning and forward line of defense for the United States. If the United States were not engaged strategically with NATO, Japan, or Israel, it would not be involved in conflicts in these areas and would be less subject to terrorism. It might still be vulnerable to some terrorist attacks, nuclear proliferation, and energy shortages, but vigilant homeland security, a basic nuclear deterrent, and national missile defense capability, along with strategic petroleum reserves, would minimize these threats. Operating from the strategic sanctuary of North America, the United States would send unmistakable signals about its intentions and avoid the ambiguities of multilateral or forward-based defense commitments. Thus, Eric Nordlinger, one of the most persuasive advocates of neoisolationism, concludes, "going abroad to ensure America's security is unnecessary, doing so regularly detracts from it."[5]

If the outside world is so unstable, however, is not the retreat to strategic immunity just a delaying tactic? Will not the conflicts escalate and eventually threaten the United States? Was that not what happened in both world wars and the Cold War? And did it not happen again in September 2001 when terrorists attacked the World Trade Center and the Pentagon?

Nationalists say no because they believe that foreign conflicts are largely self-balancing. The countries most directly involved can be counted on to deter conflict and root out terrorism. After all, these countries have the most at stake, and defense is the central imperative that drives the conduct of nations. Hence, if America is not involved, they will fight their own battles. The spread of nuclear weapons helps, not hurts, this process because these weapons increase the costs of conflict and concentrate attention.[6] When concerned with their own defense and not with vague commitments beyond their borders, nations make fewer mistakes and are less prone to use mutually destructive weapons inadvertently. Despite the disorderliness of the world, strict nationalists count on a hard-nosed capability in each country to calculate its interests rationally, particularly when the chips are down and the country's very survival is at stake.

Working from this logic, neoisolationists conclude that the United States can pull back from Europe and Asia and not only save 50 percent on defense costs (Nordlinger's estimate)[7] but expect Europe and Japan to spend more on their own defense. During the Cold War, the United States gave these countries a free ride. It provided for their defense, while economically they caught up with, and even pulled ahead of, the United States. In the world of the twenty-first century, America has to shift more defense burdens to its allies and compete with them more aggressively on the economic front.

Some neoisolationists, such as Nordlinger, favor free trade, but others, along with nationalists, worry that economic competition is now a new kind of warfare in world affairs. Geoeconomics has replaced geopolitics.[8] Nations no longer fight over territory; they fight over market share. Governments stage-manage this competition through trade barriers, industrial policies, and export subsidies, just as governments once stage-managed geopolitical competition through military forces, alliances, and wars. America, with its tendency to favor free trade and leave economic competition to the private sector, is losing out and has to take geoeconomics more seriously. In the information age, economic development is a principal source of national strength, and the nurturing of American strength is the central objective of a nationalist-oriented strategy that holds back until America is directly threatened.

Just how aggressively can America compete economically, however, if it is to stay out of foreign military entanglements? This question has posed a dilemma for neoisolationists and nationalists since the time of Thomas Jefferson. Jefferson's famous injunction to the new republic was: "Peace, commerce and honest friendship with all nations, entangling alliances with none."[9] The prescription assumed that trade could be separated from military alignments, but Jefferson himself learned that this proposition is hard to put into practice. Commerce was the only tool available to him to stop British impressment of American seamen, and so he embargoed U.S. trade. But the embargo did not end the matter; it eventually led to war with Great Britain in 1812. Trade embargoes remained a favorite tool of later isolationists—for example, the neutrality legislation of the late 1930s—but they seldom worked to keep America out of foreign entanglements. The reason for this is simple. Denying American trade is never an evenhanded policy; it helps or hurts one belligerent more than another,[10] thus entangling the United States in other nations' conflicts as surely as if America had given economic aid to one side (which, in effect, an embargo does).

Commerce cannot avoid political entanglements; it requires them. Trade flourishes in political communities, not in their absence. The post–World War II world economy grew out of the U.S.-led Cold War alliance against the Soviet Union, and now it is expanding beyond the western world under the umbrella of the United States and its democratic allies. Nothing will put an end to global markets as quickly as the emergence of a great power that opposes U.S. and western leadership.

Thus, nationalist advocates of geoeconomics are exploiting the very alliance relationships among the United States, Europe, and Asia that they seek to trim back. They welcome trade tensions, but expect that these tensions will not entangle America in traditional military rivalries. For example, economic nationalists in the Clinton administration risked security ties with Japan during auto trade disputes in 1995 because they assumed Japan would not pursue threatening security policies even if the U.S.–Japanese alliance were to weaken.[11] But if Japan is intent on "cleaning America's clock" economically, why should Washington trust it to pursue benign security policies toward the United States once the alliance has been weakened?[12] In fact, the United States can risk aggressive trade policies with Europe or Japan only if it preserves strong alliance relationships with these competitors.

The nationalist school straddles a fine line between the economic nationalism it advocates and the entangling balance of power politics it rejects. If the world is sufficiently resilient to absorb intense economic competition without provoking traditional geopolitical conflicts, then perhaps the world is not so disorderly that America needs to retreat as much as nationalists recommend. And if the world is so disorderly that America has to flee geopolitical rivalries in Europe and Asia, we might reasonably doubt that such a world will accommodate America's economic interests. Jefferson hoped that commerce would avoid or soften conflict. Such is still the hope today of libertarian isolationists.[13] But nationalist-oriented neoisolationists have no such faith in the "sweet

47

spirits" of commerce. They expect to have to fight aggressively for trade advantage, yet somehow expect to avoid the geopolitical fights that economic nationalism usually ignites.

If history is any guide, nationalists eventually will have to fight for geopolitical interests. So, at best, this strategy of "muscular stay-at-homeism"[14] delays but does not avoid foreign entanglements. Is the delay worth it? Yes, say nationalists, if delay conserves and builds up American strength. But strength is only one half of national interests. What about American identity? What kind of America is reflected in this aggressive nationalist strategy?

Most neoisolationists and nationalists do not have a demanding vision of domestic politics. They are not big domestic reformers. At best, they seek to avoid the contamination of domestic institutions by standing military forces (the threat of a garrison state) or by compromising alliances with foreign despots. In this way, they argue, America's liberal example can be more perfectly projected into international affairs. But how liberal is America likely to remain if it cuts itself off from all challenges to liberalism abroad? Many strict nationalists portray a vacuous, if not mean-spirited, image of America.

When Patrick Buchanan, an ardent American nationalist, was asked what America's national purpose was, he summed it up in a six-word toast once uttered by President Andrew Jackson: "The Union, it must be preserved."[15] Survival! But survival of what? It is well to remember that, before the Civil War, when American nationalism peaked (in the war against Mexico), the country was massively and eventually violently divided. Similarly today, when we look behind the nationalist views of American interests, we often see an unappealing American identity—one divided by nativist fears of foreign immigrants; class resentments against cosmopolitan bankers, corporate leaders, and intellectuals; and racist animosities toward nonwhite, non-European, and non-Christian Americans.[16]

Nationalists give up too much of American values as they worry too much about the preservation of American power. They reject an ambitious foreign policy in normal times, but then expect heroic national exertion in times of crisis. But will the muscles flex when they are called on? Nationalists assume that power is muscle. But power is also, in equal part, a healthy mind and spirit—in short a unifying and motivating national identity. In their hands, aggressive nationalism is likely to vitiate America's liberal self-image. When America is called on to defend its national interests, the nation itself may be divided and distempered.

Realist America

Realist advocates see the world much as nationalist Americans do—as a place of conflicts and balances. But they do not see this Old World as self-balancing.

Great powers have to do the balancing themselves, through engaged and active diplomacy, and this diplomacy requires farsighted statesmanship and a domestic willingness to sacrifice and give priority to foreign affairs. According to this logic, the United States has to remain engaged in Europe and Asia, maneuvering to preserve a multipolar balance and protect American interests.

Unlike nationalists, realists fear that other countries do not balance just to defend themselves but often seek to dominate others. As Henry Kissinger writes, "*raison d'etat* [the pursuit of national interest] can lead to a quest for primacy or to establishment of equilibrium." The quest for primacy is often inevitable, Kissinger adds, "except in the hands of a master and it probably is even then."[17]

The realist perspective straddles the nationalist and primacist positions. It does not expect automatic or near-automatic balancing, as the nationalist perspective does, because nations seek primacy, not balance. Nevertheless, although it expects primacy, the realist view does not endorse primacy as a goal. The goal is balance or equilibrium, and realism relies on the skills of the master statesman to resist primacy. Foreign policy is best left in the hands of an elite group of experts who have the wisdom, experience, and prudence to exercise self-restraint in foreign affairs—traits that ordinary people, particularly in a democracy, do not have.[18]

Because some countries seek primacy and others balance, the two motivations work in harmony. Primacy both provokes and disrupts balancing. Containment was the master balancing stroke of the United States and its allies against the imperialist drive of the Soviet Union. But now that the United States dominates the landscape, other nations will just as surely strike to counterbalance and contain the United States.[19] Realist strategists expect a multipolar world to reemerge in military affairs, even among former Cold War allies. As Henry Kissinger writes, "when there is no longer a single threat and each country perceives its perils from its own national perspective, those societies which had nestled under American protection will feel compelled to assume greater responsibility for their own security. Thus, the operation of the new international system will move toward equilibrium even in the military field, though it may take some decades to reach that point."[20] Such multipolarity is not only inevitable, it is good. The interests of all powers, according to two other realist authors, are best served "by a world order in which no power, and no combination of powers, strives for hegemony or empire."[21] This proposition apparently holds even if the dominant power or combination of powers is democratic.

In fact, according to realists, democracies do not help mitigate the balance of military power; they inflame it. Democracy and capitalism exacerbate power disparities.[22] And as George Kennan observes, democracies themselves become the problem when they fight wars to punish rather than to balance.[23] Applying this critique to foreign policy in general, realists are fond of quoting Alexis de Tocqueville: "it is especially in the conduct of their foreign relations that democracies appear to me decidedly inferior to other governments."[24]

Realists insist that foreign policy be pursued without consideration of the domestic politics of other countries. Traditional diplomacy would advise, writes James Schlesinger, "that we base our stance toward states on whether they are antagonistic or friendly toward us and not on their internal arrangements."[25] The goal of diplomacy is not democracy or even peace; it is stability and moderation. The balancing of military power is a never-ending task that is not affected by the convergence of domestic identities. Today, realists criticize U.S. policies that align with Russia because the latter is democratizing, or that favor Japan over China because Japan is already democratic. Geopolitics, they argue, dictates that we should be balancing against Russia in east-central Europe and treating Japan and China evenhandedly in Asia.[26]

Without moorings in domestic politics, realists lack direction in international politics. The world is not going anywhere, except endlessly toward equilibrium (with moderation if we get lucky). There are few standards, but certainly no moral ones, by which to judge diplomacy—tactical maneuvering to preserve options is the highest good.[27]

How does one gain support for such a diplomacy in a democratic society? The realists are truly baffled by this question. Kennan, for example, eventually concedes that sustained domestic support is not possible and calls for "a very modest and restrained [American] foreign policy."[28] He drifts toward neoisolationism, believing that America faces more serious troubles at home than abroad. Kissinger is less willing to concede the statesman's activist mantle. He grudgingly admires the Wilsonian or idealist theme in American foreign policy and is totally perplexed by the "astonishing performance" of Ronald Reagan's ideological approach to foreign policy.[29] In the end, it is unclear whether Kissinger accepts what Woodrow Wilson and Reagan certainly believed—that domestic politics defines the morality and purpose of foreign affairs and that power and balancing are means to this end, not ends in themselves—or believes that Reagan, in particular, was simply more clever than other presidents at harnessing American idealism to the requirements of geopolitics. Apparently Kissinger believes both: the latter because he concludes in one book that the ideological era of world politics is over and the world will drift back to the equilibrium politics of the nineteenth century,[30] and the former because he concludes in a later book that "in the Atlantic area, war [an ever-present possibility in equilibrium politics] is no longer accepted as an instrument of policy."[31]

Equilibrium politics, however, already contains an element of ideological politics. As we discuss in chapter 1, the balance of power does not achieve stability without the existence of some shared values, some consensus that the status quo is desirable. Metternich achieved such a consensus on the basis of conservative domestic values. Wilson tried to do the same thing on the basis of liberal domestic values. So why is a new Wilsonianism not possible at the beginning of the twenty-first century, when the entire industrial world shares common liberal values? Why is it inevitable that the world drift back to the nineteenth century's balance-of-power politics? It is not inevitable. In his later book, Kissinger himself backs away from these illogical conclusions, conceding that democracies do indeed pursue a different kind of international politics among themselves. This politics is rooted in the Wilsonian ideal of "peace based on democracy and economic progress" and is distinct from the equilibrium politics of the nineteenth century or the religious politics of the seventeenth century. Among democracies, Kissinger notes, "disputes are not settled by war or the threat of war."[32] Now, if this is the case among democracies, why should American foreign policy not aim for more than equilibrium in relations with other countries, if only like Metternich to succeed at balancing power while avoiding war with these countries? If every equilibrium depends on some consensus of values, why not seek to project American values on world order? This is the logic that leads to a more ambitious realist position in American foreign policy—a primacist role in world affairs.

Primacist America

For advocates of a primacist America, power in international affairs is a matter more of influence than of capabilities. Primacists shift the emphasis from balancing relative capabilities to influencing the goals that the balance of power serves. If realists focus on the tactical skills of conservative nineteenth-century monarchs, primacists focus on the conservative values those monarchs promoted. Primacists understand that every *balance* of power reflects some *community* of power. If one country settles for self-restraint, as realists urge, or opts out of international affairs, as neoisolationists urge, some other country will shape the moral environment of international affairs. Hence, primacists ask why their country should not shape the values and goals of that environment.[33]

Primacist America perspectives, therefore, exhibit much less ambivalence about American values than do realist or neoisolationist perspectives. They endorse Reagan's affirmation of domestic values in foreign affairs and propose "a neo-Reaganite foreign policy of military supremacy and moral confidence," which they label "benevolent global hegemony."[34] They call for increased defense budgets, a revitalized citizen military force, and more moral clarity toward authoritarian and totalitarian regimes such as China, Iran, and North Korea. Their objective is to discourage other nations, even friendly democratic ones, from challenging American leadership or seeking to overturn the established international order shaped by American political and economic values.[35]

For primacists, unlike nationalists and realists, domestic and foreign affairs do not compete with or encumber each other; they reinforce each other. As William Kristol and Robert Kagan argue, without an aggressive foreign policy, domestic preoccupations "too easily degenerate into the pinched nationalism of Buchanan's America First, where the appeal to narrow self-interest masks a deeper form of self-loathing. . . . The remoralization of America at home ultimately requires the remoralization of American foreign policy."[36] The Cold War conflict proved this complementarity. "The event that caused the greatest diversion of resources from domestic to foreign policy in our history generated unparalleled progress on our two most important domestic issues"—prosperity and racial justice.[37]

For advocates of American primacy, the world is extraordinarily turbulent. It is unlikely to balance on its own, as nationalists hope, or to equilibrate through active balancing, as realists expect. Because nations care about values, not just material survival, they may not settle for balancing. They may challenge the status quo and climb on the bandwagon rather than balance, joining the strongest or most self-confident power rather than aligning against it. Self-restraint, which realists celebrate, simply concedes the advantage to more self-confident powers. Nature abhors a vacuum of values no less than a vacuum of power.

What matters, then, is the values that great powers advocate, not that they refrain from injecting values into foreign affairs. The United States and the former Soviet Union advocated universalistic values; other nations advocate more particularistic values. But all seek to put their stamp on world order.

Hence, as Samuel P. Huntington argues, the United States, like any other country, has no choice but to promote its values in the international system. "To argue that primacy does not matter," he concludes, "is to argue that political and economic values do not matter and that democracy does not or should not matter." "A world without U.S. primacy," he warns, "will be a world with more violence and disorder and less democracy and economic growth than a world where the United States continues to have more influence than any other country in shaping global affairs."[38]

Advocates of primacy disagree about how far the promotion of domestic values should go. For all of them, it must at least condition the international environment—set the terms of the community of power (not just the balance of power) that international affairs inevitably entails. Otherwise, some other nation will set these terms. But some primacists want to see the direct export of domestic values to foreign countries. It is difficult to draw the line, they believe, because domestic and foreign affairs are so closely linked. Thus, primacy slides into an internationalist pursuit to reform the world in a nation's own image.[39]

Primacists do solve one problem of realism, namely that countries may challenge, not accept, the status quo. They create another problem, however—a yawning gap between the primacist power's ambitions and its resources.[40] Because primacists believe in the assertive use of military power, they risk a foreign policy in which burdens accumulate and eventually lead to what Paul Kennedy calls "military overstretch."[41] The hegemon becomes involved in too many commitments and conflicts, its military adventures draining resources from investment and economic growth. Other countries then sneak up on it, avoiding military entanglements and surpassing it in economic and technological preeminence.

Faced with this gap between goals and resources, primacists split in two directions. Some trim back their definition of America's goals and become more like realists. Others assume that international organizations and global historical forces make American goals possible without the significant use of American military forces and become more like internationalists. Huntington is an example of the first path, Zbigniew Brzezinski the second.

In his more recent work, Huntington backs off from the idea that American values are universal. In his widely read argument about the clash of civilizations, he contends that cultures limit the applicability of values and that democracy is relevant only in western culture.[42] Democracy and western civilization, he suggests, are valuable not because they are universal but because they are unique. He calls on the United States "to abandon the illusion of universality and to promote the strength, coherence, and vitality of its civilization in a world of civilizations."[43] The United States should concentrate on Europe and "the further development of institutional ties across the Atlantic, including negotiation of a European-American free trade agreement and creation of a North American economic organization as a counterpart to NATO."[44] Beyond the Atlantic, America faces new conflicts with other cultures, essentially "civilization clashes" with Confucian and Islamic societies.

Part of what prompts Huntington's reversal and distinguishes his liberal version of American primacy from more conservative, neo-Reaganite versions is a sense that America and the West are in decline and that American democracy itself is in trouble. In his book, Huntington details a general decline of the West in population, territorial control, number of people speaking English, number of Christians in the world, and other factors. Conversely, he documents a general rise of Islamic and Asian cultures. The most troubling evidence he finds is "moral decline, cultural suicide and political disunity in the West."[45] For him, multiculturalism and commercial interests are fragmenting American identity and national interests. "If multiculturalism prevails and if the consensus on liberal democracies disintegrates," Huntington writes, "the United States could join the Soviet Union on the ash heap of history."[46]

Like the realists, Huntington argues that the United States may need a new enemy to maintain its unity.[47] Yet, unlike realists, he calls on America not to confront rising cultures but to fall back. "The national interest is national restraint . . . and foreign policy elites might well devote their energies to

53

designing plans for lowering American involvement in the world in ways that will safeguard possible future national interests."[48] In the end, Huntington sounds more like a nationalist than a realist or primacist. He sees the primacist power slowly succumbing to counterbalancing powers, as realists predict, and urges America to husband its resources for future conflicts, as nationalists advise.

Brzezinski moves in the opposite direction.[49] He too is an ambitious American primacist who harbors doubts about American and western society, what he labels the "spiritual emptiness of permissive cornucopia."[50] But he is more positive about the universality of American openness and multiculturalism, and believes that America's "internal structure and dynamics make it organically congenial" to the new economic and communications forces that are transforming international affairs.[51] "Increasingly," Brzezinski writes, "world affairs are shaped by domestic trends that recognize no frontiers and require collective responses by governments less and less able to act in a 'sovereign' fashion."[52] This process is forging "an initial worldwide consensus that might be the beginning of a universal moral standard."[53] It "is generating progressively deepening cooperation on a global scale," and "that cooperation has to assume, and is assuming, organizational forms, expressed through the growth in number and in power of international bodies. . . ." "The result," Brzezinski concludes, "is a web of institutions that cumulatively express the reality of international interdependence."[54]

In this context, according to Brzezinski, "U.S. preponderance is both a reality and an illusion."[55] It is a reality in the sense that America's response to the information revolution is more critical than that of any other nation. But it is an illusion in the sense that America's response is a function of its domestic social and cultural values and authority, not its external military and economic exertions. Hence, America does not have to face the unipolar power's traditional gap between goals and resources because global technological forces are helping to advance U.S. goals. America's key resource in this process is not military but moral.

As a rule, primacists do not believe the United States can expect much help from its allies;[56] America carries the burdens of primacy largely alone. But what if America had more confidence in its allies, identified more with their mature democratic institutions and values, and recognized that mature democracies do not balance power against one another? Is not the peace among the mature industrial democracies a reality? As Robert Jervis, a critic of primacy, puts it, "if statesmen expect peace among the developed countries, what are the competitive reasons for seeking primacy?"[57]

Internationalists, in contrast, have always entertained the prospect that democratic nations might behave differently and provide a more secure foundation for American foreign policy in the world. But they have tended to apply the democratic label loosely (to countries that are far from democratic) and to rely too heavily on international organizations and economic interdependence to safeguard a peace that still requires the active use of military power.

Internationalist America

Internationalists are less ambivalent than realists about the universal purposes of American foreign policy, but they are more ambivalent about the use of military power to implement these purposes. They prefer a multilateral internationalism that relies on institutions, rather than a muscular internationalism that relies on military strength. They seek to transform an Old World order of balance of power and despots through a New World diplomacy of cooperative security, international law, peaceful commerce, and democratic public opinion. The means are often not commensurate with the ends.[58]

Internationalists accept the universality of democratic values and seek to structure a world environment of international law, organizations, and economic interdependence that promotes these values. Whereas early isolationists (actually nationalists—they favored unilateralism not abstention in foreign affairs), such as Jefferson and John Quincy Adams, doubted that countries in Europe or Latin America could ever become democratic, and realists wondered why it would matter if they did. Wilson, the standard-bearer of internationalism, campaigned "to make the world safe for democracy" in both Europe and Latin America.[59] For him, national self-determination was not an end in itself, as it is for realists, but a means to achieve liberal democratic societies through popular sovereignty.[60] To get there, Wilson talked about a community of power rather than a balance of power; he set forth the League of Nations as a collective security arrangement to defend national self-determination for all countries, rather than as a traditional realist alliance to defend some countries against others.

Wilson lost his battle for the League, and democracy faded in Europe as one country after another slipped into the grip of chauvinism and irredentism. But Franklin Roosevelt resurrected the idea in the United Nations, supplementing Wilson's collective security system with a traditional alliance of the five great powers, wielding veto power in the UN Security Council. The UN also failed as the Cold War ignited. But the western alliance against the Soviet Union, albeit a traditional realist structure in NATO, did go on to create a community of power that nurtured the strengthening and spread of modern democratic societies throughout the industrial world. Even after the collapse of the Soviet Union, this community practices a different kind of international politics, which Theodore Sorensen calls "a community of democracies united by their commitment to law and peace, neither threatened by hostile armies or ideologies nor dominated by any one nation politically or economically."[61]

Has Wilson's moment finally arrived? Internationalists think so. They see a movement toward democracy, markets, and the rule of law supported by powerful historical forces, none of which existed in any significant way when Wilson first tried the internationalist formula. These forces include the declining appeal of war due to nuclear weapons, the march of modernization and the communications age, the increasing influence and credibility of intergovernmental and nongovernmental organizations, an open, dynamic, multicultural global economy that reflects a universal desire for economic opportunity and at least minimal levels of respect for labor and human rights, and a planet Earth reality that elevates the common interests of population and pollution control, preservation of scarce resources, and conservation of rare forms of life.[62] In a sense, these forces make it easier and less costly for the United States to pursue the enlargement of democracy and markets. The Old World is cooperating to bring about the New—instead of producing spiraling instability, as nationalists believe, or stable balances, as realists expect, the Old World is helping to bring about a measure of natural harmony, in which a community of democracies expands and provides a peaceful alternative to international anarchy.

Because the Old World is helping, the New World does not have to exert so much effort to realize internationalist goals, even though these goals are far more ambitious than the stability that realists pursue.[63] Compared to realists, internationalists support lower defense budgets, trust more in allies and even nondemocracies to assume the burdens of local defense and stability, believe more ardently that trade and development can help to bring about democracy, and rely more on arms control and multilateral institutions to protect security and human rights. Internationalists prefer to withdraw U.S. forces from Europe and Asia. If that is not possible, they support NATO as it is but oppose expanding it. And if that is not possible, they prefer an expansion of NATO at minimal cost.[64] If the United States does withdraw, they expect that the European Union and Japan will do more.

Internationalists also expect Russia and China to behave as responsible powers, capable under UN supervision of policing regional disputes in the former Soviet republics and in Asia.[65] In both Europe and Asia, arms control, confidence-building exercises, and multilateral institutions can take care of diminishing security concerns. As long as Russia is democratizing, arms control treaties (Strategic Arms Limitation Treaty, SALT; Anti-Ballistic Missile, ABM, Treaty; Conventional Forces in Europe, CFE, Treaty; etc.) provide common security by making defensive weapon systems dominant (e.g., eliminating missiles armed with multiple weapons) and by making military exercises and planning more transparent.[66] In Asia, internationalists advocate relying on new cooperative security structures where few now exist and the ones that do are very weak.[67]

Finally, internationalists look to trade and international organizations to do the heavy lifting for them in reaching their lofty goals. In Europe, expanding the EU is far more helpful, they believe, than expanding NATO. And in Asia, admitting China to the WTO is more important than strengthening the U.S.-Japan Security Treaty, which threatens China. Economic interdependence softens external rivalries and advances the rule of law in domestic politics.

Multilateralism is the calling card of American internationalists, much as unilateralism is of nationalists. The New World is an open, inclusive, and multicultural world, and the Old World is now becoming more open and inclusive as well. Thus America's "open multiculturalism reinforces the organic linkage between America and the rest of the world,"[68] giving America a natural advantage in such a world. Multilateralism, in fact, goes to the core of American identity. As John Ruggie observes, "a multilateral vision of world order is singularly compatible with America's collective self-conception as a nation. Indeed the vision taps into the *very idea* of America."[69]

Internationalists may be on to something. As I argue in this book, the democratic peace among the industrial great powers is an astonishing, if not well understood, reality. These countries are not behaving like traditional great powers. Shared democratic values, open trade and financial markets, international organizations, and the rule of law do seem to matter, and they seem to matter far more than nationalists or realists have ever been willing to recognize. But internationalists make it seem too easy. They apply the democratic peace immediately to relations with weak democratizing countries such as Russia; they treat too cavalierly the political and security conditions that are necessary to nurture open, competitive economic markets; and they ignore the democratic deficit that many international institutions create by wielding increasing power without direct accountability. The only check on such institutions is through nationally elected institutions, such as the U.S. Congress. But internationalists regularly criticize Congress for not providing more money to international institutions.

Moreover, the democratic peace does not hold in relations between democratic and democratizing powers. It is a weak reed, therefore, on which to hang U.S.-Russian relations in Europe or U.S.-Chinese relations in Asia. Balancing power continues to be necessary to insure against a reversal of political liberalization in Russia or against aggressive nationalism in China and to consolidate democratizing movements in east-central Europe and east Asia. Over the long run, the inclusion of Poland, Hungary, and the Czech Republic in NATO and the strengthening of U.S. alliances in Asia improve the prospects for democracy in the republics of the former Soviet Union and in southeast Asia and China.

Strengthening alliances does something more, however—it makes expanding markets possible. A larger NATO in Europe and widening U.S. alliances in Asia are not alternatives to trade and economic cooperation; they are pre-requisites. As we noted in chapter 1, markets require trust, and trust requires security. An expanding NATO underpins an expanding EU, and military stability in Asia makes possible China's entry into the WTO.

Cooperative security is also a weak reed on which to hang U.S. policy in Asia. Multilateral economic arrangements, such as APEC, lack an underlying multilateral security framework. The ARF in Asia is sometimes compared to the Helsinki process in Europe during the 1970s and 1980s. But there is one big difference: ARF has no NATO to back it up. Asia has only a tenuous security infrastructure provided essentially by the American Seventh Fleet. No one with good judgment believes that Helsinki and détente would have worked in Europe without NATO and deterrence. That same judgment applies in Asia today; APEC and ARF cannot succeed without a more predictable military balance of power.

Finally, international organizations that protect the independence of sovereign nations, and particularly the liberty of democratic nations, are not automatically good things. They may become fertile arenas for new tyrannies—cabals of special interests, technical specialists, and overweening intellectuals making decisions behind the scenes and under the table. These institutions need to be accountable to democratic procedures and ultimately to the voting public in which democracies invest sovereignty. Contemporary international institutions, which are intergovernmental organizations run by national governments and are hence once removed from national parliaments, are not yet democratic. This fact fuels a lot of justified public resentment against such institutions. In Europe, the public complains about the democratic deficit, the fact that EU bureaucrats operate with little scrutiny from the European Parliament. In the United States, Congress questions the spending and lack of accountability of UN organizations, such as the IMF, World Bank, and WTO, and of blue-helmet UN peacekeeping activities. The process of democratizing international organizations will be long and arduous, easier perhaps because the most important members of today's international organizations are already democratic, but a successful outcome cannot just be assumed.

Internationalists are sometimes more concerned about democratic faults at home than democratic deficits abroad. They actually welcome international organizations to restrain American foreign policy, fearing that America does too little to mitigate inequalities both at home and abroad.[70] Unlike realists, such as Huntington, internationalists welcome multiculturalism in America and do not see it as threatening American values or weakening American unity.[71] They believe European societies and even Japan do a better job of dealing with inequality. Hence, they look to foreign countries and international organizations to provide solutions for American domestic politics. In this way, as Charles Krauthammer, a critic of multilateralism, observes, "multilateralism is the isolationism of the internationalist," the costless way of reforming both the United States and the world.[72]

* * *

How does America escape the limits of the traditional foreign policy debate among nationalists, realists, and internationalists? It can do so, I believe, only by changing its separatist self-image. This image divides America too sharply from the rest of the world and so forces a trade-off between American values and American power. Nationalists place so much emphasis on unilateral power that it eventually turns against American values. Realists seek to balance power actively, but find no basis in American values to sustain the balance of power for its own sake. Primacists enlist American values to sustain a world role, but stretch American power to the breaking point. Internationalists ease the requirement for American power by assuming that globalization and international organizations advance American values without the use of American power. Each tradition fails to integrate American power and American values.

To escape the trade-off between values and power, America has to expand its self-image. Rather than seeing itself as separate from Europe and Japan, it has to recognize that it shares a common liberal identity with other mature industrial democracies. Although the United States remains separate from those countries physically, it is no longer separate from them politically. Among these countries, self-images have converged, and they have done so independently of power. America has not lost its sovereignty—it is no weaker or less capable physically toward Europe or Japan. Identifying politically with those countries simply offers a more effective framework for exercising American sovereignty and power.

As the next chapter details, Europe has always been a part of America's struggle for freedom, and Japan is America's principal link to the struggle for freedom in Asia. America needs these countries to avoid the parochialism of nationalism, the vanity of internationalism, and the cynicism of realism. In political partnership with Europe and Japan, America might finally feel more confident and comfortable in world affairs, closing the gap between its aspirations and its power. It might finally take its proper place at home abroad.

CHAPTER THREE

National Identity

Consequences for Foreign Policy

America's identity has shaped American foreign policy just as much as American power has. This identity is a product of both internal experiences unique to America, such as the Civil War, and external interactions with other societies, especially in Europe. These internal and external dimensions of identity change, often independently of power, to influence the accumulation and use of national power. The influence of identity is evident in four distinct periods of American history.

In the first period, from 1789 to 1865, America was torn between an aristocratic republic and a popular democracy. American politics was the playground of propertied elites, including slave owners; but it was also the embryo of a liberal democracy proclaiming the freedom and equality of all people. This conflict defined the nation: Did freedom and equality apply to states, which were then free to enslave; or did they apply to individuals, including slaves, who were then protected by the federal government? American foreign policy mirrored these divisions, both in the country's expansion and fight over slavery and in the defensive and divided preferences of early American leaders regarding relations with European powers. Isolationism and unilateralism were foreign policies of a *conflicted republic* as well as the obvious alternatives for a small power trying to escape the clutches of European despots.

In the second period, from 1865 to 1930, America's identity congealed as an *electoral democracy* with legal equality for all individuals, an expanding franchise, and institutions directly elected by the people. Reflecting this new internal unity as well as growing industrial power, American foreign policy became more robust and projected progressive political reforms abroad. It set about to establish good government in foreign colonies (e.g., Cuba, the Philippines, etc.), to elect good men in Mexico and the Caribbean, and to promote self-determination in Europe after World War I.

In the third period, from 1930 to 1965, America's self-image deepened under the impact of the New Deal and World War II. It embraced a greater concern for *social democracy*—economic opportunity and social security. As a result, American foreign policy sensed that deeper social factors, not just political factors, divided nations. The Cold War between liberal and communist societies elicited more intense passions than ever before, and, for the first time, American foreign policy addressed social as well as political reforms in foreign countries—breaking up prewar elites in Germany and Japan, and pressing for rural and educational reforms in South Korea and Latin America.

In the fourth and most recent period, since 1965, the civil rights revolution and a new surge of non-European immigrants have challenged America's identity at a still deeper level. Are democracy's most fundamental roots individualistic and universal or are they social and cultural? Is America a *liberal democracy* based on equal opportunity for individuals or a *multicultural democracy* based on equal representation of diverse cultural groups? Under this challenge, American foreign policy wavers between a desire to secure democracy, markets, and human rights worldwide and a willingness to tolerate a multicultural world, even cultures that do not respect the rights and freedom of their own people.

America's self-image continues to change. Which element of its self-image will prevail in the future—the ideological one associated with the American constitution and creed; the nativist one associated with history, language, and class; the religious one linked with the Puritan and Judeo-Christian heritage; or the ethnic one tied to race and multiculturalism? Which element dominates will make a difference for foreign policy. An America divided by race and ethnicity, despite its power, is very likely to be hesitant or ineffective in foreign policy. One dominated by nationalism is likely to come into conflict with other democracies in Europe and Japan as well as nondemocracies in China and the Middle East. One focused on culture or religion is likely to gear up for a new "clash of civilizations" between the West and Islam or the West and Confucianism. This chapter explores the foundations and future of America's identity as a factor that is at least as important as American power in determining what kind of role America plays in the world of the twenty-first century.

Conflicted Republic

Is America primarily an idea of individual equality and self-government that took root in the colonial period and evolved progressively distinct from Europe? Or is it primarily a nation of Europeans, little different from the societies of Europe, which accepts non-European immigrants but only at the price of cultural assimilation to European or western values? Historically, America is both.

On the one hand, America's history is a seamless web with that of Britain and Europe. In 1790, America was 80 percent white and free; 20 percent black and slave. Of the free population, three-quarters were English, the rest Scottish, Irish, German, and other minorities. Almost all (98 percent) of the whites were Protestant. The proportion of the white population grew even as the

British character was diluted by massive waves of immigration from continental European countries. By 1960 whites constituted 89 percent of the population. It is not difficult to agree with Peter Brimelow, a senior editor of *Forbes* magazine and the *National Review*, that "the American nation has always had a specific ethnic core. And that core has been white."[1]

At the same time, America was different from Europe. It was not a "history-less people,"[2] for its history was European, but it was a people who came to think of themselves as separate and distinct. It was a New World country dedicated to the belief, despite its practice of slavery, that all human beings are created equal and have inalienable rights to participate in self-government. This belief was not mere presumption. As early as the 1770s, the average electorate in the American colonies was four times larger than in Britain.[3] As Henry Steele Commager wrote, "the American constitution was the first in history to incorporate the principle that men make government and that all government derives its authority from consent."[4] So, although the founding fathers "identified . . . the evolving American nationality with Britishness," they also gave America "a singular advantage" over Britain and other nations, namely the Constitution.[5] The country conceived in that document was "a construction of the mind, not of race or inherited class or ancestral territory."[6] It had the potential to create a new political reality, one that could hold together even as the nation became the most ethnically diverse, major democracy in the modern world.

But that possibility was hardly assured in 1790. The new nation was badly tainted by slavery and divided by class. Jefferson and other founders—George Washington, James Madison, and Alexander Hamilton—owned slaves; and although Jefferson made an attempt in the Constitution to label the slave trade an "execrable commerce," he did not free his own slaves until his death and believed that freed slaves should be resettled in Africa.[7] Nevertheless, Jefferson's soaring sentiments that all men are created equal haunted both him and his successors. Slavery tormented the country for the next seventy years, and then literally tore it apart in 1861. Class also divided America. Elites ruled, whether they governed from national institutions, as Federalists urged, or from the states, as Republicans advocated. The franchise was restricted to propertied white males. It took the expansion of the country and Andrew Jackson's Democrats of the 1830s to sanction the role of the common white man in government. And it took a civil war and the better part of another century to secure that role for white women, Native Americans, and black Americans.

To understand where America came from and what it is today, there is no need to embellish either the Constitution or the American people. America was not immunized from either the despotism or class conflict that afflicted Europe. The ideal of democratic government was little more than a glimmer in the late eighteenth century, and the struggle to realize this ideal might have ended up as mutilated and muddled as the French Revolution were it not for certain circumstances and critical choices. Three factors made the difference. The first was the colonial experience, which created a habit of self-government in America that was not possible in Europe. The second was distance. America, as Jefferson noted, was "kindly separated by nature and a wide ocean from the exterminating havoc" of Europe.[8] At the beginning, England's fleet was a threat, not a shield. But that threat did not materialize because nature and technology (the clumsiness and cost of sea power) conspired to limit the projection of British power into the Western Hemisphere.

The third and perhaps most important factor securing the American system of government was the evolution of an American liberal creed. Once the issue of individual freedom was decided in the Civil War, the U.S. political process eschewed the extremes of both left and right. Those extremes would ravage Europe over the next century and destroy Europe's political center. By default, America would become Europe's liberal center and return to Europe three times during the twentieth century to save Europe from itself. In this sense, U.S. and European identities are inextricably linked. Europe is more vulnerable to political orthodoxy and needs the emancipating energy of American liberalism to remain free. America is more vulnerable to political anomism and needs the European bookends of social egalitarianism (the fruit of socialism) and philosophical self-perspective (the product of conservatism) to bridle its individualism. Without these bookends, as Louis Hartz insightfully notes in his classic work *The Liberal Tradition in America,* America loses perspective and drowns itself in aimless legalisms.[9]

Self-government, distance, and a liberal political ideology—these three ingredients molded a new identity, even as the political ideology sharpened conflicts and put the new nation on a course to civil war.

COLONIAL SELF-GOVERNMENT

The United States was a risky experiment. Could government be entrusted to ordinary people? Would democracy lead to "mobocracy"? Nothing like self-government had been tried before. Authority in Europe depended heavily on tradition and charisma; little opportunity existed for experimentation in self-government. Revolution came either all at once, as it did in France in 1789, or very gradually from the top down inspired by an enlightened elite, as it did in England. The chance to try self-government from the bottom up by ordinary people was simply out of the question.

Yet that was precisely the opportunity offered by colonial America. Early colonial communities set up do-it-yourself governments that were not surrounded by an aura of mystery and tradition. As Daniel Boorstin recounts, these communities could not "have been more unlike the Old World governments of sanctified vice regents of God whose authority was rooted in antiquity, untouchable because of the 'divinity that doth hedge a King'."[10] Colonial communities made decisions by majority rule, their legitimacy depended on results, and their procedures blurred distinctions between private and public interests and power. American government from the beginning relied heavily on extensive voluntary associations and participation in society and local government that subsequent visitors such as Alexis de Tocqueville could not miss and greatly admired.[11]

The colonial period produced a kind of working federalism that rooted authority in the local community and made decisions from the bottom up. As Boorstin explains, "The modern nations of Western Europe, like France and England, had been founded when a power at the center succeeded in dominating the local units. But the United States was born when thirteen separate regional governments asserted their power against central authority in London. The nation was a by-product of the assertion of each colony's right to govern itself."[12]

The Declaration of Independence spoke only of the thirteen colonies, and while the Constitution in 1789 strengthened federal authority, it did so on the solid foundations of colonial and community governments. The new republic staked out a middle ground between the absolutist state in Europe that oppressed its own citizens and the anarchic state that warred incessantly against other states. The colonies clearly rejected absolutism when they broke from the tyranny of King George III, but for some eighty-five years after the Declaration of Independence they risked anarchy as they sought to define the new relationship between federal and state authorities. The struggle might have turned out very differently had America not been distant from Europe, had it not been unusually free to revolt, experiment, and fail. Paradoxically, the opportunity to fail, so vividly dramatized in the Civil War, was a key factor enabling ultimate success.

ADVANTAGE OF DISTANCE

The colonies revolted because they were free, not because they were oppressed. Samuel Eliot Morison writes, in his well-known trilogy, "British subjects in America, excepting of course the blacks, were then the freest people in the world. . . . They argued and then fought not to *obtain* freedom but to *confirm* the freedom they already had or claimed."[13] It was this freedom that allowed them to develop the sensitivities to taxes and other regulations that would spark eventual revolt. Had the colonists been truly oppressed, it would have never come down to the Stamp Act—the colonies would have been reined in, quickly and physically, like any English village that defied London's authority.

The sea was America's great protector. It was formidable enough to degrade British power so that London could strike only after long lapses of time and with clumsy supply lines. And it was inviting enough that the young republic could use it, despite repeated clashes with the British Navy, to explore new opportunities. America was less a city built on a hill than a city built in the middle of the sea. As Boorstin speculates, "how different the story of New England, or of America, might have been if [the Puritans] had built their Zion in a sequestered inland place—some American Switzerland, some mountain-encircled valley.... The sea was the great opener of their markets and their minds."[14]

The ideas of Americans were not that different from those of Englishmen. They were at best a continuation and incremental adjustment of the ideas of the Enlightenment, which had been stirring in Europe since the Reformation.[15] In this sense neither the founding fathers nor the Constitution was unexpected. Similar ideas might have appeared in Europe and did a few years later in France, Greece, and other European countries. What was astonishing was that the founding fathers got away with these ideas in America without the internecine convulsions that afflicted Europe and pitted the king's guards against the people's guillotine. America had a safe harbor in which to develop vague and even vacuous ideas. Some of these ideas failed quickly, such as the Confedera-tion of American States—which might have led to anarchy. Others endured, even after they had disappeared in Europe, and eventually led to anarchy and war—such as slavery. America had time and space to err and thus to evolve. Psychic, no less than physical, distance freed it from the feudal and frozen fra-ternities of Europe. In the end, America was free because it was far away.

THE PHILADELPHIA SYSTEM

For a hundred years, the United States struggled to dispel the conflict and vagueness in its own identity. What were the powers of the federal govern-ment? What were the powers of Congress? What was the role of the Supreme Court? How big should the country be? When did it become too ungainly for republican government? Should new states be slave or free? If heredity no longer mattered, who qualified on what grounds to participate in govern-ment? At the outset, the vagueness was protean.

The Constitution, or "Philadelphia system," created a structure in which this vagueness could be contained while it was being defined.[16] It passed power to the center or federal government, which minimized the danger of anarchy and war among the thirteen states. But it also divided power at the center, which minimized the danger of absolutism. Separated powers ensured that government could function only with the requisite majority and only after compromise protected the minority. Power was then made accountable by further dividing authority among federal, state, and local governments and by protecting the basic inalienable rights of the individual at all levels of gov-ernment. Congress passed the Bill of Rights in its first session in 1789.

The Philadelphia system was remarkably well suited for the development of a liberal, centrist philosophy of government. Expansion of the country helped as well, creating a nonzero-sum game as new territories and markets opened up. But the genius of the Philadelphia system was that it discouraged polarization. In Europe, the center was smashed between the anvil of a dispossessed elite and the hammer of the masses. Elites clung desperately to unchecked power (the stubborn staying power of the *ancien regime* in France and England), while the masses became so outraged by privileged power that they accepted government only as a process of constant revolution against domestic as well as foreign enemies (e.g., Napoleon Bonaparte and later fascist and communist regimes). To this day in Europe, liberalism, the voice of reason that limits state power and legitimates civil society and private markets, is a minority voice. Liberal parties are dwarfed on both sides of the political spectrum by conservative and confessional parties (Christian and Catholic) on the right and by social democratic, socialist, and communist parties on the left. By contrast, America has never had a serious fascist, socialist, or communist party; even social democracy is evident only in the left wing of the Democratic Party.[17]

Although history in the twentieth century discredited right and left extremes in Europe, the contrast between European and American politics persists. Although some Americans criticize the liberal conformism of American politics, too few are even aware of it, and too many hold up the European model as superior.[18] My argument here is not that one model is better than the other, but that they have developed very differently over time and today complement one another politically. It is doubtful, as I argue in the next chapter, that America can fulfill its democratic mission in the twenty-first century without a more permanent partnership with Europe. On the other hand, it is also clear that Europe would not have survived the twentieth century without the American spirit of liberty and equanimity. And Europe is unlikely to become and remain truly whole and free in the next century except in combination with American liberalism.

THE ISOLATIONIST MYTH

Given the conflicted identity of the early republic, its foreign policy was defensive and ambivalent. Contrary to conventional wisdom, this foreign policy was never isolationist—not if that adjective means separate or apart from Europe. To be sure, Washington urged the new nation to avoid entangling alliances, but the United States avoided such alliances not because it consciously separated itself from Europe but instead because its own identity was too divided to settle on permanent foreign associations. It actually formed numerous alliances, swinging back and forth in the early decades between France and England and declaring in 1823 in the Monroe Doctrine a kind of hemispheric alliance with fellow independent states in South America. But it did not form entangling or permanent alliances because its leaders were divided about what kind of country America should be and therefore who its friends and enemies abroad might be.

Hamilton and Jefferson—and their respective Federalist and Republican parties—pursued different self-images and hence different foreign policies for the new republic. As Morison explains:

> Jefferson inherited the idealistic conception of the new world to which the French *philosophes* paid homage.... To Hamilton, this was sentimental nonsense.... Hamilton believed that the only choice for America lay between a stratified society on the English model and a squalid 'mobocracy'. Jefferson, who knew Europe, wished America to be as unlike it as possible. Hamilton, who had never left America, wished to make his country a new Europe.[19]

Not surprisingly, Morison continues, "the polestar of Jefferson's policy was to cement commercial and diplomatic ties with France."[20] Hamilton, on the other hand, "believed that the essential interests of Great Britain and the United States were complementary."[21] To be sure, interests and power sometimes overrode these differences. Three-quarters of America's commerce was with Great Britain. When the British Navy impressed American sailors on the high seas, Jefferson imposed an embargo to strangle the English nemesis. Economic interests in the northern states, however, soon forced Congress to repeal the embargo, and Jefferson, against his natural sympathies, signed the repeal. Still, at other times, sentiments created interests and expanded power. Jefferson, in part because of his knowledge of France, secured the Louisiana Purchase. Whether John Adams, whom Jefferson had defeated in 1800, would have been in the same position to do so is arguable. Adams shared Hamilton's preference for England and, as president, fought a phony war with France in 1797–98 to retaliate against French insults in the XYZ affair.[22] Jefferson carried no such baggage and maneuvered deftly to avoid war with France when Napoleon tried to reestablish his empire in Haiti and Louisiana. Jefferson was then in a felicitous position to expand American territory and power when Napoleon's Hispaniola campaign faltered and France decided to sell Louisiana.

Isolationism meant not separation from or indifference to Europe but a defensive, divided reaction to Europe. When Latin American colonies rebelled against their Spanish masters, the United States did not help the colonies directly but sought to discourage European intervention. President James Monroe and his secretary of state, John Quincy Adams, announced in 1823 that "the American continents . . . are henceforth not to be considered as subjects for future colonization by any European powers." The Monroe Doctrine warned that the United States "should consider any attempt on their part to extend their system to any portion of this hemisphere as dangerous to our peace and security."[23] Although the Monroe Doctrine rejected any alignment with European powers (and at the time Jefferson and Madison were urging alignment with Great Britain to counter France and Spain in Central and South America), it was implemented over the next century not in isolationism from Europe but, in effect, in alliance with British sea power, which kept European rivals out of the Western Hemisphere.

Interestingly, isolationism, even in the limited sense, did not play a role in other areas of early American foreign policy. In continental expansion, war with Mexico and later colonization in Asia, America used power offensively, not defensively. It behaved much like the Old World powers, brutally suppressing Native Americans, neighboring Mexicans, and overseas Hawaiians and Filipinos.

It seems a stretch, therefore, to argue that early American foreign policy was either "a sophisticated reflection of the American national interest"[24] or a utopian rejection of Old World diplomacy in favor of New World ideals. America's national identity was not sufficiently coherent to support a sophisticated calculation of national interests. At the beginning of the republic, close ties with Great Britain were in the interests of the federalist North but not the republican South. By the mid-1800s, these ties had greater appeal for the agricultural South, which supplied Britain with cotton and other crops, than for the industrial North, which competed with British manufacturing. Nor was America's identity as a New World democracy so robust that American ideals rather than Old World balance-of-power maneuvering dictated hemispheric policy. In drafting the Monroe Doctrine, John Quincy Adams saw "no prospect that [the Latin American republics] would establish free or liberal institutions of government."[25] And the war against Mexico and expansion to the west were driven as much by the prospect of slave states as by the promise of manifest destiny.

The early republic was a torn country, and its foreign policy was different from the Old World's "law of brick bats and cannon balls"[26] only insofar as it was less coherent. Toward Europe the country was weak, and its policy of defensiveness was a consequence of divided sympathies. But toward the west the country was strong, and its policies created a divided empire, part free, part slave. In this period, it is difficult to argue that either national interest or manifest destiny dominated America's soul. That soul had yet to be forged in the fires of civil war.

Electoral Democracy

The Civil War resolved the core issue in the American identity struggle: Did the liberty of the Constitution apply to states or individuals? And did it apply only to white Anglo-Saxon males, or did it apply to non–Anglo-Saxon immigrants from Europe, black slaves in America, women, and Native Americans? In the three generations following the Civil War, from 1865 to 1930, the essential birthright of American freedom to participate in self-government became individual and universal—not yet as a practical reality for all Americans, especially blacks, but as a constitutional imperative that empowered the federal government to work for its realization. This imperative meant that ethnic immigrants became individual, not hyphenated, Americans and that states could not override the basic liberties of the Constitution. Combined with the outbreak of a robust and free-spirited industrial capitalism, this ideological core created the nation of Theodore Roosevelt.[27] It was a nation as yet unschooled in either the social costs of capitalism (which awaited the Franklin Roosevelt era) or the spiritual oppressiveness of government (which awaited the Ronald Reagan era). But it was a nation no longer divided, united to be free and to carry the chalice of liberty as far as its power could reach. Not surprisingly, America's foreign policy in this period set out to bring free government to other nations—to its neighbors in Mexico and the Caribbean, its colonial wards in Cuba and the Philippines, and ultimately its forebears in Europe destroyed by World War I.

After the Civil War, the American republic dropped three anchors that despite subsequent changes distinguish the country to this day from its democratic counterparts elsewhere. The first was the principle of individual liberty or emancipation on which the central government intervened in the Civil War and restored national unity. The second was a greater commitment to individualism, rooted in the stronger and more private influence of religion in America than in Europe. The third was the phenomenon of mobility in American society, the combination of greater freedom and greater risks and rewards, which results in more material wealth but also in more inequality.

LEGITIMACY OF NATIONAL GOVERNMENT

Central government was legitimated in America not by the mere accretion of institutions and power, as it was in Europe, but by the principle that the rights of individuals superseded those of states or any other subnational political grouping. The Civil War was fought over Union and power, to be sure. But national unity could not have been achieved without the principle of individual emancipation. Abraham Lincoln freed the slaves in part to inspire a flagging war effort, but emancipation worked because it altered the balance of forces. If power had been sufficient to preserve the Union, Lincoln would not have proclaimed manumission, and the country would have been reunited half-free and half-slave—a house, as Lincoln said, which would not have endured. Principle had to weigh in the balance of power to confirm once and for all the role of national government in American political life.[28]

The Thirteenth, Fourteenth, and Fifteenth Amendments, passed after the Civil War, forbade the states to deprive, deny, or abridge the rights of "any person." These rights included freedom from involuntary servitude; the rights of citizenship, life, liberty, property, and equal protection of the laws; and the

franchise to vote. Political union in America did not come before the emancipation of the individual, as it did in democratic Europe, or on grounds other
than the emancipation of the individual, as it does in nondemocratic societies. It came through the emancipation of the individual. After 1865, the federal government took the leading role in expanding individual rights—from
direct election of senators to women's suffrage and ultimately, after many false
starts, to the black civil rights revolution of the 1960s.

The central place and value of individualism in justifying American government are defining characteristics of the American creed. Because of these
characteristics, as Seymour Martin Lipset writes:

> the United States . . . compared to other Euro-Canadian polities . . . is still more
> classically liberal (libertarian), distrustful of government, and populist. It gives
> its citizens more power to influence their governors than other democràcies,
> which rely more heavily on unified governments fulfilling economic and wel-
> fare functions. Viewed cross-nationally, Americans are the most antistatist lib-
> eral (Whig) population among the democratic nations.[29]

Contemporary data support Lipset's point. If we look at current receipts
and expenditures of government (at all levels) as a percentage of gross domestic product in North America and Europe, U.S. percentages fall significantly
below those in Europe, in the low 30s compared to the mid- to upper 40s.[30]
In relative terms, therefore, the United States is a model of small government,
individualism, and anti-statism. Recognizing this fact is not the same as agree-
ing with it. The balance between the individual and the state is a hotly contested topic in the debate about America's identity; and the role of government in American life has clearly increased since the late nineteenth century.
Still, the relatively smaller government in America marks a very different starting point for the struggle between the individual and the state. The American government started with much less statist or institutional baggage and
emerged from the Civil War with much more commitment to the widening
of the individual's rights and responsibility to participate in government. This
commitment in fact underlies the central legitimacy of national government
in America, more so than is true for European governments, which benefit
from deeper cultural and historical allegiances.

RELIGION IN AMERICA

What justified this greater faith in individualism in America? Part of the
answer, at least, has to do with the different way in which two seminal historical developments—the Reformation and the Enlightenment—affected the
role of the individual and the state in Europe and America.

The Reformation empowered individuals to work out their own salvation
without the established church. In Europe, however, Martin Luther's rebellion

did not separate religion from the state; rather it divided states between the Protestant and Catholic religions and spawned bloody religious wars that eventually sapped the private spiritual appeal of religion in Europe. In America, by contrast, Puritan immigrants developed their faith apart from the central state. Religious self-reliance inspired political self-reliance and led at the federal level, in the very first article of the Bill of Rights, to a proscription: "Congress shall make no law respecting an establishment of religion." The result was that America became both a religion-soaked society and a religion-less government.[31] To this day, religious activity in the United States is as intense and sectarian (i.e., divided) as it is private, whereas in Europe it is, for the most part, perfunctory, state-managed and -financed, and publicly affiliated with confessional political parties.[32]

The Enlightenment provided individuals with the tools of reason and rational discourse to guide their participation in public life. In Europe, the rule of reason married up with the central authority and institutions to create the modern bureaucratic state. Otto von Bismarck launched the welfare state in Germany in the 1880s, decades before Lenin and Soviet communism. In America, where institutions were weak, the new rationality hooked up with factions and self-interest. In *Federalist Paper* No. 10,[33] Madison argues that the individual's ability to reason creates "different and unequal faculties of acquiring property" and "a zeal for different opinions concerning religion, concerning Government and many other points."[34] These differences, in turn, create "a division of the society into different interests and parties."[35] Since no one interest or party is sufficiently unbiased to pass judgments, that task, Madison concludes, must be the function of republican or representative government. Such a government divides interests horizontally (separation of powers) "to guard against the cabals of a few" and extends interests vertically (federalism) "to guard against the confusion of a multitude."[36] or ensure that no representative will be captured by the narrow interests of local constituents.

Thus, reason in America checked the passions of both interests and religion. In Europe, it killed the spirit of religion and fueled the growth of bureaucracy. America got along with less government and more private initiative; Europe functioned with more government and less religious or moral zealotry.

MOBILITY IN AMERICA

The third anchor of electoral democracy in America after the Civil War was mobility. From the start, America was on the move. As Boorstin reports, "English observers in the mid-19th century admired the ease with which American laborers moved around the country, from one job to another. They were amazed at the general freedom from fear of unemployment, at the vagueness of social classes, at the facility of moving from one class to another."[37]

This mobility became a crucial factor in the second half of the nineteenth century. Mobility ended the last vestiges of aristocratic class in America and accommodated the first great wave of foreign immigration. The old Federalist and Republican elites, who could not stomach the "mobocracy" of Jackson's Democrats, fought a lost battle to preserve the union based on class and national manufacturing. As the Whig Party died and a new Republican Party emerged, America's aristocrats gave up Hamilton's suspicion of popular government, but they kept his capitalist dream of national industry. After the Civil War, industrial expansion, railroad development, and tariff protection created a national market for the first time. Hamilton's legacy now merged with Jefferson's concept of equal opportunity: a highly mobile and individualistic capitalism created opportunities for entrepreneurs and robber barons, immigrants and merchants supplied the new captains of industry, and wealth became both a great leveler and a great divider of American society. The result was the myth of Horatio Alger and the American dream: that with hard work, good temper, and much luck, any American could become an aristocrat. Wealth did not solidify class in America; it became the conveyor belt to higher (or sometimes lower) class. To this day, Americans resent the wealthy less than Europeans do because wealth is perceived as earned, not inherited.

The "moving pot" of territorial expansion and the "money pot" of capitalist expansion made possible the melting pot of America's growing ethnic diversity. Still predominantly British in 1850, America now began to lose its Anglo-Saxon majority as immigrants poured in first from northern Europe and then at the turn of the century from southern and eastern Europe. Change in this period took place in both the industrial might and the cosmopolitan character of the new nation. No doubt, both factors—rising power and a more worldly identity—contributed to the projection of American power onto the world stage in the decades before and after 1900.[38]

ASSERTIVE FOREIGN POLICY

Between the Civil War and the 1920s, American foreign policy ran the gamut from the self-absorption of Reconstruction to military imperialism in Latin America and Asia to Wilsonian idealism in Europe and back again to self-absorption in the Great Depression. American power was increasing throughout this period, and so it is difficult to account for these changes solely in terms of American power.

It was the mood and confidence of the country that shifted. National energies first poured into Reconstruction and western expansion. Then, influenced by colonial competition and Darwinist themes of rugged individualism and survival of the fittest, the country plunged into foreign imperialism. But American imperialism had an ideological, not just a cultural or military, face. The Progressive Era inspired missions to clean up local and national government in America and expand the democratic franchise, especially to women. This same spirit inspired American foreign policy, which set about to elect good governments and good men in Latin America and the Philippines and to make the world safe for democracy in Europe. Quickly, after World War I, national energies imploded again, and Wall Street became Main Street as financial markets rocketed and then suddenly crashed.

There was one constant in American identity throughout this period, however. It was the focus on democracy, seen primarily as honest administration, popular elections, good leaders, and universal suffrage. The nation was no longer divided between free and unfree societies, but it was not yet committed to social reforms or equality of opportunity for all of its citizens or for the colonial peoples for which it assumed responsibility. U.S. imperialism did not dislodge local elites in colonial territories such as Cuba, the Philippines, and Puerto Rico. Military intervention in the Caribbean and Mexico sought primarily to improve administration to pay debts, not to transform society. And Wilson's program of self-determination at Versailles created a clutter of new nations in eastern Europe—all of which were elected democratically, but few of which had the underlying social and economic conditions necessary to sustain democracy. The nation's identity expressed a thin version of democracy—one that increasingly extended formal rights to all citizens, but did not follow up with legal enforcement, land reform, education, or economic opportunity.[39]

Social Democracy

The Great Depression and America's total mobilization for World War II dramatically altered American identity. Franklin Roosevelt's New Deal opened up an era of activist national government, welfare capitalism, and industrial regulation; and America's foreign policy after World War II "amounted to a promise to extend the New Deal . . . to the world."[40] In postwar reconstruction, America pressed social and economic reforms in both West Germany and Japan. In the Cold War, it confidently juxtaposed its version of New Deal democracy against the more socialist and communist versions of governance in Europe and the Soviet Union. And in Vietnam, it crafted an international version of the Great Society programs, a social engineering mission that ended in disaster.

LIBERTY AND EQUALITY

All democracies seek a balance between liberty and equality. But they strike this balance differently, and there are different kinds of equality. America has always had more equality than European societies in terms of class. On the other hand, America has always had less equality in terms of income. If we look at the ratio of family income of the highest income group to that of the lowest income group, the United States has the largest ratio—5.78, compared to 2.75–4.67 in the other major democracies.[41] In a sense, a greater income inequality was tolerated in America because it did not imply frozen categories of class. By the same token, greater class distinctions were tolerated in Europe because they did not imply significant income disparities.

The balance in America between liberty and equality shifted after 1930. America discovered social and economic inequalities in the marketplace. Not everyone started from the same point or had the same advantages and opportunities; government had to give individuals a more equal chance. The New Deal legitimized the national government's role in socioeconomic areas, just as the Civil War had secured the central government's role in individual liberty.

Socialism and communism in Europe carried this socioeconomic role to the extreme. It not only envisioned government regulation of the market, it went on to establish government domination of the market; government became the primary or sole owner of production and property. Nationalizations swept western Europe, both before and, briefly, after World War II. Communist governments created command markets, economic systems that ran on central government plans and orders and strictly prohibited private market activities.

The era of social democracy in America changed the face of American identity and made American foreign policy much more conscious of the social dimensions of domestic and international politics. But it did not diminish the differences between American and European society.[42] American identity drew the line at equality of opportunity. It may be possible to help everyone or almost everyone up to the starting line, but it is not possible to guarantee that they can all run equally fast—American individualism rejected equality of results. At Howard University in 1965, Lyndon Johnson declared a more extreme version of social equality, "We seek not just freedom but opportunity—not just legal equity but human ability—not just equality as a right and a theory, but equality as a fact and a result."[43] This version was inconsistent with American exceptionalism. As Aaron Wildavsky points out, "when the argument goes beyond the prevention of cumulative inequalities to claim that inequality *per se* is incompatible with self-government, so that substantive equality must be achieved before equal opportunity (and hence the political system itself) may be deemed legitimate, exceptionalism American-style is over."[44]

For all its faults, the market in America was not only an essential part of the country's capacity to grow and accommodate immigration (as it had done in the melting pot era), it was also an essential part of its liberty. As Madison points out, "the most common and durable source of factions, has been the various and unequal distribution of property."[45] Try to equalize this distribution of property and diminish the role of factions, he argues, and you have also diminished if not extinguished liberty itself.[46]

ENTANGLING FOREIGN POLICY

As Europe's offshore liberal center, America had escaped the battles of the early twentieth century between the dying feudal empires of Europe and the rising nationalist ideologies of fascism and socialism. Wilson's America had been unprepared for the tumult that convulsed Europe in World War I and had understood little about the political passions and extremes that tormented Europe at Versailles and in the decades that followed. At that time, America, with its thin electoral approach to democracy, was still innocent of the deeper and darker struggles that threatened to extinguish liberty in Europe.

The Great Depression and World War II changed all that. They brought America face-to-face with the extremes of feudalism and socialism. The Depression, although it drew America inward, also deepened America's democratic identity and made it more aware of both friends and foes of democracy abroad. Without the Depression and America's own schooling in the balancing of equality and liberty, the United States might have stayed on the sidelines in World War II for at least as long as it had in World War I. True, the Japanese attack on Pearl Harbor jump-started America's entry, but a Hitler victory in the Battle of Britain in winter 1940–41 would have probably done the same thing. There was no escape from the political extremes of Europe. Fascism and then communism would now all but destroy the liberal center in Europe and bring the challenge directly to the doorstep of America.

America's rediscovery of its political lineage in Europe was evident even before the U.S. entry into the war. The Atlantic Charter, negotiated by Franklin Roosevelt and Winston Churchill in August 1941, set out the common democratic goals of Europe and America in the war and initiated a process of planning for the postwar period that ultimately established the United Nations and the Bretton Woods international economic system. This postwar system reflected a compromise between the U.S. preference to err on the side of liberty and the western European (at the time, especially British) preference to err on the side of equality. The United Nations system struck a blow for liberty by installing a trusteeship system to end European colonialism. Colonialism was a moral blot on both European and American liberty, but it weighed more heavily on Europe, and it was among the factors that had discouraged America from joining the League of Nations, which created mandates for European colonialism. The Bretton Woods system struck a blow for economic equality. It initiated the postwar free trade regime and took governments progressively out of international markets, at least in terms of border barriers such as tariffs and quotas. But it also confirmed a role of "enlightened liberalism" for governments in domestic markets, a step toward more stable and equitable markets that America had resisted before the New Deal.[47]

The new postwar Atlantic solidarity was barely in place before European and American democracy was tested again by extremism, this time from the left—international communism. Had America's self-image as a social, not just electoral, democracy not been deepened by the Depression and World War II, it is at least arguable that America might not have perceived the Soviet Union in the late 1940s as a dire threat to western liberty. Roosevelt hoped to deal with Soviet interests after World War II through electoral processes in Poland and other liberated countries, much the way Wilson had sought to deal with national grievances after World War I, but American and western democracy was now more than elections. From a western perspective, elections in Poland and elsewhere required not just votes and nominal parliaments, but competitive parties, markets, media, and social classes. Communist elections did not meet these deeper requirements. These dramatically different conceptions of political elections and political society came to a head in the postwar reconstruction of Germany. Unable to agree on a single system, the West and the Soviet Union divided the country, and the Iron Curtain descended across the political landscape of Europe.[48]

The Cold War was always as much about these differing and hostile political identities as about a struggle for material power. It aroused deeper passions than World War I or previous balance-of-power conflicts because it involved deeper conceptions of what democratic and totalitarian societies were like and how they differed. As such, the Cold War drove America back to its European roots. In NATO, America established for the first time an entangling, indeed perhaps a permanent, alliance with European powers; and in the Marshall Plan, it set about strengthening European democracy, shoring up its vital center against political extremism. The marriage was anything but artificial or convenient. It put America right back in the center of its political heritage, and it gave Europe its best chance to hold the democratic center against nondemocratic extremes and to spread and unite democracy.

NATO, the Marshall Plan, and the European and Atlantic institutions of cooperation that they spawned—the NATO Council and Assembly, the European Community and then Union, the Organization for Economic Cooperation and Development (OECD), the General Agreement on Tariffs and Trade (GATT), the Group of Seven (G-7)—constituted the first institutional lineaments of what may become in the twenty-first century a new political community of western industrial democracies.[49] We explore the contemporary and future prospects for this community in the next section and more thoroughly in chapter 4. Suffice it here to note that the deepening and spread of democracy in the Atlantic world constituted the single greatest achievement of post–World War II diplomacy and the reason, in the end, that the West won the Cold War.

This emerging community of industrial democracies does not end political divisions between the United States and Europe. The United States and Europe continue to differ over many foreign policy issues, in part because their domestic systems differ in the balance they strike between liberty and equality.[50] But as European democracies stabilized around more centrist "liberal" politics, and liberal institutions spread to transform the lingering authoritarian regimes in Spain, Portugal, and Greece, the United States and Europe no longer disagreed about the most fundamental issues of domestic political governance that had divided them for centuries.[51] They did not pose a military threat to one another and therefore did not deploy or threaten to use military force in their relations with one another. That agreement persists even after the military threat of the Soviet Union has disappeared. The sinews of democracy, which permit a more peaceful style of international relations, appear to have grown stronger than the historical differences of nationality, culture, ethnicity, and religion. It may not always stay that way, but how it became that way is the most important legacy of America's foreign policy in the era of social democracy.

Liberal or Multicultural Democracy

Four events began in the mid-1960s that once again challenged America's identity and eventually altered its foreign policy. Two of these events reached deep into the cultural dimensions and civil society of American democracy. Civil rights legislation in 1964–65 addressed the unfinished business of the Civil War and began the full political, economic, and social emancipation of black Americans. In the same period, immigration laws significantly opened America's portals for the first time to non-European citizens, particularly Latin American and Asian immigrants. These two events raised the profound issue of whether American democracy applied to all races and cultures or only to white Europeans. While this issue struck deeply at the heart of American identity, two other events weakened America's self-confidence, sending the country into a political and economic tailspin from 1965 to 1980. The Vietnam War escalated, casting doubt on the U.S. political character and purpose in the Cold War as well as on its democratic system at home. In addition, the economy, which had catapulted America forward after World War II and fueled the U.S. crusade against communism, began to sputter and crash in the 1970s, reaching extremes of inflation and unemployment unseen since the Great Depression.

As the country reeled under the impact of these events, America's leadership foundered. A dangerous chasm emerged between the democracies in America and western Europe. Doubting America's will, Europe—France and then Germany and Britain—initiated détente with the Soviet Union, even as Moscow gained nuclear parity with the West and threatened, in the late 1970s, through the deployment of theater nuclear missiles, to separate Europe from U.S. nuclear guarantees. Oil crises, the Vietnam and Watergate debacles, and intensifying crime and income inequalities in the United States further alienated European allies. Meanwhile, for the first time, the Soviet Union projected military power beyond its borders into Angola, Ethiopia, Vietnam, Afghanistan, Cuba, and Central America. Only a decade before it would disappear, the Soviet

Union looked like it was winning the Cold War, less because of its own political and economic performance than because of the floundering fortunes of its American adversary.

Post-1965 events challenged previous dimensions of American identity (individual liberty and social equality) and added a third—racial or multicultural integration. Did liberty still matter enough to motivate the American republic to stand firmly against totalitarian communism? Did social equality require more government regulation and welfare even at the risk of less growth, or was less government regulation and welfare necessary to spur more growth? And did multiracial and multicultural democracy require more integration along the lines of the old melting pot model of cultural assimilation, or did it demand new rules of affirmative action, which provide equal opportunities for individuals not in spite of their race or culture but because of it?

By the end of the millennium, the first question of liberty versus totalitarianism had been resolved. Although it may be tacky to say it, America and the West won the Cold War. Any other conclusion is false modesty. The second question of more versus less government also appeared to be resolved. President Clinton and social democratic leaders in Europe declared the era of big government to be over. And dramatic welfare reforms in the United States moved millions of families off the government payroll into productive jobs in a revitalized private marketplace. But the third issue remained wide open. How America grapples with the multicultural and multiethnic dimension of democracy will decide not only how self-confident American foreign policy is in the future, but whether democracy is relevant to the nonwestern world— in Russia and other former Soviet republics, in the Confucian countries of Asia, in the Islamic states of the Middle East, and among the ethnic groups of Africa.

LIBERTY AND THE COLD WAR

If the Civil War decided whether liberty applied to all Americans, the Cold War decided whether it applied to all Europeans. For the first time, America confronted political extremism directly. America entered the two world wars late. In the Cold War, however, America was there at the beginning. It experienced what Europe had already learned: political extremes wipe out the political center. When Harry Truman met Joseph Stalin at Potsdam in 1945, Truman explained that Italy should be admitted to the United Nations because it was a free country but that Romania, Bulgaria, and Hungary, which Soviet forces controlled, should not until they had open and democratic governments. Stalin's response was direct and simple: "If a government is not fascist, a government is democratic."[52] For Stalin and communism, there was no political center.

Truman understood immediately and picked up the challenge. In a speech to a joint session of Congress in March 1947, which became known as the

Truman Doctrine, he outlined what the confrontation with communism was all about:

> One way of life is based upon the will of the majority, and is distinguished by free institutions, representative government, free elections, guarantees of individual liberty, freedom of speech and religion, and freedom from political oppression.
>
> The second way of life is based upon the will of a minority forcibly imposed upon the majority. It relies upon terror and oppression, a controlled press and radio, fixed elections, and the suppression of political freedoms.[53]

Truman had it right. The Cold War was a choice between liberty and tyranny, no less than the Civil War was between liberty and slavery. Both wars were fought through power—a contest of nuclear arms and deterrence in one case, a struggle over union in the other. But neither war was about power alone—each was also about identity, what political goals power would ultimately serve.

No American president after Truman understood that point better than Reagan. Although Reagan pursued the arms race with renewed—some thought shocking—vigor, he knew that arms alone did not decide great conflicts. In his now well-known "democracy speech" in Great Britain in June 1982, Reagan said it best, "We maintain this strength in the hope it will never be used, for the ultimate determinant in the struggle that's now going on in the world will not be bombs and rockets, but a test of wills and ideas, a trial of spiritual resolve, the values we hold, the beliefs we cherish, the ideals to which we are dedicated."[54]

Communism was a particularly serious challenge to democratic ideals because it coincided with more moderate socialist and social democratic efforts, especially in Europe, to achieve greater equality in western societies. For many socialists, communism did not seem that dangerous, and they worried more about belligerent overreaction from the right than about subtle oppression from the left.[55] On the other hand, western democracy could not have won the Cold War had it not achieved greater justice, both economic and civil, among its own citizens. Reagan, on whose watch the Cold War turned, did not repudiate the New Deal or the civil rights revolution. Quite the opposite, he defined a new combination of social justice and economic entrepreneurship that preserved liberty and simultaneously made it available to a larger number of U.S. citizens—not least through the more than 18 million jobs created on Reagan's watch and another 14 million created in the 1990s.

LESS GOVERNMENT AND ECONOMIC RENAISSANCE

Perhaps no aspect of the recent U.S. domestic experience is more controversial than its economic recovery. The recovery began in 1983 and continued, except for the mildest recession of the postwar period in 1991–92, into the late

1990s. No one denies any longer—although many Americans did right through the elections of 1992—that America is back on top. What is now disputed is how it got there. Partisans on the right attribute it to Reagan, his tax cuts, and the "magic of the marketplace." Partisans on the left attribute it to Clinton (and also George H. W. Bush), who raised taxes and reinvented a "kinder, gentler" but more activist government.

A longer view offers a less partisan explanation. In retrospect, the 1970s marked the beginning of the end of the manufacturing era and the end of the beginning of the information age. Computers inaugurated a massive shift of employment from manufacturing to services, just as one hundred years earlier railroads and cars had moved employment from agriculture to manufacturing. This process began first and went fastest in the United States. As early as the 1960s, the United States had fewer workers employed in agriculture and manufacturing (16 percent compared to 18–26 percent) than most of Europe did. By the mid-1990s, the United States along with Canada had the lowest percentage of workers employed in manufacturing and the highest percentage employed in services (73 percent compared to 59–70 percent).[56]

In a market economy, this kind of shift takes place through prices. To computerize manufacturing, employers substituted capital for labor; labor moved to new employment in services. Two factors kept labor prices more attractive in the United States than in Europe and facilitated this transfer. First, the supply of labor expanded dramatically as women and, after 1965, immigrants entered the workforce in large numbers. In Europe, women entered labor markets more slowly, and governments were less welcoming toward immigration. Second, labor mobility in the United States was higher. For historical reasons, as we have noted, American markets are more individualistic and competitive. Industry lays off workers more easily, and workers move more easily to take advantage of wage differentials. Deregulation and tax cuts in the early 1980s accelerated this process. Deregulation stopped and moderately reversed the government intervention that had built up in the postwar pursuit of social democracy. Tax cuts created incentives for investment to start new companies in the service sector. As large firms in manufacturing were laying off workers, attracting all the media attention, small firms in the service sector sprouted and silently created millions of new jobs. Excessive regulation and taxes stymied this same development in Europe, with the exception of Great Britain under Margaret Thatcher.

Price mechanisms for labor, capital, or product markets do not work well if inflation exists. A second major step, therefore, was one the United States had taken in the early 1980s to restore discipline over the money supply and reduce the double-digit inflation of the 1970s. The Federal Reserve Board, under Paul Volcker from 1979 to 1987 and Alan Greenspan thereafter, deserves credit for this contribution, although it could not have succeeded without strong support from the White House—from Reagan, who accepted a long and serious recession in 1981–83, to Clinton, who opposed calls for easier money policy from the liberal wing of his party. The consequence was a long, slow, so-called jobless recovery that did not return large benefits until the late 1990s when U.S. unemployment hit postwar lows of 4.0 percent.

A third factor, which also helped account for the slow pace of the recovery, was the budget deficit. Deregulation and tighter money stirred partisan controversy, but tax cuts and budget deficits stirred even more. Reagan's budgets lowered taxes significantly across the board but reduced expenditures only in domestic discretionary accounts, largely welfare programs and industrial subsides. Meanwhile, defense expenditures soared, and entitlement expenditures, which account for nearly half the budget (New Deal programs such as Social Security and Johnson's supplements such as Medicare and Medicaid), increased automatically as the population aged, health costs spiraled upward, and more and more immigrants entered the country. The results were large and chronic budget deficits and spiraling national debt. The government borrowed resources from the private sector at home, which slowed growth, and from foreign countries, which led to massive trade deficits, a volatile dollar, and vulnerable international financial markets.

Presidents George H. W. Bush and Clinton and a Republican-controlled Congress after 1994 (which ended early any Clintonite hopes of big spending programs such as a national health system) finally stanched the budget hemorrhage. They raised some taxes and preserved, much as Dwight D. Eisenhower had for New Deal programs, the basic consensus on social programs even as government downsized. This last step in the recovery released savings for private use and sharply accelerated business investment, which had been growing steadily, albeit slowly since 1983. This last step alone, however, would have never worked without the previous two steps. Earlier deregulation, monetary discipline, and tax cuts had created the incentives to deploy capital more efficiently and to use subsequent budget savings to accelerate growth. The United States made these adjustments a full decade or more before most of western Europe and Japan began to introduce such incentives. In addition, defense budget increases in the 1980s undoubtedly contributed to the demise of the Soviet Union, which in turn made possible the large defense savings in the 1990s after the Cold War ended. Not unlike the Roosevelt administration, which ran up a major national debt (about 140 percent of GDP) to win World War II, the Reagan and Bush administrations ran up a somewhat smaller national debt (approximately 75 percent of GDP) to win the Cold War.[57] And the end of the Cold War opened up world markets and societies, giving an impetus to economic competition, efficient markets, and global growth that the world had not seen since before World War I.

In the end, despite the hyperbolic debate about the U.S. economic recovery, the money borrowed in the 1980s was, by and large, well spent. Republicans deserve credit for reversing economic course in the early 1980s, and

Democrats deserve credit for finishing that course in the 1990s. Both parties contributed to this achievement and the related Cold War victory, much as both parties can take credit for the New Deal and victory in World War II.

MULTICULTURALISM AND AMERICAN FOREIGN POLICY

Will the American economic miracle last? Probably not. The economy slowed sharply in 2001. Economies, even the New Economy, still have business cycles. Even more important, however, politics continues. Cultural wars have broken out where economic feuds have subsided. The cultural issues not only supersede economic issues; they go to the core of American identity. In time, they may shatter the economic policy consensus, which accounted for the good economic times of the 1980s and 1990s.

Even as the New World spread to the Old, consolidating liberal democracy in Europe after World War II, the Old World is now descending on the New. After 1965, the Civil Rights revolution and the third great wave of immigration from Latin America and Asia created ethnic, racial, and cultural divisions in the United States, the likes of which had been more common in Europe than America. As late as 1960, America was still 89 percent white. Two decades later, it is barely two-thirds white, and only 15 percent trace their ancestry back to Britain.[58] The ratio is shrinking each decade. America is losing its ethnic core.

Can America survive as a nation? The large democracies in Europe and Japan are racially homogeneous (see table 4.1 in chap. 4).[59] They are held together by blood and culture. America has no single race, culture, or even language. What holds such a diverse nation together? As Brimelow points out, "there essentially is no precedent for a successful multiracial society."[60] In the past, multiethnic societies—the Austro-Hungarian, Ottoman, and Russian empires (the last reincarnated as the Soviet Union)—were old-fashioned despotisms, not democracies.

The diversity of America is a fact; whether whites and Europeans will become a minority is not yet a fact. Most likely, the third wave of non-European immigration will ebb in the years ahead, just as the first two European waves did. But America will still remain the most diverse large democracy in the world. If it survives, it will do so on the basis of ideas, not blood. Three ideas compete to supply the binding core for the American republic. The first is the traditional idea of a liberal constitutional democracy rooted in the value of the individual human being, who is both free and equal under the law regardless of his or her race, creed, or culture. The second is the idea of multiculturalism, that, in Arthur Schlesinger's words, "America is not a nation of individuals at all but a nation of groups, that ethnicity is the defining experience for most Americans, that ethnic ties are permanent and indelible, and that division into ethnic communities establishes the basic structure of American society and the basic meaning of American history."[61] The third is the idea of nationhood, that America is a nation with "a concrete historical community, defined primarily by a common language, common folk ways, and a common vernacular culture."[62]

Each of these ideas of American identity has vastly different consequences for American foreign policy. The first implies, in Ben Wattenberg's phrase, "the first universal nation," a country that strives to integrate diverse cultures and religions around common values and institutions of democratic individualism and holds out the prospect that not only basic human rights but also democracy are relevant to all peoples, nonwestern as well as western.[63] According to this idea, a nation is held together not by common race or culture; rather, "the free and equal individual with moral responsibility is the basis of communal solidarity."[64] Individuals are born into racial, ethnic, cultural, or religious communities, but they need not be defined by their communities. Through critical reason (the benefit of the Enlightenment) and belief in individual autonomy (ultimately the benefit of the Reformation), they can rise above community constraints. They can critique, reform, even reject inherited communities and create new voluntarist associations. On this basis, individuals in America escaped race, gender, and ethnicity in the past and forged voluntarist groups to free slaves, emancipate women, and open the American dream to non-European immigrants. The same is possible for individuals in all countries. The traditional liberal notion of America underwrites an internationalist foreign policy, which promotes the spread of basic human rights, democratic institutions, and nondiscriminatory markets to all societies.

The multicultural view of American identity rejects the traditional view that the individual is the bedrock of pluralist society. European religions and cultures may value the individual, multiculturalists point out, but other cultures value the society more. Given their experience with slavery, many, although not all, black Americans are more group oriented. Together with Asian immigrants, they assert more collectivist values. A multicultural democracy, they contend, allows for multiple, often incompatible moral and cultural claims. No one view takes precedence, especially not the universalist western view that proclaims only one standard applicable to all. What holds such a society together is not common moral (let alone religious) or cultural claims but reasonable political standards of fairness, which include equal rights and respect for differences of diverse cultures.[65]

Racial issues go to the heart of the multicultural debate in America today. Multicultural advocates insist that race or ethnicity is the defining basis of American law. They support legal discrimination in favor of black Americans to make up for centuries of legal discrimination against black Americans— quotas for school admissions, government contracts, employment, seats in Congress (by drawing districts based on racial demographics), and other social and economic benefits. When the Supreme Court cautioned against the legality of drawing Congressional districts by race, Justice Anthony M. Kennedy warned that "at the heart of the constitution's guarantee of equal protection lies the simple command that the Government must treat citizens as individuals." Justice Ruth Bader Ginsburg shot right back that "to accommodate the reality of ethnic bonds, legislatures have long drawn voting districts along ethnic lines."[66]

Class divisions also animate the identity debate. Recent economic growth has reduced inequality for many Americans, particularly the black middle class, which has achieved substantial progress.[67] But it has increased inequality for other Americans, especially the unskilled black or Hispanic worker in the inner city. This group at the bottom of the income ladder is seen to constitute a growing underclass in American society.

The nativist or nationhood view of American identity is particularly animated by these class differences. The concern is not only that national elites manipulate social programs—welfare, quotas, immigration, national education standards, and so on—to divide Americans and preserve their power, but also that a cabal of multinational corporations, banks, and internationalist intellectuals use free trade and global economic integration to widen the economic gap among the classes. This class consciousness fuels opposition to globalization, free trade agreements such as NAFTA, and international institutions such as GATT, WTO, IMF, and the UN.[68]

The multicultural and nativist views of American identity suggest a less internationalist and more nationalist approach to U.S. foreign policy. An America divided by race or class is not an America that will act with great self-confidence and effectiveness in foreign affairs, however preeminent its power may be. Increasingly, internal divisions and preoccupations will draw America home and transform its foreign policy into a patchwork of ethnic and commercial particularisms. National interests will erode.[69] In past periods when America was divided at home—the early republic, 1920s and 1930s, and late 1960s and 1970s—its foreign policy was weak and ineffective. Proponents of racial and class divisions do not want an activist foreign policy. They may support episodic interventions abroad to protect and assist racially or class-related nations. Jewish and Slavic Americans have supported past interventions on behalf of Israel or countries in eastern Europe. Pressure may grow from black, Hispanic, and Asian minorities to intervene in Africa, the Caribbean, Central America, or the Pacific. But a foreign policy driven by race, class, or ethnicity is not likely to congeal into a coherent or sustained American role in world affairs.[70]

Thus, American foreign policy in the early twenty-first century faces its principal challenge at home, not unlike American foreign policy after World War I. In both periods America had just absorbed a massive influx of new immigrants. It had also just come home from a victorious foreign war—World War I then, and the Cold War now. In the first period, domestic exertions to sustain the melting pot distracted from international leadership. This same possibility exists today. But the United States may also be in a better position to avoid a trade-off between domestic and foreign challenges. It faces a world in which all the major industrial powers are mature democracies. Unlike the situation after World War I, western Europe, Japan, Canada, and the United States do not threaten or arm militarily against one another. A permanent partnership between the United States and these countries is within reach. This partnership promises the best chance America has ever had to integrate its domestic ideals and international power in world affairs.

CHAPTER FOUR

Permanent Partnership

America and the Other Industrial Democracies

America's relations with the mature democracies of Canada, France, Germany, Italy, Japan, and the United Kingdom (the G-7 countries) take place under the structural conditions of converging democratic identities and growing, although not existing, equality of power. Under these conditions, history suggests strong democracies do not threaten one another and engage in military competition. In partnership with these countries, therefore, the United States can avoid costly arms races with the world's richest nations and sustain a role in the world that would not be bearable if America had to rely on its own resources alone. By such structural logic, these countries are or should be the cornerstone of American foreign policy.

But will the United States recognize and strengthen the democratic ties that enable it to feel more at home abroad? Much depends on America's future self-image. If this self-image gives priority to America's national sovereignty and to cultural differences with Europe and Japan, the democratic peace will weaken. Strategic considerations will become more important than political or moral ones; America will draw back and exploit its geographic separateness, pursuing various realist strategies of offshore balancing against its former allies. If, on the other hand, the United States recognizes the unprecedented political ties with Europe and Japan, a permanent partnership may emerge. NATO and the U.S.-Japan Security Treaty will effectively eliminate balance-of-power politics among the democratic nations and facilitate continuing military cooperation against third countries. Similarly, G-7 institutions will contain economic disputes and widen markets. Such a G-7 partnership will give democratic values and institutions an overwhelming influence in the rest of the world and create strong encouragement for other countries, especially Russia and China, to liberalize opportunities for their own people.

Traditional perspectives discount democratic ties between the United States and other G-7 countries. The nationalist perspective counsels U.S. withdrawal from European and Asian alliances because there is no enemy; the realist perspective advocates strengthening these alliances because it anticipates new enemies, such as Russia and China. Both emphasize independent American initiatives, and both subordinate economic issues to strategic concerns. Internationalist perspectives, by contrast, give priority to multilateral and economic initiatives. They advocate arms control agreements, such as the Anti-Ballistic Missile (ABM) Treaty and Comprehensive Test Ban Treaty (CTBT), to preserve peace in Europe and Asia. And they call for centralized international institutions, such as the WTO and IMF, to coordinate economic policies and address common problems of poverty, global warming, terrorism, and AIDS. Traditional perspectives, in short, focus on military and economic initiatives and neglect political ties. They assume that the structural conditions of anarchy prevail among the mature democracies when, in fact, the political identities of these countries have converged and so constrain military and economic rivalries.

U.S. policies in the 1990s suffered from traditional misconceptions. On the one hand, the United States expanded its security commitments in Europe and Asia—enlarging NATO and broadening defense guidelines with Japan. On the other, it exacerbated economic rivalries with these same countries, even threatening at one point to sever security commitments over trade differences.[1] U.S. security and economic initiatives, in short, worked at cross-purposes. If the United States faces divisive trade conflicts with Europe and Japan, it has no business expanding security commitments with these countries. And if it does expand security commitments, it has no business threatening to reduce economic ties, which reinforce security commitments and offset security costs. Military and economic relations do not exist in a vacuum. They reflect the common or divided political purposes for which states deploy military and economic power. In America's relations with other mature democracies, the strengthening of common democratic values and institutions is the starting point for America's national interests.

America's national interests, therefore, call for a permanent partnership with the European Union and Japan.[2] The purpose is not to fight old (or new) enemies but to build the democratic security community. The partnership has three aspects. The first aspect is to continue to coordinate American military and economic initiatives through the common loosely confederated institutions of NATO, the U.S.-Japan Security Treaty, and the G-7. The second is to strengthen underlying political, especially parliamentary, contacts that reinforce peaceful, law-governed relations among the G-7 countries. And the third is to promote nongovernmental and civil society relationships among the mature democracies that constitute the foundation of liberal political systems.

The democracies of western Europe and Japan should always get the benefit of the doubt in American foreign relations. Contrary to what traditional perspectives counsel, Asia, which is less democratic, is not an alternative to Europe; and China, which is nondemocratic, is not a substitute for Japan, which is now a mature democracy.[3] Economic engagement with China cannot succeed without further security and trade integration with Japan. And stronger security ties in Europe require a deepening of U.S.-EU economic relations, not a threat to shift the economic emphasis to Asia.

Partnership does not mean centralization of international institutions or loss of American sovereignty. The partnership is primarily with major democracies through existing decentralized organizations such as NATO, the U.S.-Japan Security Treaty, the G-7, and bilateral U.S.-EU summits. The G-7 is the most important link because it is the only institution that brings together the major democracies in both Europe and Asia and discusses both economic and military affairs. This G-7 process is informal and centered on nations. It does not involve a centralized bureaucracy as does the EU, nor does it involve institutional ties with nondemocracies as do the United Nations and WTO. Hence, it does not threaten American sovereignty, nor does it dilute American values to accommodate countries that do not guarantee their citizens basic democratic freedoms.

America's partnership with other major democracies does not require new or stronger institutions; it requires a new American self-image. The new self-image would embrace other mature democracies in a community based on converging national identities and increasingly equal military and economic power. Although the United States continues to dominate the G-7, the trend is clearly toward greater economic equality and a larger European and Japanese military contribution (the United States and EU are roughly comparable in population and economic size, while Japan is somewhat less than half the size of the other two; see table 4.1). The G-7 is already an informal association of equal and like-minded states, similar, in conception at least, to the loose confederation that emerged among the thirteen colonies of the original United States. Both associations were born in war, but both persisted, transcending traditional alliances to become democratic security communities. The G-7 countries, to be sure, are more diverse and diffuse than the original thirteen colonies. They are not likely to move soon toward a states-union, as the thirteen American states did in 1789. Nevertheless, the European democracies are uniting, and the United States faces a critical choice in the twenty-first century. Does the United States try to influence a stronger and more assertive Europe from the outside, or does it embrace the democratic union in Europe and coordinate its policies on a regular basis with other mature democracies? Like Great Britain in the twentieth century, the United States may have to choose in the twenty-first century between Europe (and Japan) and insularity. At the very least, America needs to recognize what is already a reality—it cannot act successfully, not to mention morally, in international economic or military affairs if its actions are systematically opposed by the other mature democracies.

Permanent partnership does not preclude unilateral actions; it actually requires such actions. A loose confederation of democratic states depends on initiatives by individual countries, just as democratic institutions at home depend on initiatives by individual citizens. National initiatives compete with and counterbalance one another in an open international political and economic community. These initiatives provide checks and balances at the international level, just as individual and group initiatives do at the domestic level. No nation threatens another nation by force, just as no group within a nation threatens another group by force. A kind of constitutional order emerges among states that are themselves subject to such constraints at the domestic level. What distinguishes this order or democratic security community is not the absence of unilateralism but the absence of violence. There exists in effect, although not in fact, the equivalent of a domestic community; states share a common identity, which precludes the legitimate use of force in their interstate relations with one another.

The rest of this chapter explores the institutions and politics of relations among the G-7 countries. It argues that recent U.S. policies have mischaracterized the political ties and trade competition among the mature democracies. U.S. policy has treated globalization as economic warfare against other democracies and a threat to American sovereignty and jobs, it has focused excessively on specific trade disputes and short-term financial crises, and it has missed the opportunity to portray globalization as the economic outgrowth of a world dominated by great-power democracies. These democracies shape the way the world economy functions; they are not threatened by it. They trade and invest abroad much the way they do at home and compete with one another through a loose process of international market and policy competition regulated by the rule of law. This chapter outlines a nationally centered or inward-first approach to G-7 economic policy competition called *competitive multilateralism*. This approach relies heavily on national initiatives, open markets, intensive but not institutionalized multilateral diplomacy, and increasing interparliamentary interactions. It advocates initiatives, such as a single market exercise, which reduce regulatory barriers by national policy competition and parliamentary oversight. Such initiatives contrast sharply with traditional outward-first initiatives, such as direct exchange rate coordination, which rely on intergovernmental diplomacy and involve less immediate parliamentary oversight.

Democracy in Europe and Japan

How does America recognize mature democracies and work to enhance ties among them? As we discuss in chapter 1, the features of a mature democracy that correlate with peaceful external relations are multiple. These features go beyond popular elections to include opposing parties rotating periodically in power, divided institutions accountable to elected officials, and protection of the basic individual rights of voting, assembly, free speech, religious choice, and the due process of law. These features vary across democratic countries. Where they diverge substantially, military threats and conflicts may reemerge. Hence, it is no easy task to figure out where democracy is sufficiently strong that we should expect nonmilitary forms of peaceful interstate relations.

Nevertheless, the task of assessing political conditions in foreign countries is no less necessary than assessing military and economic threats. Indeed, external threats are in part a function of internal politics. In recent years, statistical measures have been developed to rank and compare countries in terms of the internal dimension of identity. Table 4.1 provides such measures, along with the traditional measures of power capabilities, for the industrial democratic nations. Although imperfect, just like power measures, identity data facilitate a public debate about the degree of democracy in various countries.

All twenty-five industrialized nations in table 4.1 rank highest on the Freedom House scale of political rights. All but France and Cyprus score highest on the Polity IV scale. These political rights include the existence of free and fair elections; the right to organize and compete in opposing political parties; the existence of elected officials with real power, especially over military, religious, economic, and other institutions; and provisions for reasonable cultural, ethnic, and religious autonomy of minorities. Such rights cover essentially the first two features of democracies that live in peace with one another, namely democratic elections and divided institutions accountable to elected officials. The Freedom Rating CL column of table 4.1 covers civil liberties: the protection of basic individual rights. Here some industrial democracies rank lower than others. Greece is the weakest among the industrial democracies. It became democratic in 1974 after a decade of military rule and continues to contend with the legacies of that military rule, including an ongoing military confrontation with Turkey on the island of Cyprus. Seven other countries get a reduced rating on civil liberties. Perhaps the most unexpected country on this list is the United Kingdom, which ranks lower because of the absence of a constitutional bill of rights and the existence of libel laws that significantly restrict the media.[4] Belgium has the most culturally diverse and divided population, with 55 percent French-speaking Walloons, 33 percent Dutch-speaking Flemish, and 12 percent other ethnicities. France has no habeas corpus law, and Italy constitutionally forbids prewar fascist parties and detains defendants without trial. The most important countries ranking lower on civil liberties, however, are Germany and Japan. Given their history and material power, they represent perhaps the critical links in the chain that holds democratic states together.

Under contemporary conditions, Germany is a stable and mature democracy. Opposing parties rotate regularly in power, albeit remaining in office for relatively long periods of time. The military, which in Wilhelmine and Weimar Germany eluded strict parliamentary control, is today fully accountable to elected institutions. Conscription and the principles of self-responsibility (*innere Führung*) ensure a citizen soldier who accepts the use of force only in the defense of liberal democratic values. The civic culture, especially in the former West Germany, is open and pluralist.[5]

Germany ranks somewhat lower on civil liberties than some other democracies because it bans extremist right-wing parties and maintains citizenship laws that discriminate against foreign immigrants.[6] In addition, a recently united Germany copes with nondemocratic legacies in the former East Germany, both a persisting and perhaps revitalized communist party and accelerating neo-Nazi violence, especially among unemployed youths. Nevertheless, extremist activities are no more of a problem and probably less of one in Germany than elsewhere in Europe. In France, Switzerland, and Austria, for example, the far right commands approximately 15, 20, and 25 percent of the vote, respectively, and the far right party in Austria entered a government coalition in early 2000, sparking a political crisis in the EU and EU sanctions against Austria.[7]

Democracy in Germany is still the key to democracy in Europe. Contemporary German democracy has grown in the hothouse of western European economic and political integration. It may survive a stalling of the movement toward deeper European union, but a backsliding of European integration would thrust German democracy into virgin territory in a way that is not the case for British or French democracy. In addition, it would expose German democracy more directly to the vicissitudes of the democratizing process in central and eastern Europe, as well as in the still nondemocratic polities of the Balkans and the former Soviet republics. Ethnic and authoritarian nationalism is alive and well in much of the formerly communist part of Europe. Only eight of twenty-seven countries in this part of Europe rank highest on the Freedom House scale of political rights, and none ranks highest on civil liberties (see table 5.1). Most fall at the lower end of the civil liberties scale, although the Czech Republic, Hungary, Poland, Romania, the Slovak Republic, Slovenia, and the Baltic states rank no worse than Germany on these scales. Hence, these eight countries constitute a first crescent of eastern neighbors that share Germany's democratic identity. Their democracies are more recent and less tested than Germany's, and they border on countries that are or may easily again become nondemocratic (e.g., Belarus and Ukraine). Thus, they live in an environment in which military power may have to be contested and balanced. That prospect weighs heavily on countries, such as Germany, that have worked for decades if not centuries to discipline the military dimension of their political systems.

No one is more aware of these dangers than the Germans. As a consequence, the country has been the leading supporter of both deepening and widening the EU. Its unification in 1991 was premised on further European unification.[8] And Germany has been the most vocal of all EU members in making clear that its political identity is more European and democratic than

Table 4.1. Power and Identity Indicators in Industrial Democracies

| | | Political | | | | Economic | | Military | | | Social |
	Population, 1999[a] (millions)	Freedom Rating[b] PR	Freedom Rating[b] CL	Polity IV Rating, 1999[c]	Minority (%)[d]	PPP GNI, 1999[e] (billions of dollars)	Economic Freedom, 2001[f]	Budget (% GDP)[g] 1985	Budget (% GDP)[g] 1999	Weapons of Mass Destruction and Delivery Systems[h]	Human Development Index, 1998[i]
						European Union					
Austria	8.1	1	1	10	2	199	2.05	1.2	0.8		0.908
Belgium	10.2	1	2	10	31, 11	263	2.10	3.0	1.5		0.925
Denmark	5.3	1	1	10	1j	136	2.05	2.2	1.6		0.911
Finland	5.2	1	2	10	6, 1	117	2.15	2.8	1.4		0.917
France	59.1	1	2	9	7j	1,349	2.50	4.0	2.7	A, S, M, L	0.917
Germany	82.0	1	2	10	2, 6	1,930	2.10	3.2	1.6		0.911
Greece	10.5	1	3	10	2	166	2.70	7.0	5.0		0.875
Ireland	3.7	1	1	10	NA	84	1.65	1.8	0.9		0.907
Italy	57.6	1	2	10	2	1,268	2.30	2.3	2.0		0.903
Luxembourg	0.4b	1	1	10	NA	NA	1.75	0.9	0.8		0.908
Netherlands	15.8	1	1	10	9	386	1.85	3.1	1.8		0.925
Portugal	10.0	1	1	10	1	158	2.30	3.1	2.2		0.864
Spain	39.4	1	2	10	2j	367	2.40	2.4	1.3		0.899
Sweden	8.9	1	1	10	NA	196	2.25	3.3	2.3		0.926
UK	59.1	1	2	10	10, 9	1,322	1.80	5.2	2.6	A, S, M, L	0.918
EU TOTAL	375.3					7,941					
					Other European Industrial Democracies						
Cyprus	0.8b	1	1	9	18, 4	NA	2.15	3.6	6.1		0.886
Iceland	0.3b	1	1	10	0	NA	2.15	NA	NA		0.927
Malta	0.4b	1	1	NA	NA	NA	2.80	1.4	0.8		0.865
Norway	4.5	1	1	10	4j	126	2.45	3.1	2.2		0.934
Switzerland	7.1	1	1	10	18, 10, 7	205	1.90	2.1	1.3		0.915

				North American Democracies							
Canada	30.6	1	1	10	28, 26, 23, 15, 6, 2	776	2.05	2.2	1.2		0.935
United States	272.9	1	1	10	12, 9, 8[k]	8,878	1.75	6.5	3.1	A, C, S, M, L	0.929
					Pacific Industrial Democracies						
Australia	19.0	1	1	10	7, 1	452	1.90	3.4	1.9		0.929
Japan	126.6	1	2	10	1	3,186	2.05	1.0	0.9	C, S	0.924
New Zealand	3.8	1	1	10	10, 5, 12	67	1.70	2.9	1.6		0.903
TOTAL (ALL)	841.3					21,604					

Note: NA, not available.

[a] World Development Report 2000/2001: Attacking Poverty (New York: Oxford University Press, for The World Bank, 2001), 278–79.

[b] Freedom in the World 1999–2000 (New York: Freedom House, 2000), 596–97. Ratings are based on a scale of 1–7, with 1 signifying the most free in the categories of Political Rights (PR) and Civil Liberties (CL). Population data are taken from respective country page.

[c] Polity IV: Political Regime Characteristics and Transitions, 1800–1999, Center for International Development and Conflict Management, University of Maryland at College Park, 2000. Rating is based on Democracy Score (scale of 0–10, with 0 signifying low democracy) minus Autocracy Score (scale of 0–10, with 0 signifying low autocracy).

[d] U.S. Central Intelligence Agency, The World Factbook 2000, http://www.cia.gov/cia/publications/factbook/index.html. Single minority groups with at least 5% of the population are listed separately, with the final number including all minority groups with less than 5%. Minority refers to ethnic origin.

[e] World Development Indicators 2001 (Washington, D.C.: World Bank, 2001), 12–14. GNI equals GNP plus net receipts of primary income from nonresident sources. Conversions are at Purchasing Power Parity (PPP) exchange rates, not current exchange rates.

[f] Gerald P. O'Driscoll Jr., Kim R. Holmes, and Melanie Kirkpatrick, 2001 Index of Economic Freedom (Washington, D.C.: The Heritage Foundation, 2001), 8–14. Rankings are based on a scale of 1–5, with 1 signifying the most freedom. The score is based on trade policy, fiscal burden of government, government intervention in the economy, monetary policy (inflation), capital flows and foreign investment, banking, wage and price controls, property rights, business regulations, and black markets.

[g] The Military Balance, 2000/2001 (London: Oxford University Press, for The International Institute for Strategic Studies, 2000), 297–301.

[h] Countries proven or suspected to have Atomic, Biological, or Chemical weapons and Short-range, Medium-range, or Long-range military missile capabilities, as cited in the following sources and from interviews with government officials. Federation of American Scientists, http://www.fas.org; Center for Non-Proliferation Studies, Monterey Institute of International Studies, http://www.cns.miis.edu; Henry R. Stimson Center, http://www.stimson.org; Stockholm International Peace Research Institute, http://www.sipri.se; U.S. Department of Defense, Proliferation: Threat and Response (Washington, D.C.: Department of Defense, 1997); U.S. Department of Defense, http://www.defenselink.mil/pubs.

[i] Human Development Report 2000 (New York: Oxford University Press, for the United Nations Development Programme, 2000), 157–60. Rankings are based on life expectancy, real GDP per capita, and a combination of adult literacy and school enrollment ratios. The highest possible index value (better off) is 1.0, while the lowest possible value is 0.

[j] The World Book Encyclopedia, vols. 1–21 (Chicago: World Book, Inc., 1995).

[k] John W. Wright, ed., The Universal Almanac, 1997 (Kansas City: Andrews and McMeel Co., 1996), 524.

national. Within this context, Germany has pursued reconciliation with its neighbors and resumed a more normal military role, not only in the traditional NATO area but also more recently through contributions (including combat units) to NATO forces in out-of-area conflicts such as Bosnia and Kosovo. Some analysts believe that these commitments are now rooted in strong domestic beliefs and values that could withstand significant external change.[9] Indeed, even after reunification, Germany continues to forswear nuclear weapons, and German forces operate only under NATO or multilateral command. But no country's domestic politics is immune from external contingencies—if the environment in east-central Europe deteriorates, German democracy will be further tested.

By historical standards, Japan is also a solid and practicing democracy. Compared to 1945 and to any other country in Asia, Japan has an open, competitive, accountable, and constitutionally protected democratic political system. Its place in the democratic peace is somewhat more exposed and fragile, however. Unlike Germany in Europe, it exists alone in Asia, without democratic partners in a region that has not been historically hospitable to democracy. Its own democracy is young and in crucial ways still untested. And it has not done much since 1945 to reconcile its military past with former adversaries in the region.

Japan has competing political parties, but analysts question how much these parties actually oppose one another.[10] Since 1955, Japanese parties have rarely rotated in power; only once in 1993–94 did a coalition of opposition parties briefly replace the dominant Liberal Democratic Party (LDP). And despite a decade-long economic slump in the 1990s, the LDP remained in power and opposition parties languished. Japan's political culture encourages compromise, not confrontation. Personalities and patronage seem to matter more than policy differences and open clashes among interest groups or political representatives.

The clientelist style of Japanese politics makes for a relatively weak parliament. A weak parliament, in turn, leads to doubts that the Japanese bureaucracy is effectively controlled by elected politicians.[11] Many U.S. complaints about Japanese trade and economic policy focus on the power of Japanese economic ministries and the collusive backdoor politics they pursue with Japanese interest groups—collusion that effectively undercuts the control of both the parliament and the prime minister.[12] Some of these perceptions of Japanese bureaucratic influence are probably exaggerated; the literature suggests a wide range of interpretations about how Japanese politics really works.[13] Moreover, Japanese politics is changing, and bureaucratic influence may be on the wane. Nevertheless, the relative impotence of Japan's parliament and prime minister does raise legitimate questions about how Japan may handle controversial issues in the future relating to its military role and its foreign policy more generally.[14]

Japan is much less far along than Germany in resuming a more normal military role, despite its alliance with the United States. In the short run, Japan's military policy remains under tight civilian control,[15] but Japan's military role is expanding. In 1999, the Japanese parliament approved new defense guidelines under the U.S.-Japan Security Treaty, which permit Japanese military forces to assist U.S. forces in areas surrounding Japan (left undefined, but expected to cover conflicts on the Korean peninsula and perhaps in the Taiwan Strait). Such assistance includes search and rescue operations, logistical support such as medical and transport assistance, and naval operations such as minesweeping and sanctions-monitoring. In 2001, Japan sent medical and logistical support to U.S. forces in Afghanistan. Each step in the enlargement of Japan's military role raises questions about Japan's constitution and what authority the cabinet and parliament will have in deciding when Japan can use force.[16] To implement new legislative authority, for example, Japan has to amend the Self Defense Force law, change the laws governing civilian ministries that may be involved in rear area support, and possibly strengthen the emergency power of the prime minister's office—all without diluting democratic controls by a parliament that is already weaker than parliaments in other democratic countries. The new guidelines also raise issues for U.S.-Japan military relations. Japanese and U.S. forces are not integrated in a joint and combined command structure, as national forces are in NATO. The guidelines clearly require closer coordination. But while national tasks are evolving, Japan resists joint command. The bureaucratic and political aspects of a larger Japanese military role are far from settled.[17]

Much depends on when and under what future circumstances the questions of Japan's military role arise. Japan's political culture is consensus-oriented. It is often hard to figure out in advance the alternatives that Japanese society is considering;[18] there is much less open confrontational debate. And although individual rights are protected, the culture discourages strongly advocated individual opinions, particularly unconventional or critical ones. Chie Nakane, a Japanese anthropologist known for her study of Japanese character, puts it bluntly:

> The Japanese way of thinking depends on the situation rather than principle. . . . Some people think we hide our intentions, but we have no intentions to hide. Except for a few leftists or rightists, we have no dogma and don't know ourselves where we are going. This is a risky situation, for if someone is able to mobilize this population in a certain direction, we have no checking mechanism. . . .[19]

The absence of strong individual or collective accountability makes it difficult for Japan to acknowledge and apologize for its past military excesses. It also creates the concern that the military may gain influence again in the future. As Edward J. Lincoln, a very sober student of Japanese politics, worries, "once given an enhanced role, the military would be in a position to push an agenda—whatever it might be—to which other interests might have to give way."[20] So far the Japanese public itself fears this possibility and resists a more "normal" role for the Japanese military. Some foreign analysts agree and urge the United States not to press Japan for larger military contributions.[21] But strategic developments are necessitating such a role, and they include the reality that America cannot fight future wars in Asia without more direct assistance from Japan. The present situation, in which Japan's military role is growing yet the political acceptance of this role is still unsettled, is probably not sustainable. The Japanese people will have to address this issue in the future. They will do so themselves, but if it is true that they think largely in terms of situations rather than principles, it will matter greatly what the circumstances are. In this sense, Japan's ties with the United States may be crucial. Japan can take on a larger military role within a close and deepening relationship with the United States, or it can do so outside such a relationship.

Institutions among Democracies

The principal policy-making institutions that unite the industrial democracies are NATO, the EU, and the annual summits of the heads of government and state known as the Group of Seven (G-7). The Organization for Economic Cooperation and Development (OECD), the successor of Marshall Plan cooperation in Europe, is primarily a research organization and now also includes democratizing states such as South Korea and Mexico. The Council of Europe and the Organization for Security and Cooperation in Europe (OSCE) include numerous nondemocratic states and focus primarily on human rights, election monitoring issues, and the like.

NATO is the most consequential institution among democracies because it involves binding commitments on the central issue of when it is legitimate to use military force against third parties. Article 5 of the NATO Treaty obligates the members to assist one another if one or more of them suffers armed attack. Although this commitment to assist is both automatic and unconditional, it need not involve the use of force. Each member decides "such action as it deems necessary, including the use of armed force, to restore and maintain the security of the North Atlantic area."[22] Nevertheless, during the Cold War, a credible deterrent required the United States to position American forces along the central frontier with the Soviet Union. This forward positioning ensured that any aggression would be met by collective military action. NATO developed an integrated military-force structure and logistical command to carry out such action. Although U.S. officers commanded NATO forces and were also the commanders of U.S. forces, they acted under collective NATO, not sovereign American, control. Since 1955 and the establishment of integrated NATO military forces, therefore, the United States has been, in effect, sharing sovereignty with other democracies in the most critical area of U.S. national security.[23]

The article 5 commitments apply to the territories of the member states (including the North Atlantic sea-lanes) previously threatened by the Soviet Union, the NATO area defined in article 6 of the treaty. The withdrawal of Soviet and then Russian forces from central Europe sharply reduced the military threat, yet article 5 did not become irrelevant. It was invoked for the first time in NATO's history in the wake of the terrorist attacks against U.S. territory in September 2001. The automatic and unconditional commitment to assist against armed attack also applies to new NATO members—Poland, Hungary, and the Czech Republic. NATO now borders on an enclave of Russia territory, Kaliningrad, and faces Russian forces in Ukraine, not on the central Polish border but in the south, in the Crimea where Russia naval forces remain. A U.S. commitment to use force in Europe is still very much intact.

NATO is also evolving common military practices outside the NATO area. Here the threats involve smaller actions, and there is no binding obligation to act collectively (only to consult). Nevertheless, NATO forces have been reconfigured as rapid reaction forces that can be deployed with air and naval support in the Balkans, Persian Gulf, and perhaps other areas. In redirecting NATO cooperation to out-of-area concerns, the industrial democracies demonstrate a double reality: that their interests outside the NATO area are not fundamentally opposed, and that their resources to conduct separate foreign policies are limited. Since the end of the Cold War, they have used significant force in several out-of-area conflicts. Although it was not a NATO operation, the United States fought the Persian Gulf War, not only with allied approval and essential support (including direct military support from the British, French, and others), but also with the approval of the UN. After the EU and UN failed to quell the Bosnian crisis in former Yugoslavia, NATO undertook its first out-of-area operation, initially to strike Serbian forces in Bosnia and then, after the Dayton Accords, to monitor a cease-fire. Subsequently NATO intervened in Kosovo, waging a massive and successful air campaign inside the sovereign country of Serbia to stop ethnic cleansing.

NATO operates under the political authority of the North Atlantic Council, which brings together the elected civilian leaders of the NATO states. These leaders, in turn, answer to democratically elected national parliaments. Independent but related to NATO is the North Atlantic Assembly, a gathering of parliamentarians designated from national parliaments to consider North Atlantic issues. At present, the North Atlantic Assembly has no real powers.[24] Eventually, as NATO assumes more collective military assignments, the member countries may wish to tighten the accountability of the NATO Council. One way to do so would be to elect directly the representatives of the North Atlantic Assembly and give them certain oversight responsibilities for NATO policy. In economic areas, the European Community did this in 1979 when it authorized the first direct elections of the European Parliament and gave the parliament increasing authority in relations with the European Council and Commission. The NATO countries are still a long way from that point, and it would not be wise to subject a military alliance to a weak and fragmented North Atlantic parliament. But among democratic countries, it is never too early to consider the requirement of direct representation. After all, democracies are constructed on republican principles. Why should the international organizations among them not apply these principles as well? For the foreseeable future, NATO might strengthen interparliamentary relations among its members, both bilaterally and through the North Atlantic Assembly, and use occasional joint parliamentary committees to review and advise on broader NATO strategic and procurement issues.

A key issue in NATO's future, and in the EU's future, is how the United States reacts to greater European cooperation in security affairs. From the beginning, the United States has both feared and promoted European military cooperation. While seeking to integrate European resources against the Soviet Union, the United States worried that if Europe provided more of its own defense, it would not need the United States or it would act in ways that would draw the United States into European conflicts. For decades, of course, Europe worried about the reverse, that the United States might make deals with the Soviet Union that would ignore European interests, or precipitate conflicts with the Soviet Union or in the Middle East in which Europe would not choose to be involved. In fact, all of these possibilities are quite remote. When the stakes are significant, the United States and Europe usually end up acting together, or at least not in opposition. The trepidations on both sides of the Atlantic are overwrought.[25]

Increasing European unity in defense policy is not incompatible with growing NATO unity. Since the end of the Cold War, both EU and NATO defense cooperation have strengthened. In 1994, France, which had withdrawn from NATO's military command during the Cold War, rejoined parts of NATO's military structure (e.g., the Defense Planning Committee and Military Committee, although not the integrated military command). In 1996, NATO agreed that European countries might use "separable" forces in NATO without U.S. participation as long as these forces were not "separate" from NATO. Then, in 1999, NATO expanded to include new members. Similarly, under the Maastricht Treaty, the EU adopted a Common Security and Foreign Policy (CSFP) and European Security and Defense Identity (ESDI). It upgraded the role of the Western European Union (WEU), a smaller defense group created in 1964, and expects to fold this institution into the EU as the European link to NATO. In 1997, under the Amsterdam Treaty, the EU members agreed that the European Council, the highest organ of the EU, could not only request but mandate WEU operations to support peacekeeping activities outside their territories. In December 1998 Britain, which had been most reluctant to support military operations outside NATO, issued a joint statement with France that the "European Union must have the capacity for autonomous action, backed by credible military force, the means to decide to use them, and a readiness to do so, in response to international crises."[26] EU members subsequently appointed a High Representative for External Relations and Common Security and agreed to establish by 2003 a 60,000-strong European military force along with appropriate political and military committees in Brussels to command this force.

Thus, the EU is edging toward a capacity to take military action without the United States. But the EU is not likely to use force and succeed in opposition to U.S. wishes, just as the United States is not likely to succeed in independent military actions if Europe and Japan are strongly opposed. Most allies agree that NATO should decide first if it wants to act (whether formally or informally is still an issue), meaning that the EU forces are not "separate" from NATO. Then, if the United States chooses not to participate, the EU uses "separable" NATO units to act on its own, undoubtedly with some U.S.-supplied NATO intelligence and logistical support.

There are practical complications to working out a more balanced, joint security arrangement between the United States and Europe. As table 4.2 shows, membership differs in NATO, the EU, and the WEU. Of the fifteen EU members, Denmark belongs to NATO but not to the WEU. The neutral EU countries—Ireland, Austria, Sweden, and Finland—belong to neither. Until the membership of the WEU or EU overlaps with NATO, military actions by these organizations will take place separately from NATO and could lead to a decoupling of the United States from European security. The assumption of WEU defense responsibilities by the EU, which Britain and France now support, would bring the neutrals on board. The widening of the EU might then include new or old NATO members and further close the gap between NATO and European defense organizations. In the meantime, non-EU NATO members, such as Turkey and possibly others, worry that a EU force might plan regional security operations that affect their interests without their direct participation.

Another practical complication is the reluctance of European countries to spend what is needed to build a truly equal European military partner in NATO. As table 4.1 shows, the major European military powers—the United Kingdom, France, and Germany—spend less of their GDP on defense than the United States (in 1999, 2.6, 2.7, and 1.6 percent, respectively, compared to 3.1 percent). In absolute terms, all European allies combined spend only 60 percent of the amount the United States spends on defense. It would weaken the alliance substantially if Europe established a largely symbolic force with lots of committees but with military structures that were essentially empty shells. The United States is right, therefore, to press for real capabilities that add to, not subtract from, NATO's capabilities. On the other hand, the United States is naïve to expect that, if the Europeans make a real contribution, they

Table 4.2. Membership in International Organizations among Democracies, 2000

Countries	EU[a]	WEU[b]	NATO[c]	G-7[d]
Austria	X			
Belgium	X	X	X	
Denmark	X		X	
Finland	X			
France	X	X	X	X
Germany	X	X	X	X
Greece	X	X	X	
Ireland	X			
Italy	X	X	X	X
Luxembourg	X	X	X	
Netherlands	X	X	X	
Portugal	X	X	X	
Spain	X	X	X	
Sweden	X			
UK	X	X	X	X
Canada			X	X
Iceland			X	
Japan				X
Norway			X	
Turkey			X	
United States			X	X

[a]European Union, http://www.europa.eu.int. Denmark, Sweden, and the UK are not included in the Economic and Monetary Union.

[b]Western European Union, http://www.weu.int/eng/index.html. Observer status: Austria, Finland, Sweden, Denmark, and Ireland. Associate members: Czech Republic, Hungary, Iceland, Norway, Poland, and Turkey. Associate partnerships: Bulgaria, Latvia, Estonia, Lithuania, Romania, Slovakia, and Slovenia.

[c]North Altlantic Treaty Organization, http://www. nato.int. Also includes new members: Poland, Czech Republic, and Hungary.

[d]Group of Seven, http://www.state.gov.

will not also demand greater influence within the alliance. If NATO persists, a European commander of NATO is likely. A European general currently commands the NATO force in Bosnia, which includes American troops, and France in particular has long argued that a European commander should be in charge of the southern area of NATO, which includes the U.S. Sixth Fleet.

These obstacles are not insurmountable. The road to take involves overlapping membership and an Atlantic alliance with two equal pillars. In theory, each pillar and perhaps each nation retains the legal right to opt out of common arrangements. In practice, however, opting out is not likely, especially on the most critical national security interests in which neither Europe nor America can act alone militarily and succeed.

Unlike NATO, the U.S.-Japanese alliance in Asia stands by itself and has no unified command structure. It is one of several separate U.S. bilateral security treaties in the region. As chapter 6 details, this bilateral diplomacy in Asia is not viable over the longer run. The U.S.-Japan Security Treaty will either eventually build out on a multilateral basis to include South Korea and perhaps other emerging democracies in Asia, or gradually lose credibility as a practical military organization.

In the meantime, the G-7 is the primary institution that links Japan, NATO, and the EU.[27] (In addition to the heads of state and government of the seven major democracies, the G-7 includes the presidents of the European Council of Ministers and the European Commission.) This link is critical for at least four reasons. First, the G-7 discusses both military and economic issues. It provides the only political link between the EU and NATO.[28] Second, the G-7 brings Japan into the larger world of democratic nations. Japan is not only a potential weak link in the democratic peace, as we have discussed; it is also the only nonwestern advanced democratic nation. Its presence in the G-7 suggests that democracy reaches out beyond cultural lines and offers a precedent for including other nonwestern nations. Third, the G-7 provides an arena to coordinate U.S. and European expectations toward Japan and Asia. The trade and financial links between Europe and Asia are weaker than those between the United States and Asia; at times, these varying stakes create unnecessary conflict. The G-7 ties together the triangle of Asian, European, and North American diplomacy and interests. Fourth, Japan is a critical economic player in international financial institutions, and the G-7 plays the key role in global monetary and financial affairs, including the oversight of international financial institutions such as the IMF and World Bank.

The G-7 is the indispensable institution for overseeing the democratic peace, yet it is not used very effectively for this purpose. It is viewed either in symbolic terms as an arena of traditional great-power politics or in substantive terms as a forum for detailed negotiations. In fact, it is neither. The symbolic view creates pressure to include nondemocratic powers in the G-7, such as Russia and possibly China.[29] This inclusion of nondemocratic or democratizing states in the G-7 is inconsistent with the structural features of a democratic security community. The most distinctive feature of the G-7 is that it is a community of great powers that do not engage in traditional great-power politics. Russia and China may be great powers, but they are not mature democracies that do not threaten or use military force against the G-7. The democratic countries must relate effectively to them, to be sure, but the G-7 is not the appropriate forum in which to do so. The UN Security Council is a better venue. It is a traditional great-power institution and already accords special status to Russia and China as permanent members. If the great powers agree in the Security Council, the United Nations can act decisively to deal with world problems. But if the permanent members cannot agree, the G-7 is the main instrument the democratic states have for defending their interests. Including Russia and China in the G-7 either disables this institution, if Russia or China objects to G-7 action, or exacerbates a crisis, if the G-7 acts against the objections of these countries. The latter situation happened in NATO in 1999 when Russia objected to the Kosovo campaign and walked out of the Russia-NATO Joint Council, suspending U.S.-Russian relations in a wide range of areas.

The second view of the G-7 casts the annual summit exercise as a negotiating forum for specific economic issues among the advanced industrial democracies.[30] This view, as I discuss later in this chapter, misjudges the proper role both of heads of state and government and of high-level national bureaucrats. Heads of state and government are not particularly well suited to negotiating details of complicated policy issues in the few hectic hours of a summit meeting. And the national bureaucrats who prepare these details in secret meetings before the summits are not sufficiently accountable to national parliaments, which, in the absence of international parliaments, have a major stake in these issues.

The G-7 is not a negotiating institution operating under a treaty, as is the EU. It is best seen as an informal forum for broader strategic initiatives among the major democratic nations. The leaders set overall policy directions for the world economy and international institutions, such as NATO, the IMF, the World Bank, and the WTO, and commission studies by experts, bureaucrats, and (perhaps in the future) joint parliamentary committees to work on the details. If the G-7 does this job properly, it enhances the transparency of world markets and holds a spotlight on the work of international bureaucracies that may become complacent and sometimes corrupt.[31] The Williamsburg Summit in May 1983 offers an example of this type of G-7 role. Williamsburg solidified strategic commitments in NATO to deploy intermediate-range ballistic missiles in western Europe in fall 1983. This strategic decision countered the deployment of Soviet SS-20 missiles in eastern Europe and hastened the end of the Cold War. Williamsburg also initiated the convergence of G-7 economic policies toward lower inflation, fiscal restraint, and more competitive domestic and international markets.[32] In subsequent years, this convergence became the bedrock of global economic expansion and the globalization phenomenon that exists today.

The G-7 countries face critical security and economic challenges in the early twenty-first century. The most divisive may be the issue of antiballistic missile defenses. America under President George W. Bush is determined to press ahead with such defenses, amending and even abrogating, if necessary, the 1972 ABM Treaty with the former Soviet Union, which limits missile defenses. Europe and Japan fear antagonizing Russia and China, both of which oppose U.S. anti-missile plans. Over the long run, anti-missile defenses, combined with smaller numbers of offensive weapons, offer a more humane and acceptable nuclear strategy to deter aggression than the mutual destruction of civilian populations by large numbers of offensive weapons and limited defenses. The transition to the long run, however, will be tricky. The United States, although it may take unilateral initiatives along the way to display resolve, cannot succeed unless it gains multilateral consent. Deploying such systems without Europe and Japan would shatter the alliances, and going ahead without consultations and perhaps even sharing the technology with Russia would unnecessarily jeopardize strategic stability. The missile defense issue nicely illustrates the structural constraints of a security community. Unilateralism does not disappear, but it is circumscribed by multilateral commitments to work out differences short of breaking up the community (the practical equivalent of a domestic community that resolves differences without the threat or use of force).

Other challenges confront the G-7. The Asian economic recovery is still fragile; world trade negotiations flag; and initiatives to combat terrorism, nuclear proliferation, drugs, pollution, and ethnic conflicts need regular attention. The G-7 forum is the most appropriate institution to lead on these issues. To be sure, it is a rich-country club, and it will be resented, but if it does not act, the consequences will be worse. When the Asian crisis hit in 1997–98, the G-7 did not convene to exercise overall leadership. G-7 ministers worked behind the scenes to quell the crisis, but a G-7 summit meeting, enlarged to include relevant Asian nations, might have reinforced confidence and demonstrated that governments were dealing with globalization, not being overrun by it. Instead, the IMF and unaccountable international bureaucrats took charge and left the impression that globalization and international institutions threatened national sovereignty—the most vivid political symbol of the Asian crisis being a picture of the IMF director towering over a seated Indonesian head of state signing an economically punishing IMF agreement.[33]

The most important institution among the democracies in Europe is the European Union (EU). This institution arouses the most ambivalence in Washington.[34] Unlike the G-7, the EU is a treaty-based institution with significant centralized powers in trade and monetary areas.[35] U.S. and EU leaders meet regularly at bilateral summits, in addition to their annual contacts in the G-7 summit. But Washington complains that the evolving authority of the EU creates uncertainty and sometimes makes cooperation more difficult than it would be without the EU. There is no common economic institution between the United States and the EU to match the common military institution of NATO. Thus, the United States feels excluded from the decision-making process in Brussels. It is unsure whether to encourage further integration of the EU, at the risk that U.S. interests may not be fully taken into account, or to contain and circumvent the EU by dealing bilaterally with major European partners. It conveys simultaneously both envy and disdain for European unification.[36] The United States wants a seat at the table of European Union but, as we discuss later, it is not ready to assume the treaty-based responsibilities of such a seat.

Politics of G-7 Cooperation

U.S. diplomacy in the 1990s missed an opportunity to refashion G-7 politics. Influenced by traditional foreign policy perspectives, Clinton officials pursued inconsistent military and economic initiatives and in the process weakened political ties among the major democracies.[37]

In Europe after the Cold War, the George H. W. Bush and Clinton administrations pressed ahead to reform and expand NATO.[38] Simultaneously, however, the United States deemphasized closer economic ties with Europe and warned Europe that Asia was becoming more important economically to the United States.[39] Although it did complete multilateral trade negotiations under GATT (the Uruguay Round), the Clinton administration gave top priority thereafter to bilateral and regional trade initiatives in Asia. No comparable initiatives were undertaken toward Europe. In spring 1995, transatlantic business leaders and European officials became alarmed by the contradictions between U.S. expanding security commitments and declining economic interest in Europe. They recognized that politically the United States could not sustain new security commitments in Europe if its economic stake and interest in the region declined. They called for a Trans-Atlantic Free Trade Agreement (TAFTA) and other initiatives to bring economic relations more in line with expanding military commitments.[40]

In Asia, U.S. officials did just the opposite. They pressed economic initiatives and neglected security alliances. The Clinton administration pioneered a more aggressive bilateral trade strategy toward Japan and the Asian tigers (such as South Korea) and initiated a new leaders' meeting in the APEC forum (not called a summit because Taiwan cannot be recognized as a state). Meanwhile, security relations languished. From 1993 to early 1996, the U.S.-Japanese alliance was neglected even in the face of the worst security crises in Korea and Taiwan since the 1950s. Eventually, a scandal involving U.S. military forces in Okinawa forced the president to visit Japan and South Korea and reaffirm U.S. security treaties with these two countries.

Under the influence of traditional perspectives, America pursued initiatives in both Europe and Asia that weakened democratic solidarity. Tokyo, for example, was expected to open markets further to U.S. products at the very moment American officials were threatening to reconsider security ties with Japan.[41] If countries are uncertain about their security relationships, they are not likely to open their markets. Similarly, the U.S. Congress and the American public cannot be expected to pay more for closer security ties with Europe if Europe and the United States are not cooperating to expand mutual economic opportunities.

Traditional perspectives work best in two circumstances—when there is a serious threat, which forces consistency between military and economic initiatives (as in the case of the Marshall Plan and NATO in the Cold War); and when there is no threat, which allows economic conflicts to be pressed with no apparent harm to security interests (as in the Clinton administration's early policies toward Japan). Most real events do not meet these ideal conditions. With the end of the Cold War, the United States faces diminished but nevertheless real threats. It cannot expect external threat (the external dimension of G-7 identity) to drive its economic and military relationships with other democracies. On the other hand, it cannot afford military or economic initiatives that weaken political ties (the internal dimension of G-7 identity) with these countries.

Aggressive trade tactics with Japan, for example, called for market-share agreements to increase Japanese imports of American products. But this approach encouraged the very practices, bureaucratic intrusion and industrial cartelization, that kept American products out in the first place. It reinforced bilateralism and elevated trade disputes to high-level intergovernmental negotiations that threatened security ties. A better strategy, more consistent with the structural realities of a democratic security community, is to press for direct contacts between foreign businesses and closed Japanese cartels (e.g., regular meetings between steel associations, construction unions, professional associations, and other market participants in the two countries) and thereby open up civil society relations. U.S. negotiators can continue to work for immediate results, but their efforts would now be reinforced by wider societal contacts.

Similarly in Europe, preoccupation with individual trade issues—bananas, hormone-treated beef, export tax subsidies—played into the hands of EU bureaucrats and widened the democratic deficit in Europe. Clubby relationships between Brussels bureaucrats and special interest groups decided trade policy, and broader initiatives languished. A better approach, again more consistent with the structural realities of converging democratic identities, is to push a bigger agenda that requires European leaders to take the initiative away from bureaucrats and special interests. Such an agenda would include a new trade round with emerging nations and a single market exercise among democratic nations. Both initiatives strengthen transnational and civil society contacts between Europe and the United States and involve national, international, and supranational parliaments more directly in the G-7 and the process of globalization.

An identity and power perspective reverses the logic of traditional thinking. In the old thinking, great power rivalries shaped political relationships. Countries grouped together to balance power, regardless of their internal preferences. In the new thinking, shared internal identities matter more and diminish the sense of external military and economic rivalry. Shared democratic identities produce an entirely new kind of peaceful, law-governed international relations. Mature liberal democracies reserve a large space in their societies for private, nongovernmental activity. They project this same space for markets and civil society in their relationships with one another. Democracies relate peacefully to one another through this healthy transnational economy and civil society. In relations with other mature democracies, U.S. policy needs to strengthen this private transnational space even more than it needs to strengthen public intergovernmental institutions.

Globalization in this light is no threat to democratic society. It is instead a manifestation of democratic life among the G-7 countries. This characterization is a far cry from conventional wisdom, and it requires a better understanding of the nature of domestic markets and international competition among the G-7 countries.

Rival Capitalisms—Diverse Domestic Institutions

The contemporary debate about trade and competitiveness between the United States and its industrial partners no longer centers on policies at the border, such as tariffs, quotas, and export subsidies. More important are behind-the-border or domestic policies, both government policies such as macroeconomic, industrial, and regulatory policies, and private-sector business practices such as domestic cartels.[42] Even more broadly, this debate addresses deeply ingrained cultural institutions and habits that exist in the private sector of particular societies and are not necessarily subject to direct policy controls. Through free trade practices over the past fifty years, industrial nations have stripped away border measures affecting trade and created more direct competition among behind-the-border policies. Business practices, such as the tendency of Japanese firms to buy only from other Japanese firms, and macroeconomic policies, such as a change in monetary policy by the European Central Bank, have more to do with how much American firms sell in Japan and Europe than do traditional tariff barriers or health and safety standards enforced at the border.

Behind-the-border policies in western countries come in many variations. Figure 4.1 provides a pictorial display of the major differences in capitalist institutions among the principal industrial nations. Countries are placed near the institutions that have greater relative strength in their economies. The United States has an economy in which state and labor are relatively weak and consumers are relatively strong. In all other industrial societies, consumers are relatively weaker. In Japan, producers dominate in collusion with government bureaucrats. In France, the state dominates; in Britain, labor is stronger. Germany has both strong producers and strong labor, but a weaker federal state and less active consumers.

Supplementing these institutional differences are deeply ingrained cultural habits. Americans are more individualistic, Japanese and Germans more communitarian, French more provincial, and British more class-oriented.

Figure 4.1. Diversity of Capitalist Institutions among Major Democracies

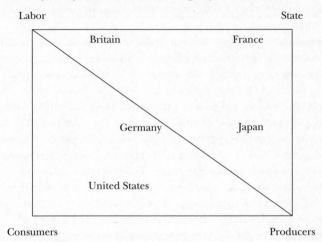

Source: Adapted from Jeffrey A. Hart, *Rival Capitalists* (Ithaca: Cornell University Press, 1992), 281.

These institutions and habits contribute to different capacities to compete and perform.[43]

Experts debate endlessly which set of institutions and habits is more efficient and leads to leadership in world markets. This debate reflects an obsession in the 1990s with international competitiveness as the key to national economic success.[44] President Clinton came into office in 1993 proclaiming that in the post–Cold War world national security depended primarily on economic competitiveness. He set up a high-level National Economic Council in the White House as the equivalent of the National Security Council and proclaimed a new "national economic security" strategy to boost American exports and generate higher national living standards.[45] This strategy was directed at the G-7 countries and later at the industrializing countries or big emerging markets. But, above all, it was targeted at Japan and the rapidly growing countries of Asia, countries thought to epitomize a new and more effective model of competitiveness.[46]

The Asian model (sometimes called the Asian-German model) claimed that the key to economic success was no longer comparative advantage but competitive advantage. That is, instead of reducing barriers to allow comparative advantage to emerge, governments aggressively intervened to create it by protecting and subsidizing industries to help them develop new technologies, grab market share, exploit economies of scale, and establish market leadership.[47] Countries in which governments and producers played a stronger role had an advantage, and they were not going to give up this advantage to level the playing field. Hence, the United States and Britain would have to imitate

107

the more successful Asian and German models of industrial targeting or be driven out of the global marketplace (see also the discussion of the Asian model in chap. 6).

This obsession with a government-led geoeconomic struggle for international economic supremacy misreads the realities of economic relations among diverse capitalist democracies. The unique feature of liberal capitalist democracies, in contrast to all other economic systems, is the existence of a separate market and civil society and so a limitation on the government's role. Even in Japan, the government's role is small compared, for example, to China or prewar Japan. Governments may have deep pockets but, in market economies, they do not escape the laws of competitive economics. Japan spent unwisely in the 1980s and entered a decade-long slump in the 1990s. Among market economies, societal differences do not obstruct trade; they are the principal reasons that trade flourishes and enhances competitiveness. As Robert Lawrence points out, "cross-border trade is valuable because the playing field is not level."[48]

Nevertheless, international trade and capital flows can be disruptive. Labor is displaced, capital is lost, and companies go out of business. The point at which a country decides to limit international competition is arbitrary. Some countries, such as the United States, tolerate greater flexibility and mobility to adjust to externally induced changes; others tolerate less. As noted in chapter 3, the mix of individualism (liberty) and community (equality) in democratic countries varies.

Since 1981, America has run current account deficits, importing more goods, services, and investment income than it exports. These deficits reflect faster growth and a higher marginal propensity to import in the United States than in Europe or Japan. In 2000, the deficit reached $369 billion, the largest ever in the history of the country. At first glance, such a deficit seems to suggest that the United States is losing more jobs from imports than it is gaining from exports. But the current account deficit is only part of the story—a current account deficit is always offset by a capital account surplus. Countries with current account surpluses, such as Japan, have to lend money to countries with current account deficits, such as the United States. This capital inflow increases jobs and consumer welfare in the United States. On balance, the United States gains because capital inflows go into new, higher-paying jobs in which the United States is more competitive, whereas imports displace old, lower-paying jobs in which the United States is no longer competitive.[49] Nevertheless, the job shift displaces some producers and labor and constitutes a social cost. And the fact that the United States accumulates foreign debts is potentially a political and economic cost—a political cost if the United States fears that a foreign country may use its lending leverage to harm America's political interests, an economic cost if the United States fails to invest wisely what it borrows today and is unable to pay back what it owes tomorrow.

What then does the United States, or indeed any democratic country, do when international economic diversity and competition produce intolerable domestic social or foreign political costs? Level the playing field by negotiating market shares that balance exports and imports with countries such as Japan? No. Trade policies are not the cause of the problem; domestic policy is. As Paul Krugman argues, "national living standards are overwhelmingly determined by domestic factors rather than by some competition for world markets."[50] If a country experiences a massive current account deficit or surplus, the culprits are macroeconomic, regulatory, and private-sector policies in the country concerned, which reduce or increase savings and lower or raise productivity. Although international competition can enhance domestic performance at the margin by stimulating competition in industries that engage in trade, it cannot substitute for more influential domestic policies and has only an indirect effect on the 75 percent of the U.S. economy that is not engaged in international trade. According to Krugman, "the rate of growth of living standards essentially equals the growth of domestic productivity—not productivity relative to competitors."[51]

Less is at stake in international trade and economic relations than meets the eye. U.S. policies made a mistake in the 1990s by placing too much emphasis on global competition, frightening American citizens that globalization was getting out of control. The expansion of global markets was not the source of economic growth in the United States and other industrial nations. The expansion was itself the result of the dramatic transformation that took place in the domestic policies of democratic as well as emerging nations. One after the other, these countries adopted the Williamsburg Summit consensus of 1983 and reduced inflation, increased incentives, liberalized labor and capital markets, and practiced more restrained fiscal policies. Globalization resulted from this revolution of domestic economic policy governance, not from an internationalization of trade and capital flows that circumvented domestic control. Globalization is a product of national sovereignty in democratic and free market economies, not a threat to it.

Globalization and National Sovereignty

Traditional perspectives squeeze all international relations into two boxes: national autonomy without centralized institutions (anarchy) and centralized institutions without national autonomy (hierarchy). Sovereignty and international institutions are seen as trade-offs. Between these two boxes, however, many other forms of international relations exist. The United States has many choices about how to associate with other democracies, and most of them do not threaten national sovereignty.[52]

First, the United States might coordinate its policies with other democracies through a competitive process known as *mutual recognition*. In this process, each country pursues different policies but lets the open marketplace decide which policies prevail. For example, a product that meets environmental regulations in one country can be exported to any other country, even if the latter country has tougher regulations. Or a bank licensed to do business in one country can do business in any other country. This is the method the European Community used with great success to reduce regulatory barriers in its Single Market Exercise (SME) in the late 1980s. Second, the United States might reach an agreement with other democracies on common policies and then monitor these agreements through *decentralized processes*. This is what it does at the annual economic summits with the G-7 countries. The summits set goals, for example, to reduce budget deficits or lower interest rates, but then rely exclusively on national institutions to implement these decisions. Third, the United States might agree to establish *common intergovernmental institutions* to implement agreements in specific areas, as it did after World War II when it established the Bretton Woods institutions to promote economic integration—the IMF, World Bank, and GATT. Fourth, it might agree to set up *integrated* or *federal institutions and policies* with other democracies. This is what the original European Community did in trade policy and the EU has done in monetary policy as well.

Only the last form of association—integrated institutions, which the EU is implementing—would significantly constrain American sovereignty, but, among the major democracies, the United States does not belong to any integrated economic institutions. The G-7 has no formal authority or weighted voting procedures. American national sovereignty is legally unconstrained. The United States does belong to some common intergovernmental institutions, and these institutions include nondemocratic members. But these institutions have modest powers, and in most of them the United States and other major democratic powers enjoy special rights. In the IMF and World Bank, for ex-ample, the United States has voting rights based on the size of its contributions. In the UN Security Council, the United States has veto rights. (This is the right the United States compromised slightly in NATO, obligating itself by treaty law to act collectively under certain circumstances, albeit in specific ways that it will still decide independently.) The GATT was only an executive agreement, not a treaty, and operated by consensus.

The WTO, however, is a slightly different and more integrated institution. Like the original International Trade Organization (ITO), which the U.S. Congress rejected in 1947 (GATT became the nonlegally binding successor), the WTO has legally binding authority in dispute-settlement decisions. After cases have been heard by the Dispute Settlement Body and appealed to the Appellate Body, the decision can be overturned only by a consensus vote (an unlikely event because the country winning the appeal is certain to vote

against its rejection). NAFTA settlement procedures have similar legal implications and allow not only governments but also private-sector actors to appeal
violations.[53]

The WTO and NAFTA agreements sparked a heated debate about the loss
of American sovereignty. This debate was particularly charged because it
reflected the fear that America was ceding sovereignty both to nondemocratic
and democratizing states, which do not practice the rule of law to the same
degree in their home markets, and to international bureaucrats, who are often
beyond the reach of democratic parliaments and direct political accountability. The debate was overdone because the WTO has no power to change
American laws or to enforce such changes if it did. (If a member loses a case
in the WTO, it is legally bound to pay compensation to the offended member
in another area, but it need not change the law that caused the offense in the
first place.)

The protests against globalization illustrate the costs of U.S. policies, which
fail to distinguish between institutions among democracies, such as the G-7,
and institutions that include nondemocracies, such as the WTO. Working
through the WTO, particularly if the United States and other democratic
countries do not coordinate policies vigorously beforehand, portrays globalization as a threat to American sovereignty from outside the democratic community, and this is exactly what happened when the United States attended
the WTO ministerial meeting in Seattle in December 1999 without a leadership agenda and careful prior preparations with other G-7 democracies.

As I argue in chapter 1, globalization is best conceived in two stages: cooperation among the mature democracies and relations with emerging nations.
The first is more important—these countries are not only the most important
ones in the operation of the global economy, they are also the most directly
accountable to their citizens and parliaments. Hence, the G-7 countries have
a special responsibility to lead the broad international economic institutions.
Democratic institutions do not just require more participation; they also
require more accountability. Traditionally, the G-7 has led the international
economic institutions through the quadrilateral mechanism in the GATT and
WTO and through the G-7 finance ministers and summit process in the IMF
and World Bank. This cooperation becomes more, not less, important as international institutions expand to include formerly communist and emerging
nations.

Working with other democracies in the G-7 is not easy. Contrary to what
internationalists expect, multilateral decision making is neither guaranteed
nor always better. Sometimes decision making requires leverage. The major
countries, especially the United States, may have to act unilaterally to move
the process forward. The best system for G-7 coordination, therefore, is a
loose process of inward-first or nationally centered policy competition, more
akin to the mutual recognition and summit processes previously discussed

111

than to the integrated or intergovernmental models followed by the EU, IMF, and World Bank.

Inward-First vs. Outward-First Economic Cooperation

The traditional tendency to define U.S. national interests in terms of external economic and military interests has created a preference in U.S. diplomacy for an outward-first style of foreign economic leadership.[54] This style of diplomacy places the emphasis first on negotiating common policies with other countries in international institutions and then on implementing these agreements by adjusting domestic policies in national institutions. It conforms with a more institutionalized view of the G-7: a large central secretariat, permanent interbureaucratic or transgovernmental bargaining mechanisms, and detailed cross-issue policy packages negotiated by heads of state and government at the annual economic summit. This view is very critical of national initiatives, equating them with unilateralism, and falls toward the intergovernmental, if not integrated, end of the spectrum of institutional cooperation. Democratic countries agree to pursue and monitor common policies increasingly supported and overseen by centralized institutions and civil servants. The Bonn Summit meeting in 1978 is often taken as a classic example of this approach to international policy making. There three major interlinked agreements were reached: Germany and Japan agreed to reflate their economies, the United States promised to curb inflation and oil imports, and other participants agreed to support significant liberalization of world trade in the Tokyo Round. These commitments went beyond what each country was ready to do domestically and had to be sold to domestic constituents after the summit.[55]

An alternative approach, which draws more from the identity perspective and reflects greater sensitivity to domestic institutions, advocates an inward-first style of economic leadership. In this approach, the United States (or another democratic country) takes domestic actions first to implement a certain policy course and then uses competitive policies in the international marketplace to press other countries toward an international consensus or agreement. This approach falls toward the autonomy or mutual recognition end of the spectrum of mechanisms for sharing sovereignty. It allows for greater unilateral action to achieve consensus and does not immediately condemn national action as uncooperative. Policies pursued by the Reagan administration in the early 1980s and by the European Community in its Single Market Exercise in the late 1980s are examples of this more decentralized approach. Reagan initiated assertive national policies of deregulation, tight money, and tax cuts that sparked American economic recovery and competitiveness and eventually encouraged a consensus among G-7 and other countries to pursue similar policies. The Single Market Exercise encouraged competition among national policies to narrow differences among European Community countries in regulatory areas, such as environmental, transportation, and health standards.[56]

Both approaches have advantages and disadvantages, and both are being used today in contemporary relations among industrial countries.[57] The European Union is clearly moving toward the more centralized approach in areas of regulatory, trade, and monetary policy. The United States says it wants a seat at this table, but it has never been willing to accept the obligations that go along with the more integrated approach. The American record of implementing agreements reached even in the looser summit process is not exactly stellar.[58] Japan is a latecomer to multilateral institutions. Like the United States, it does not formally share sovereignty with other countries, even in its own region; and its policies are often considered to be the most unilateralist in trade and economic areas.

Thus, the prospect of more centralized G-7 institutions or a North Atlantic Economic Organization comparable to NATO is not likely. What is more, this prospect is not necessary, given the structural features of G-7 relations. The institutional form of G-7 economic relations is less important than the substantive policy of G-7 cooperation. For the United States, the key issue is not whether Europe integrates but what kind of policy an integrated Europe pursues. Will it be a more open and liberal Europe or a more protectionist and statist one?

The United States can best ensure a more open Europe by pursuing an inward-first style of G-7 economic policy coordination. This inward-first style has two indispensable advantages. First, it avoids granting powers to an international bureaucracy that is not directly accountable to democratic parliaments and thereby avoids a democratic deficit in Atlantic economic relations (comparable to the democratic deficit in EU affairs). This step avoids, in turn, a political backlash against globalization caused by the fear that international institutions threaten national sovereignty. Second, the inward-first style maximizes the negotiating leverage of America's more individualistic style of capitalism and ensures that economic liberalism, not social democracy or nationalism, has the best chance to prevail in twenty-first-century relations among the industrial democracies.[59]

An inward-first style of economic leadership gets the priorities straight. It starts with domestic policies, which, as noted earlier, are more important than international policies for determining productivity and economic growth. If the United States gets these domestic policies right, it projects incentives through international markets to encourage open and more competitive economies abroad. The United States, in effect, lets the international marketplace do most of the heavy lifting of economic diplomacy. The trick, of course, is to keep the international marketplace open.

Here the agenda for future international economic negotiations becomes crucial. At the top of this agenda, new multilateral trade negotiations figure prominently. These trade negotiations are important, not because trade itself is so significant economically but because open markets and interlocking civil societies are the political hallmarks of democracies. The agenda I discuss in what follows is not arbitrary. It follows from a U.S. strategy to exploit structural conditions of a great-power democratic security community. Such a community minimizes the risk of unaccountable international institutions by promoting nationally centered policy initiatives and maximizes the opportunity for democratic and market reforms in emerging nations by expanding nongovernmental and civil society contacts.

Trade Priorities

The United States has become absorbed in a search for new trade policy instruments at the same time that it has become more ambivalent about the direction in which it wants to apply these instruments. For four decades after World War II, America gave priority to multilateral freer trade and the global trading system. Through eight broad-based trade rounds, the GATT reduced average tariffs on manufactured trade among the industrialized nations from an average of 40 to 4 percent. These reductions coincided with a sixteen-fold expansion of world trade. But this success increased the visibility of behind-the-border barriers. The United States strengthened or invented a war chest of unilateral, bilateral, and regional trade policy instruments to attack these barriers.[60] Meanwhile, it put multilateral trade talks on the back burner.

The proliferation of new or strengthened trade policy instruments is not itself the problem. Behind-the-border issues require more intensive and focused negotiations. The United States has to be able to threaten or to carry out unilateral, bilateral, and regional initiatives to break multilateral stalemates. Such bilateral and regional trade moves are consistent with an inward-first style of economic leadership; the United States decides the overall direction in which it seeks to achieve a multilateral consensus (e.g., new WTO talks) and then uses its unilateral, bilateral, and regional muscle to move other countries in this direction.

The problem is that the new trade policy instruments are increasingly seen as ends in themselves or as substitutes for a global trading system. Early Clinton administration officials had no faith in multilateral solutions to trade problems.[61] Laura D'Andrea Tyson, Clinton's head of the Council of Economic Advisers and then National Economic Council, referred to enforceable multilateral rules as "utopian . . . any time soon,"[62] and Jeffrey Garten, Clinton's undersecretary of commerce for international trade, argued that "a multilateral system . . . is not there yet" and "it will be quite a while before [such a system] is effective in areas that really matter to us."[63] They called for a more realistic, results-oriented approach to close the trade deficit, especially with Japan. But the results-oriented policy they implemented in the mid-1990s failed on its own terms. The current account deficit in 2000 was larger than it had ever been. In addition, the policy sabotaged multilateral talks by stoking fears of loss of competitiveness. In Seattle in December 1999, the WTO meeting, convened to launch a new trade round, blew up as mobs protesting against globalization forced the ministers to leave town. During President Clinton's second term, U.S. trade policy deconstructed, even though the U.S. economy did better in this period than it had in its entire history—the crucial cornerstone of the democratic peace, open markets, threatened to disintegrate.[64]

This loss of direction in U.S. trade policy is a serious problem. It contravenes both U.S. economic and, more important, political interests. Economically, the United States is the only major industrial country that depends equally on all regions of the world for its markets—Europe, Asia, and North America.[65] Regional trade blocs, therefore, could potentially disrupt U.S. trade more than the trade of any single industrial nation. But economic costs are not the most important factor.[66] The most serious threat of regionalism to U.S. interests is political. If the world drifts into regional trading blocs without significant new global initiatives, America, Europe, and Japan will disengage, losing intimacy and political empathy with one another. Such divergence damages much more than U.S. economic interests; it threatens the democratic peace.

President George W. Bush recognized the dangerous drift in U.S. trade policy and succeeded in 2001 in both launching a new WTO trade round in Doha, Qatar, in November and securing legislative approval to negotiate multilateral agreements that cannot be amended by Congress. The United States can continue to pursue unilateral and bilateral initiatives to pressure trade partners, but these initiatives now serve multilateral goals, not the parochial interests of specific trade lobbies or bilateral relationships.

The new trade round exploits the structural opportunities in a global system dominated by liberal democratic great powers. It reinstates the democratic great powers as the leaders of globalization, and it extends a helping hand to emerging nations, many of whom are struggling to introduce democratic and market reforms. The new round will help these countries lock in liberalizing reforms and open up markets for their exports in agricultural, textiles and clothing, steel, and other low-end manufacturing sectors. In return, the industrial democracies secure further access to service, investment, and technology markets in emerging nations.[67] The new trade round is potentially the single most important instrument for winning the post–Cold War peace, successfully integrating the emerging economies of the formerly communist states in Europe, China, and the developing world.

Dollar and World Finance

Regardless of how important it is for political reasons, free trade policy alone cannot carry the load of economic policy coordination in the contemporary global economy. When it did under the GATT immediately after World War II, capital transactions were restricted. Today, capital flows are liberalized. Capital flows dwarf trade transactions and dramatically increase interdependence.

Exchange rate and macroeconomic policies have the greatest influence on short-term capital flows. Microeconomic or structural policies have the greatest influence on long-term capital flows. The G-7 countries have to get these policies right, or they cannot sustain the free trading system.

Unless the macroeconomic policies of major countries are aligned with one another, exchange rates fluctuate wildly and speculative capital flows distort trade competition and invite the re-imposition of barriers to trade at the border. The breakdown of Bretton Woods rules for exchange rates and macroeconomic policies had much to do with the rise of trade protection in the 1970s and 1980s and the accompanying shift to more discriminatory bilateral and regional trade initiatives. The Asian financial crisis had the same effect in 1997–98, raising demands to re-impose restrictions on capital flows, particularly short-term bank loans.

Most analysts, even those who prefer fixed exchange rates, agree that it is impractical politically to return to the fixed rate system of the early postwar period.[68] Such a system requires an enormous degree of international commitment and domestic self-discipline. In fixing and then unifying their currencies and monetary policies, the member states of the European Monetary Union (EMU) accepted severe limits on domestic inflation rates, fiscal deficits, and national debt—inflation and interest rates of no more than 1.5 percent and 2 percent, respectively, above the levels of the three best performing member states; fiscal deficits of no more than 3 percent of GDP; and public debt of no more than 60 percent of GDP. That they were able to follow these limits and implement the EMU in 1997, despite high unemployment in Europe, is still a mystery to many observers. What is not a mystery, however, is that the United States, its independent Federal Reserve Board, and, above all, the U.S. Congress are not ready to accept similar limits on U.S. domestic policies.

For the United States, therefore, the choice is not to fix rates but to seek stable or gradually adjusting exchange rates somewhere between fixed limits (which threaten sovereignty) and no limits (which threaten prosperity). There are two, non–mutually exclusive ways to accomplish this task: intervention in exchange markets to maintain certain target zones for exchange rates and direct coordination of macroeconomic policies. Normally, intervention can have lasting effects on exchange rates only if underlying macroeconomic policies change.

An outward-first style of economic leadership emphasizes exchange rate coordination and accompanying macroeconomic policy adjustments. An inward-first approach prefers domestic policy reforms and competitive market adjustment of exchange rates. The EMU employs the first approach. Advocates of the inward-first approach prefer the second and fear that the EMU approach may make domestic policy reform in Europe more difficult.[69] Critics believe that the strict monetary and fiscal rules of the EMU will slow European growth, making structural adjustments in labor and agricultural markets more difficult and less likely; the restructuring of domestic industry will slow. This inflexibility, in turn, will encourage renewed trade barriers and create a Fortress Europe keeping out U.S. and other non-EU exports. In short, the cost of slower growth will be displaced onto outside countries in the form of increased protectionism.

To avoid such protectionism in Europe, some commentators urge European countries (and, for that matter, Japan as well) to stimulate their economies through macroeconomic expansion, lower interest rates, and more fiscal spending.[70] But U.S. interests are not served by an inflationary Europe any more than by a protectionist Europe; macroeconomic stimulus without needed microeconomic reforms is eventually inflationary. The alternative, clearly, is to push structural or microeconomic reforms.

A case can be made that the EMU will accelerate, not slow, microeconomic reform. Structural reform was one of the early motivations for both the Single Market Exercise and EMU. The removal of barriers to internal trade and capital flows facilitates a broader consolidation and restructuring of European industries, information and financial services, and infrastructure. In the late 1990s, the pace of restructuring in Europe picked up; for example, Germany, France, Sweden, Italy, the Netherlands, and other European states slashed tax rates and privatized telecommunication and other services. This fact is overlooked by critics of EMU.[71] The entry of Great Britain, a country with more flexible labor and capital markets and policies, into the EMU would accelerate this restructuring even more. And a positive U.S. initiative, such as an Atlantic Single Market Exercise, would compound the pressure on Europe to remain open and make the necessary social adjustments. Structural changes are difficult politically and do not produce short-term gains, as a fiscal or monetary stimulus does. The restructuring option for Europe, therefore, will be more like the "jobless recovery" of the United States in the early 1980s—it will be slow but steady. The long-term payoff, however, would be enormous.

Nevertheless, if Europe and Japan do not restructure sufficiently or in a timely fashion, they will have to stimulate or protect. Stimulus policies will torpedo the EMU, and protectionist policies will severely weaken if not shatter the democratic peace among the G-7 countries. Currency volatility will follow. After its introduction in January 1999, the euro, Europe's new unified currency, fell by more than 20 percent against the dollar. This drop reflected slower growth and the more sluggish pace of structural change in Europe than in the United States. Such wide swings in exchange rates are usually unsustainable. The weak euro potentially creates inflation in Europe due to surging exports and rising import prices; and the strong dollar exacerbates the already large current account deficit in the United States, due to surging imports and declining exports. Domestic-led growth in Europe (and Japan) will have to pick up, especially as U.S. growth slows from its unprecedented pace in the late 1990s.

Structural or microeconomic reform is the only policy option that avoids inflation. Monetary policy options in Europe and Japan are either used up or potentially inflationary—the European Central Bank cannot lower interest rates further without threatening to weaken its currency further, and Japan is already sitting on the lowest interest rates in the postwar period, its economy still sputtering because of structural constraints, especially in manufacturing and banking. In Japan, fiscal policy is also used up—since 1992, Japan has implemented eight fiscal pump-priming packages totaling more than $1 trillion; in 2000, it was running a fiscal deficit of 7–9 percent of GDP, and its total public and private debt exceeded 200 percent of GDP. The fear is that Europe now will also turn to fiscal stimulus, despite EMU constraints. Social democratic parties, which in mid-2001 controlled all the major European governments, except Spain and Italy, are more sympathetic to stimulus policies. They may accelerate fiscal spending and also test the independence of the new European Central Bank by pressing for lower interest rates, just as the Japanese government has done successfully with the Japanese central bank.

With all the signs pointing toward stimulus, the time is not ripe for new exchange rate or macroeconomic policy coordination initiatives. In this situation, outward-first approaches to the coordination of economic policies are particularly dangerous. They would almost certainly accelerate stimulus and reduce restructuring.[72] The United States would do well to stress inward-first initiatives and keep the focus on competitive national policy reforms, particularly in microeconomic policy areas such as capital and labor markets.

A Single Market Exercise

The main obstacle to the economic success of the G-7 and global economies is the slow progress of structural and microeconomic reform in Europe and Japan. As we have noted, Europe and Japan have just begun the transition from a manufacturing to an information and service economy. They are a decade behind the United States in shifting production abroad, deregulating telecommunications and service sectors, and reforming workplace practices. The United States should exploit its lead in structural reforms. It can do so by initiating a Single Market Exercise (SME) with Europe and Japan to leverage deregulation in these societies more directly.[73] Such a G-7 SME would focus precisely on the behind-the-border issues of deeper integration that now make up the heart of trade disputes.

The United States faces a situation in 2001 that may be comparable to Britain's relationship with Europe in the 1980s. At the earlier time, Europe was suffering from Eurosclerosis (slow growth and high unemployment) and was in no mood to adopt new multilateral trade initiatives. In 2001, Europe, Japan and the United States face slower growth and are also reluctant to accept new trade openings. Great Britain favored an open Europe in the 1980s, just as the United States favors an open Europe and Asia in 2001. But Britain, like the United States, was divided internally and could not persuade its European partners to move swiftly on new trade initiatives. As an alternative, Britain backed the competitive deregulation of standards and restrictive business practices through the European SME. At the same time, it opposed direct fiscal and monetary policy coordination and the creation of a single currency and exchange rate, just as the United States in 2001 fears the EMU and is not prepared to accept more direct monetary and fiscal policy coordination with Europe. The European SME unlocked the European situation for both Britain and the other European countries. It liberalized over three hundred technical rules and regulations and did so through a process of mutual recognition and competition that did not require a level playing field or more centralized EU bureaucracies.[74] A successful SME further paved the way for the conclusion of the Uruguay Round and the launching of the EMU, even though Britain decided, at least initially, to opt out of the common currency system. The European SME, nevertheless, drew the British and European political systems closer together, engaging national parliaments and courts in the process of ratifying liberalized regulatory practices.

A G-7 SME might serve U.S. interests in similar ways at the beginning of the twenty-first century. It would address the root causes of domestic structural immobility in Europe and Japan and accelerate the progress of a new trade round. It would draw the U.S. Congress and European parliaments more directly into the process of economic entanglement. The European parliaments and the U.S. Congress would hold hearings and draft new legislation, and courts in the industrial nations would be empowered to monitor and enforce the liberalized system. Political and civil society relations among the democracies would draw closer. The process might be launched and monitored by the G-7 summits and assisted by the OECD, and it might be conducted in parallel with the new trade round launched in Doha, Qatar, in November 2001. Regulatory reform would ensure that the most important prerequisite exists for countries to continue to liberalize trade—namely, more flexible economies to accommodate change and growth.

* * *

This chapter has outlined the way forward in U.S. relations with other stable and mature democracies in Europe and Asia. The payoff of permanent partnership with these countries is massive just in terms of the military and economic benefits the United States would gain. These benefits alone would seem to justify some sharing of U.S. sovereignty with these countries, preferably in a form that maximizes policy competition through open markets. But other benefits would also follow. In the next chapter, we examine the prospects for U.S. relations with the formerly communist states of Europe, particularly Russia. These relations will depend to a large extent on the unity and strength of America's partnership with the industrialized democracies.

CHAPTER FIVE

Winning the Peace

America and the Formerly Communist States of Europe

For the fourth time in the past two centuries, the whole of Europe (east and west) is undergoing reconstruction after devastating conflicts. The first reconstruction came after the Napoleonic wars, at the beginning of the nineteenth century, when the Congress of Vienna convened in 1815 to restore the balance of power in Europe. For realists, this balance-of-power approach, which pays no attention to domestic affairs, remains the classic prescription for world order. The second effort came after World War I when the Treaty of Versailles instituted a collective security system under the League of Nations. This model epitomizes an internationalist prescription for world order—all countries are prepared to defend others against external aggression, for no country is anathema to any other as a consequence of its domestic politics. The third effort followed World War II when Europe was reconstructed on the basis of containment, a bipolar balance of power that identified and defended divisions between communist and liberal societies.

The fourth attempt is now under way, in the wake of the Cold War. How will the United States and other industrial democracies organize to reintegrate the "defeated" powers of the Cold War—the formerly communist countries of central and eastern Europe and many of the fifteen republics of the former Soviet Union? Which prescription for world order will they follow—balance of power, collective security, or containment?

The answer is "none of the above." Containment cannot work because it justifies American engagement in Europe on the basis of ideological divisions. Today, the communist enemy is gone, at least in its old virulent form of Marxist-Leninism; and without an actual and persistent enemy, there is no one to contain. Collective security is likewise a nonstarter. The domestic affairs in the formerly communist countries and republics, especially Russia, are too uncertain to support collective defense commitments. These countries may never be sufficiently liberal to solidify a democratic peace across the whole of Europe. Finally, the traditional bipolar or multipolar balance of power is also unlikely. Since the collapse of the Soviet Union, Russia does not pose an immediate threat of military aggression to its neighboring states. Without external military threats, the traditional balance-of-power model has no compass.

America needs some new thinking to cope with the challenge of transition in the eastern half of Europe. It needs an approach that anticipates but does not depend on military threat, that balances power to consolidate internal political change, not to stop external military aggression, and that encourages economic growth as a prerequisite but not a guarantee of democratization. Such an approach may never produce a democratic peace, but it does not balance power just for its own sake. It addresses domestic instability as a potential source of external aggression and, by mitigating such instability, moderates the balance of power.

Structural conditions in Europe are changing. During the Cold War, anarchy prevailed across Europe while a democratic security community flourished in western Europe. Today, anarchy remains in U.S.-Russian relations; power has to be balanced. But, because external, if not yet internal, identities have converged, the two countries no longer see one another as implacable enemies. Meanwhile, the democratic security community in western Europe is slowly inching its way across the former Iron Curtain to embrace the formerly communist countries. This process of democratic transition alters internal identities and prepares the way for future relationships without a military balance of power. The transition is tricky and calls for an approach that accepts the possibility of change, but does not count on it.

Power and Democratization

The identity and power model offers such an approach. It pays attention simultaneously to balancing power and to domestic politics. When domestic societies converge, power becomes less relevant in international affairs—the case of the mature industrial democracies. When domestic societies diverge, the balance of power becomes primary—the case of the Cold War. When countries are democratizing, however, both power and domestic politics become equally relevant. Democratizing countries are unstable and tend to fight against democratic states, more so than mature democratic states fight against one another, and so the democratic peace is not yet applicable between democratic and democratizing states. Power must be balanced, but it must be balanced to nurture and stabilize democratizing states, not to defend them against immediate military threats. Structural conditions dictate a strategy of balancing power that narrows identity differences and transforms anarchic relations eventually into a potential security community.

Realism defends against *actual* external threats. When those threats disappear, realism loses its compass. Then it either creates a new enemy, for instance a resurgent Russia, or it counsels America to come home because there is no enemy. By contrast, an identity perspective focuses on *potential* sources of threat in international affairs. Threat emerges from shifting domestic identities, not shifting power balances. When Russia ceased being communist, an identity shift, the Cold

War ended in central Europe. The next identity shift may involve Russia becoming less authoritarian, and in such a case Russian imperialism would end.

The end of Russian imperialism will improve prospects of democratic evolution in other formerly communist societies. Unlike Russia, many of these countries have weak national traditions. They are struggling to unite as well as to become free. Sometimes these struggles conflict. To become more democratic, for example, some Baltic states (Estonia and Latvia), Ukraine, and central Asian republics (Kazakhstan and Kyrgyzstan) are obliged to grant equal rights to ethnic Russians, who make up a significant proportion of their population. Yet these same ethnic Russians, some of whom might favor a restoration of the former Soviet Union, are the residue of Russian imperialism and a threat to national unity. Even in countries where Russians do not reside (e.g., the former republics of Yugoslavia), other ethnic divisions tear at the fabric of national unity and militate against democratic equality. These simultaneous struggles to develop new nations and to democratize domestic politics are a cauldron of instability from which new threats may emerge in the formerly communist half of Europe.

Unlike internationalism, however, the identity perspective does not assume that these internal political struggles have an inevitably democratic outcome or that U.S. and western foreign policy can influence that outcome directly. This perspective distinguishes between external and internal identities. U.S. and western diplomacy can soften decades-long images of adversarial relations with formerly communist states, but it cannot change significantly internal identities rooted in centuries of cultural and historical differences. Democracy is by definition the outgrowth of local conditions and choices. It will be won or lost by indigenous groups and traditions. From this perspective, most of the formerly communist countries are ill-prepared for democracy. Like Japan in 1945, these countries—Russia, most other former Soviet republics, the former Yugoslav republics, Romania, and Bulgaria—have no significant democratic traditions. And, unlike Japan and Germany in 1945, they have not been occupied after defeat and are therefore much less subject to foreign, especially American, influences. Unlike Japan or Germany, they have also never been rich or fully industrialized, a possible prerequisite for democratic development (see chap. 1). Hence, the opportunities for democracy in these countries and of direct U.S. or western influence are considerably less than they were in Japan and Germany in 1945.

Nevertheless, domestic systems can change. After all, totalitarianism did give way in the former Soviet Union to authoritarianism.[1] Authoritarianism may now evolve further toward more democratic practices. The process may be long and complicated, to be sure, but much depends on economic growth and whether an authoritarian elite can be bought off by the fruits of capitalism (e.g., the models of Chile, South Korea, and Taiwan).

The real issue, then, is not whether but how America pursues the goal of a democratic Europe, a "Europe whole and free." Traditional perspectives emphasize government-led military and economic initiatives. Realists call for traditional alliances to protect borders, whereas internationalists call for arms control agreements and massive economic assistance to promote reforms. U.S. initiatives in the early 1990s mirrored internationalist concerns—remove Soviet nuclear weapons from the former Soviet republics of Ukraine, Belarus, and Kazakhstan; reduce and dismantle warheads; clean up nuclear wastes; safeguard weapons-grade nuclear materials; and provide substantial loans and economic assistance for democratic reforms, especially in Russia. Subsequently, NATO expansion reflected realist concerns—preempt Russian imperialism and secure Germany's eastern borders.[2] Neither set of initiatives focused on the crux of the security dilemma when structures are changing from anarchy to a potential security community. The tasks in these circumstances are to consolidate democratic reforms in countries that are farthest along, such as Poland, Hungary, and the Czech Republic, not in countries that are way behind, such as Russia; and to protect these advancing democracies from extremist domestic elements, not from direct Russian military aggression.

Traditional perspectives get it wrong on both counts. Realists defend NATO expansion by exaggerating the threat from Russian imperialism. Internationalists oppose NATO expansion by exaggerating the threat to Russian democracy, the adverse impact on liberal forces in Russia. By realist logic, the countries to defend, because they are most exposed to Russian aggression, are the Baltic states, Ukraine, and Belarus, not Poland, Hungary, and the Czech Republic. And by internationalist logic, the key country to democratize is Russia, not Poland, Hungary, and the Czech Republic, because Russia is central to creating a collective security arrangement that supplants NATO. The result is confusion; and, predictably, U.S. policy comes up with contradictory initiatives. NATO expands as a traditional alliance *and* as a collective security arrangement. It adds new members to preempt Russian imperialism, and it adds a new council that incorporates Russia, the NATO-Russia Permanent Joint Council. The two initiatives are not compatible. The NATO-Russia Joint Council dilutes the credibility of NATO alliance guarantees to new members, and it stretches the credibility of U.S.-Russian cooperation as partners in collective security institutions.

From an identity and power perspective, I suggest a more durable solution— NATO expansion to consolidate democracy incrementally along the gradient from Germany to Russia and a vigorous U.S.-Russian partnership through the United Nations (especially the OSCE), not through NATO. In the United Nations, Russia already enjoys great-power status; and, through UN involvement, the United States and the West could gain some influence over Russian military activities in the former Soviet republics (e.g., Armenia, Georgia, and Moldova), where NATO forces could not intervene without causing a crisis with Russia.

From an identity and power perspective, however, NATO expansion is only the first half of the task of preempting potential threats in former communist

Europe. The second half is economic growth through trade expansion and the enlargement of the European Union. Realists overlook the second half, internationalists the first half. Predictably, economic initiatives, aside from external aid, have languished. Enlargement of the EU is on a slow track. New members are not due to be admitted until 2003, if then. Without the transparency of open markets, economic reforms languish. Capital flows out of former Soviet republics because these countries lack vibrant entrepreneurial and financial markets. Privatization passes assets from state enterprises to state managers, often the same elite, because these countries have no capitalist class. Economic growth depends on responsive domestic groups, and the countries that are succeeding in the formerly communist half of Europe are those that had or have developed more extensive private sectors (e.g., Poland in agriculture). Nothing would promote this private sector development more than faster economic integration with the West. Imagine how little western Europe might have developed after World War II if the United States had not pressed trade liberalization programs through the Organization for Economic Cooperation and Development (OECD) and the General Agreement on Tariffs and Trade (GATT).

A Strategy of Consolidation

The strategy that follows from an identity and power perspective is consolidation; this strategy differs from containment. Containment defended advanced democracies in the West against actual territorial aggression from the East. Consolidation stabilizes emerging democracies in the East and preempts potential territorial aggression. Containment stopped at the Iron Curtain in Europe; détente sought to stabilize the ideological division of Europe, not to overcome it. Consolidation, by contrast, recognizes that identity differences can be overcome and that balancing power becomes much easier as identities converge, even if those identities never converge fully toward strong liberal democracies.

Key to the consolidation strategy is Russia. This is not a tilt toward or against Russia. Realists prefer to tilt against Russia, giving priority to the central European countries and Ukraine in the hopes of weaning these countries from Mother Russia.[3] Internationalists tend to tilt toward Russia, arguing that Russian inclusion and eventual liberalization is the key to democracy and independence in other formerly communist countries.[4] A consolidation strategy recognizes both realities. Russia is the country whose domestic evolution bears the greatest consequences for external affairs in Europe. Simultaneously, Russia, along with Belarus and some of the central Asian republics, is the country least likely to become stably democratic, at least in the medium term. Russia, therefore, has to be balanced against while it decides how much it wishes to converge with the West.

Russia's opportunity to converge is enhanced by strong democracies in the West. These democracies are the anchor that moors democratizing countries in the East. This anchor stabilizes first those countries closest to the West that have the best early chance to achieve mature democratic development. Then, with this first group of countries stabilized, the anchor exerts a stabilizing effect on countries farther away. Thus, a consolidation strategy establishes a gradient of prospective reform from central European countries with the most immediate prospects of reform (Poland, Hungary, and the Czech Republic) to Russia and central Asian countries with the least immediate prospects of reform. In between fall the Baltic countries (Lithuania, Latvia, and Estonia), Slovakia, and Slovenia with moderate prospects for reform, and Ukraine, Belarus, Romania, Bulgaria, Moldova, Albania, Croatia, Macedonia, Yugoslavia, and the Caucasus republics (Azerbaijan, Armenia, and Georgia) with weak possibilities for reform.[5]

Western assistance to encourage democracy and markets becomes less important as one moves along this gradient from west to east. The best thing the West can do for democracy in Russia in the near term is to stabilize it in central and eastern Europe. Similarly, the best thing western diplomacy can do to preempt Russian meddling in the Caucasus republics is to stabilize ethnic clashes and preempt great-power conflicts in Bosnia and Kosovo. U.S. diplomacy sometimes gets these priorities reversed—U.S. officials worry too much about democracy at the eastern end of the gradient and too little about military and balance-of-power considerations at the western end. Washington invests too much in every poll and election in Moscow, and reacts too slowly to military conflicts in the Balkans.

The war against terrorism in southwest Asia does not alter these priorities. The prospects for democracy or even stable nation-building in Afghanistan and Muslim republics in central Asia are not very good; and once terrorism is rooted out, policing this region with large international forces is considerably less vital for U.S. and western interests than policing stability in regions, such as the Balkans, which are much closer to the heart of Europe. These realities do not counsel against an effort by the industrial powers to stabilize Afghanistan, perhaps along the lines that was done in Cambodia in the 1990s. But the task is primarily for the United Nations and close U.S., Russian, and Chinese cooperation, not for the United States and western or NATO forces.

Potential Domestic Threats

The primary security threat to democratic evolution along the gradient from central Europe to Russia is the potential instability of domestic affairs. Table 5.1 provides the basic indicators of power (security) and identity (democracy) for the formerly communist countries in Europe. The second through fifth columns (Freedom Rating, Polity IV Rating, and Minority) of the table suggest the rather fragile political conditions that prevail in this part of the world. The three new members of NATO, Poland, Hungary, and the Czech Republic, score as high on the Freedom House democracy scale of political rights and civil liberties (1 and 2, respectively) and on the Polity IV scale (9 and 10) as some democracies in western Europe. On a par with these new NATO members are Slovenia, the Slovak Republic, and the Baltic countries—countries that are next in line to join western institutions. From this point east, however, the gradient falls off sharply. Romania, Bulgaria, and Moldova score 2 on political rights and 2–4 on civil liberties. Romania and Moldova also drop lower on the Polity IV scale, 7 and 6, respectively. Macedonia, Georgia, and Ukraine fall further to a level of 3 on political rights, 3 (for Macedonia) or 4 (for Georgia and Ukraine) on civil liberties, and 5 or 6 on the Polity IV scale. The rest of the republics of the former Yugoslav and Soviet areas, including Russia, rank 4 or below on Freedom House measures and, except for Croatia, 5 or below on the Polity IV scale. Some, such as Turkmenistan and Uzbekistan, rank as low as −8 and −9. These democracy measures for the formerly communist part of Europe are well below such measures for Latin American countries (see table 7.1) and place the prospects of democracy in much of the Balkans, central Asia, and the Caucasus region on a par with prospects in Africa, the Middle East, and parts of Asia.

Also noteworthy about the formerly communist countries in Europe and contributing further to their potential instability is the high level of ethnic diversity in most of these countries. This diversity, suggested by the Minority column in table 5.1, contrasts sharply with the relative homogeneity of democracies in western Europe, North America, and Japan. In fact, diversity is least in those countries in the formerly communist part of Europe that have the best chance of becoming durable democracies—Poland, Hungary, the Czech Republic, the Slovak Republic, and Slovenia. (Albania, Armenia, Azerbaijan, Bulgaria, and Romania are the exceptions with relatively homogenous populations, but still low prospects for becoming democratic.) The presence of large ethnic minorities in the other countries complicates the process of democratization. As studies show, elites in these countries like to play the nationalist card, stirring up ethnic hatreds to hold on to power.[6] Until recent improvements, these patterns were self-evident in Croatia, Bosnia, Kosovo, and Serbia. But they influence domestic politics in Bulgaria, Slovakia, and Romania as well, and they are pervasive throughout the former Soviet area where more than 20 million ethnic Russians live outside the present borders of Russia.

Whereas the political gradient drops off sharply from west to east, the power (military and economic) gradient is more dumbbell-shaped. As the other columns of table 5.1 show (columns 1 and 6–10), Russia, despite its current weakness, remains a dominant power among the formerly communist countries. This is the case in terms of size (Population column), GNP, which is more than 40 percent of the total in the region (PPP GNI column), and military,

Table 5.1. Power and Identity Indicators in the Formerly Communist Countries in Europe

		Political				Economic		Military			Social
	Population, 1999[a] (millions)	Freedom Rating[b] PR	CL	Polity IV Rating, 1999[c]	Minority (%)[d]	PPP GNI, 1999[e] (billions of dollars)	Economic Freedom, 2001[f]	Budget (% GDP)[g] 1985	1999	Weapons of Mass Destruction and Delivery Systems[h]	Human Development Index, 1998[i]
Eastern, Southern, and Southeastern Europe											
Albania	3.4	4	5	5	5	11	3.50	5.3	3.6		0.713
Bosnia and Herzegovina	3.8[b]	5	5	NA	31, 44, 17, 5, 2	NA	4.00	20.0[j]	8.4		NA
Bulgaria	8.2	2	3	9	9, 3	42	3.30	14.0	3.3	S, M	0.772
Croatia	4.5	4	4	7[k]	12, 12	32	3.45	9.8[j]	4.1		0.795
Czech Republic	10.3	1	2	9	13, 7	132	2.15	2.7[j]	2.3	S	0.843
Hungary	10.1	1	2	10	10	111	2.55	7.2	1.6		0.817
Macedonia	2.0	3	3	6	23, 11	9	NA	NA	2.0		0.763
Poland	38.7	1	2	10	2	324	2.75	8.1	2.1		0.814
Romania	22.5	2	2	7	7, 2	134	3.65	4.5	1.8		0.770
Slovak Republic	5.4	1	2	9	11, 2	56	2.85	2.9[j]	1.9	S, M	0.825
Slovenia	2.0	1	2	10	8	32	2.90	1.9[j]	1.8		0.861
Yugoslavia	10.6[b]	5	5	−6	NA	NA	NA	3.8	12.4		NA
Former Soviet Union											
Armenia	3.8	4	4	5	7	9	2.95	5.9[j]	8.6		0.721
Azerbaijan	8.0	6	4	−7	10	20	3.95	5.0[j]	4.4	S	0.772
Belarus	10.2	6	6	−7	13, 9	69	4.25	4.8[j]	5.0		0.781
Estonia	1.4	1	2	6	28, 7	12	2.05	2.8[j]	1.5		0.801
Georgia	5.5	3	4	5	10, 8, 6, 6	14	3.55	3.5[j]	2.4		0.762
Kazakhstan	15.4	6	5	−3	35, 14, 7	71	3.75	2.4[j]	3.5	S	0.754
Kyrgyzstan	4.7	5	5	4	18, 13, 5, 1, 2	12	3.65	3.5[j]	3.5		0.706

Former Soviet Union

Latvia	2.4	1	2	7	30, 4, 9	15	2.65	3.3[j]	1.0		0.771
Lithuania	3.7	1	2	10	9, 7, 4	24	2.55	4.2[j]	1.0		0.789
Moldova	4.3	2	4	6	14, 13, 9	9	3.60	3.8[j]	.5		0.700
Russia	146.5	4	4	5	18	1,022	3.70	7.4	5.1	A, C, S, M, L	0.771
Tajikistan	6.2	6	6	−1	25, 10	NA	3.95	10.1[j]	7.6		0.663
Turkmenistan	4.8	7	7	−8	9, 7, 7	16	4.40	2.8[j]	3.3		0.704
Ukraine	49.9	3	4	6	22, 5	168	3.85	2.2	2.9	S	0.744
Uzbekistan	24.5	7	6	−9	6, 5, 10	54	4.45	3.8[j]	3.9		0.686
TOTAL	412.8					2,398					

Note: NA, not available.

[a] *World Development Report 2000/2001: Attacking Poverty* (New York: Oxford University Press, for The World Bank, 2001), 278–79.

[b] *Freedom in the World 1999–2000* (New York: Freedom House, 2000), 596–97. Ratings are based on a scale of 1–7, with 1 signifying the most free in the categories of Political Rights (PR) and Civil Liberties (CL). Population data are taken from respective country page.

[c] *Polity IV: Political Regime Characteristics and Transitions, 1800–1999,* Center for International Development and Conflict Management, University of Maryland at College Park, 2000. Rating is based on Democracy Score (scale of 0–10, with 0 signifying low democracy) minus Autocracy Score (scale of 0–10, with 0 signifying low autocracy).

[d] U.S. Central Intelligence Agency, *The World Factbook 2000,* http://www.cia.gov/cia/publications/factbook/index.html. Single minority groups with at least 5% of the population are listed separately, with the final number including all minority groups with less than 5%. Minority refers to ethnic origin.

[e] *World Development Indicators 2001* (Washington, D.C.: World Bank, 2001), 12–14. GNI equals GNP plus net receipts of primary income from nonresident sources. Conversions are at Purchasing Power Parity (PPP) exchange rates, not current exchange rates.

[f] Gerald P. O'Driscoll Jr, Kim R. Holmes, and Melanie Kirkpatrick, *The 2001 Index of Economic Freedom* (Washington, D.C.: The Heritage Foundation, 2001), 8–14. Rankings are based on a scale of 1–5, with 1 signifying the most freedom. The score is based on trade policy, fiscal burden of government, government intervention in the economy, monetary policy (inflation), capital flows and foreign investment, banking, wage and price controls, property rights, business regulations, and black markets.

[g] *The Military Balance, 2000/2001* (London: Oxford University Press, for The International Institute for Strategic Studies, 2000), 297–301.

[h] Countries proven or suspected to have Atomic, Biological, or Chemical weapons and Short-range, Medium-range, or Long-range military missile capabilities, as cited in the following sources and from interviews with government officials. Federation of American Scientists, http://www.fas.org; Center for Non-Proliferation Studies, Monterey Institute of International Studies, http://www.cns.miis.edu; Henry R. Stimson Center, http://www.stimson.org; Stockholm International Peace Research Institute, http://www.sipri.se; U.S. Department of Defense, *Proliferation: Threat and Response* (Washington, D.C.: Department of Defense, 1997); U.S. Department of Defense, http://www.defenselink.mil/pubs.

[i] *Human Development Report 2000* (New York: Oxford University Press, for the United Nations Development Programme, 2000), 157–60. Rankings are based on life expectancy, real GDP per capita, and a combination of adult literacy and school enrollment ratios. The highest possible index value (better off) is 1.0, while the lowest possible value is 0.

[j] 1995 data (1985 data unavailable).

[k] 2000 data (1999 data unavailable).

especially nuclear, assets (Military columns). Since the collapse of the Soviet Union, Russia no longer has the capability to threaten western Europe directly, except with its nuclear arsenal, which remains significant. But it would be incorrect to conclude that Russia no longer has the resources to threaten its more immediate neighbors in what Russia calls the "near abroad" (the former Soviet republics). All of these countries, with the possible exception of the Baltic states, are poor countries with low levels of social development, education, health, and so on (Human Development Index column), and minimal opportunities for economic advancement (Economic Freedom column). In these circumstances, military power, even at reduced levels, looms large as a means to suppress local minorities and to agitate across national boundaries.

Political and military meddling in the former Soviet area is endemic; Russia is the main culprit. In all the former Soviet republics, except the Baltic countries and Georgia, old-line communist leaders ran the governments in 2000. What is more, former Soviet KGB operatives remained active in these countries, and a former KGB operative was president in Russia. Although localized after 1991, the security agencies in the former republics maintained "back channels" through the KGB's "old-boy networks," gathered at summits under Russian leadership and staffed by a permanent secretariat in Moscow, and helped through Russia's Federal Border Service to patrol the outer borders of the old Soviet Union.[7] As Eduard Shevardnadze, the president of Georgia, told *Washington Post* reporters in February 1999, "you mustn't think these are weak groups.... They have serious funding," and "in all these countries—Azerbaijan, Uzbekistan, Ukraine—the main problem they have is retaining their independence." Moscow "will try to make them walk the path that Belarus has walked," toward full reintegration with Russia.[8] The Russian government continues to station military bases or troops in some of the former republics and maintains a heavy hand on the control of key energy supplies and routes in Ukraine, Moldova, the Caucasus, and central Asia (see later discussion).

Hence, although Russia is weak, it is by no means incapable of intervening and exploiting instability.[9] It bears repeating that the danger is not immediate aggression by Russia; it is festering domestic deadlock, economic frustrations and setbacks, eventual local violence, and then intervention by outside powers. Bosnia and Kosovo offer textbook cases of such scenarios. After the collapse of the former Yugoslavia, political institutions dissolved, ethnic conflicts resurfaced, instability weakened moderates, radicals turned to force, civil war erupted, neighboring groups or governments intervened, and outside powers, specifically NATO and Russia, were drawn into the conflict. In Kosovo, for example, Russia protested NATO's air campaign and then in April 1999 entered the country unilaterally and blocked NATO troops for several days from occupying the main airport at Pristina.

Why is such instability in the formerly communist countries of Europe a vital national interest of the United States? If NATO were not present in this area, the chance of conflict between Russia and the United States would be zero. And instability, even ethnic cleansing, is not a direct physical threat to America's security. As deplorable as it is, ethnic violence has occurred in other parts of the world—Sudan, Nigeria, Rwanda, and so on—yet America did nothing about it in those places, and this did not jeopardize vital interests. Moreover, the Balkan region is Europe's front yard, not America's. Withdrawal seems inviting. Why is it unwise?

The answer is straightforward. As I have emphasized, America's vital interests consist of two things—self-image and power. When only one of these things is at stake, the logic of intervention is not fully compelling. Rwanda offended America's values, but did not threaten its basic capabilities. Brutality in the Balkans threatened both—America's values were at stake, and Bosnia and Kosovo threatened escalating violence and the weakening of NATO on the very borders of democratic Europe. A bare sixty years ago, such brutalizing violence started small and eventually consumed all of Europe. America stood by then and paid a big price later. Would it be wise to do so again today?

Maybe western Europe can take care of the crisis. It is now united and all democratic. In 1991, America deferred to Europe in the Balkans, but Europe failed to stop the bloodshed. An American withdrawal is not a solution; it is just a rain check. It postpones the reckoning until another day. And when that day comes, America inevitably will face bigger threats, have fewer friends to cope with these threats, and pay a higher price in blood and treasure to redeem its interests. It is much cheaper and more effective to stay involved today when America has no actual enemies and can preempt potential ones.

Security without Enemies

A consolidation strategy focuses on domestic instability, not external aggression. The task, as in the former Yugoslavia, is to preempt instability or, failing that, to contain it and then try to mediate and police it. Which organization is best suited to accomplish this task? In the euphoria at the end of the Cold War, European and global institutions seemed to be the preferred instruments.[10] In the Yugoslavian conflict, the EU grabbed the initiative, and when that effort soured the UN moved in. Neither institution, however, had the decisive political leadership or the credible military capabilities to succeed. Eventually the United States and NATO became involved in a more central way.

NATO has both the political and military clout to make a difference, but its role is controversial. It excludes Russia, and its expansion to preempt political instability in central and eastern Europe exacerbates political instability in Russia in the short run. Nationalist and nondemocratic forces in Russia gain ground, claiming that NATO represents an aggressive threat against Russia.[11] Of course, NATO might also include Russia. However, this prospect not only dilutes the significance of NATO protection for central and eastern European countries; it also involves the United States and the West in potential domestic conflicts in Russia. The threat to Russian domestic politics is not from outside meddling, as it is for domestic politics in Ukraine or the Baltic states, but from warring factions inside the country.

Thus, NATO inevitably threatens Russia with the fear of outside intervention in Russian domestic affairs if Russia is included in NATO or a powerful military alliance on the Russian border if Russia is excluded. At the same time, NATO remains the only organization able, at least for the moment, to preempt, contain, and mediate political instability in other democratizing countries in Europe. What to do? As usual, when confused, American leaders took contradictory actions and pushed the issue into the future. They expanded NATO to include the first wave of new members, gave Russia a special agreement with NATO (and quickly gave a similar, although slightly less special, agreement to Ukraine, lest it feel neglected), and left the issue open to be debated again in the next wave of new members.

A consolidation strategy recommends a less conflicted approach. NATO expands to include the countries most likely to become stable democracies. Poland, Hungary, and the Czech Republic became NATO members in April 1999. Slovenia and the Baltic states are next in line. A third group may include Slovakia, Romania, and Bulgaria. The chances of other states seem remote (although Macedonia and Albania have Membership Action Plans with NATO, portending possible membership in the future); these states are unlikely to meet NATO requirements for either democratic control of the military (civilian control responsive to parliament and the protection of minorities) or the development of meaningful military capabilities (ability to contribute to NATO defense).

NATO should not consider membership for Russia at any time in the foreseeable future.[12] Even the NATO-Russia Permanent Joint Council was ill conceived and goes too far. If NATO acts only with Russian consent, it gives Russia a veto and nullifies the alliance. If it acts without Russian consent, the Joint Council becomes ineffective and even counterproductive. In the Kosovo crisis, Russia walked out of the Joint Council to protest NATO bombing. In a severe crisis, involving a possible confrontation with Russian troops, Russia would have to be kicked out. NATO could not have Russian generals swarming around the halls of NATO in Brussels.[13] Dissolving the council in such a crisis might make the crisis even worse. This would be true especially if the United States had developed no alternative venue for working with Russia. Hence, even if the NATO-Russia Joint Council remains in place (and, now that it exists, I am not recommending that it be abolished), the United States and other western countries need a parallel security relationship with Russia that does not depend solely on NATO. This parallel relationship could be built up around the United Nations and its European counterpart, the OSCE.

The United Nations already gives Russia a status and influence that distinguishes it from other formerly communist countries without diluting NATO commitments to those countries.[14] A special U.S.-Russian relationship in the United Nations would accomplish four objectives. First, it would compensate and assuage Russia for the expansion of NATO, making the latter more acceptable and less threatening to Moscow's pride. Second, it would involve western forces under UN auspices in security activities closer to Russia, where NATO forces could not operate in any case without Russian consent and where information about Russian military activities at the present time is lacking. Although the OSCE monitors military and political activities between the two parts of Europe, including supervision of the Conventional Forces in Europe (CFE) agreement that limits conventional arms, its supervision of Russian activity in the Caucasus region and central Asia is inadequate. In 2000, for example, Russia continued to violate promises under the revised CFE agreement to remove equipment from Moldova and Georgia. Third, cooperation through the United Nations might continue even if nationalist or communist elements regained control in Moscow, whereas cooperation in NATO would have to be curtailed. UN cooperation could thus temper the immediate revival of a new Cold War— Russia would be reluctant to walk out of the United Nations, as it did from the NATO-Russia Joint Council, because the United Nations gives it influence in areas beyond the near-abroad, such as Kosovo. Finally, in some areas, the United Nations and NATO might be able to work together operationally. Such cooperation was troubled in Bosnia, and today NATO operates independently in both Bosnia and Kosovo. Nevertheless, UN Security Council resolutions legitimate these peacekeeping operations. Down the line, after some strengthening of UN peacekeeping machinery and experience, it is not inconceivable that the UN and NATO might cooperate again, albeit under different guidelines and perhaps more able UN (and U.S.) leadership.

An effective security strategy in Europe necessarily entangles the United States in multilateral organizations and initiatives. The United States prefers NATO because the United States provides the decisive leadership and commands the military structure of that organization. But NATO is not enough; and, in the future, NATO too will change. The United States will have to share more influence with European members. As we have observed in chapter 4, a European pillar is emerging in NATO. The European Union is gradually absorbing the Western European Union (WEU), Europe's principal defense arrangement. In the future, Europe may decide to act in certain military situations without the United States. If Europe acts often without the United States or against U.S. wishes, the European pillar will weaken and perhaps end the alliance. On the other hand, if Europe assumes larger defense burdens and acts separately with NATO consent, the alliance as a whole will clearly benefit. In all cases, a NATO consensus will be essential because it is unlikely that the United States,

WEU, UN, or OSCE, were they to act outside of NATO, could function effectively without the cooperation of all the major industrial democracies.[15]

How then do NATO, European, and UN security organizations respond to the challenge of security in the formerly communist half of Europe? The discussion that follows distinguishes among four areas of potential instability. In central and eastern Europe, NATO remains the primary military and political organization. In southeastern Europe, NATO (acting either as a whole or through its emerging European pillar) plays the key military role, but the United Nations plays an increasingly important supplementary role to gain wider support for NATO operations and make them less threatening to Russia. In northeastern Europe, NATO also plays the key military role, but a European defense capability, should it develop, might play a significant parallel role. Finally, in the former Soviet republics excluding the Baltic states, the United Nations or OSCE might become the indispensable political and military institution, monitoring Russian military activities and potentially legitimating peacekeeping activities in specific situations.

CENTRAL AND EASTERN EUROPE

One argument against NATO expansion was that the new members, Poland, Hungary, and the Czech Republic, being more advanced democratically and economically, were least in need of NATO security guarantees.[16] The argument was flawed—based on this logic, NATO would also not include the western European democracies because they are the most stable countries of all and in need of protection even less than the three new members. Such logic assumes that the only threat to security is the narrow realist conception of a military attack across territorial borders.

But the central and eastern European countries need NATO protection precisely because they are the most advanced and stable countries of the formerly communist world. They need the assurance that they are part of the mature democratic world, in which extremist parties are marginalized inside their borders; and they need the confidence to cope with political instability in neighboring countries across their borders. Considering the war in Kosovo, imagine for a moment how instability across the border and extremist parties inside the border might have destabilized Hungary if it had been excluded from membership in NATO. Ethnic Hungarians populate Vojvodina, the northern province of Serbia. Belgrade might have cracked down hard on this ethnic group, as it did on Muslim Albanians in Kosovo. Center-right parties in Budapest, which came to power in 1995, might then have reacted to defend the rights of ethnic Hungarians in Serbia. In a Hungary outside NATO, extremist elements might have fanned the flames of a wider war. Instead, with Hungary joining NATO at the time of the Kosovo crisis, wider war was not only averted, but Hungary also hosted a logistical base for U.S. forces operating in the Balkans. Further, Hungary and other eastern European countries denied transit rights to Russian forces, which moved unilaterally into Kosovo after the bombing halted.

Poland too has unstable borders. Indeed, it borders on Russia. Kaliningrad (formerly East Prussia) lies on the Baltic Sea to Poland's north; in 2000 this Russian enclave hosted four divisions and an air regiment of Russian troops, as well as the headquarters of the Russian Navy's Baltic fleet. To the east, Poland shares borders with Belarus and Ukraine, which also have Russian bases and troops. If any of these areas were destabilized, Poland would be immediately and seriously threatened. To be sure, instability is not the same as invasion, but uncertainty in neighboring countries feeds uncertainty in domestic politics and leaves a dangerous opening for extreme nationalist and xenophobic forces. No one is aware of these vulnerabilities more than the new NATO countries themselves. They have been persistent advocates of early entry into NATO, even under governments led by former communists in Poland and Hungary.

The same logic of weakening extremists and consolidating the democratization process applies to other eastern European countries. NATO stabilizes democracy in Poland, Hungary, and the Czech Republic. That consolidation, in turn, helps to weaken political extremists in Slovakia (which borders the Czech Republic), Romania (which borders Hungary), and Bulgaria (which borders Romania and the former Yugoslav republics, where NATO actively contains extremist groups). After NATO decided in 1997 to include Poland, Hungary, and the Czech Republic, the neighboring countries of Slovakia, Bulgaria, and Romania all experienced a moderation in their domestic political affairs. NATO expansion acted as a political balm as much as, if not more than, a military bulwark. Although NATO membership requires enhanced and compatible military capabilities, democratic controls over the military and democratic development more generally are equally important. NATO is not expanding as a traditional alliance and has indicated that it has no intentions, plans, or causes to deploy NATO forces in the territories of new members.[17] It is expanding primarily to weaken extremist and strengthen democratic groups in countries struggling to moderate authoritarian political systems.

NATO expansion in this guise poses no threat to Russia, especially in eastern European countries that do not border on Russia. NATO expansion into the Baltic states or the northeastern European theater, on the other hand, might be more difficult for Russia to swallow.

NORTHEASTERN EUROPE (THE BALTICS)

Lithuania, Latvia, Estonia, and the Russian enclave of Kaliningrad create a different set of security challenges in northeastern Europe. Like central and eastern Europe, this area has experienced no open violence or civil war since the fall of the Soviet Union. And the Baltic countries are relatively stable and democratic, and compare favorably with the new NATO members in central and eastern Europe. Why, then, weren't these countries admitted early into

NATO to consolidate democracy? There are two reasons: the Baltic states border on Russia, and Latvia and Estonia have large ethnic Russian minorities. Thus, Russia is particularly sensitive about its relations in northeastern Europe, more so than about its ties with Serbia in the Balkan region, which does not border Russia or include Russian minorities.

Russian minorities make up approximately one-third of the populations of Estonia and Latvia (in Lithuania, the figure is only 9 percent). Most ethnic Russians arrived after the Soviet Union annexed the Baltic states in 1940. They took over the jobs, homes, and privileges of local elites and made Russian the dominant language, while the local elites were deported forcibly to Siberia. Understandably, native Estonians and Latvians (and, to a lesser extent, Lithuanians) resented this takeover and saw ethnic Russians as the consequence and abiding symbol of Russian imperialism. After independence, the Baltic states passed laws that revoked the citizenship of ethnic Russians who entered the country after 1940 and required five years of residency and knowledge of the local language and constitution to acquire new citizenship. Although these laws have since been relaxed, ethnic Russians see them as apartheid, especially in Estonia where much of the Russian minority is concentrated in a single area (the northeastern corner of the country) and speak only Russian (giving them little opportunity or incentive to learn Estonian). Russia strongly defends the rights of ethnic Russians and uses allegations of mistreatment to threaten sanctions and intervention in the Baltic states.[18]

Because of intense Russian feelings, NATO moved cautiously in this area. It concluded Partnership for Peace (PFP) agreements with the Baltic states, which involve joint military exchanges and training but not necessarily prospective NATO membership. In 1997, it consolidated these agreements with those of other countries under the Euro-Atlantic Partnership Council. Poland's entry into NATO in 1999 brought the alliance to the border of both Russia and Lithuania. But at this point, Russia declared a "red line," strongly opposing NATO membership for the Baltic states. NATO is far from deciding how to proceed to provide security for these countries if Russia intervenes.

While NATO deliberates, European organizations have stepped into the vacuum. These organizations are much weaker militarily than NATO, but make important contributions to increase transparency and facilitate political reconciliation in the area. The OSCE monitors ethnic disputes in Estonia and Russian military base agreements in Latvia (closing down the Russian early warning facility in August 1998). The Council of Europe tracks human rights violations. The EU concluded a European Security Pact in 1995, which includes the three Baltic and six central and eastern European states (the new NATO members plus Slovakia, Romania, and Bulgaria). The pact encourages political reconciliation and stability as a prelude to membership in the European Union. The Nordic Council (Denmark, Finland, Iceland, Norway, and Sweden) established the Council of Baltic Sea States to include Estonia, Latvia, and Lithuania. The Council holds periodic summits and fosters cooperation in airspace, coastline, peacekeeping, and rescue operations. It also promotes multilateral military cooperation, including a Baltic peacekeeping battalion (which sent troops to participate in UNPROFOR, the original UN peacekeeping operation in Bosnia), a Baltic naval squadron for mine clearance, a Baltic air surveillance network, and a proposed Baltic air force.[19] The EU expanded in 1995 to include two non-NATO countries in the Baltic area, Sweden and Finland, and has initiated accession discussions with six other European states, one of which is Estonia. If the EU develops its own defense capabilities and policy, the EU's presence in the northeastern European area could add measurably to security arrangements in the future.

In the meantime, however, and even if the EU develops a more coherent defense force and policy, NATO remains the indispensable organization to deter and, if necessary, defend against potential Russian aggression in this area. Russian forces in Kaliningrad, Belarus, and Russia itself already surround these countries. In 1996 Russia proposed extending bilateral or multilateral (with western countries) security guarantees to the Baltic countries. These proposals are threatening. Russia is the only potential aggressor in the Baltics (or elsewhere in the formerly communist part of Europe); what is more, Russia continues to insist that the arrangements under which the Soviet Union incorporated the Baltic countries in 1940 are legal.

Given the proximity, although not immediacy, of the Russian threat, there is no substitute for deterrence, and credible deterrence requires practical defense measures. At some point, NATO membership is a prerequisite for the Baltic states. Lithuania is considered to be the best prospect because it has fewer ethnic problems and a better relationship with Russia (in part because of the need to coordinate transit issues between Russia and the separated enclave of Kaliningrad).[20] Estonia is in a first group of countries to join the EU, but EU membership is no substitute for NATO membership. Economic growth requires security. Without stable domestic politics and accepted borders, economic growth may actually widen ethnic differences or at least fail to improve them (as happened, for example, in former Czechoslovakia and Yugoslavia in the early 1990s). On the other hand, Russian sensitivity cannot be ignored.

A better approach would be to proceed over the next decade at three levels simultaneously. First, NATO proposes membership for all Baltic states based on an agreed timetable related to internal improvements on ethnic Russian issues. Second and simultaneously, the EU negotiates accession for Baltic states. Whether membership negotiations in the two organizations take place on exactly the same time schedule is less important than making it clear that the EU is not substituting for NATO. The EU/WEU may eventually provide important defense supplements in the Baltic region, such as the bulk of conventional forces if there is violence (as it is doing in Kosovo in 2001). Such an arrangement would be both effective and more acceptable to Russia. But the EU will not be able to act alone in this region—NATO is the indispensable link. And third, the United States and other G-7 democracies initiate closer links with Russia, not through direct association with NATO or the EU (the NATO-Russia Joint Council and the G-8) but through the individual Partnership for Peace agreements collected under the Euro-Atlantic Partnership Council (which includes all NATO, WEU, and former Soviet-bloc countries except Tajikistan) and through the UN's OSCE (which includes all the members of the Euro-Atlantic Partnership Council plus Tajikistan and other European entities, such as Bosnia, Croatia, and Ireland). Presently, Finland, Sweden, and the three Baltic countries are not part of the OSCE regime for monitoring conventional arms in Europe, the CFE. They might be drawn in, especially as the Baltic countries prepare for membership in NATO.[21]

SOUTHEASTERN EUROPE (THE BALKANS)

With civil wars in Bosnia and Kosovo, the security challenge in southeastern Europe is of a different order of magnitude than that in central, eastern, or northeastern Europe. The task is not primarily to preempt violence but to contain and eventually overcome existing violence. Because conflict already exists, NATO's military role is even more immediate and central than it is in the new NATO member states (where the issue is contingency planning, not actual crisis management). NATO's military role in this out-of-area situation, however, is new. NATO is not defending borders, as it does under article 5 of the NATO treaty. Rather, it is managing conflicts through peacekeeping, peace enforcement, humanitarian intervention, and institution-building, sometimes inside a country itself, as in the case of Kosovo. This role is more delicate politically because it involves issues of sovereignty. It, therefore, requires greater multilateral legitimation.

UN and European institutions help to provide this legitimation. None of these institutions can substitute for NATO, as the Bosnian experience proved decisively. The EU alone was unable to muster the necessary military force and political cohesion, and the United Nations, with the double-key arrangement in which both it and NATO had to approve military strikes, undercut military effectiveness.[22] And even if the EU could play such a role, it too would require UN legitimization. A UN role, at least on the European level (i.e., the OSCE), is indispensable, if not always to legitimate force before the fact (e.g., the failed experience in Bosnia), then certainly to legitimate the peace after the fact (as it did in 2000 in Kosovo).

NATO has undertaken substantial reforms to play this new behind-the-border (as opposed to cross-border) role in out-of-area conflicts.[23] Three issues potentially divide the United States and its allies in such conflicts: who commands NATO forces, whether prior UN authorization is needed to use NATO force, and the future expansion of NATO and NATO-Russian relations in this area.

Regarding the first issue, the United States has always held the major NATO commands, including the critical command in southeastern Europe (based in Naples) that controls the U.S. Sixth Fleet in the Mediterranean. In 1995, France demanded, as a condition of rejoining NATO's military structure, that NATO's future commander in the southeastern European sector be a European. The United States rejected the demand, arguing that Europe's contributions were not sufficient to warrant command. In Kosovo, however, where European states provided the bulk of NATO's forces, the United States accepted a European commander—as of 2001, a British and then a German general. If Europe becomes a more equal contributor in NATO, it will eventually command major regional headquarters, including the southern command.[24]

The second issue is also manageable. In the Kosovo crisis, NATO conducted the air campaign against Serbia without UN authorization, even though NATO was intervening, for the first time, in the affairs of a sovereign state without being invited by the relevant parties. The United States argued that existing UN resolutions in connection with Bosnia provided sufficient authorization. The major European democracies disagreed. Nevertheless, they went along with air strikes in October 1998 as part of the diplomatic effort to secure Serbian acquiescence to the Rambouillet Accords, and they ultimately supported the bombing campaign in March 1999 after Serbian intransigence created a looming refugee disaster. The issue, therefore, is not UN authorization but U.S. and allied agreement. UN authorization may help to obtain allied agreement outside the European area, as it did in the Persian Gulf conflict, but inside Europe it may be unnecessary, as it was in the Bosnia and Kosovo conflicts. If the major democracies agree, that is sufficient justification to use force. The U.S. acting alone against allied wishes, on the other hand, especially in sensitive areas such as the Balkans and Persian Gulf, would not only fail; it would shatter the alliance. The same would hold true if a future European force acted against U.S. wishes.

The third issue is NATO-Russian relations in the Balkans. Russia was incensed by NATO attacks against Serbia and suspended its participation in the NATO-Russia Joint Council and other military cooperation with the alliance. Russia insisted that the use of such force was illegal without UN approval and threatened to counter NATO actions by forging a new alliance with China, Iran, and other countries against the American and NATO hegemony. In the end, Russia accepted NATO's role in Bosnia and Kosovo, not because it had no choice (a nationalist government that rejects cooperation with the West is always a possibility) but because, on balance, it benefits from what NATO is doing in the Balkans. NATO was correct to include Russian forces in Bosnia and to accept Russian diplomacy and troops in Kosovo. Russian participation provides transparency and preempts U.S.-Russian rivalries that would divide the United States and its NATO allies. The specific mechanism for gaining Russian cooperation is secondary. The NATO-Russia Joint Council proved useless in the

Kosovo crisis, although Russia did work with the western powers in the G-8. Cooperation through the United Nations offers better prospects, especially in the European area, including the former Soviet republics.

OTHER FORMER SOVIET REPUBLICS

Russia's reference to the former Soviet republics as the "near-abroad" reflects the fact that most of these republics have been an integrated part of imperial Russia since the early eighteenth century. All post-Soviet leaders in Russia have claimed special responsibility for this area. Even as the Soviet Union dissolved, Boris Yeltsin created the Commonwealth of Independent States (CIS), which now includes all of the former republics except the Baltic states.[25] In 1992 he negotiated a collective defense pact at Tashkent with some of these countries (later transformed into a Defense Council) and subsequently intervened in secessionist conflicts in Azerbaijan and Georgia to compel those republics to accept defense arrangements. In 1993, both Yeltsin and then Foreign Minister Andrei Kozyrev spoke openly about the need for a Russian Monroe Doctrine in the near-abroad.[26] In March 1996, Yeltsin's communist opponents, dominating the parliament, passed a resolution rescinding the 1991 accord that dissolved the Soviet Union.[27] Yeltsin rejected this resolution, but later signed a union treaty with Belarus that called for restoring the old union relationship between the two republics.[28]

Two of the principal former Soviet republics, Belarus and Ukraine, border NATO territory in central and eastern Europe (with Poland and Hungary). Three others—Armenia, Georgia, and the Nakhichevan enclave of Azerbaijan—border NATO territory (Turkey) in the southeast. And a sixth, Moldova, will border NATO territory if Romania joins NATO in the future. Russian army or naval forces are or have been stationed in all of these countries. Unrest in these countries might spark once again a direct conflict between NATO and Russia. Ukraine is the most explosive point of potential confrontation. Divided internally between the southern and eastern regions, which were a part of Russia and the Soviet Union for 350 years, and the western half, which became a part of Russia only in the nineteenth century, Ukraine remains unstable. Its prospects are closely tied to those of Russia.[29]

The former republics, Azerbaijan, Georgia, and the central Asian republics, encompass or border areas that are vital to U.S. and G-7 interests in oil supplies (both in the Caspian Sea and via Iran in the Persian Gulf) and in combating terrorism along the southwest Asian border with Afghanistan, Pakistan, India, and ultimately China. Sizable Russian ethnic minorities live in Kazakhstan and Kyrgyzstan (35 and 18 percent, respectively). In these as well as other southern republics, Muslim majorities contend with fundamentalist secessionist movements supported by Iran and terrorist sympathizers in Afghanistan. Russian forces actively supported the Tajikistan government in a civil war against fundamentalists in that country and monitor cease-fires in Georgia and Azerbaijan where secessionist conflicts fester. Uzbekistan, fearing a spillover of the conflict, fought alongside Russian forces in Tajikistan. Only Kazakhstan, Kyrgyzstan, and Turkmenistan are at peace; but these republics are much less developed than the Baltic states or Ukraine and face continued threats of economic instability and Russian intervention, particularly related to Caspian Sea energy supplies. The oil and gas reserves in the Caspian Sea (perhaps 100–200 billion barrels, or the size of another Kuwait) and ethnic conflicts and terrorism in the region—principally the Kurds in Turkey, Armenia, Iraq, Iran, and Syria and Taliban remnants in Afghanistan and Pakistan—raise the stakes for the great powers and link the area to the highly volatile Middle East and Balkan conflicts. In addition, of course, Russia fights civil conflicts within its own territory in Chechnya and Dagestan, provinces that border on the Caucasus states and reflect the internal stake that Russia has in the future of the Transcaucasian republics.[30]

Unrest in the southern and central Asian republics is not as destabilizing as it would be in Ukraine, Belarus, or Moldova. But, as the terrorist attacks against the United States on September 11, 2001, suggest, instability in this region and bordering areas breeds extremism and poses direct dangers for American and western societies. Such extremism will have to be contained, if not eliminated. In the wake of the September 11 attacks, the United States, with NATO and UN political support, declared war against the Taliban government in Afghanistan and inserted forces in the region to pursue terrorists, such as Osama bin Laden and his Al Qaeda organization, accused of carrying out the September 11 events. Russia and China cooperated with this U.S.-led effort, Russia even consenting to let U.S. forces use military facilities in Uzbekistan and Tajikistan. As welcome as this cooperation is, strengthening Russia's influence in the central and southwest Asian region has its potential costs. If politi-cal developments went off track in Moscow, Russian imperialism would most likely reconstitute itself initially in this region. Thus, the central Asian and Caucasus region provides the trip wire or early warning signal for NATO of the kinds of identity changes (i.e., from Russian authoritarianism to Russian imperialism) that could redirect Russian power and once again bring about serious external conflict between Russia and the West in the European arena.

Through its Partnership for Peace agreements and special agreements with Russia and Ukraine, NATO has a presence in the former Soviet republics, but this presence is limited and will undoubtedly remain so. It seems unlikely that the United States or NATO would be able to keep troops in these areas for extended periods of time without precipitating eventual conflict with Russia (in contrast to the situation in Bosnia and Kosovo or the possibility that EU members of NATO might position forces one day in the Baltic states).

At the same time, the United States and NATO have a growing stake in former Soviet republics and bordering areas, especially after the events of September 11. Long-term policing and peacekeeping functions will be required in Afghanistan and perhaps other countries (e.g., potentially Georgia). For this purpose, UN forces may be indispensable, organized under the auspices of the OSCE. The United States missed an opportunity in 1993 to deploy UN peacekeeping forces in the Caucasus region. Distracted by efforts at the time to cooperate with Russia through NATO, the United States dismissed Russian appeals for UN intervention.[31] In the aftermath of the anti-terrorist campaign in Afghanistan, the United States has a second chance to deploy UN forces in this region, both to suppress terrorist activities on the borders of the former Soviet Union, and to monitor Russian military activities in central Asia and the Caucasus.

Development without Authoritarianism or Anarchy

In traditional perspectives, military security is either unnecessary or an end in itself. Isolationism and internationalism consider it unnecessary—the first because there is no threat, the second because all countries are presumed to be friendly enough to practice collective security. Realism pursues military balancing for its own sake. But in an identity and power perspective, balancing military power is a means, not an end. The end is to protect diverging and nurture converging identities. In Europe, the identity gap is no longer between democracy and communism; the gap is now between mature democracies and authoritarian (as opposed to totalitarian) countries, some of whom are democratizing. As identities change in the formerly communist half of Europe, two specters haunt stability and signal potential danger for European democracies and the United States—resurgent authoritarianism and anarchy.

Independence, national unity, and individual rights are all necessary to support stable democracies. Traditional perspectives generally focus on only one or two of these requirements. Internationalism focuses on independence or self-determination and assumes that unity, if not democracy, will follow; the European Community recognized the independence of the separate provinces of the former Yugoslavia (Slovenia, Croatia, and Bosnia) and then expected erroneously that these independent states would hold together and respect minority rights. Realism focuses on national unity and downplays self-determination and democracy; the George H. W. Bush administration was initially reluctant to see either the former Yugoslavia or the former Soviet Union break apart, fearing that anarchy might follow self-determination and eclipse any hope for democratic development. Thereafter, realists doubted that democracy was actually possible in most of these countries and concentrated primarily on helping these countries secure their independence from their former Russian master.

Traditional perspectives confuse tactics and strategy. It may have been good tactics to caution Ukraine against precipitous separation from the former Soviet Union, especially when Soviet nuclear weapons still existed on Ukrainian soil, but it was not good strategy because independence was the basic prerequisite to end the Soviet threat. Similarly, it might have been good tactics to support Bosnia's independence when it was threatened by Serbian and Croatian aggression, but it was poor strategy because such independence could not succeed without national unity and respect for minority rights. An identity and power perspective integrates tactics and strategy and nurtures all three prerequisites of independence, unity, and individual rights. The strategy of consolidation aims for a community of sovereign and unified nation-states that mutually respect the basic democratic rights of their individual citizens. In the formerly communist world of Europe, such a community is without doubt a long way off—hence the need in the interim, as we have just discussed, of a viable balance of power. But balancing power works toward repositioning identities—a transition, however distant, to democracy and markets.

TRANSITION TO DEMOCRACY

The crucial characteristics of democratic states that live together in peace without a military balance of power are competitive and fair elections that rotate opposing parties in government institutions, which in turn divide powers and exercise effective authority over all significant state functions and protect individual rights. Most formerly communist countries in Europe have held competitive elections since 1989. Many have also held fair elections, at least by the standards of monitoring institutions such as the UN and OSCE. Fewer, however, have seen a transfer of authority from one major party to the chief opposition party. And fewer still have the basic institutions that ensure divided and accountable bureaucracies (especially police, military, and intelligence agencies) and the protection of civil liberties.

Table 5.2 provides rankings of the formerly communist countries in Europe on democracy and market transition scales. The countries divide into three groups, reflecting a gradient of progressive democratization as we move from west to east.[32] The first group is identified in the source for table 5.2 as consolidated democracies and includes the new NATO members (Poland, Hungary, and the Czech Republic) and the early candidates for membership in the European Union (Slovenia, Slovakia, and the Baltic countries). (I use the term *evolving* rather than *consolidated* democracies to refer to this first group of countries because, in my judgment, it is still premature to classify these countries as being fully on a par with the mature democracies of western Europe.) These countries have made steady progress toward democracy. They have competitive parties and, through elections, have experienced at least one peaceful parliamentary transfer of power between opposing parties.[33] They also have relatively effective institutions to protect civil liberties, including a free media, market economy, and independent judiciary. Problems remain, to be sure. Ethnic Russian issues, as we have noted, fester in Estonia and Latvia; and the rights of gypsies and Sudeten Germans stir controversy in the Czech Republic. Slovakia got a late start

Table 5.2. Democracy and Market Transition in the Former Communist States of Europe, 1999

	Democracy Rank	Economy Rank
Evolving Democracies		
Poland	1.44	1.67
Czech Republic	1.75	1.92
Hungary	1.75	1.75
Slovenia	1.94	2.08
Lithuania	2.00	2.83
Estonia	2.06	1.92
Latvia	2.06	2.50
Slovakia	2.50	3.58
Unstable Transitions		
Romania	3.19	4.17
Bulgaria	3.31	3.75
Macedonia	3.44	4.58
Moldova	3.88	4.00
Georgia	4.00	3.67
Croatia	4.19	3.67
Russia	4.25	4.33
Ukraine	4.31	4.58
Albania	4.38	4.50
Armenia	4.50	3.58
Kyrgyzstan	4.88	3.83
Yugoslavia (Serbia and Montenegro)	4.90	4.83
Bosnia	5.13	5.58
Kazakhstan	5.35	4.50
Azerbaijan	5.55	5.00
Tajikistan	5.69	6.00
Reassertive Autocracies		
Belarus	6.44	6.25
Uzbekistan	6.44	6.25
Turkmenistan	6.94	6.42

Note: The rankings are similar but not identical to the Heritage Freedom House scale of democracy (1 being highest) and the Heritage Economic Freedom Index (1 being highest).
Source: Adrian Karatyncky, "Nations in Transit 1999–2000: From Post-Revolutionary Stasis to Incremental Progress" in *Nations in Transit 1999–2000,* ed. Adrian Karatnycky, Alexander Motyl, and Aili Piano (New Brunswick, N.J.: Transaction Publishers, 2001), 19.

and is still the weakest democracy in this first group. Because of a highly fragmented party structure, governments change frequently between elections; from 1990–98, Poland had eight governments and the Czech Republic six. But the early fear that right-wing nationalist parties would fill the vacuum left by the collapse of communism or that opposition parties, particularly ex-communist ones, would abandon reforms when they came into office has not been borne out on a broad scale. Poland and Hungary, which are furthest along in the reform process, have both had leftist governments for periods since 1991.

One reason the frequent government changes and even ex-communist governments have not destabilized these countries is the existence of a highly supportive international environment in which all of the countries in Europe to the west are solid democracies. As Anatol Lieven, a student of Baltic politics, reports, "the major strength of Baltic democracy . . . is the hegemony of democratic ideas in contemporary Europe." If extremism reemerges in western European countries, the fragile balance in some of these new democracies may be lost. "All the extreme nationalist parties in Latvia and Lithuania have taken great encouragement from the rise of Jean Marie Le Pen and Front National in France."[34] In 1997, Le Pen's party garnered 15 percent of the vote in elections in France. The rise of rightist parties in Austria (which provoked EU sanctions in 1999), Germany, Italy, and other European democracies poses similar dangers. As this chapter has emphasized, the future of democracy in the eastern half of Europe depends in good part on the existence and health of democracy in the western half.

By the same logic, the progress of democracy in central and eastern Europe influences political consolidation and the prospects for democracy in a second group of formerly communist countries. As table 5.2 shows, this second group includes some countries that have taken partial steps toward democratic and market reforms—Romania, Bulgaria, Russia, and Ukraine. But it includes others who have not made much progress at all, such as some central Asian, Caucasus, and former Yugoslav republics. In this second group, only Romania, Bulgaria, Ukraine, Moldova, Macedonia, Serbia, and Croatia have experienced peaceful transfers of power to opposing parties. The transfers in Romania (1996 and again in 2000) came late in the decade and had not led by mid-2001 to significant reforms, as earlier transfers in Poland, Hungary, and the Baltic states did. Ukraine's transfer in 1995 was in the president's office, not the parliament, and an autocratic president sacked a reformist prime minister in 2001 and continued to dominate Ukrainian politics.[35] Bulgaria's parliamentary transfers in 1994 and 1997 did little to ignite economic reforms. Moldova's experiment with opposition government ended in early 2001 when the communist party regained full control and announced intentions to retain Russian forces and join the planned union between Russia and Belarus. Macedonia elected an opposition president in 1999, after its founding president stepped down, but its prospects were clouded in 2001 by new ethnic violence. And Croatia chose an opposition parliament and president in early 2000 after its strongman, President Franjo Tudjman, died. Serbia followed suit in late 2000, deposing Slobodan Milosevic and sending him off to The Hague for trial as a war criminal.

Russia, the key country in this second group, has yet to experience a peaceful transfer of power between opposing parties. Yeltsin won successive presidential elections in 1991 and 1996 and handpicked his successor, Vladimir Putin, who was elected in 2000. In mid-2001, the lower house of parliament, or Duma, was still controlled by the communists. Democracy in Russia is clearly a long way off.[36] Whereas Yeltsin's tenure witnessed the unprecedented strengthening of political freedoms and local authority in parts of Russia, Putin has reversed decentralization, suppressed rebellions in Chechnya and Dagestan (both provinces of Russia), replaced the elected regional governors with regionally appointed legislators in the upper house, cracked down on the independent media, and deployed old KGB associates to monitor and harass political opponents.[37] Russia is the pivotal state. If it evolves politically toward greater authoritarianism, the prospects for more liberal politics in the second group of countries in table 5.2 drop dramatically.

Other countries in this second group—Armenia, Azerbaijan, Kazakhstan, Georgia, Kyrgyzstan, and Albania—have held elections, but these elections were controversial and have not resulted in peaceful transfers of power between opposing parties. Force is still an instrument of politics in all of these countries. Armenia and Azerbaijan wage a bitter secessionist struggle in Nagorno-Karabakh. Moldova and Georgia confront separatist movements, and the president of Georgia, Shevardnadze, has survived two assassination attempts. Albania is in the middle of ongoing ethnic strife in the former republics of Yugoslavia.

The third group of formerly communist countries in Europe is the most despotic or retrograde. This group includes Belarus and the two central Asian states of Turkmenistan and Uzbekistan. None of these countries has held competitive and fair elections or contemplates doing so. Belarus is the archetypal old-line communist state, reconstituting central control over many aspects of society and legitimating an aggressive secret police. Uzbekistan fights domestic insurgents. Turkmenistan boasts a one-man autocracy. In all of these countries, Soviet-style leaders win in weakly contested or uncontested national elections by large margins.

U.S. efforts to promote democracy in the formerly communist states in Europe are helpful in exposing a new generation of leaders to alternative political institutions and practices.[38] These efforts should be maintained and accelerated, but they should follow rather than lead the process of transition. As leaders (e.g., Václav Havel in the Czech Republic) retrieve or create democratic aspirations that fit the local culture, western countries should accelerate exchanges of all types—sister city relationships, party officials, parliamentarians, professional associations, and educational and religious groups. In countries where leaders are more ambivalent, however, as in Russia or Ukraine, democracy-promotion efforts might be soft-pedaled.[39] In these cases, the United States and other western countries must exercise patience. Democracy cannot be sold, like a pair of shoes. It may or may not happen in certain countries, such as Russia. And the identity and power approach does not depend on it happening, as the internationalist approach does. But the identity and power approach also does not dismiss the possibility, as realist approaches do. To nurture liberalization, a strategy of consolidation relies much more on a stable, thriving, expanding zone of democracy *outside* authoritarian countries than it does on intensive democracy promotion activities *inside* these countries.

TRANSITION TO MARKETS

As long as elites compete for a pie that is not growing, economic issues immediately become political ones and vice versa. Relative gains dominate because there are no absolute gains. Elites divide and polarize the masses, delaying reforms and squandering foreign assistance. A start has to be made to break this vicious cycle.

The key obstacle in most formerly communist countries is state-owned microeconomic structures. Macroeconomic, trade, and exchange rate policies cannot stimulate output as long as state institutions dominate property rights. Privatization programs were an essential first step to break up state dominance, but these programs were short-circuited. They benefited primarily the old elite, who then blocked further reforms. In the Czech Republic, for example, which had perhaps the fairest privatization program of all the formerly communist countries, vouchers were distributed to every citizen representing a stake in the old state-owned enterprises. However, banks and investment fund managers bought up most of these vouchers, and these institutions remained under the control of the state. By the end of the 1990s, Czech banks controlled about two-thirds of the financial assets of Czech industry, and the Czech Republic trailed Poland and Hungary in economic growth and transformation. Privatization in Russia followed a similar course and also benefited the old elite. Former officials acquired state assets at bargain basement prices, even as those industries continued to benefit from massive state subsidies. By one estimate, roughly 80 percent of Russia's wealth is based in Moscow in a parasitic relationship with the state.[40]

If economic reform stops with elite privatization, market Bolshevism, to use the term coined by Peter Reddaway and Dimitri Glinski,[41] simply replaces ideological Bolshevism. Highly concentrated and corrupt industrial and financial structures continue to snuff out macroeconomic incentives. Price liberalization, for example, which is designed to free prices and stimulate production, cannot do so because concentrated industrial structures do not respond to price incentives. The result, instead, is massive inflation and more corruption. Partial price reforms in Russia in 1992 generated a 24-fold increase in prices in one year and opened up opportunities for elites in the old state industries, particularly in the energy sector, to sell raw materials abroad at world prices well above domestic prices. The same results prevailed in Russian agriculture. Collective farms dominated short supplies and squeezed out private production. Production was further constrained by the lack of private ownership of land, a legal situation that persisted even after a presidential decree in 1993 authorizing private ownership of farms. (In 2001, Putin signed a law permitting sale of urban but not farm land; the latter constitutes more than 90 percent of all land.) Throughout the economy, an entrepreneurial sector of small and medium-size businesses, which might respond to price incentives, was missing. Liberalization did stimulate one source of supply, namely imports. It also stimu-lated capital flight. External accounts rapidly deteriorated, and Russia, along with other republics, experienced deteriorating currency and financial markets culminating in a currency crisis in summer 1998.[42]

Not surprisingly, in Russia, Ukraine, and other countries that failed to undertake significant structural reforms, early market-oriented policies produced havoc and a popular backlash against democracy. Russia paid all of the social price of liberalization and got none of the economic benefits. Criminal syndicates flourished and controlled as much as 40 percent of the Russian economy and half or more of its banking assets.[43] Following a sharp drop during the financial crisis of 1998, Russia began to grow in 2000 for the first time since 1991. But this growth reflected primarily price increases for oil and gas, which Russia exports, and a sharp devaluation of the Russian currency, which boosted domestic substitution for imports.

Market reforms produced quite different results in countries that had more competitive state industries or significant private industrial and agricultural sectors. Poland undertook price liberalization, or shock therapy, much like Russia. Industrial production in the old state sector declined sharply, but price increases now provided powerful incentives to stimulate production in Poland's alternative private economy. Eighty percent of Polish agriculture was already private, and small business activities mushroomed to increase output in retail, tourism, transportation, finance, and other service sectors. Employment shifted rapidly out of declining into advancing sectors, although not fast enough to prevent unemployment from skyrocketing. By 1992, however, Poland was growing again with more than 50 percent of its production coming from the private sector.[44] In 2001, it was the leading economy in the East, having grown in 1994–2000 at an average real rate of 5.4 percent per year. Only in 1995 did it launch a significant privatization program that benefited from greater market transparency and pricing competition. Throughout this transition, Poland still suffered the social costs of transition; the political backlash brought the ex-communists back into power from 1993 to 1997. But Poland also gained the economic benefits, and those benefits are now spreading beyond the old elite to the broad spectrum of Polish workers and shopkeepers.

In Hungary, Slovenia, and the Baltic states, where the state sector was less dominant under communism, transition to the market followed the Polish pattern. In Romania, Bulgaria, and most of the former Soviet republics, where the state sector controlled almost everything under communism, market policies followed the Russian experience. After finally voting out the old-guard communist parties, Romania and Bulgaria tried to break the Russian pattern, but macroeconomic reforms do not work well in the absence of microeconomic entrepreneurial structures. In Romania, the new government elected in 1996 failed completely, and the ex-communists returned to power in 2000.[45] After a bout of hyperinflation, Bulgaria staked its economic future on a radical monetary policy, which pegged the Bulgarian currency to the new euro. But economic hard times led to the fall of the noncommunist government and the election of a new party founded and led by Simeon II of Saxe-Coburg-Gotha, the former exiled king.[46]

The lessons from these experiences of transition to the market economy are clear. Aid is not the answer—from 1992–99, the West provided over $100 billion to Russia alone.[47] Market policies are the demonstrated means to increase the overall economic pie. But they work only in an institutional environment in which farmers, industries, and workers are free to establish enterprises protected by law that can respond to price signals. If there is no competitive sector or if the state insists on controlling this sector by limiting the ownership of capital and land, restricting the flexibility of labor and capital markets, or tightly regulating the establishment of new businesses, market policies become a means to enrich the elite and the state.

As we note in chapter 4, there is a wide variety of capitalist economies that reforming states can aim for. The Czech economy is a model of continental capitalism, in the mode of the French and German economies. The British, Dutch, and American economies, on the other hand, are more decentralized, individualistic, and less state regulated. Most of the formerly communist countries in Europe are likely to follow the continental model. What distinguishes a Czech economy from a Russian or Chinese economy, however, is the widespread existence of private property and the greater accountability of political institutions. Ownership of private property is a critical factor that facilitates the spread of economic benefits in a capitalist economy, and greater political accountability is due, at least in part, to the fact that private citizens, because they have greater access to economic wealth and power, can protect their rights and interests in the political arena.

The principal contribution that the United States and western countries can make to economic growth in the eastern half of Europe is to open markets for both goods and foreign investment. So far the United States and EU have been inexcusably slow in doing this, much slower than they were to expand NATO. And, in this case unlike NATO, there was no opposition from Russia. The opposition has all been from domestic groups in the western countries. Farm groups in the EU and labor and environmental groups in the United States strongly oppose widening trade. As a result, the EU did not even begin negotiations to add new members until November 1998, and no decisions on membership are expected to be made until at least 2003.

The first wave of potential members from the formerly communist countries includes the new NATO members (Poland, Hungary, and the Czech Republic),

Slovenia, and Estonia. The EU signed interim or association agreements with these countries plus Slovakia, Bulgaria, Romania, Latvia, and Lithuania. These association agreements call for free trade over a period of ten years. But the commitment does not apply to farm products or sensitive industrial products, such as textiles and steel, precisely the products that these countries can export competitively in the near term. Altogether, the association agreements exclude some 40 percent of the exports of transition countries. The United States has not been any more generous. As we have seen in chapter 4, its trade policy is stalled, consumed by sector quarrels with western Europe and Japan and obsessed with the requirement to raise labor and environmental standards to western levels before the reforming countries can access U.S. and western markets freely. This trade agenda asks reforming countries, in effect, to forgo their basic comparative advantage, making it less likely that trade can contribute to their economic advance.

$$* * *$$

Democracy and markets in western Europe failed after World War I and would have failed after World War II if the United States had not taken the unprecedented initiative under GATT to liberalize trade and, subsequently, investment relations among western countries. Reforms will fail today in eastern Europe and the former Soviet republics if the United States does not lead a similar effort in the WTO. In the early stages, reforming countries need capital. Wages are too low to generate sufficient domestic saving or spending. But foreign capital will not move into these countries in sufficient magnitude unless businesses can export and import freely from these markets. Thus far, foreign private capital has gone only to a few select countries in the area (Hungary has attracted the largest amount), not surprisingly those with the best access to western markets. Even in those countries, foreign direct investment continues to operate under widespread burdens imposed by tax, welfare, and regulatory systems that remain as relics of the old, state-centered economies.[48] Growth accordingly suffers, and authoritarian elites consolidate their control of a stagnant or only marginally growing economic pie.

America needs to do more in Europe, but it cannot do so until it builds more support at home to liberalize trade. Open markets abroad do not compete with jobs and growth at home. Just the opposite. The United States and its allies won the Cold War because they created opportunities for emerging democracies abroad at the same time that they created diverse and prosperous societies at home.

Despite these obvious links between domestic and foreign prosperity, U.S. and western diplomacy continues to obscure the relationship. Debates persist about costs and burden sharing; yet the industrial democracies have never been richer, stronger, or more capable, individually and collectively, to build an international environment sympathetic to the transition to democracy and markets in Europe. If they default on the historic moment before them, they will pay a price in later turmoil and ill will. The western democracies essentially have three choices: they can import the products of the democratizing countries; failing that, they can import the people of those countries as immigrants stream out of the desolate and hopeless economies in the East; or, failing to import either products or people, they will import the lasting hostility of those in the East who have been excluded from western prosperity. The burdens of re-armament and new military conflicts will follow, as democracies square off once again with authoritarian states in Europe in a deadly balance of power. Jeane Kirkpatrick summed up the choices well: "whatever it costs to restructure these economies, societies and politics, it will be cheaper than fighting another war."[49]

The first half of the strategy of consolidation is working. NATO expansion insulated Hungary from the conflict in Kosovo. NATO stabilization in Bosnia assisted the consolidation of democratizing forces in Slovenia and, more recently, a hopeful political transition in Croatia and Serbia. NATO's efforts in Kosovo precipitated the fall of Yugoslav strongman Slobodan Milosevic and a potential turn toward more moderate Yugoslav and Serbian politics. Ethnic violence in Macedonia poses new challenges, but consider how much worse the situation in Macedonia might be if Kosovo and Serbia were still in the hands of extremist groups. Stabilization and the marginalization of extremist groups, however, are only the first steps. The second half of the strategy of consolidation is not doing as well. Economic reforms and market-opening initiatives are lagging. The EU delays expansion and the United States forfeits leadership of the world trading system. The rich industrial democracies are acting pusillani-mously. They are missing the opportunity to win the peace after the Cold War.

How identities evolve and realign in Europe will be more important for peace than specific new institutional arrangements for European security. After the last great upheavals in Europe, diplomacy focused primarily on inter-national institutions (the Concert of Europe, League of Nations, and United Nations). Traditional perspectives urge us to think again about new security designs. But international architecture assumes stable domestic foundations. What matters most is what happens domestically in Russia and other formerly communist countries and whether democracies in the United States and west-ern Europe remain vital and open. Security arrangements influence these domestic developments, but only at the margins. They exist primarily to defend against reversals and setbacks. When ethnic violence erupted in Kosovo and threatened to engulf neighboring countries, the expansion of NATO proved to be an invaluable investment. If Russian democracy falters, NATO's expansion will look even more prescient. But NATO cannot build democracy in Kosovo or Russia. That will be done by the indigenous peoples and by the example of successful and self-confident democracies in the West that open markets to their eastern neighbors and generate prosperity in the world economy.

CHAPTER SIX

From Bilateralism to Multilateralism

American Policy in Asia

America derived its identity from relations with Europe, and it projected this identity onto relations with Asia. Hesitant to use force toward Europe, America used force readily to expand to the Pacific and Far East. It conquered natives and neighbors alike, forced open markets in Japan and China, and championed a civilizing Christianity for the pagan multitudes of Asia. If Europe encountered a relatively weak and wary America, Asia endured a potent and proselytizing one.

Manifest destiny left little time for self-reflection. America never agonized over the denial of fundamental rights to Native Americans, Mexican immigrants, Chinese workers, or Japanese-American citizens, as it did over slavery or the rights of European immigrants. Vietnam eventually produced such nationwide anguish. It unleashed a flood of new Asian immigrants, and it compelled America to reexamine its self-image. Was America the New World after all? Or did it use power for imperialist and even racist reasons just as the Old World powers of Europe did? And, if it was a New World, did its ideals apply universally, to Asians also, or only to Europeans?

The question persists today. America is ambivalent about Asia, and this ambivalence produces wild swings in U.S. expectations. On the one hand are ever new threats coming from Asia, from the falling military dominoes of Korea and Vietnam during the Cold War to the rising economic dynamos of Japan and China after the Cold War; on the other hand are boundless opportunities—prospects of markets and democratization for three-quarters of the world's population. In assessing both threats and opportunities, America exaggerates and betrays its lack of rootedness and self-perspective in Asia.

Traditional perspectives on American foreign policy in Asia perpetuate this ambivalence. Realist perspectives focus on threats, internationalist perspectives on opportunities. American policy cycles from one to the other. In World War II, China was our friend and Japan was our foe. During the early Cold War, China was our enemy and Japan was our friend. Later, China became a strategic friend and Japan became an economic foe. Today, U.S. policy makers cannot decide. Is China a strategic partner or competitor? Is Japan an economic or also a strategic rival? In all the confusion, isolationism gains ground as America ponders whether Asian nations should manage their own conflicts.

The identity and power approach offers a way to transcend this ambivalence and anchor U.S. participation in Asia. It highlights two structural features of the Asian subsystem, signposts to shape a more enduring American presence in Asia. The first is contemporary American military hegemony in Asia. This structural feature predicts more stability over the next decade than realist perspectives expect, but also more need to balance power than international perspectives predict. Since the demise of the Soviet Union, U.S. air and sea power is unchallenged in the Pacific and will remain so for at least another generation. On land, as the wars in Korea and Vietnam suggest, the U.S. position is more precarious. China's military capability is growing and may become sufficient in the next two decades to deter U.S. intervention in Taiwan or even South Korea. In addition, China's internal and external identity—nondemocratic and dissatisfied—diverges significantly from that of the United States (and, for that matter, Japan). Hence, balancing rising Chinese power remains a requirement for stability in Asia. The issue is not whether America can handle such balancing in material terms. Given its overwhelming sea and air power, it almost certainly can. In the next decade or so, U.S. policy makers would do well not to exaggerate China's material challenge. The issue is whether America has the will to balance power in Asia; this depends on whether America recognizes the second structural feature of post–Cold War Asia.

The United States and Japan form an incipient democratic security community in Asia, one that includes the distant democracies in Australia and New Zealand and, increasingly, the emerging democracies in South Korea, Taiwan, and southeast Asia. This security community, the second structural feature, offers for the first time a mooring or anchor for American identity in Asia. As I argue in chapter 4, Japan is the first industrialized Asian country to become a strong democracy. Although it continues to adapt its democracy to a more normal military role, more frequent rotations of government power between opposing parties, and more aggressive defense of individual civil liberties, it resolves issues with the United States peacefully with no threat of military planning or power balancing. This peace between strong democracies, expanding to include new democracies, is the starting point of a new and more enduring American presence in Asia. This presence is key both to stabilizing the growth of Chinese power and to offering China a secure place in the peaceful and prosperous world community.

The structural features of American hegemony and of an emerging democratic security community argue for an American grand strategy in Asia that places more emphasis on multilateralism. Hegemonic U.S. power facilitates multilateral cooperation. Even if China eventually challenges U.S. power, it needs U.S. and global markets to do so. At the same time, an emerging democratic security community between the United States, Japan, and possibly other Asian democracies disciplines U.S. power and makes it more transparent and accountable. In this structure, U.S. power in 2001 is much less threatening to China than Soviet power in the 1960s was. In addition, a democratic security community promotes open trade and encourages confidence-building to reduce suspicions. Tensions persist but they are less likely to spiral out of control, as they might in a structure of bilateral power balancing among several independent powers.

The possibility of multilateralism in Asia is new. After World War II, America built its presence in Asia on a foundation of bilateralism. Driven by specific military threats and economic opportunities, the United States underwrote a series of separate bilateral security and economic arrangements with Asian countries. These arrangements included six original bilateral treaties—with Japan, South Korea, Taiwan, the Philippines, Australia, and New Zealand. Bilateral pacts created a hub-and-spoke pattern of relationships in which the United States sought to have closer military and trade ties with Asian countries than Asian countries had with one another.[1] Initially, for example, Japan needed the United States not only to balance Soviet power, but also to mediate relations with Asian neighbors, such as South Korea and China. Later, China needed the United States not only to balance power against the Soviet Union, but also to manage unresolved tensions with Japan and South Korea. Meanwhile, China and Japan, Japan and South Korea, and China and South Korea had fewer ties with one another. Japan and the four original Asian tigers—South Korea, Taiwan, Singapore, and Hong Kong—grew economically largely through bilateral ties with the United States. Each shipped more goods to the American market than to any single Asian market. Subsequently, other Asian tigers, Malaysia, Thailand, the Philippines, and Indonesia, followed the same course; and the latest and largest tiger, China, perpetuates the pattern (in a sense also developing under the protective shield of the U.S. Seventh Fleet). In 2000, it shipped almost 30 percent of its exports to the United States. Despite some Asianization of trade and investment in recent years, Asian countries still ship a disproportionate share of their exports to the United States (see table 6.2 later in the chapter).

Cold War politics also had the consequence of excluding India from American bilateral alignments, even though India is the oldest democracy in Asia. Locked in border disputes and regional rivalry with China, India moved closer to the Soviet Union, while Pakistan aligned with the United States. Pakistan and India—one Muslim, the other predominantly Hindu—clashed in a rivalry that persists today, threatening south Asia with nuclear confrontation.

This bilateral hub-and-spoke pattern of U.S. relations in Asia is obsolete. It reflects structural conditions from the Cold War, when American power was contested by the Soviet Union and political cohesion (or democratic convergence) in Asia was much weaker. But American military power is now more dominant, and the political and economic stakes for America have increased. Greater cohesion with Japan and a democratizing South Korea and Taiwan offers a way to anchor and diffuse American power, making it both more effective and more acceptable in the region.

Bilateralism assumes that the United States could fight a future war in Asia without the help of its allies in the region. It is doubtful, however, that the American people would support such a war. Yet until new defense guideline revisions were ratified in 1999, the bilateral security treaty with Japan did not obligate Japan to help the United States except in the case of a direct attack against the Japanese homeland. This was the case even though the United States provided the major market for the development of Japan and other Asian nations. Congress and the American people are not likely to support such go-it-alone policies indefinitely. They will expect greater multilateral support from U.S. allies in both security and trade relations, or they will insist that America reduce its commitments in Asia.

The United States needs a new strategy that recognizes the structural changes in Asia, particularly the emerging security community with Asian democracies and the long-term growth of Chinese power. I call this strategy concentric multilateralism. *Concentric multilateralism* starts with a core group of countries that share greater similarities in domestic identities and builds out to construct a more stable balance of power with more disparate political cultures. The core group includes the United States, Japan, and South Korea. Within this core, America has to restructure military and economic relations. The key step in restructuring is to trilateralize security treaties with Japan and South Korea and undergird security commitments with more integrated and equitable economic relationships. This trilateralization is necessary not only to ensure that defense commitments are credible and publicly supported, but also to promote political reconciliation between Japan and South Korea, which continue to have difficult political relations due to unresolved historical grievances. A second circle of multilateral ties extends to democratizing countries, Thailand, the Philippines, and, indirectly, Taiwan. These ties also incorporate, loosely, the distant and strong democracies of Australia and New Zealand, as well as the closer but weaker democracies of India and Bangladesh. In this second circle, the United States needs to refurbish alliances with Australia and New Zealand (the latter essentially defunct due to differences over nuclear weapon issues) and associate India more closely with sea-lane defense in south and southeast Asia. The core and second circles need not threaten China, any more than NATO threatens Russia in Europe. A third circle complements the first two and draws in nondemocratic or transition countries, such as China, Russia, Malaysia, Indonesia, and perhaps eventually North Korea. This third circle involves, first, the liberalization and multilateralization of economic relationships through the Asia Pacific Economic Cooperation

(APEC) forum and the WTO and, second, a confidence-building diplomatic and security dialogue through the ASEAN Regional Forum (ARF).

The three concentric circles supplement and reinforce one another. The core trilateral alliance ensures a credible balance of power and begins to construct the deeper political community between American and Asian democracies that establishes a permanent basis for peaceful nonmilitary relations among these countries. This political community, in turn, provides the confidence to expand aggressively trade and security ties with nondemocratic countries. The confidence-building and security dialogue through ARF makes the core alliance transparent and supports economic engagement (much as the Helsinki Accords and OSCE agreements did in Europe). This dialogue softens and may, in some cases, preempt potential military tensions that would otherwise destabilize markets. Ultimately, the key threats in the region, North Korea and the China-Taiwan dispute, may be reduced as countries recognize that military force cannot succeed and that economic and political objectives can be achieved by cooperative means.

The concentric strategy is one of deepening U.S. engagement in Asia. Because multilateralism in Asia is weak, however, the strategy risks the appearance of reducing commitments. In Asia, as Yoichi Funabashi notes, "the historical pattern has been one of domination by the strongest power."[2] If the dominant power does not dominate, it appears to retreat. Thus, concentric multilateralism must build on, not substitute for, the existing bilateral relationships. It should not involve any early reductions of U.S. military or economic stakes, but it also does not need to involve any significant increases. What it calls for is the political restructuring of current military and economic stakes from bilateral to multilateral mechanisms.

This restructuring will result in deeper political engagement over the long run. It will reduce U.S. ambivalence toward Asia, an ambivalence that has led America either to ignore the region in favor of Europe or to run roughshod over the region with unilateral military and economic initiatives. In short, the strategy allows America to sink roots in Asia, initially with Japan, South Korea, Taiwan (indirectly), and some ASEAN states as security partners and eventually with other ASEAN states, Russia, China, and perhaps even North Korea as economic partners.

Political Geography of Asia—Internal Identity

Following World War II, political cohesion in Asia was weak, much weaker than it was in Europe. This structure of more divergent identities created an unstable and unpredictable foundation for economic and military relations. It accounted for the fact that historically military and economic alignments dominated and frequently shifted in Asia (not unlike the situation in Europe in the eighteenth and nineteenth centuries). Whatever stability emerged was due to temporary regional balances or external global alignments. For a brief moment after 1970, for example, Asia united through American alliances with both China and Japan against the former Soviet Union. But this externally induced regional coalescence collapsed once the Soviet threat receded, and it never entailed significant rapprochement between Asia's two biggest powers, China and Japan.

This regional structure of greater political divergence persists into the twenty-first century and makes balancing power a more enduring element of stability in the Pacific than in the North Atlantic. Economic exchanges, consequently, are more vulnerable. Structural realities limit economic regionalization in Asia and suggest why it is important to consider structural constraints before looking at specific state behaviors. Trade ties with nondemocratic states such as China (not unlike trade ties with Russia in Europe) can become significant only as political identities further converge.

Table 6.1 provides identity and power indicators for the Asian states. The internal dimension of identity is measured along a democracy/nondemocracy scale (Freedom Ratings and Polity IV Ratings columns). The South Pacific nations of Australia and New Zealand rank highest in terms of democracy, and Japan almost as high. By these measures, Japan compares favorably with many European democracies, including Belgium, France, Italy, Germany, Spain, and the United Kingdom. Slightly behind Japan come South Korea and Taiwan. Farther back come Mongolia, India, the Philippines, and Thailand. Hong Kong, now a part of China, is not ranked, and its democratic future is uncertain. The rest of the states in Asia fall toward the nondemocratic end of the scale. China, North Korea, Cambodia, Laos, Vietnam, Pakistan, Afghanistan, Myanmar (formerly Burma), Brunei, and Bhutan are least free. Malaysia, Singapore, Sri Lanka, Nepal, Bangladesh, and Indonesia are only partly free.

As table 6.1 further shows, the major countries in north Asia are ethnically homogeneous. China is almost totally Han, with a small Muslim population in the western provinces. Japan, except for minuscule Korean and indigenous minorities, is, as Edwin Reischauer observes, "the most thoroughly unified and culturally homogeneous large bloc of people in the world, with the possible exception of the Northern Chinese."[3] Korea, both North and South, is ethnically unified. The south and southeast Asian states are more diverse; subjected to periodic invasions, these states are riven with cultural and religious differences. Throughout Asia, racial prejudice is commonplace, and minorities in most countries—Koreans in Japan, overseas Chinese in Malaysia and Indonesia, Muslims in the Philippines and China—are not well integrated. Four major religions in the region compound the divisions—Islam in Pakistan, the insular states of southeast Asia, and western China; Buddhism in Tibet, China, and Japan; Shintoism in Japan; and Hinduism in India.

Table 6.1. Power and Identity Indicators in Asia

	Political				Economic			Military			Social
	Population, 1999[a] (millions)	Freedom Rating[b] PR	Freedom Rating[b] CL	Polity IV Rating, 1999[c]	Minority (%)[d]	PPP GNI, 1999[e] (billions of dollars)	Economic Freedom, 2001[f]	Budget (% GDP)[g] 1985	Budget (% GDP)[g] 1999	Weapons of Mass Destruction and Delivery Systems[h]	Human Development Index, 1998[i]
North Asia											
China	1249.7	7	6	−7	8	4,452	3.55	7.9	5.4	A, B, C, S, M, L	0.706
Hong Kong	6.9	NA	NA	NA	5	152	1.30	NA	NA		0.872
Japan	126.6	1	2	10	1	3,186	2.05	1.0	0.9	C, S	0.924
Mongolia	2.6	2	3	10	10	4	3.00	9.0	1.9		0.628
North Korea	21.4[b]	7	7	−9	0	NA	5.00	23.0	14.3	A, B, C, S, M, L	NA
South Korea	46.8	2	2	8	0	728	2.25	5.1	3.0	C, S	0.854
Taiwan	22.1[b]	2	2	9	NA	NA	2.10	7.0	5.2	C, S	NA
Southeast Asia											
Brunei	0.3[b]	7	5	NA	15, 17, 6	NA	NA	6.0	6.7		0.848
Cambodia	11.8	6	6	2	5, 5	16	2.85	5.9[j]	5.1		0.512
Indonesia	207.0	4	4	8	45, 14, 8, 8, 26	550	3.55	2.8	1.1		0.670
Laos	5.1	7	6	−8	22, 9, 1	7	4.65	7.8	2.3		0.484
Malaysia	22.7	5	5	4	26, 7, 9	173	3.00	5.6	4.0		0.772
Myanmar	45.0	7	7	−7	NA	NA	NA	5.1	5.0	C	0.585
Philippines	76.8	2	3	7	9	296	3.05	1.4	2.1		0.744
Singapore	3.2	5	5	−2	14, 8, 2	88	1.55	6.7	5.6		0.881
Thailand	61.7	2	3	9	14, 11	358	2.20	5.0	1.9		0.745
Vietnam	77.5	7	7	−7	3	144	4.10	19.4	3.1	C, S	0.671

South Asia

Country	Population	PR	CL	Polity	Ethnic groups	GNI	Econ. Freedom			WMD	HDI
Afghanistan	25.8[b]	7	7	-7	38, 25, 19, 6	NA	NA	8.7	14.9	S	NA
Bangladesh	127.7	3	4	6	2	196	3.80	1.4	1.9		0.461
Bhutan	2.0[b]	7	6	-8	35, 15	NA	NA	4.9	5.3		0.483
India	997.5	2	3	9	25, 3	2,226	3.85	3.0	3.4	A, C, S, M, L	0.563
Nepal	23.4	3	4	6	NA	30	3.50	1.5	0.8		0.474
Pakistan	134.8	7	5	-6	NA	250	3.45	6.9	5.7	A, C, S, M	0.522
Sri Lanka	19.0	3	4	6	18, 7, 1	61	2.70	3.8	5.1		0.733
South Pacific											
Australia	19.0	1	1	10	7, 1	452	1.90	3.4	1.9		0.929
New Zealand	3.8	1	1	10	10, 5, 12	67	1.70	2.9	1.6		0.903
TOTAL (all)	3,340.2					13,436.0					

Note: NA, not available.

[a] *World Development Report 2000/2001: Attacking Poverty* (New York: Oxford University Press, for The World Bank, 2001), 278–79.

[b] *Freedom in the World 1999–2000* (New York: Freedom House, 2000), 596–97. Ratings are based on a scale of 1–7, with 1 signifying the most free in the categories of Political Rights (PR) and Civil Liberties (CL). Population data are taken from respective country page.

[c] *Polity IV: Political Regime Characteristics and Transitions, 1800–1999*, Center for International Development and Conflict Management, University of Maryland at College Park, 2000. Rating is based on Democracy Score (scale of 0–10, with 0 signifying low democracy) minus Autocracy Score (scale of 0–10, with 0 signifying low autocracy).

[d] U.S. Central Intelligence Agency, *The World Factbook 2000*, http://www.cia.gov/cia/publications/factbook/index.html. Single minority groups with at least 5% of the population are listed separately, with the final number including all minority groups with less than 5%. Minority refers to ethnic origin.

[e] *World Development Indicators 2001* (Washington, D.C.: World Bank, 2001), 12–14. GNI equals GNP plus net receipts of primary income from nonresident sources. Conversions are at Purchasing Power Parity (PPP) exchange rates, not current exchange rates.

[f] Gerald P. O'Driscoll Jr., Kim R. Holmes, and Melanie Kirkpatrick, *2001 Index of Economic Freedom* (Washington, D.C.: The Heritage Foundation, 2001), 8–14. Rankings are based on a scale of 1–5, with 1 signifying the most freedom. The score is based on trade policy, fiscal burden of government, government intervention in the economy, monetary policy (inflation), capital flows and foreign investment, banking, wage and price controls, property rights, business regulations, and black markets.

[g] *The Military Balance, 2000/2001* (London: Oxford University Press, for The International Institute for Strategic Studies, 2000), 297–301.

[h] Countries proven or suspected to have Atomic, Biological, or Chemical weapons and Short-range, Medium-range, or Long-range military missile capabilities, as cited in the following sources and from interviews with government officials. Federation of American Scientists, http://www.fas.org; Center for Non-Proliferation Studies, Monterey Institute of International Studies, http://www.cns.miis.edu; Henry R. Stimson Center, http://www.stimson.org; Stockholm International Peace Research Institute, http://www.sipri.se; U.S. Department of Defense, *Proliferation: Threat and Response* (Washington, D.C.: Department of Defense, 1997); U.S. Department of Defense, http://www.defenselink.mil/pubs.

[i] *Human Development Report 2000* (New York: Oxford University Press, for the United Nations Development Programme, 2000), 157–60. Rankings are based on life expectancy, real GDP per capita, and a combination of adult literacy and school enrollment ratios. The highest possible index value (better off) is 1.0, while the lowest possible value is 0.

[j] 1995 data (1985 data unavailable).

Ethnic diversity in Asia does not correlate with political democracy; unlike the situation in the formerly communist states of Europe (see table 5.1), homogeneous Asian states are not more inclined to be democratic. Homogeneous states in north Asia include both democratic and nondemocratic regimes (Japan and South Korea; China and North Korea). Nonhomogeneous states in southeast Asia do as well (India and Thailand are democratic; Malaysia, Laos, Vietnam, and Cambodia are nondemocratic). Homogeneous states do seem to enjoy a higher level of social development. This is true regardless of type of political regime. North Asian states rank highest in this regard, southeast Asian states are mixed, and south Asian states have a relatively low level of social and human development.

The structure of internal identities in Asia suggests several conclusions. Politically, Japan identifies much more closely with the United States than it does with China. This gap is as wide as the Freedom House and Polity IV scales themselves. Japan and the United States fall at one end of the scale, and China at the other end. If the structure of internal identities matters at all, and this book argues that it matters as much as the structure of power, this divergence is fundamental to understanding American foreign policy in Asia. Compared to Japan, China is a secretive, authoritarian state. The inner workings of China's policy-making processes are, in good part, inaccessible and hard to predict, even on such basic things as succession of leaders. These differences in domestic political identities impose significant obstacles to determining when and for what purpose China may consider the use of force to be legitimate, both against its own citizens and against other societies.

The vast differences in internal identities do not necessarily make China an adversary. States also relate along an external dimension of identity, in which they cooperate or conflict based on historical relations with one another. The United States has often collaborated with closed societies to balance power against third countries—the U.S.-China alliance in the Cold War is but one example. What the divergence of internal identities does mean is that America has to relate differently to China than it does to Japan. The two countries are not substitutable or alternative allies. Even if the United States cooperates with both, as this study suggests it should, the relationship with Japan is qualitatively different from the relationship with China. The United States will have to balance military power with China, even as it engages China economically. It does not have to balance military power against Japan, even as it competes vigorously with Japan in economic relations.

Traditional perspectives completely miss this overriding feature of the structure of internal identities in Asia. Realists call for a conventional balance-of-power approach to U.S. relations in Asia. Henry Kissinger, for example, advocates a Bismarckian strategy of power balancing, which foresees equal bilateral ties between the United States and both China and Japan. In these parallel alliances, "the American role," according to Kissinger, "is the key to helping

Japan and China coexist despite their suspicions of one another."[4] This is the classic approach of bilateralism, of keeping potential adversaries closer to the United States than they are to one another. It assumes that the United States can be, and indeed should be, completely indifferent to the internal politics of Japan and China. Internationalists, on the other hand, go to the other extreme. They argue that the centerpiece of U.S. strategy toward Asia should be economic engagement with China. Despite the absence of the rule of law in China and despite great difficulties in economic relations with a much more law-abiding Japan, internationalists are optimistic that economic liberalization can become the cutting edge of political reform in China and narrow the identity gap between China and the United States. What is more, to the extent that they neglect the need to balance Chinese military power, internationalists reflect no or at most little concern that China might exploit the opportunities of economic liberalization to expand its military power and disrupt the balance of power in Asia. For the most part, this internationalist approach was the strategy of the Clinton administration toward Asia. Clinton began and ended his two-term administration with economic initiatives to liberalize trade with Japan (bilateral agreements) and China (WTO entry). He ignored U.S.-Japanese security ties during his first term (until North Korean nuclear ambitions and Chinese missile launches brought alliance issues back to the front burner), and he gave diplomatic priority to China over Japan in his second term.

Traditional approaches will fail because they do not acknowledge the structural constraints of identity and power in Asia. At the moment, Japan is part of a democratic security community with the United States and other western countries. These countries compete with one another economically, but do not balance power among themselves militarily. This behavior is dramatically different from what we expect between the United States and China or between Japan and China. Now, identities may change, but they do not always change in one direction, as traditional perspectives assume. As I discuss in chapter 4, Japan's democracy is still evolving. If Japan becomes a more normal state, wielding military power not only for self-defense but also for multilateral and collective defense, Japan's relationship with the United States could change. Because of their democratic affinities, the two countries may deepen their military cooperation, as the democracies of the North Atlantic have done. On the other hand, because the democratic relationship between the two countries is relatively new and not as historically tested as U.S. relationships in Europe, the two countries could slip back into military rivalry.[5]

Much depends, therefore, on how democracy evolves in the Pacific and Asia, first in the U.S.-Japan relationship; second in the widening of the U.S.-Japan security community to include democratizing states such as South Korea, Thailand, the Philippines, and, indirectly, Taiwan; and finally in the prospects for political liberalization in nondemocratic countries such as China.

Japanese democracy has evolved without the protective or nurturing womb of a larger Asian democratic community. Unlike Germany in Europe, Japan was the democratic exception in Asia. As a result, its relationship with the United States was and remains critical. But now the opportunity exists to expand the democratic security community in Asia; South Korea and Taiwan are democratizing. This development vindicates Japan's democratic evolution and facilitates Japan's reconciliation with its neighbors in Asia.

There is still much less trust of Japan in Asia than of Germany in Europe. The most popular novel in South Korea in 1995 was a story not about war between South and North Korea but about how South and North Korea cooperated to develop nuclear weapons and save South Korea in a war against Japan.[6] This visceral distrust of Japan, perhaps most evident in Korea, is only slightly less evident in China.[7] All of these countries endured Japanese occupation—Korea for thirty-five years, Taiwan for fifty years, and parts of China and Southeast Asia for more than a decade.

Authoritarian institutions in Asia are another source of this historical distrust. Traditionally, Asian political institutions made decisions secretively. The dominant form of government was authoritarian one-party rule. China and Japan had multiple parties in the 1920s, and Japan today is pluralizing, at least in form, but the overwhelming political tendency inside the countries of the region has been toward consensus and unifying institutions.[8] Not surprisingly, four of the five remaining communist regimes in the world are in Asia—China, Vietnam, Laos, and North Korea. And knowledgeable analysts believe communism has lasted and will probably be absorbed rather than rejected in China because it is organically consistent with that country's enduring traditions and values.[9]

Political authoritarianism within countries, coupled with political divergence among countries, contributed to different patterns of conflict in Asia. The major countries, accustomed to hegemony at home, sought to impose it abroad.[10] The Chinese historically perceived themselves as the Middle Kingdom with tributary relations stretching from the Indian Ocean to the Yellow Sea. Japan similarly perceived the need for hierarchy and place in the world around it, just as it revered station and status at home.[11] These self-images projected superiority and subordination, as opposed to equality (as in Europe), and necessitated the pursuit of maximum power, not just security. In Europe, the concepts of anarchy and sovereignty made dominance unacceptable and temporary. In Asia, dominance was expected, and one country, usually China, imposed its imperial order.[12]

Prospects for Democratization in Asia

Can the emergence of democratic institutions in Asia alter these traditional patterns of authoritarianism and eventually open up the region to somewhat more egalitarian practices? They could, but it may be an uphill struggle. Today, democracy is not an important determinant of relations in Asia. The only long-standing democracies are in the South Pacific, and Australia and New Zealand are too small and too far away to exert significant influence, particularly in northeast Asia. A big test of Japan's democracy will come when it indigenizes its security policies, including possibly those dealing with nuclear weapons. At the moment, Japan's democracy is strong enough to relate peacefully with more powerful and mature democracies such as the United States. But Japan's society is not yet sufficiently open and accountable to reassure its own citizens, let alone the citizens of neighboring countries, that it can be trusted with the exercise of normal military power. Although far ahead of other Asian countries in the process of democratization, Japan still has a lot of work to do to become the center of a nonviolent, democratic peace community in Asia.

Asia's emerging democracies suffer from deficiencies in all three areas that support a democratic peace—peaceful rotation of opposing parties in power, divided and accountable institutions, and protection of civil liberties. Only in the late 1990s did South Korea and Taiwan experience a first peaceful transition of power between significantly different political parties. In 1997, the center-left candidate for president, Kim Dae Jung, a preeminent pro-democracy leader during the military era (imprisoned and nearly executed by the military government), ousted the incumbent president from the party of the previous military government. In coalition with other parties, Kim's Democratic Party also gained a majority in the parliament in 1998. In Taiwan, an opposition candidate won the presidential elections in 1999, but the long-ruling Nationalist Party, or Kuomintang, still controlled the parliament in 2001. Both presidencies face numerous obstacles to establishing a tradition of peaceful power transitions. In the Philippines, since the ouster of the dictator Ferdinand Marcos in 1986, elections have been contested more by opposing personalities than by well-established parties, and democratic governance remains vulnerable to military intervention (six coup attempts against Corazon Aquino from 1986 to 1992) and popular instability (the impeachment and removal of Joseph Estrada in 2000). Thailand has also held competitive elections among multiple parties, but it too faces military instability. Indonesia held its first elections in thirty years in 1999, but the results were inconclusive and criticized by many as fraudulent. The new leader, Abdurrahman Wahid, was impeached and driven out of office in 2001, and Megawati Sukarnoputri, the daughter of the former dictator Sukarno, took office. One province of Indonesia, East Timor, violently separated in 1999, and secessionist struggles persisted in Irian Jaya, Aceh, and other places in the sprawling archipelago.

Bureaucratic politics in Asian democracies is elitist, highly personalized, and often corrupt. Even in India, which has competitive parties that rotate in power (twelve elections and several transfers of power since independence), democratic accountability is weak. Indira Gandhi ruled by emergency decree from 1975 to 1977, and religious as well as regional tensions fragment governmental institutions and civil society. South Korea has powerful corporate and government institutions, much like Japan, but unlike Japan it also has a large military establishment that only recently dominated Korean politics. To its credit, the new democratizing government in South Korea has attacked some of these problems, prosecuting former presidents for corruption and pressuring large industrial corporations to become more open. Taiwan has stronger medium- and small-size business institutions, but it has a powerful military establishment, and business relations tend to be dominated by family networks. Relatively closed and often corrupt family ties are a dominant way of doing business and influencing politics throughout Asia, particularly among overseas Chinese communities in Indonesia, Malaysia, Singapore, and Taiwan.

Civil society and institutions are also weak in Asia's new democracies. In South Korea, a draconian national security law results in hundreds of arrests each year, with many still detained even after the new democratic administration released some prisoners. In most of the young democracies in Asia, the media are heavily subsidized, and authorities regularly pressure editors to kill critical articles. Judicial proceedings are rife with corruption, police treatment is often brutal, and human rights violations are commonplace.

The lack of full protection for civil liberties in Asia reflects the significantly different traditions regarding the relationship of the individual to society.[13] Nowhere in Asia is there a celebration of political individualism as we know it in the West, either in political thought or in historical events such as the Reformation or Enlightenment. Authority patterns infuse all social relationships—in the family (Confucianism), in religion (Buddhism and Islam), and in the state (Shintoism). This authority is personalized, informal, and less institutionalized or publicly accountable than constitutional and legal authority in the West. At the top, authority is unconstrained or arbitrary, not so much in the sense of being irresponsible as in the sense of knowing what is best for lower subjects, whether children in the family or citizens in the realm. As Lee Kwan Yew, the former prime minister and elder statesman of Singapore, suggests, "the main object is to have a well-ordered society."[14] "What a county needs to develop," he adds, "is discipline more than democracy."[15] Malaysia's prime minister, Mohammed Mahathir, puts it more bluntly, "The group and the country are more important than the individual."[16]

Asian democracy also labors under the authoritarian shadow of China. China looms over the prospects for democracy in Asia, much the way Russia does in Europe. But Russia is part of European and western history; China is not. And today Russia elects its leaders and tolerates political opposition; China does not.

In China, the state supplies the unifying and moral purpose of society. There is no church, as there is in Russia, or other national institution that provides alternative sources of inspiration and guidance. For 2000 years, as Kenneth Lieberthal writes, the traditional Chinese polity "was a profoundly non-pluralistic system, based squarely on the notions of hierarchy, centralization and the state as the propagator of the correct moral framework for the society."[17] This fact makes the reform of the Chinese state a particularly delicate and potentially destabilizing endeavor.

Economic reforms begun in 1979 represented the first significant steps in two millennia to reduce the state's dominance of at least part of Chinese society. Reforms sanctioned provincial and local economic activities in agriculture and light industry and created special economic zones in urban coastal areas to attract foreign investment and encourage foreign exports. China's economy exploded, growing at annual rates of 10–12 percent from 1980 on. In the meantime, however, communism collapsed in the Soviet Union and elsewhere around the world. The Chinese party lost a major source of its political legitimacy, even though it had already distanced itself from the Soviet party in the 1960s. In the rapidly growing economic sector, the Chinese state no longer provided a moral compass. Was political reform now inevitable?

China experts divide on this question. Lowell Dittmer predicts that "under such circumstances, previous experience suggests that a full-blown civil society—albeit still with distinctive Chinese cultural characteristics—is apt to emerge as quickly as bamboo shoots after a spring rain."[18] Zbigniew Brzezinski agrees: "It is impossible to envision a long-term process of increasing economic pluralism without the appearance of civil society in China that eventually begins to assert its political aspiration."[19] But other experts are less sanguine. Lieberthal notes that "more power in the hands of local cadre has not meant a comparable increase in the opportunities for local social forces to coalesce."[20] And Andrew Nathan cautions that economic reforms may serve more as "an instrument of mobilization whose function is to strengthen the links of the citizen to the state, rather than a set of procedures for limiting state power to protect individual rights."[21]

Chinese politics is changing, but it is doing so glacially. In December 1998, the first-ever election occurred in a Chinese township. Townships have real powers to tax citizens and run schools, unlike villages, where noncompetitive elections have been held since 1980. But the township election in 1998 was not explicitly authorized by Beijing and was even called illegal by the party newspaper; moreover, the party candidate won, albeit barely. With migrants pouring into townships from rural villages, China sits on a powder keg of dislocated labor clamoring for attention but not trusted to exercise new political freedoms.[22]

It is clear that more Chinese people live better today and have more private choice in their lives than they have ever had before. What is less clear is what will hold them together, what ideology or institution will fill the moral gap left by the decline of state and communist ideology? Will China implode? The release in early 2001 of secret documents revealing how Chinese leaders decided to crush the widespread protests in Tiananmen Square and elsewhere in 1989 dramatizes the divisions that simmer just below the surface of Communist Party rule in Beijing.[23] The party, then and since, remains determined to hold the line against open political opposition. In ordering the crackdown, Deng Xiaoping called the democratic opposition "scum of the Chinese nation" and declared that political reform was possible only under the Four Basic Principles—the political thought of Marx, Lenin, and Mao; socialism; the people's democratic dictatorship; and leadership by the Communist Party.[24] At the Party Congress in 1997, Jiang Zemin, Deng's successor, reaffirmed the hard line: "It is imperative that we uphold and improve [China's] fundamental political system, instead of copying Western models."[25] Subsequent repression of the Falun Gong spiritual movement and of various underground Christian movements in effect restored totalitarian controls, at least in religious areas of Chinese civil society.

Hong Kong confirms the reluctance of Chinese authorities to liberalize. When Beijing took control of the former British colony in 1997, it disbanded the partially elected Legislative Council (LegCo), changed the laws, and elected a new council. Pro-democracy parties still won fourteen of the twenty directly elected seats (the other forty seats are reserved for functional constituencies such as business) and polled more than 60 percent of the vote. But Beijing selects the committee that appoints the chief executive, and no LegCo members serve in the Hong Kong government. In LegCo elections in 2000, turnout dropped ten percentage points, and the pro-Beijing party gained relative votes. At the turn of the millennium, Hong Kong's emerging democracy was dispirited, and its economy faced increasing uncertainty as China's expected entry into the WTO raised questions about the future importance of Hong Kong as an intermediary or entrepôt economy.[26]

How should the United States react to this political landscape? Two conclusions seem inescapable. It would be foolhardy to expect that China will evolve quickly into a transparent democratic state. And it would be foolhardy to undervalue the less individualistic democratic system that exists in Japan, however short Japanese democracy may fall in comparison to its western counterparts. Because international diplomacy starts with domestic politics, which positions the weather vanes of economic and military power, America has to maintain and build its position in Asia on the foundation of a strong partnership with Japan. It can then work through this relationship to construct a more solid political community with other countries, especially China.

Military Seismology of Asia—External Identity

The military tremors in Asia center around China. China borders on fifteen countries, more than any other country in the world. (Germany, for example, borders on nine.) And all along its border, China faces territorial claims, dis-

Figure 6.1. Threat Map of Asia

INTERNAL IDENTITIES

	Converge	Diverge
Cooperation	United States-Japan-Australia-New Zealand	United States-Pakistan China-South Korea China-Pakistan-Islamic Nations China-Russia
	1 (no threat)	3 (more threat)
	2 (some threat)	4 (high threat)
Conflict	Japan-South Korea Japan-Southeast Asia China-Vietnam China-North Korea United States-India	United States-China China-Japan India-Pakistan China-India North Korea-South Korea China-Taiwan Japan-Russia

EXTERNAL IDENTITIES

putes and uncertainties—from past tensions with Russia, the central Asian republics, and India; to the military occupation of Tibet; to past conflicts with Vietnam; to a paranoid neighbor in North Korea; to claims on Taiwan and a series of islands in the South China Sea; and finally to the bitter historical rivalry with Japan. In addition, historical subrivalries proliferate in the region—in south Asia between India and Pakistan, in Indochina between Vietnam and Cambodia, and in north Asia between Russia and Japan. This historical legacy of conflict shapes the structure of social or external identities in the Asian region and compounds the suspicions generated by divergent internal identities.

Putting together the structure of external and internal identities in Asia yields a threat map for the region. As figure 6.1 suggests, most relationships fall into the high-threat space (box 4). They are marked by a divergence of internal identities and a history of external conflict.

China sits at the epicenter of this threat seismology. It is a stirring great power. Historically, as we have noted, it is accustomed to hegemonic orders, usually its own. And its strategic culture has been described as hard realpolitik.[27] It clearly opposes American hegemony in the region and seeks to revise the existing status quo. NATO's bombing of the Serbian province of Kosovo in spring 1999, coupled with the accidental strike against the Chinese embassy in Belgrade, exposed a very broad and deep layer of suspicion in China that America is bent on world hegemony. Unchecked, Beijing feared, America might intervene with similar dispatch in sovereign territorial disputes elsewhere, such as that between China and Taiwan. The midair collision over

Hainan Island in early 2001 between a Chinese fighter plane and an American reconnaissance aircraft reinforced this paranoia. At the very least, hard-line military and other groups in Beijing exploit these incidents to accelerate China's military modernization. At worst, China may be preparing for a series of power struggles in Asia.

Whatever its intentions, China is not unalterably belligerent. Its behavior in many respects has been moderate. There has been no challenge to American or western interests on the scale of the Berlin blockade or the proxy war in Korea in 1950. For the most part, China has acted circumspectly in North Korea, Indochina, and recent Indian-Pakistani confrontations. And in recent years, its diplomacy has reached out to promote cooperation with South Korea and Russia. Its acquisition of arms from Russia and its support of Pakistani and wider Islamic efforts to develop nuclear missiles is more ominous. Although China supported the U.S.-led coalition against terrorism in Afghanistan, China's desire to counterbalance U.S. hegemony no doubt remains. Realists in America, who expect such behavior, should not overreact to it. As we discuss next, American power dominates in Asia today, as it never did in central Europe.

Thus far, we have looked only at the structure of relative internal and external identity in Asia. This structure establishes threat. Now we look at the structure of relative power. This structure tells us how dangerous the threat is. Asia possesses some unique features of stability. America's military, especially naval and air power, is preeminent. An imperial order prevails, and such an order is more predictable than anarchy. Under the security treaty with the United States, Japan, despite its impressive power, threatens no one militarily. Russia no longer menaces China's border. Neither China's power nor grievances compare to those of the Soviet Union during the Cold War. Containment in a military sense is inappropriate in Asia—no immediate threat equivalent to Soviet divisions in central Europe in 1947–48 needs to be contained.

By current measures of economic and military power, the United States alone, and especially in combination with Japan, dwarfs China. As tables 4.1 and 6.1 show, China's GNP, despite China's enormous population, is only about one-third that of the United States and Japan combined, even at more reliable purchasing power parity exchange rates. To be sure, projections abound, including some by the respectable World Bank, that purport to show that, at present rates of growth, China's GNP will surpass that of the United States within the next several decades.[28] But the chances of that happening are very small. Countries do not grow at 10 percent per year for long periods of time. In the late 1980s, pundits forecast that Japan would grow at 10 percent per year, but in the 1990s, Japan's average growth was less than 1 percent per year. It would be not only wrong but counterproductive to base U.S. policy on such projections. China's military and economic power is growing and bears watching, but this power is not an immediate threat to the United States, as Soviet power was in Europe.

China is a declared nuclear power. It has missiles, both land- and sea-based, that target cities in the United States. At present, these missiles number in the dozens, not the thousands of weapons that characterized the U.S.-Soviet stand-off. But China conducted vigorous nuclear testing from 1992 to 1996 to minia-turize nuclear warheads, which it seeks to deploy eventually on mobile, solid-fuel, silo-busting missiles. And according to initial estimates, this is the area in which China arguably gained most from its systematic pilfering of U.S. nuclear secrets over the past two decades.[29]

China's weapons may not threaten the United States directly, but they do threaten China's neighbors and could complicate U.S. decisions to help defend those neighbors. The Taiwan Strait confrontation in 1995–96 tells us how. When a former Defense Department official and China specialist warned top Chinese military officers in early 1996 (before the strait confrontation in March) that a Chinese attack on Taiwan would provoke an American military response, a senior Chinese officer replied, "No you won't.... In the 1950's, you three times threatened nuclear strikes on China, and you could do that because, we couldn't hit back. Now we can. So you are not going to threaten us again because, in the end, you care a lot more about Los Angeles than Taipei [capital of Taiwan]."[30]

This kind of thinking in Beijing explains the strong Chinese opposition to U.S. plans to develop and deploy national missile defenses. U.S. defenses would potentially nullify China's small number of intercontinental ballistic missiles and provoke Beijing to build a much larger missile force. But this situation is catch-22. If the United States does not deploy missile defenses, it remains defenseless in face of the kind of threat spelled out by the senior Chinese official, except to threaten a devastating retaliatory strike against Chinese cities. What is more, China has reasons to increase its missile capabilities whether or not the United States deploys missile defenses. To deter the United States, China needs an invulnerable second-strike capability. Such a capability requires enough missiles to survive a U.S. first strike. This number is considerably greater than what China currently has, although the final number may be larger still if Chinese missiles have to survive a first strike and also penetrate U.S. missile defenses.

China is also modernizing its conventional capabilities. It has 2.2 million men under arms and is reconfiguring its forces to deploy rapidly and fight wars of shorter duration along and beyond its border. It aspires to develop a blue-water navy (with aircraft carriers) and long-range bomber capability.[31] It has installed naval and air facilities in the South China Sea, Hainan Island, the Paracel Islands (which it seized from Vietnam in 1974), and the Spratly Islands (which it claimed, along with the Senkaku Islands, in 1992). It is building a railroad link through Myanmar to the Bay of Bengal. And it operates a listening post on Coco Island, a possession of Myanmar in the Indian Ocean.[32] The size of its total military budget is unknown, but conservative estimates place it in the range of $30–40 billion, more than the published figures of approximately $10 billion.[33] In fiscal year 2001, China increased its defense budget by 17 percent, the twelfth year of double-digit growth in military outlays.

The most ominous buildup is taking place in the area of the Taiwan Strait. As of 2001, China has deployed three hundred ballistic missiles on its side of the strait and was adding fifty missiles more per year. It has also strengthened its army and naval forces in the area. As Chas W. Freeman, a China expert, concludes, "China's armed forces have begun a decade-long effort to acquire the capabilities and do the planning required to have a serious chance of overwhelming Taiwan's formidable defenses."[34] Although China still lacks important assets (intelligence, air refueling, and amphibious equipment) to conduct an invasion of Taiwan, a Pentagon study reported that its buildup could give it an "overwhelming advantage" over Taiwan as early as 2005.[35]

None of these capabilities approaches those of the United States, nor will it in the future. China is still a poor country; its economy is not the juggernaut some believe it to be. And if China spends heavily on military equipment, it will reduce its economic potential even further. Still, China's military capabilities dwarf those of its immediate neighbors (including Japan, at least in the nuclear area) and have sparked an arms race in Asia.[36] If the United States fails to respond to these military changes or, worse, withdraws from the Asian balance of power, the "cork in the bottle," a term once coined by a U.S. commander to refer to the U.S. military presence in Asia, may indeed pop out.

Four seismic fault lines threaten to pop the cork out of the bottle, even if America stays. The most volatile is North Korea. The one with the most direct consequences for U.S.-Chinese relations is Taiwan. The third is China's growing presence and interest in the South China Sea, south Asia, the Indian Ocean, and, because of a growing dependence on imported energy, the Middle East. The fourth is China's relations with Russia.

Consider first the situation in North Korea. The volatility of this situation is truly breathtaking. After test-firing missiles over Japan in 1998 and engaging in a naval gun battle with South Korea in 1999, North Korea suddenly and unexpectedly agreed in June 2000 to a summit meeting with South Korea. The two leaders met in Pyongyang and began a limited program of family exchanges and economic cooperation. Heartening though it is, this breakthrough has not changed any of the facts on the ground, in North Korea or along the highly militarized border between North and South Korea. In 2000, in the midst of the summit euphoria, North Korea conducted its largest military exercises in years.

North Korea is a completely totalitarian society, dominated by the cult of a top leader who is apparently deified even beyond the likes of Mao and Stalin. Although the county is starving, it has a huge military (1.1 million men in arms out of a population of 20 million, the largest per capita military in the world), which is poised in a state of extreme readiness to invade South Korea within a matter of hours. North Korea also has a program to develop nuclear weapons. In 1993, it threatened to withdraw from the Nuclear Non-Proliferation Treaty. When the United States insisted on inspecting facilities suspected of producing nuclear materials, the confrontation almost led to war. The crisis was defused in October 1994 when North Korea signed a framework agreement to freeze the operation and construction of graphite nuclear reactors, which produce weapons-grade plutonium, and the United States, Japan, and South Korea agreed to build and finance in their place light-water reactors, which do not produce weapons-grade materials. From 1994 to 2000, North Korea staged a series of crises with its nuclear weapons and missile programs to extort more food, fuel, and financial aid from the United States and others. Although it suspended production of nuclear materials and the testing of ballistic missiles, North Korea continued to develop missiles that could eventually target Alaska and Hawaii and admitted shipping missile technology to Iran, Pakistan, Iraq, and Syria. Despite its economic collapse, it has not reduced its enormous military expenditures and battle-ready deployments along the tense border with South Korea. In effect, the United States and its allies have been paying North Korea not to make the situation worse, rather than requiring North Korea to make the situation better by reducing its military forces on the border.

Why does this situation persist? All the countries involved, including perhaps North Korea itself, hope to avoid war, but none is particularly eager to see a quick solution to the Korean problem. For China, such an outcome might confirm U.S. power on China's border, especially if U.S. forces remain in the southern part of Korea after reunification (as they did in the western part of Germany after German reunification). For South Korea, reunification would be extremely costly and politically disruptive.[37] For Japan, reunification might mean a wave of refugees and huge outlays of foreign aid. And for the United States, it would call into question the long-term need for American forces in Korea and, by extrapolation, perhaps in Japan as well. Consequently, the principal parties prefer more gradual improvements.

This configuration of interests probably explains the at times unseemly willingness of all parties, especially the United States, to tolerate inexcusable behavior on the part of the North Koreans and to postpone the hard issues into the distant future. Meanwhile, some 37,000 U.S. forces remain directly exposed across the 38th parallel in Korea, and the United States could be involved any day in another land war in Asia. That war would be fought without Japanese combat help, although changes in U.S.-Japan defense guidelines in the late 1990s permit Japan to provide modest logistical support. How China might react to such a war would have profound significance for U.S. interests.

Taiwan is the most incendiary issue in Asia because it threatens to bring the two nuclear powers in the region, China and the United States, into direct confrontation. Taiwan is part of China, although it was occupied by Japan from 1895 to 1945. In 1949, the Nationalist Chinese forces, fleeing communist victory on the mainland, seized control of the island. Today, Taiwan is a separate entity with a thriving, independent economy and an evolving democratic political system. Neither Taipei nor Beijing denies that the island is part of China. They disagree, however, about both the external and internal identity of a single China. The "one country, two systems" formula disguises this disagreement. By advocating state-to-state relations and independence, Taiwan threatens the external or "one country" part of the formula; by insisting on the use of force and rolling back democratization in Hong Kong, China threatens the internal or "two systems" part.

The evolution of democracy in Taiwan also widens the gap between the two systems and pushes the prospect of one country further into the future, after, say, mainland China also liberalizes. For this reason, Beijing has upped the ante, indicating that it might use force not only if Taiwan declares independence, but also if it delays too long to negotiate reunification. Democracy in Taiwan ups the ante for the United States as well. As President Clinton observed in March 2000, whatever happens in Taiwan must now occur with the assent of the people of Taiwan.[38] America has converging identity as well as geostrategic interests at stake. If it fails to support Taiwan should Beijing provoke a crisis, U.S. commitments to other democracies in the region would look suspect, and Washington's ability to persuade the U.S. Congress and people to support the U.S. presence in Asia would revert to a more crass balance-of-power logic, which has never been enough to motivate American power except in case of direct threat.

When Washington normalized relations with Beijing in 1978, it severed the bilateral defense treaty with Taiwan, concluded in 1954. It withdrew American troops, but retained the right to sell limited quantities of defensive arms to Taipei. Congress passed the Taiwan Relations Act, which supported arms sales and declared that any resort to force or other forms of coercion (such as a blockade) by China against Taiwan would constitute a threat to peace in the Pacific and cause grave concern in the United States. Since then, Beijing has pressed Washington to terminate arms sales, while Washington has pressed Beijing to forswear the use of force against Taiwan. In April 2001, the United States approved the biggest sale of defensive weapons to Taiwan since the early 1990s. This decision, coming on the heels of the downing of an American reconnaissance plane off the coast of China, raised U.S.-Chinese tensions to new levels.[39]

If China eventually incorporates Taiwan, as it has Hong Kong, China will sit astride the East and South China seas. This is the third seismic fault line threatening stability in Asia. These bodies of water northeast and southwest of Taiwan are the main highway for commerce and communications in the region. Japanese exports and raw materials, including all of its oil imports, flow up and down this highway. The U.S. Seventh Fleet patrols the sea-lanes. Choke points exist at the narrow Straits of Malacca between Malaysia, Singapore, and Indonesia and the Lombok Straits in Indonesia, used by heavier oil tankers. China's explosive growth is concentrated in the coastal areas along these sea-lanes. This growth is demanding larger amounts of energy. In late 1993, China became, for the first time, a net oil importer and, by the year 2010, expects to import as much as 3.0 million barrels of oil per day, approaching by 2015 a level close to current Japanese oil imports of 4.5 million barrels per day.[40]

Thus, expanding commerce, as well as geostrategic interests, ensures a Chinese presence on the high seas, reaching in the case of oil imports, through the Indian Ocean, all the way to the Persian Gulf and Middle East. In 1992, China passed a maritime law that laid claim to 80 percent of the South China Sea, including portions of the Spratly Islands that are also claimed by Malaysia, the Philippines, Vietnam, and Brunei; and, in the East China Sea, the Senkaku Islands, which Japan also claims. By some estimates, this area may contain as much as 65 billion tons of oil and gas reserves.[41] China's military push into the Paracel and Spratly islands derives in part from this prospect of oil and gas deposits. Its search for outlets in the Indian Ocean, confrontation with Vietnam in Indochina, rivalry with India in South Asia, and arms sales in the Middle East, including nuclear and missile technology—all reflect the appetite of a spreading power that needs resources and seeks influence among the countries that control these resources.

The fourth seismic fault line threatening stability in Asia is China's interior border with Russia. This border traces a long arc across the north and west of China from Russia to Mongolia to the central Asian states—it is the old border with the former Soviet Union, which was China's most pressing concern during the Cold War and which led to strategic alignment with the United States. The western part of this border now traces a frontier with the newly independent republics of Tajikistan, Kyrgyzstan, and Kazakhstan. This interior area of China, the Xinjiang Province, is sparsely populated and contains most of China's Muslim minorities. It also contains the Tarim Basin, China's largest potential indigenous source of oil and gas. The central Asian republics next door harbor further major oil resources and represent obvious land routes for pipelines.

At the beginning of the twenty-first century, this fault line is inactive. In the 1990s, China and Russia demarcated and demilitarized the interior border. They also signed agreements with the central Asian republics to guarantee borders, reduce arms, and limit military exercises. Russia sold arms to China, and rhetorically the two countries cooperated to denounce hegemonism in Asia, a code word for American dominance. China and Russia have a common interest in combating fundamentalist Muslim rebels in central Asia and Afghanistan and signed a pact in Shanghai in 2001 to cooperate against terrorism and separatism. Muslim insurgency on their border is the equivalent of ethnic violence in the former Yugoslavia on the border of Europe. Thus, Russian-Chinese cooperation in the Asian periphery need not signal heightened conflict with the United States any more than U.S.-EU cooperation on the European periphery caused new conflicts with Russia. Russian-Chinese cooperation is no substitute for their links with the West. Trade between the two countries is minuscule compared to their dependence on the United States and other G-7 countries, and unstable domestic politics in either country could once again spark new frictions between them.[42]

The military fault lines in Asia are dangerous, but they are also diffuse. They have no core, such as the central front in Europe during the Cold War, and they involve more ambiguity than defense arrangements in Europe, both toward potential adversaries (e.g., under what conditions the United States will defend Taiwan) and among allies (e.g., whether and how Japan will assist the United States in conflicts surrounding Japan). For all these reasons, America deals with Asian security threats on a piecemeal and bilateral basis. But bilateral initiatives often catch allies and adversaries by surprise; they conflict with one another, as when U.S. initiatives toward Japan concern China or vice versa. And they are no longer compatible with changing identity and power structures. Bilateralism ignores the emerging security community with Japan and other democracies in the region, and it places the United States ultimately on a collision course with rising Chinese power.

Multilateralizing Security Ties

A strategy more consistent with evolving structures would reposition America's military profile. It would capitalize on converging identities to create a greater sense of collective security and confidence among democratic countries in the region. This confidence, in turn, would underwrite more vigorous economic initiatives toward other countries, such as China, whose identities continue to diverge and whose power, without such economic engagement, might be threatening in the future.

This repositioning involves three simultaneous steps to multilateralize security relations. The first and most crucial step is to trilateralize security treaties with Japan and South Korea, reinforced by the South Pacific democracies of Australia and New Zealand. The second step is to close the gap in security expectations between this core alliance and south and southeast Asia (India and ASEAN). And the third step is to bridge the security gap with China.

The first step, trilateralizing security ties with Japan and South Korea, has two purposes—one external and one internal. The external purpose is to deter the use of force by either China or North Korea. This purpose can be achieved quietly and proceed simultaneously with rapprochement with China. The internal purpose is to accent and deepen U.S. solidarity with the new democracies in Asia and encourage these new democracies to reconcile their historical animosities. This purpose can be pursued more openly and calls eventually for formalizing alliance ties among democratizing states in Asia. This objective of formal multilateral alliance is not urgent, but it is as vital in the long run for new democracies in Asia as NATO expansion is for new democracies in Europe. Alliance cements in the minds of the people of democracies that these countries are safe not only against the resurgence of extremist, especially military, groups in their own societies but also against the threat or use of force in their relations with one another.

America's allies in Asia are not themselves allies. Japan and South Korea have no commitments to help one another. Because of its constitution, Japan cannot contribute significantly to the defense of South Korea, but, even if it could, South Korea would not be particularly comfortable with such help. The two nations remain deeply divided over historical atrocities. Their external identities diverge, even as their internal identities converge toward democracy. A trilateral initiative by the United States would reinforce the internal convergence and encourage both countries to accelerate external reconciliation. Exchanges of all sorts could be expanded, including large-scale student exchanges, sister city programs, joint business, parliamentary and governmental contacts, and high-level diplomatic initiatives to heal historical wounds. Franco-German reconciliation in the 1960s is a model. Many experts, American as well as Japanese and Korean, will object. They will argue that this is not America's business, Asia is not Europe, and economic interactions are sufficient to bridge political differences. These objections are unconvincing. Neither deeper economic integration nor military cooperation is possible without greater political trust. This political offensive should be conducted visibly and energetically.

The trilateralization of defense ties can proceed more gradually and less visibly. These ties are not intended to threaten anyone, let alone contain China. They are intended, in the first instance, to preserve a credible defense commitment against North Korea. And they are intended to preempt the use of force in Asia's vital sea-lanes, where various countries have territorial claims: China on Taiwan, the Senkaku Islands, and the South China Sea; and Japan and South Korea on Takeshima Island in the Sea of Japan. Most important, and this is above all in China's interest, trilateral ties are intended to preempt independent nuclear aspirations in South Korea and Japan and prepare a more cooperative, localized security framework for the day when Korea is reunited.

In 1994–95 Japan revised and adopted a new National Defense Program Outline (its chief military document), and in 1996 Japan and the United States signed a joint security declaration and negotiated a new set of guidelines under the U.S.-Japan Security Treaty. These changes, passed by the Japanese Diet in April 1999, enable Japan to provide significant logistical and non-combat support for conflicts in "areas surrounding Japan" (not named in the guidelines, but including Korea and possibly Taiwan) and authorize low-key military and logistical exercises between the United States and Japan.[43] Although a strict interpretation of Japan's peace constitution permits military (including noncombat) activities only in the case of an attack against Japan, Japan relaxed this interpretation in the 1990s and participated in UN peace-keeping activities in Cambodia, Mozambique, Rwanda, and East Timor.[44] In addition, in response to Chinese and North Korean missile launches, the United States and Japan began in 1998 joint research on a ship-based theater missile defense (TMD) system, which would not only protect Japan, but might also cover the island of Taiwan. This program should be developed apace, but the United States and its allies might agree to open and even share TMD technology if China and North Korea accept verifiable commitments to stop and reduce their ballistic missile programs.[45]

Quietly, Japan and South Korea have also initiated military contacts. In 1995, the two countries began joint training exercises for peacekeeping missions and conducted naval exchange programs. In 1997, they inaugurated a formal Military Information Consultative System, and, in 1999, they carried out a joint naval drill in the sea-lanes between their respective territories. South Korea halted all of these military contacts in July 2001, protesting the way a new Japanese school textbook glossed over Japanese wartime atrocities in Korea.[46] The suspension suggests how fragile relations are between Asia's two most important democracies and how critical the U.S. role remains.

The United States, Japan, and South Korea have collaborated since 1998 on policy toward North Korea in the Trilateral Coordination Group, and officials have proposed formal trilateral consultative meetings on broader policies among defense and foreign ministers of the three countries.[47] Closer consultation among trilateral parliamentary leaders might also be helpful. Trilateral relations are the key to resolving both the Korean question and long-term stability with China. Just as NATO proved indispensable to reunite Germany peacefully and stabilize post-unity relations in Europe, a virtual, if not formal, trilateral alliance among the United States, Japan, and South Korea is indispensable as the bedrock of peaceful evolution in Asia.

China strenuously objects to this deepening and widening of U.S.-Japanese-South Korean alliance relationships. For Chinese officials, a trilateral alliance smacks of containment and reduces China's military leverage in the Taiwan Strait. But China's use of force against a democratic Taiwan would be far more destabilizing in Asia than a responsible balance of power to prevent such use. A failure to counter China's missile threat in the Taiwan Strait would undermine America's defense commitments in Korea and even in Japan. And U.S. alliances do not prevent China from changing the status quo peacefully. China has to face a simple choice: Is it better to manage the gradual normalization of Japanese and South Korean military activities in the context of an alliance with the United States, which stabilizes the Asian region, or is it preferable to deal with Japanese and South Korean remilitarization outside the U.S. alliance and face possible open rivalries with Japan and the two (or one) Koreas? Given the deep-seated animosities among the key east Asian countries, American military power may be less threatening to China than the alternatives.

The second step in multilateralizing security relations is to extend security cooperation to south and southeast Asia. ASEAN was founded in 1967 as an economic association among smaller countries—the Philippines, Indonesia, Malaysia, Singapore, and Thailand. Brunei, Cambodia, Laos, Vietnam, and Burma joined later. In the 1980s, ASEAN began to discuss political issues, particularly in connection with the situation in Cambodia. In 1989, it launched the ASEAN Post-Ministerial Conference (PMC), which involves discussions, after regular ASEAN meetings, with the United States, Japan, South Korea, Canada, Australia, New Zealand, and the European Union. In 1993, partly in response to China's claims in the South China Sea, the PMC discussed security issues for the first time and created a still wider forum for security and confidence-building talks, the ASEAN Regional Forum (ARF), which includes China, Russia, and since 2000 North Korea.

The PMC security discussions provide a vital link between the trilateral core of northeast Asia and the smaller countries of southeast Asia. And they provide this link without tying these smaller countries too closely to either U.S. or Japanese military power. The PMC also draws in other U.S. allies with defense commitments in the region, particularly Australia, which signed a security agreement with Indonesia in 1995 and is part of a Five Power Defense Arrangement in the region with Great Britain, New Zealand, and the former British colonies, Malaysia and Singapore. Informally, some security cooperation already takes place in this larger context.[48] Thus, the PMC serves as a broad political forum for reviewing both security and economic issues. It might function as a much weaker but nevertheless useful equivalent of U.S.-EU consultations in Europe—consultations among like-minded countries that are separate from but do not preclude wider discussions with less like-minded states, such as Russia in Europe and China in Asia.

Some southeast Asian states, while they require U.S. defense assistance, object to becoming too closely associated with U.S. policies. In 1991, Malaysia proposed an East Asian Economic Group that would have excluded the

United States, and, in 1997, ASEAN actually set up an "ASEAN plus three" (China, Japan, and South Korea) ministerial forum that did exclude the United States. In Asia, as in Europe, the United States is skeptical of such regional groupings because they isolate the United States and may provoke a reduction in U.S. forces. But, in Asia as in Europe, the United States will have to accept such regional groups and learn to work with them. A strategy of concentric multilateralism encompasses these groups in a wider cooperative framework (as NATO does the EU in Europe) and makes it less likely that these groups will compete with or substitute for one another.

The third step in multilateralizing security relations is the ARF, which includes China and North Korea. The ARF has met annually since 1994 and has established four working groups—confidence building, peacekeeping, search and rescue operations, and disaster relief. It aims at greater transparency in military budgets, plans, exercises, and arms sales. It serves the enormously important function of building political confidence and trust in Asia, as the Helsinki process did during the emergence of détente in Europe. It does not substitute for or subtract from concrete defense treaties and commitments, just as Helsinki did not substitute for NATO. Nor does it need to monopolize all negotiations. It should become a place where bilateral, plurilateral, and other types of governmental and nongovernmental negotiations can be vetted and blessed and their implications assessed.[49]

Highest priority in the ARF, as in the case of Helsinki, should go to arms and technology control agreements to cap the spread of nuclear weapons and missile technologies. For this purpose, America needs to upgrade its relations with India, which is a member of ARF. The Cold War divided the United States and India; the United States allied with India's rivals—Pakistan to counter Soviet ambitions in Afghanistan, and China to balance the Soviet Union globally. In turn, India relied on the Soviet Union for arms and other support. These circumstances have changed, yet China continues to provide nuclear and missile technology to Pakistan, the United States gives priority to China over India, and India continues to buy arms from Russia. Meanwhile, the India-Pakistan conflict threatens to engulf the region in nuclear war.

As part of a strategy to curb China's technology exports and moderate India-Pakistan tensions, U.S. policy should become more evenhanded, drawing India, Pakistan, and China into a nuclear and arms control regime in Asia that reduces tensions and creates a framework for future peaceful nuclear programs in Japan and the two Koreas. In 1995, ten southeast Asian nations concluded a nuclear-free-zone treaty. The United States and China opposed the treaty; and such a treaty is undoubtedly premature, given the need for U.S. naval deployments in the region. Nevertheless, the nuclear powers need to consider a region-wide nuclear organization for Asia, an Asiatom (patterned after Euratom in Europe), that could safeguard and support future civilian nuclear programs.[50]

The security multilateralization recommended here cannot be put in place overnight, and there will be many pitfalls along the way.[51] But, given the new structural realities in Asia, it is clearly the right direction for U.S. policy. It anchors the U.S. presence in Asia in an emerging democratic security community, and it provides a long-term strategy to narrow differences with nondemocratic countries. In this sense, concentric multilateralism goes beyond traditional balance-of-power politics in Asia but stops well short of a collective security system that treats all counties, democratic and nondemocratic, alike.

Asia's Economic Miracle and the U.S. Market

Asia has one of the weakest security communities in the world, yet it also has one of the fastest growing and most interconnected economic communities. Does this mean that a security community is unnecessary for trade and investment ties? Hardly. The view that countries trade to get rich, whatever the consequences for their security or political values, is not only unduly cynical, it is wrong. Asia's postwar economic success did reflect a political community. The common Soviet threat brought together the external identities of Asian states, even as their internal identities diverged. Now, unless internal commonalities, such as widening democratization, replace external exigencies, Asia's political community will weaken and Asia's economic future will be much less bright than its past.

The old Cold War community in Asia had three principal components, none of which is likely to exist in the future: the bilateral U.S. strategic alliances against the former Soviet Union, which we have just discussed; bilateral access to the U.S. market, first for Japan and then for each subsequent Asian tiger, including, now, China; and an Asian model of development that exploited authoritarian politics at home and technological and industrial advances abroad to power Asia's development. Each of these components needed the others. Without the security alliances, the United States would not have opened its markets so generously to each Asian tiger. Without the unique features of the Asian model of development, the Asian tigers could not have exploited U.S. markets so effectively. And without rapid economic growth, Asia's fragile political community may have splintered, spawning superpower wars like those in Korea and Vietnam.

The move from bilateral to multilateral security ties in Asia would enhance the prospects of multilateral economic arrangements. Such arrangements in Asia are minimal compared to Europe and, as in APEC, reflect a more cautious attitude toward open, competitive trade and investment markets. The fear is that if Asia multilateralizes, it will do so on the basis of the Japanese or Asian model of development, emphasizing state-led industrialization and managed trade and investment markets. The Asian model of development, however, is being radically transformed. It is no longer a viable model and was successful in the first place only because the American model of development existed and opened markets widely to Asian exporters.

Table 6.2 tells much about the history of economic development in Asia after World War II. This development was underwritten in substantial part by access to the U.S. market. As the first group of five columns shows, the United States absorbed at least 10–15 percent and as much as 30–50 percent of the exports of the Asian tigers from the beginning of the 1970s. In 1999, it continued to take in 16–31 percent of these exports, including now also exports from China. This is an astonishingly high dependence on one market over multiple decades, especially when some of the exporters are highly industrialized. Japan, the most industrialized, shipped almost one-third of its exports to the United States in both 1970 and 1999. Revisionist interpretations of Japan's postwar development see these numbers as proof that the United States paid too high an economic price for security benefits in Asia (imports from Asia being evaluated as an economic cost);[52] it opened its market to help unstable allies, but those allies did not reciprocate. After 1970, some Asian exporters, such as South Korea and Hong Kong, reduced their dependence on U.S. markets substantially. But the rest maintained a high degree of dependence, even as Asian markets grew more rapidly in the 1970s and 1980s than U.S. markets.

The middle five columns of table 6.2 show that the proportion of trade Asian countries do with one another grew only modestly during 1970–1999. Except for South Korea and Hong Kong, other countries did approximately 30–60 percent of their trade with one another in 1970 and approximately 40–60 percent in 1999. Some commentators saw this modest regionalization of trade as the harbinger of a new Asian trading bloc led by Japan. Japanese investments in Asian countries grew rapidly, as Japan sought lower cost platforms in Asian countries to maintain its export competitiveness.[53] But, unlike U.S. industrial expansion in Asia in the 1970s, it was argued, Japanese overseas plants did not export back to Japan (as U.S. subsidiaries in Asia exported back to the United States). They exported instead to other Asian countries and to the United States. The result, it was feared, was an Asianization of the Japanese development model. The entire region, under Japanese leadership, was reorganizing as an export platform, shipping goods to the U.S. market, not only from Japan but also from other Asian countries as well. This export push from Asia, it was believed, came at the expense of U.S. exports to Asia.[54]

This Asianization thesis is not borne out by the facts. I do not dispute that an increasing share of production and trade in Asia is now regional. It would be startling if this were not the case, given the progressive and regionwide development of Asian countries. As Edward Lincoln, an economist at the Brookings Institution and longtime student of U.S.-Asian economic relations,

Table 6.2. Asian Countries' Share of Exports to Indicated Markets

	United States					Asia[a]					Industrial Europe[b]				
	1970	1980	1990	1994	1999	1970	1980	1990	1994	1999	1970	1980	1990	1994	1999
China[c]	1.4	6.4	8.4	17.7	21.5	42.5	59.6	68.8	59.4	51.3	18.2	15.8	10.3	13.2	16.0
Hong Kong	35.6	26.1	24.1	23.2	23.9	25.0	28.7	48.1	52.8	51.8	25.2	26.7	19.7	16.0	17.0
Indonesia	15.7	19.6	13.1	16.8	16.0	62.7	66.4	69.5	58.4	60.5	29.5	6.6	12.2	17.5	15.4
Japan	31.1	24.5	31.7	29.9	31.0	29.0	27.3	34.2	42.5	40.0	12.0	15.9	21.7	16.3	18.7
Malaysia	20.0	16.4	17.0	21.2	21.9	41.1	56.4	61.8	58.1	56.6	22.3	18.0	15.6	14.5	15.9
Philippines	38.8	27.7	38.5	38.8	30.0	42.5	43.9	39.5	39.2	46.5	9.6	18.3	18.8	17.9	19.2
Singapore	11.1	12.5	21.3	18.8	19.1	54.5	55.5	54.4	60.3	59.2	19.9	13.2	15.5	14.1	12.4
South Korea	46.7	26.4	29.9	21.4	20.5	10.1	32.5	38.7	47.7	47.2	8.6	20.0	16.2	11.7	16.0
Taiwan	38.1	34.1	32.4	26.2	25.4	37.8	28.7	38.2	49.4	48.7	10.1	15.8	18.2	13.9	16.7
Thailand	13.6	12.7	22.7	23.2	21.5	60.5	42.8	41.1	48.8	52.4	19.7	28.5	19.5	17.7	17.8

Note: Percent of total exports.

[a] Includes Japan, Australia, New Zealand, and the Asia group in DOT Statistical Yearbook; and the Asia region in Taiwan Statistical Data Book.

[b] Includes Austria, Belgium, Denmark, Finland, France, Germany, Greece, Ireland, Italy, Luxembourg, the Netherlands, Norway, Portugal, Spain, Sweden, Switzerland, and the United Kingdom in DOT Statistical Yearbook; and the Europe region in Taiwan Statistical Data Book.

[c] 1970 figures from 1972.

Source: Direction of Trade (DOT) Statistics Yearbook (Washington, D.C.: International Monetary Fund, 1970–2000); data for Taiwan from *Taiwan Statistical Data Book,* 2000 (Taipei: Council for Economic Planning and Development, 2000).

writes, there is "something that could be termed a 'soft' economic regionalism centered on Japan," in which are evident both more trade among Asian countries and a larger regional trade role for Japan.[55] But, as Lincoln hastily adds, this phenomenon does not add up to a regional bloc that discriminates against the United States. Japan's exports as a share of world exports actually fell from 10.5 percent in 1986 to 7.5 percent in 2000.[56] Meanwhile, Japan's imports from overseas subsidiaries grew substantially from 4.0–4.6 percent of total imports in 1986–90 to 11.2 percent in 1996. And although Japan's foreign investment in Asia grew rapidly, it grew even faster in the United States (at an annual pace of 45–50 percent in the 1990s, compared to 20–25 percent in Asia).[57]

The correct way to read table 6.2 is to note the astonishing continued dependence of Japanese and Asian trade on the U.S. market. (This bilateral trade dependence mirrors the bilateral security framework in Asia—security is vital for trade.) After 40 years, the United States still absorbs over 30 percent of Japanese exports and roughly 20–25 percent of the exports of other Asian countries (30 percent for the Philippines). After the United States, which took 31 percent of Japan's exports in 1999, Japan's next most significant export markets were Taiwan, South Korea, and Hong Kong at a share of 6.0–6.5 percent each, less than one-fourth the share accounted for by the United States. For South Korea and Hong Kong, which shipped 20.5 and 23.9 percent, respectively, of their exports to the United States in that same year, the next most significant market was Japan at a share of 11.0 and 5.9 percent, respectively. For Singapore, Malaysia, Thailand, and China, dependence on the U.S. market actually grew from 1970 to 1999, in China's case reaching almost 30 percent in 2000.

Asian growth has not diminished American influence in Asia. A country's market is its negotiating leverage. When it comes to negotiating trade agreements in Asia, no country has more negotiating leverage than the United States.

Thus, the Asian development model was closely linked to the American model. The American model, sometimes called the Anglo-American model, of economic growth is an open one that emphasizes liberal trade and competitive business relations. The Asian model is a protected system that emphasizes government-targeted trade and corporatist business relations. The Asian model succeeded as much because the U.S. market was open as because skillful bureaucrats in Japan and other Asian countries chose correct policies. Advocates of the Asian development model not only miss this point, they negate it when they advocate U.S. government targeting. Without the open U.S. market, there would have been no Asian economic miracle. And if the United States had emulated the Asian development model, there would have been no open U.S. market.

End of Asian Model

The U.S. market was also open to Latin American countries, and they did not fare as well as the Asian tigers. So the Asian model of development did have something to do with Asia's success. This model had three principal features: government selection and stimulation, through subsidized and long-term loans and grants, of leading industrial and technological sectors, usually accompanied by side payments to industries that were not selected or favored by government policies; government protection of home markets for all sectors, not only through multiple layers of direct government trade and investment restrictions, but also through the indirect, personalized, closed, and consensus style of bargaining characteristic of Asia's business culture; and an all-out, government-promoted export drive, often at subsidized (or dumping) prices to penetrate foreign markets and accumulate market share. The model depended on several political conditions. Authoritarian governments, or in the case of Japan highly centralized democratic ones, extracted massive savings from citizens at low interest rates in return for broad-scale educational and employment benefits. These savings were then channeled, again at below-market rates, to the favored industrial sectors that produced primarily for export, not for domestic consumption. Consumers and workers paid a high price for this model. Exports constrained domestic consumption, and the resulting domestic savings earned below-market returns. In addition, as Lester Thurow notes, Japan's workforce got the lowest share of national income among the five leading industrial countries, and in the fifteen years prior to 1992, wages rose in Japan only half as fast as the rate of productivity.[58] Today, Japan's aging population faces an underfunded pension system largely locked up in a government-controlled postal savings system that pays paltry interest rates. Even much-valued social benefits, such as lifetime employment, had to be trimmed back.

Why exactly did the Asian model of industrial development work? Here there are almost as many answers as there are analysts.[59] Most of the hype about the Asian model attributes the success to skillful government direction. In the early 1990s, when the United States was recovering slowly from the economic recession of 1990–91, many studies proposed government targeting as a solution for U.S. woes. With its competitive style of capitalism, the United States, it was argued, was out of step with the future. The Asian model was inherently superior.[60]

Time, a sustained recession in Japan, and a severe Asian financial crisis have produced a more critical evaluation of the Asian model. The model did succeed in its place and time, but it was no model for other countries, especially technological leaders. The model, in fact, was closely connected with the particular stage of development Asian countries were passing through. All of these countries were undergoing rapid manufacturing development in which they were either initiating industrialization or, in the case of Japan, aggressively catching up with industrial and manufacturing standards around the world. They were followers, not leaders, in world markets. The leading sectors and technologies into which they sought to advance were known; these sectors did not have to be invented. Instead, in most cases, the Asian countries simply imported and improved on technology from abroad, by licenses in the case of Japan or by foreign direct investment in the case of China today. This strategy did not require particularly smart or sophisticated bureaucrats (that is, compared to bureaucrats in other countries). It required sound macroeconomic policies, which Asian countries generally pursued (including, for many Asian countries, exchange rates pegged to the dollar, which disciplined monetary policy), and a consensus-oriented business and political culture, which Asian countries generally have.

As Japan and other Asian tigers moved up the ladder of industrial and technological sophistication, however, the model began to falter. Dominant market shares in existing technologies, emphasized by the Asian model, were supposed to lead to first-mover advantage in developing new technologies. But once Asian countries drew closer to the technological frontiers, they no longer knew what technologies to target and develop. As Scott Callon, a critic of the model, notes, "funding concentrated on 'catch-up' targeting of known technologies was much easier than having to push out along an uncertain technological frontier." At that frontier, "it was no longer clear where and how to spend the money, since future technologies by definition did not exist yet and it was very hard at times to figure out which technologies would prove to be important and which would not."[61] The Asian model was not well suited to inventing new information technologies or developing new applications for the Internet. It is a lesson that Asia is still learning.

The Achilles' heel of the Asian model proved to be its financial system and the high levels of investments for which it was so widely admired.[62] Throughout the 1980s and early 1990s, advocates of the Asian model pointed out how much Asian countries saved and invested, compared to the United States. What they did not point out was how much of that investment was redundant and unproductive. Studies in 1996 by the respected global consulting firm McKinsey and Co. showed convincingly that the productivity of capital in Japan (as well as in Germany) was only two-thirds that in the United States.[63] Although Japan invested almost twice a much as the United States in terms of the percentage of its GNP and used more labor, it got back far lower returns than the United States did from smaller investments. Other Asian countries got back even less. The so-called Asian miracles, Paul Krugman, a well-publicized economist, concluded, were not miracles at all. They were simply the consequence of "an astonishing mobilization of resources—driven by extraordinary growth in inputs like labor and capital rather than by gains in efficiency."[64]

The inefficient use of capital brought on the financial crisis that crippled Japan in the early 1990s and spread to other Asian countries in 1997. Forced savings at low interest rates generated massive overinvestment in manufacturing capacity and speculation in land and real estate holdings. Banks become overextended, and central banks hesitated to raise interest rates for fear of exposing mounting bad bank loans. With exchange rates tied to the dollar, Asian countries such as South Korea, the Philippines, Malaysia, and Thailand borrowed cheaply abroad. Foreign banks stepped in willingly, unaware in some cases of the mounting bad debt (which was not disclosed under the crony banking system in these countries) and convinced in other cases that Asia's economic expansion was unstoppable. The bubble inflated for some time, but then it burst. Banks and other financial institutions stopped lending and propping up real estate and stock markets, which had become highly leveraged against speculative loans. Foreign money fled, and local institutions repatriated their investments abroad to cover mounting liquidity requirements.[65] Japan and other Asian countries responded by expanding exports. But, for countries with tied exchange rates, a rising dollar in 1996–97 led to overvalued currencies and deteriorating trade accounts. Fixed rates could not be sustained, and currencies depreciated. Competitive depreciations unleashed a scramble for foreign markets and put the U.S. market, the only market growing steadily throughout the 1990s, directly in the crosshairs of another Asian export assault.

The next assault of Asian exports on American markets, however, is likely to be the last. Not only is the United States unlikely to permit it (although Japan has continued to run a huge trade surplus throughout its sustained recession), but the Asian development model is at the end of its rope. What Asian economies need, more than anything else, is thorough-going structural reform, especially in the financial and banking sectors. Japan has run out the string of stimulus policies, both interest rate reductions and fiscal deficits. All that is left is deregulation or eventually insolvency. At the beginning of the millennium, Japan is still struggling to make the choice.[66]

What lessons should America draw from the Asian crisis? Generally speaking, the old debate continues, but in a different form. Those who are sympathetic to the Asian development model blame capital markets and the IMF for the Asian crisis. According to this school of thought, short-term borrowing, not fundamental flaws in the Asian economies, created instability and precipitated the currency crises. The IMF stepped in and compounded the problem by requiring excessive devaluations and restrictive macroeconomic policies.[67] Those who are critical of the Asian model trace the problem to structural deficiencies, particularly in the banking system. According to this school, international capital markets exploited these deficiencies, but did not create them. The IMF stepped in to provide emergency liquidity in return for concessions from both borrowers and lenders that improved creditworthiness.[68]

There are problems in private capital markets, such as the moral hazard that private banks lend excessively because they know the IMF will step in to prevent default. And IMF policy conditions for loans are certainly not above criticism. But, again and again, countries that follow the IMF's advice fare better than those that do not. The problem is not economics; it is politics. Within as well as among countries, the fight goes on between special interest groups that stand to lose from economic change that improves efficiency and those that stand to gain. The United States and international institutions need to be sensitive to these domestic conflicts—as Asian countries democratize, these conflicts are, after all, the substance of liberal, pluralistic democratic politics. But donor countries do not have to abandon good sense and stop advocating policies that they know work in the long run to raise the standard of living of most, if not eventually all, domestic groups.

A Plurilateral Trade Strategy

America's open market gave birth to modern Asia, and the U.S. market remains the best hope to bring the last Asian tiger, China, into the peaceful and prosperous world of industrialized nations. To keep its market open, however, America needs better access to Asian markets. For that reason, it should persist in a strategy to reform and liberalize Asian economies. It should do so by working across a broad front, using regional and global as well as bilateral initiatives to encourage adaptation to the new information economy. At first, it can continue to press the bilateral agenda it has emphasized in recent years, particularly with the Asian democracies of Japan, South Korea, Taiwan, and the Philippines. But what bilateral negotiations gain in focus, they lose in leverage.[69] And bilateralism is now metastasizing in Asia—Japan, Singapore, South Korea, and other Asian countries are discussing bilateral free trade agreements with an enthusiasm that has accelerated after the failure of the WTO talks in Seattle in December 1999.[70] To regain leverage and balance, the United States has to complement bilateral talks with a more vigorous and visible regional and multilateral strategy. The APEC is an ideal forum to revitalize free trade talks with Japan, and WTO is the proper forum to press ahead with the slow emancipation of the Chinese economy and society.

In contrast to its bilateral diplomacy, U.S. policy in the APEC forum has been pusillanimous. The United States was dragged reluctantly into the APEC forum,[71] and it remains in that organization with no consistent strategy to deepen Asian-Pacific integration beyond the symbolism of initiatives, such as the leaders' summits inaugurated by President Clinton in Seattle in 1993—a symbolism that Asia craves and is happy to focus on. In APEC negotiations, the United States has deferred to Asian lowest-common-denominator consensus building and encouraged Japan to take the lead in opening Asian markets. Predictably, little of substance has happened. APEC agreed in 1991 to create a free trade area over the next fifteen years, but pushed the goal back in 1994 to the year 2010 for advanced countries and 2020 for developing countries. Even these goals are no longer realistic. Overall, APEC has focused almost exclusively on process, not substance. The annual meeting of leaders begun in 1993 created numerous working groups and a small secretariat in Singapore. But since 1993, it has spent much of its time wrangling over the techniques to govern trade negotiations. The symbolism of APEC is not to be dismissed. China attends the leaders' meeting with Taiwan's economics minister (although not with its president, which is why the meetings are not called summits), and the procedures APEC has developed are needed in a region that lacks a basic multilateral infrastructure. Nevertheless, APEC is going nowhere unless the United States makes it a more central instrument of its trade diplomacy.

Neither Japan nor any other Asian country can lead in economic areas until these countries themselves become more open. The yen, for example, has not challenged the dollar's role in Asian or global trade, despite repeated predictions that it would. The reason is simple. Traders and investors cannot use the yen in Tokyo markets as freely as they can use dollars in New York markets. What is more, Asian countries are reluctant to borrow in yen, instead of dollars, because they cannot export as easily into the Japanese market to pay off yen debt as they can into the U.S. markets to pay off dollar loans. Looking to Japan to lead APEC is therefore a nonstarter.

Instead, the United States should use APEC to further open Japan's market. It can do so by forming minicoalitions with other APEC members. For example, the United States might offer to phase in liberalizing agreements with South Korea and Taiwan if South Korea and Taiwan back U.S. proposals for an immediate or earlier liberalization in Tokyo. Similar bargaining strategies might be applied to other sectors, always aiming to do as much to open Japanese markets for all Asian countries as for U.S. exporters. In this way, the United States can turn APEC from an institution in which Japan poses as a free trader, criticizing American unilateralism and bilateralism, to one in which Japan is put on the spot to act as a free trader.

China is one of the lowest-income yet fastest-growing countries in Asia. As such, it presents a unique dilemma for U.S. trade policy. China's entry into the WTO does not resolve the issue of opening China's market; the battle over how China enforces WTO rules is still to be fought. Nor does economic engagement with China solve the issue of China's political development. With the help of the WTO, China may simply become a more powerful, repressive country.

In dealing with China, American democracy is messy. No government strategy can avoid the numerous and committed interest groups that weigh in on China policy. But government policy does have the obligation to outline the larger goals. In the case of China, as this chapter has argued, the larger goal is to balance China's potential military and political aggressiveness in order to encourage a gradual evolutionary convergence between China, on the one hand, and the United States and its Asian democratic friends, on the other. The latter goal cannot be achieved by cutting trade and commercial contacts with China. And if the United States does reduce such contacts and its democratic friends in Asia do not, the United States only weakens its competitive position vis-à-vis Japan and other Asian rivals in Chinese markets. In the end, it also weakens its military position, as quarrels over trade with China divide the allies. Thus, rolling back Chinese trade is not a realistic option.

On the other hand, U.S. trade with China is following a course that has already reached its limits in other Asian countries. China is the latest Asian tiger exploiting unusual access to the American market. In 2000, China enjoyed a $83 billion trade surplus with the United States, larger even than Japan's surplus of $81 billion. The weaknesses of this export-led strategy are beginning to show. China has a government-dominated banking system that pumps out loans to selected enterprises based on government objectives, not market prospects. Big, inefficient state enterprises still produce one-third of China's GDP and, what is worse, employ two-thirds of China's workers. These enterprises manufacture goods that pile up in warehouses. If inventories are subtracted from growth, estimates of recent Chinese growth at the turn of the millennium are 2–3 percent per year, rather than the official 7–8 percent per year. Returns on capital are minuscule. Bad loans in China are estimated at $200 billion, or 20 percent of GDP, and may grow to as much as 55 percent of GDP in 2008.[72]

This overinvestment syndrome is beginning to affect China's export industries. Unlike Japan, China opened its market to foreign investment. Foreign producers charged into special export zones along China's coastal regions. When Asian countries devalued in the financial crisis of 1997, Chinese exports became less competitive. In subsequent years, China increasingly subsidized exports, achieving by one estimate an effective 15 percent devaluation of its currency.[73] Foreign investment remains high, but is coming increasingly at the expense of investment elsewhere in the region, suggesting slower net growth in Asia overall.

The export-led strategy is not only faltering, it has created a huge division in wealth between China's booming coast and its impoverished interior, complicating China's political life. An estimated 100–200 million Chinese have left the interior looking for work in the urban and coastal boomtowns. To date, Chinese economic reforms have compounded the problems. Provincial authorities have become more powerful and resist central government efforts to collect taxes, restrain bank lending, and so on. Cronyism and corruption now dominate local relationships, revealing the weaknesses of the Asian development model at this level as well.

The United States does China no favor by encouraging it to continue down the path of U.S.-market-dependent, export-led growth. It should bargain hard to open China's market and to embed China in a wider network of multilateral trade and investment relations. Above all, the United States needs to be patient. China will not change quickly, and repeatedly threatening retaliation, as the United States did in trade relations with Japan, is self-defeating.

* * *

China is important to U.S. interests in Asia. But it is not that important, either as a threat or as a market. Much more important, given the wide divergences in political cultures and national identities in the rest of Asia, are Japan and the newly democratizing countries of South Korea, Taiwan, the Philippines, Thailand, and, eventually, Indonesia. These countries, along with the mature democracies in Australia and New Zealand and stable, albeit poor, democracies in India and Bangladesh, are the principal nations for an American strategy in Asia. If these relationships falter, especially the ties with Japan, America has no foundation in Asia and can hardly expect to build bridges to the authoritarian states in southeast Asia (Malaysia, Singapore, Vietnam, etc.), let alone to the biggest and potentially most dangerous authoritarian state, China. A strategy of concentric multilateralism can build this more enduring framework and sustain American engagement in Asia for the decades it will require to develop the most populous region of the world.

CHAPTER SEVEN

Beyond Indifference

American Relations with the Developing World

America's foreign policy traditions serve it least well in the developing world. By the "developing world" I refer primarily to the Middle East, Latin America, and Africa. (Developing nations in Asia, on average wealthier and more industrialized than other developing nations, are treated in more detail in chap. 6.) Realism dictates intervention in developing nations only if great-power stakes are involved—keeping European powers out of Latin America, insisting on equal great-power access or an "open door policy" in Asia, and containing Soviet power in Africa and the Middle East. Internationalism fosters the missionary impulse in American foreign policy—pursuing manifest destiny in Asia, Wilsonian democracy in Latin America, and human rights in Africa and the Middle East. Isolationism counsels indifference, confining America's interest to its immediate borders and sea-lanes.

In the post–Cold War world, all of these traditions are obsolete. American power is supreme in the developing world. With the demise of the Soviet Union, there are no great-power conflicts and no need, in realist thinking, to intervene in developing nations.[1] In the absence of counterbalances to American power, internationalism overreaches. America intervenes everywhere—in Haiti, Somalia, Bosnia, Kosovo, Colombia, Panama, and Kuwait. In most of these crises, America's military and moral energies first surged and then sagged. In the absence of persisting threat, America lacks staying power. Before the terrorist attacks on September 11, 2001, the George W. Bush administration looked for ways to trim American commitments in the developing world. After the war against terrorism, the United States may repeat the cycle once again, overreaching and then retreating.

The power and identity approach offers a way out of this morass. It takes account of America's structural preponderance, which allows it to intervene at will, but also emphasizes diverging identities, which limits America's moral right to intervene. It counsels intervention only when U.S. military and moral interests are equally engaged and when U.S. values overlap with those of developing nations or great-power stakes are high. The combination of moral and material interests ensures that the United States is not intervening for frivolous moral reasons (e.g., to feel good morally) or for crass material reasons only (e.g., to secure raw materials). Exceptions to this rule arise in two cases. The first is when American values overlap with those of local nations, such that American intervention reinforces local institutions and values even if America has few material interests at stake (the case, perhaps, in Haiti but not in Somalia). And the second is when great-power moral commitments outside the developing world, such as the Cold War or defense of international law, dictate intervention to protect material interests even if the United States has little in common with local political institutions (the case, perhaps, in the Persian Gulf).

This calculus takes into account several new and crucial realities. First, the U.S. self-image is changing. For almost two centuries, U.S. identity was Eurocentric. Since the mid-1960s, however, a third great wave of immigrants has been arriving, predominantly from Latin America and Asia. America's citizenry is now almost one-third non-European, and this ratio is projected to grow to as much as one-half by 2080. America has cultural reasons to relate more sensitively to developing countries, reasons that go beyond the traditional Eurocentric world of great-power rivalry and universalistic values.

Second, threats to American interests in the developing world now derive less from immediate military confrontations or economic resource requirements and more from political instability. Many developing nations are weak, or what some call "failed" states. They face civil wars and local interstate conflicts, which elevate the significance of military power in these areas and potentially invite future great-power rivalry and intervention. Until other unifying sources of identity emerge to override ethnic and tribal divisions, balancing military power is a reality of life within, between, and outside many developing countries—whether warring factions separate into independent states or remain inside multiethnic states.

Third, democratization, a most promising if distant process, may eventually override ethnic factionalism, interstate animosity, and the resulting threat of great-power intervention. This process is already well advanced in Latin America, which enjoys some features of the democratic peace. It is emerging in key developing nations in Asia, such as South Korea and Taiwan. But it is just beginning in Africa, most important, in South Africa, and is no more than a remote aspiration in the Middle East, except in Israel and perhaps Turkey. If Mexico succeeds in its democratic transformation and the North American Free Trade Agreement (NAFTA) can be expanded, a democratic security community may emerge in the Western Hemisphere over the next several decades. Given the frequent use of military power in this hemisphere over the past several centuries, this development alone would be a major achievement.

Figure 7.1 illustrates graphically the new calculus of power and identity to guide American intervention in developing nations. The vertical axis lays out the material (power) or realist incentives to intervene, from political threats to American interests abroad (such as violations of international law) at the bottom to direct threats to U.S. territory at the top (for more details on the

Figure 7.1. Threats to and Opportunities for American Values and Power
(brackets indicate no U.S. military intervention; parentheses indicate interventions during Cold War; question mark indicates ambiguous commitment)

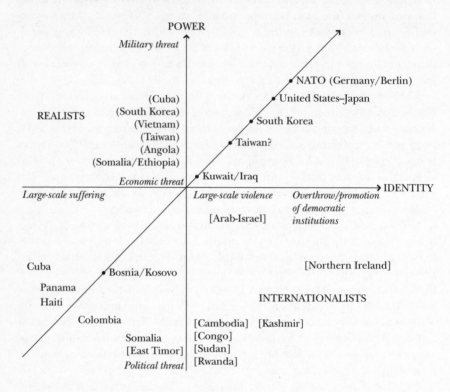

vertical and horizontal axes in Fig. 7.1, see Fig. 1.1 in chapter 1). The horizontal axis depicts nonmaterial (identity) or internationalist incentives to intervene, from large-scale suffering in developing nations (offensive to American values) on the left side to the overthrow of democracy on the right side. When realist incentives dominate, interventions fall in the upper left-hand quadrant. When internationalist incentives dominate, interventions fall in the lower right-hand quadrant. In neither of these quadrants, however, are American material and nonmaterial interests balanced. In the realist quadrant, America's values are sometimes trampled, as in Vietnam; in the internationalist quadrant, America's material strength may be dissipated, if the United States intervenes in any crisis that offends American values.

The diagonal arrow running from the lower left-hand quadrant to the upper right-hand quadrant identifies the line along which American material (power) and nonmaterial (identity) interests are equally engaged. This arrow defines U.S. interventions that are likely to be both supported at home and effective abroad because they involve in equal measure American values and American power. The classic example is America's commitment to defend Germany and western Europe since 1945. This commitment persists even though great-power conflicts have waned because the preservation of a democratic and rich western Europe is central both to American values and to American security. Post–Cold War interventions in developing nations that fall along this line include Bosnia/Kosovo and Kuwait/Iraq. In both cases, America had important strategic interests (threats to stability in Slovenia, Hungary, and other border areas of western Europe, and oil in the Persian Gulf) and moral affinities (identification with democracy in western Europe and Israel). Interventions in Somalia and Rwanda do not fall along this line. Rwanda might have warranted American intervention because genocide was a bigger reality there than it was in Kosovo or Somalia. But Rwanda and Somalia, unlike Kosovo, did not involve strategic stakes for the United States. Even the moral stakes were less, at least in the sense that America's democratic identity converges only weakly with tribal and warlord-dominated politics in eastern and central Africa, whereas it converges strongly with western European nations potentially threatened in the Balkans or Persian Gulf. The danger in Bosnia and Kosovo is that U.S. intervention may drift to the right of the diagonal line. Mission creep might expand U.S. moral commitments beyond the task of ending violence on the border of democratic Europe to that of building multiethnic, democratic societies where the costs (e.g., more forces to integrate and defend ethnic groups) exceed the realistic possibilities.

When global great-power conflicts intensify in developing nations, U.S. interventions get pushed up the vertical axis. That happened during the Cold War, in Korea, Vietnam, Taiwan, Cuba, Central America, Lebanon, and parts of Africa (interventions in parentheses in fig. 7.1). When democratic identities converge between the United States and developing nations, U.S. interventions get pushed to the right side. That is happening now in South Korea and, perhaps, in Taiwan. With the end of the Cold War, superpower conflict in Asia recedes, but American values overlap more with those of the emerging democracies of Asia. Moral stakes rise, while material stakes decline. In the Middle East, materialist incentives remain high because local instability may be just as disruptive as great-power intervention to oil flows. America's moral stake in Israel is real, but wider modernization and political liberalization in the Middle East would better balance the U.S. moral and material interests in this region.

U.S. incentives to intervene in Cuba and the rest of Latin America dropped after the Cold War. With the spread of democratization in Mexico and other Latin American countries, however, the American moral stake increased. No such convergence of identities tempered America's withdrawal from Vietnam or Africa. Once the Cold War stakes were gone, America had little reason to remain. The prospects of U.S. intervention in southeast Asia and Africa in the future, therefore, depend less on abstract claims about universalistic human rights than on the practical progress of democratization in these areas, foremost perhaps in countries such as Thailand, the Philippines, and South Africa.

Latin America

Of all developing areas, Latin America (South America, Central America, and the Caribbean, unless otherwise indicated) is closest to the European and western heritage. Unlike Asia, its culture is largely Christian and individualistic (albeit a more Catholic and paternalistic variety than the Protestant version found in the United States or in some former British and Dutch colonies in the Caribbean). Unlike Africa, it escaped colonialism much earlier, and, although some Latin American countries had slaves, the Latin American people themselves were never formally enslaved.

In light of these facts, U.S. policy toward Latin America is a paradox. Although the region is culturally and politically more like the United States than Asia, Africa, or the Middle East, the United States has related to Latin America more by military and economic than by political or cultural means. It intervened initially to expand and shape the boundaries of the U.S. republic. Mexico absorbed the brunt of U.S. conquest, losing roughly half of its territory in the nineteenth century. But beyond its continental borders, the United States intervened in Latin America mainly to ward off intervention by other great powers. From the Monroe Doctrine to Theodore Roosevelt's corollary to Wilsonian democracy and Cold War containment, the United States said, in effect, to Latin American countries, "manage your affairs so as not to attract foreign intervention, or we will manage those affairs for you." Even the intervention in Colombia to create Panama was driven by extra-regional concerns and the U.S. ascent to global power with a two-ocean navy. Beyond Mexico, Puerto Rico, and Cuba, the United States did not need or want Latin American territory or resources. It never intervened militarily, for example, in South America, where the major resources are. The worst crime of the United States over the years has not been imperialism but indifference, caring about Latin America only if extra-regional powers cared. Its political identification with the republics of the south has always been abstract and awkward.[2]

This pattern of indifference is now being swept away by two forces. The first is the change in the U.S. self-image, which is most dramatic with respect to Latin America. Eighty-six percent of all immigrants to the United States since 1960 have come from Latin America, two-thirds from Mexico and the other third from the Caribbean basin (including Central America). Southern Florida and southern California now have Hispanic majorities. Nationwide,

Hispanic Americans made up 13 percent of the population in 2000, and are expected by 2100 to be the largest single minority group in America. They will generate a much greater natural affinity with Latin American history, language, and culture. Already U.S. citizens have family ties with almost half of Mexico's population of 85 million. Given also the identification by black Americans with parts of Latin America, particularly countries where large slave populations existed (such as Haiti and Brazil), more and more Americans will look at Latin America and see themselves.

The second force is democratization. After waxing and waning for a century, democracy in Latin America, especially in key countries such as Mexico, Brazil, and Argentina, may have reached a tipping point. Opportunities have never been greater. If the United States remains indifferent, it will tell us more about the decline of the democratic ethos in the United States than in Latin America.

DEMOCRACY IN LATIN AMERICA

The Cold War, not the development of democracy, dictated U.S. policy toward Latin America after World War II. From 1948 to 1954, six democracies in Latin America fell to military dictators, reversing a wave of new democracies established right after World War II. The United States not only tolerated this reversal; it abetted it by intervening to overthrow a potential communist government in Guatemala in 1954. Thereafter, U.S. policy helped democratic developments at times through the Alliance for Progress and hurt it at others, notably by covertly assisting the overthrow of a democratic, albeit leftist, government in Chile. It is wrong to conclude, however, that the U.S. preoccupation with communism was anti-democratic. It was quintessentially pro-democratic—a policy that opposed the major threat to democracy in Europe and required trade-offs in other areas.[3] Stopping communism in Europe and in Cuba had its costs, but few would argue today that letting communism spread would have been better for democracy. The U.S. sin was to care more about democracy in Europe than in Latin America, but that legacy is not a heavy burden to shed. Latin American countries always had more room to maneuver on their own and to influence U.S. policy than conventional realist or Marxist perspectives allow.[4]

What is more, the U.S. defense of democracy in Europe had an important indirect effect on democracy in Latin America. The final success of democracy in Spain and Portugal, the former colonial and cultural parents of South America, provided the decisive breakthrough for democracy in Latin America.[5] With the demise of Francisco Franco's Spain and António de Oliveira Salazar's Portugal, dictators in Latin America no longer had role models in the industrial world. Dictators on both the right and left became anachronistic and illegitimate. The left is permanently compromised by the dismal failure of communism in the former Soviet Union. And the right is equally compromised by the inherent limitations of authoritarian governments in an information age.[6]

None of this means that crude military or communist dictatorship lies on the ash heap of history in Latin America, at least not yet. On two of the three criteria necessary for democracies to live peacefully both at home and with their neighbors (elections, divided and accountable institutions, and civil society), Latin America strikes out, at least for the moment. Table 7.1 summarizes identity and power indicators for the Latin American countries. As the Freedom Rating and Polity IV Rating columns suggest, only the Bahamas, Barbados, and Trinidad and Tobago, the small English-speaking Caribbean islands; Belize, Costa Rica, and Panama in Central America; and Bolivia and Uruguay in South America rise to the standards of mature democracies in North America or Europe. On the whole, Latin America democracies are weak, both institutionally and culturally.[7]

While democratic elections in Latin American countries are well established, the continuous, stable transfer of power among opposing political parties is not.[8] Since the advent of mass politics, all countries have endured interruptions of constitutional rule. Over a stretch of seventy-five years or so, only Colombia and Costa Rica have had fewer than ten years of nondemocratic rule. All the other countries have clocked at least two decades of intermittent authoritarian government. The Central American countries (except for Honduras), Argentina, Brazil, Ecuador, Bolivia, Mexico, and the Dominican Republic have clocked four decades or more. Some countries, such as Haiti, have never experienced a peaceful transfer of power from one democratic party to another. The lone exceptions to this turbulence are the small English-speaking countries of the Caribbean.

This situation is improving in the most recent wave of Latin American democratization. Of more than thirty elections held from 1978 to 1992 in fifteen Latin American countries previously under authoritarian rule, half represented second, third, or fourth elections, and four-fifths of these elections involved victories by opposition parties.[9] By contrast, in Asia, as we have seen in chapter 6, Japan has had only one opposition party victory since 1955 (in 1993, and that government lasted less than one year). And Korea and Taiwan had their first peaceful transfer of presidential power in 1997 and 1999, respectively.

Since 1992 there have been both setbacks and further progress. Setbacks occurred in the Andean states. Peru had a dictatorial president, Alberto Fujimori, for nearly a decade before he was driven into exile in Japan. Colombia and Ecuador fought destabilizing wars against drug lords and guerrillas. And Venezuela in effect acquiesced in a new dictatorship under Hugo Chávez. Haiti, Nicaragua, Guatemala, and Paraguay also experienced instability. On the other side of the ledger, Mexico took unprecedented steps toward democracy. In 1997, the people of Mexico elected a National Assembly controlled for the first time by opposition parties. And in 2000, a center-right opposition party, the National Action Party (PAN), won the presidential elections and took power for the first time in seventy years from the ruling party, the Institutional Revolutionary Party (PRI).[10]

A major cause of democratic impermanence in Latin America is weak political institutions. Colombia, Costa Rica, Chile, Uruguay, and Venezuela have the most settled institutions in the region. But even in these countries, legislatures, parties, and court systems are not sufficiently strong to discipline presidential power, make legislatures responsive to the people, integrate pluralist interests, or protect human rights and civil liberties. Presidential offices dominate in most countries, and a proportional representation system keeps parties and legislatures fragmented and weak.[11] Parties exist to elect presidents or dispense patronage, not to exercise day-to-day governance through parliamentary legislation and public debate. Where legislatures are strongest, they may block executive initiatives or even impeach presidents, such as Fernando Collor de Mello in Brazil and Carlos Andrés Pérez in Venezuela. But they cannot provide alternative government. And even established legislative institutions may be undercut by populist leaders (e.g., Hugo Chávez in Venezuela) or shadow power brokers (e.g., Augusto Pinochet Ugarte and the military in Chile). More often, divided parties and legislatures lead to paralysis, inviting violence by guerrillas and drug lords, as in Colombia, or extra-constitutional measures, such as the two attempted military coups in Venezuela in 1992 and Chávez's autocratic takeover after his election in 1998. In weaker systems, the military often rules in fact if not in form, as in Guatemala.

Judicial and police systems in Latin America are highly politicized, inefficient, and often corrupt. Municipal and local authorities are also weak. The consequence is poor protection of human rights and basic civil liberties. In 1995, despite widespread electoral democracy, only eight of Latin America's twenty-two principal countries protected civil liberties sufficiently to qualify as liberal democracies, down from thirteen in 1987.[12] Large groups remain excluded from the political system, including indigenous populations in Mexico, Guatemala, and Peru, blacks in Brazil, and women throughout Latin America. Other institutions of civil society are also weak or excessively politicized— media, churches, universities, and professional societies. The opportunity to generate initiatives from grassroots organizations, debate and contest these initiatives through the media and voluntary interest associations, aggregate such ideas through stable policy-oriented party structures, decide issues through open competitive public debate and parliamentary procedures, and hold elected and bureaucratic officials accountable for implementing decisions is all too infrequent. We cannot yet conclude that democracies in Latin America will endure. The chief obstacle remains a political culture rooted in personalism, charisma, and traditional sources of authority (class, family, church, etc.) rather than in rational discourse, compromise, and legal adjudication.

Table 7.1. Power and Identity Indicators in Latin America

		Political				Economic		Military			Social
	Population, 1999[a] (millions)	Freedom Rating[b] PR	Freedom Rating[b] CL	Polity IV Rating, 1999[c]	Minority (%)[d]	PPP GNI, 1999[e] (billions of dollars)	Economic Freedom, 2001[f]	Budget (% GDP)[g] 1985	Budget (% GDP)[g] 1999	Weapons of Mass Destruction and Delivery Systems[h]	Human Development Index, 1998[i]
North America											
Mexico	97.4	3	4	6	30, 9, 1	780	2.95	0.7	0.9		0.784
Caribbean											
Antigua and Barbuda	0.1[b]	4	3	NA	NA	NA	NA	0.5	0.6		0.833
Bahamas	0.3[b]	1	1	NA	12, 3	NA	2.15	0.5	0.7		0.844
Barbados	0.3[b]	1	1	NA	4, 16	NA	2.40	0.9	0.5		0.858
Cuba	11.2[b]	7	7	−7	37, 11, 1	NA	4.75	9.6	4.8		0.783
Dominican Republic	8.4	2	3	8	16, 11	44	2.85	1.1	0.9		0.729
Haiti	7.8	5	5	6	5	11	3.90	1.5	1.3		0.440
Jamaica	2.6	2	2	9	9	9	2.80	0.9	0.8		NA
Trinidad and Tobago	1.3[b]	1	2	10[j]	43, 40, 18, 2	10	2.50	1.4	0.9		0.793
Central America											
Belize	0.2[b]	1	1	NA	44, 31, 9, 6, 10	NA	2.70	1.4	2.5		0.781
Costa Rica	3.6	1	2	10	6	28	2.65	0.7	0.6		0.797
El Salvador	6.2	2	3	7	10	26	1.95	4.4	1.1		0.696
Guatemala	11.1	3	4	6	44	40	2.70	1.8	1.1		0.619
Honduras	6.3	3	3	6	7, 3	14	3.35	2.1	1.8		0.655
Nicaragua	4.9	3	3	9	17, 9, 5	10	3.45	17.4	0.9		0.631
Panama	2.8	1	2	7	14, 10, 6	15	2.55	2.0	1.3		0.776

South America

Argentina	36.6	2	3	7	3	437	2.25	3.8	1.9	0.837
Bolivia	8.1	1	3	8	30, 30, 25, 15	19	2.40	2.0	1.7	0.643
Brazil	168.1	3	4	8	38, 6, 1	1,148	3.25	1.8	2.7	0.747
Chile	15.0	2	2	7	5	126	2.00	10.6	4.0	0.826
Colombia	42.0	4	4	8	20, 14, 8	232	2.95	1.6	2.8	0.764
Ecuador	12.4	2	3	8	25, 7, 3	35	3.45	1.8	2.3	0.722
Guyana	0.7[b]	2	2	6	30,14, 5	NA	3.35	6.8	0.9	0.709
Paraguay	5.4	4	3	6	5	23	3.20	1.3	1.4	0.736
Peru	25.2	5	4	3	45, 37, 15, 3	113	2.50	4.5	1.6	0.737
Suriname	0.4[b]	3	3	NA	37, 31, 15, 10, 7	NA	3.85	2.4	5.5	NA
Uruguay	3.3	1	2	9	8, 4	29	2.35	3.5	2.3	0.825
Venezuela	23.7	4	4	7	NA	129	3.55	2.1	1.5	0.770
TOTAL	463.4					3,046				

Note: NA, not available.

[a]*World Development Report 2000/2001: Attacking Poverty* (New York: Oxford University Press, for The World Bank, 2001), 278–79.

[b]*Freedom in the World 1999–2000* (New York: Freedom House, 2000), 596–97. Ratings are based on a scale of 1–7, with 1 signifying the most free in the categories of Political Rights (PR) and Civil Liberties (CL). Population data are taken from respective country page.

[c]*Polity IV: Political Regime Characteristics and Transitions, 1800–1999*, Center for International Development and Conflict Management, University of Maryland at College Park, 2000. Rating is based on Democracy Score (scale of 0–10, with 0 signifying low democracy) minus Autocracy Score (scale of 0–10, with 0 signifying low autocracy).

[d]U.S. Central Intelligence Agency, *The World Factbook 2000*, http://www.cia.gov/cia/publications/factbook/index.html. Single minority groups with at least 5% of the population are listed separately, with the final number including all minority groups with less than 5%. Minority refers to ethnic origin.

[e]*World Development Indicators 2001* (Washington, D.C.: World Bank, 2001), 12–14. GNI equals GNP plus receipts of primary income from nonresident sources. Conversions are at Purchasing Power Parity (PPP) exchange rates, not current exchange rates.

[f]Gerald P. O'Driscoll Jr., Kim R. Holmes, and Melanie Kirkpatrick, *2001 Index of Economic Freedom* (Washington, D.C.: The Heritage Foundation, 2001), 8–14. Rankings are based on a scale of 1–5, with 1 signifying the most freedom. The score is based on trade barriers, tax rates, government consumption, monetary policy (inflation), capital flows and foreign investment, banking, wage and price controls, property rights, business regulations, and black markets.

[g]*The Military Balance, 2000/2001* (London: Oxford University Press, for The International Institute for Strategic Studies, 2000), 297–301.

[h]Countries proven or suspected to have Atomic, Biological, or Chemical weapons and Short-range, Medium-range, or Long-range military missile capabilities, as cited in the following sources and from interviews with government officials. Federation of American Scientists, http://www.fas.org; Center for Non-Proliferation Studies, Monterey Institute of International Studies, http://www.cns.miis.edu; Henry R. Stimson Center, http://www.stimson.org; Stockholm International Peace Research Institute, http://www.sipri.se; U.S. Department of Defense, *Proliferation: Threat and Response* (Washington, D.C.: Department of Defense, 1997); U.S. Department of Defense, http://www.defenselink.mil/pubs.

[i]*Human Development Report 2000* (New York: Oxford University Press, for the United Nations Development Programme, 2000), 157–60. Rankings are based on life expectancy, real GDP per capita, and a combination of adult literacy and school enrollment ratios. The highest possible index value (better off) is 1.0, while the lowest possible value is 0.

[j]Data for Trinidad only.

Nevertheless, democracy in Latin America is not fighting uphill against deeply ingrained collectivist and group traditions, as it is in Asia. Nor does it suffer from virulent ethnic conflict, as it does in Africa; nor is it considered a pagan and materialistic philosophy, as it is in the Muslim world. Latin America is, in a sense, the next logical frontier of the European or western struggle for individual freedom and political pluralism. If this struggle is won, Latin America may become democratic as naturally and convincingly as southern Europe has. If Asia is, or was until the financial crisis of 1997, the economic miracle of the developing world, Latin America may be on its way to becoming the political miracle—the first developing region to democratize successfully and durably.

While the struggle goes on, however, two implications follow. First, there will be setbacks in consolidating and deepening democracy in Latin America. Although military budgets are down since 1985 (with some exceptions—see table 7.1), the use of force has not yet been expunged from Latin American politics, as it has within and among the industrial democracies. And because countries on their way to becoming democratic are more prone to conflict than fully democratic countries, interstate conflict is still a possibility in Latin America. Interstate wars in the past twenty-five years have occurred between Ecuador and Peru, El Salvador and Honduras, and Argentina and Great Britain (over the Falklands/Malvinas); border disputes exist between Colombia and Venezuela and between Venezuela and Guyana, and there is also a dispute about access to the sea between Bolivia and Peru. The democratic peace, in short, is not yet applicable in this region. The use of force is, moreover, not solely or even primarily a consequence of intervention by outside powers; it is also a product of indigenous politics and a culture of authoritarianism. Second, the continued role of violence has implications for U.S. policy. Given the prospects for democracy but also the continuing, sometimes violent, struggle to achieve it, what is the role of military force in U.S. relations with Latin America? If violence remains a threat, how does the United States deal with it while simultaneously advancing the cause of democracy and economic development in Latin America?

MULTILATERALIZING THE USE OF FORCE

Unilateral intervention by the United States in Latin America has not been just a tendency of the U.S. government. It has also been a tendency of U.S. nongovernmental groups. During the Cold War era, leftist groups in the United States made common cause with revolutionary groups in Latin America, while conservative elements in the United States supported right-wing forces. Divisions in the United States reinforced divisions in Latin America. One factor affecting U.S. policy toward unilateral intervention in Latin America, therefore, is the health and unity of U.S. politics—that is, U.S. identity. Whether larger and more activist Hispanic and black American groups will intensify or moderate the passion to intervene remains to be seen. But a second factor affecting U.S. intervention is the growing democratic convergence with Latin American countries. This factor may permit U.S. policy making to move in the direction of multilateral cooperation with Latin American countries, characteristic of the way more fully democratic countries behave toward one another.

Recent multilateral initiatives in U.S.–Latin American diplomacy and trade reflect an emerging democratic security community in the region. This community is more important than globalization in drawing the Americas together and diminishing an excessive concern with national sovereignty. An unqualified insistence on national sovereignty is misplaced when countries are converging toward respect for individual rights and democratic institutions. If Latin American countries no longer insist on an inviolable right of nonintervention in their domestic affairs, an insistence that once served as a cover for despotism and protectionism, the United States may no longer insist on an unrestrained, unilateral right to intervene militarily in the region or to settle trade disputes by reference solely to U.S. domestic law.

The Organization of American States (OAS) has become the multilateral rallying point for dealing with democracy and military force in Latin America. Although founded at the outset of the Cold War to defend democracy, the OAS was not always seen in this light. For many Latin American countries, it looked like a convenient tool for American diplomatic and military strategy vis-à-vis the former Soviet Union. For the United States, it was often an unwieldy and unreliable collection of weak allies, many of whom were not democratic or interested in the defense of democracy. Nevertheless, the OAS Charter, unlike the UN Charter, did state that hemispheric solidarity required "the political organization of [member] states on the basis of the effective exercise of representative democracy."[13] When the Cold War ended, this provision became the central commitment of a revitalized and more independent OAS.

At Santiago, Chile, in 1991, the OAS approved a commitment to uphold representative democracy by specific steps. A Resolution on Representative Democracy called for an automatic meeting of the OAS Permanent Council "in the event of any occurrences giving rise to the sudden or irregular interruption of the democratic political institutional process or of the legitimate exercise of power by the democratically elected government in any of the Organization's member states."[14] The meeting must convene an ad hoc gathering of the ministers of foreign affairs, or a special session of the General Assembly—all within a period of ten days. This procedure recognizes that an interruption of democratic governance, so common in Latin America's historical experience, is no longer a matter of domestic interest only. It is also an occasion for international concern—and potentially for international intervention.

Intervene is exactly what the OAS did several months after the Santiago Declaration, when a military junta overthrew the democratically elected government of Jean-Bertrand Aristide in Haiti. The OAS met immediately and imposed sanctions. When sanctions proved ineffective, the OAS requested in June 1993 that the UN Security Council take supporting steps. Eventually, the UN authorized force, and the United States prepared a military invasion of Haiti. At the last moment, the junta backed down and abdicated power. UN, including U.S., peacekeeping forces entered Haiti to enforce the agreement. Since the restoration of democracy, Haiti has had two elections, in which Aristide ceded power peacefully to a handpicked successor, René Préval, and then won it back in 2000. Opposition parties and international observers considered the 2000 elections flawed, and Haiti's democracy remained highly elitist and one of the most suspect and fragile in the region.

The OAS also reacted swiftly to disruptions of democracy in Peru (1992), Guatemala (1993), and Paraguay (1996)—Peru demonstrated the limits of multilateral action, Guatemala and Paraguay the benefits. After President Alberto Fujimori closed the congress and courts in Peru, the OAS pressured him to hold elections for a constitutional congress. This congress subsequently revised the political system and gave even more power to the presidency. Fujimori then stage-managed elections to win another term in office. With popular support and in the absence of a credible threat of outside military intervention, Fujimori effectively sidestepped international diplomatic pressure. In Guatemala, where President Jorge Serrano also suspended constitutional guarantees but had much less popular support, OAS pressure led to change. Civilian groups backed a military coup that ousted Serrano and installed a new civilian president. Similarly, in Paraguay, OAS intervention helped preserve the elected administration of President Juan Carlos Wasmosy when he was pressured by army commanders to resign.

OAS action alone is clearly not enough. OAS economic sanctions are often ineffective because countries outside the hemisphere remain free to supply the targeted state, as happened in the case of Haiti. Sanctions generally do not succeed without the supporting threat to use military force. The OAS, for historical reasons, is reluctant to authorize the use of force, which inevitably involves U.S. troops. A UN authorization of force is more acceptable, but also more difficult to achieve because the UN has numerous members uninterested in the defense or consolidation of democracy.

Much depends on the popularity of the nondemocratic governments against which force is threatened. Haiti's military junta was broadly unpopular. Fujimori's government was not; when it became increasingly unpopular in 1999–2000, Fujimori left office even though the OAS did not invoke the Santiago Resolution and intervene. Fidel Castro's continuing hold on Cuban loyalties is waning, but his popularity still dilutes effective economic sanctions against Cuba and diminishes any outside threat to intervene militarily. The same is the case with Chávez in Venezuela. Despite his trashing of democratic institutions, he retains broad support and leads a diplomatic effort to counterbalance U.S. and democratic influence in Latin America, collaborating with Cuba, violent opposition groups in Bolivia, Ecuador, and Colombia, and antidemocratic forces in Peru and El Salvador.

The popularity of nondemocratic governments, even if that popularity is suspect because it is not registered openly and freely, is not necessarily an inappropriate constraint on U.S. or OAS military intervention. Because great powers outside the region pose no threat, the perpetuation of despotism does not pose an immediate military danger to surrounding countries or the United States. On the other hand, the existence of popular despotism in Cuba, Venezuela, Peru, or wherever is not acceptable in a region committed to representative government. Such regimes reinforce the need for U.S. and OAS political and economic pressure.

Multilateral political and economic pressures can help, and even unilateral U.S. sanctions may play a role if they help to bring about multilateral sanctions. The current unilateral sanctions against Cuba (the Helms-Burton Act), however, do not meet these criteria.[15] U.S. allies strongly oppose sanctions against Cuba, and the United States hesitates to apply the most controversial provisions. Rather than lead to a consensus, the sanctions isolate U.S. diplomacy. These sanctions need to be recast and linked with specific conditions that strengthen indigenous reformers. For example, the United States might authorize civilian and mail connections with Cuba as Castro relaxes constraints on who can travel. Or the United States might ease restrictions on medical and food assistance as Cuba opens up its hospitals and domestic facilities to international volunteers. If allies cannot support the sanctions, the United States should get them on board to support the objectives that the sanctions are designed to achieve, namely the need for free and fair elections and an OAS presence to assist and monitor such elections. None of these steps is likely to achieve immediate agreement or results, but they would put the sanctions in a framework that might eventually produce a multilateral consensus. In the meantime, they would clarify for the Cubans, Latin American democracies, and European allies why sanctions are being pursued.

Popular despots in Latin America are one thing; failed or failing states are another. Colombia is a classic example of the latter, and other Andean countries—Ecuador and Bolivia—may follow suit. In these states, revolutionary guerrillas and paramilitary forces square off against one another; drug traffickers rather than Cold War rivals finance the weaponry and wars of mutual self-destruction. This situation provides the greatest temptation for U.S. unilateral intervention. To combat drugs, the United States has offered large military and financial assistance to Colombia and established air surveillance facilities in Ecuador and several Caribbean countries. The use of force is not avoidable unless Colombia surrenders to the guerrillas and drug lords, but unilateral U.S. intervention is. Colombia is a case in which U.S. moral interests should not supersede its material stake. If it intervenes directly in domestic politics, it should do so only with broad regional approval and legitimacy. It may complicate efficiency, but the United States needs to involve the OAS and the United Nations. Unilateralism is effective and justified only if it leads to multilateralism, especially in a democratizing region.[16]

What would help in the long run in Colombia and Cuba is a hemispheric policy on the use of force. Such a policy, to be realistic, would have to be built around the establishment of a standing OAS military force. An OAS peacekeeping force would reinforce economic sanctions as well as OAS election monitoring and other political efforts. International pressure backed by such a force might be enough in most cases to deter or contain violent regimes. It would not only reduce the prospect of unilateral military intervention by the United States, but also encourage and make more effective economic sanctions that enjoy a wider multilateral consensus.

Clearly, the hemisphere is not yet ready for such a force. The Rio Group in the OAS (the large South American countries plus Mexico) opposes the idea.[17] Until Latin American countries are more democratic and self-confident, and the United States becomes more aware of its own evolving multicultural identity, democracies of different degrees and depth will contest the issues and rules for the use of force. The Western Hemisphere is not likely to enjoy the democratic peace to the same extent as Europe and North America. Be that as it may, democracies, even weak ones, limit the use of force in their own societies more than nondemocratic countries do. And that prospect opens up opportunities for peaceful economic and social competition that have never existed before.

MARKETS AND NAFTA

As this book has stressed, economic arrangements both within and between countries tend to reflect the political communities among countries. The political communities in Latin America feature weak democratic institutions and personalistic political cultures. Not surprisingly, economic relations exhibit wide income inequalities and extensive corruption. Latin American countries lack Asia's collectivist traditions and unified, technocratic administrative experience. Wealth is acquired by privilege, not by initiative or merit, and it is transferred by paternalistic as opposed to rational bureaucratic mechanisms (such as modern tax and welfare systems). As a consequence, economic development in Latin America has been driven by elitist policies of protection for the favored and of exclusion for the masses, and by nationalist ideologies that fulminate against foreign exploitation and imperialism. Few Latin American countries score high on the Heritage Index of Economic Freedom (fig. 7.1). U.S. policies, particularly during the earlier days of resource extraction in Latin America, did much to reinforce Latin American insularity, but U.S. policies were not the principal cause of Latin America's inequities or meager economic results. To this day, privileged elites and a badly skewed and, more important, inefficient distribution of domestic wealth do more to impede rapid growth in Latin America than U.S. neocolonial policies.[18]

In the first half of the twentieth century, many Latin American elites found rising Marxist and socialist economic policies congenial to their political interests. Socialism justified elite privileges in terms of historic missions, and arguments about the adverse terms of trade for developing countries (producing commodities whose prices were falling and importing manufactured goods whose prices were rising) resonated with nationalist fears. Even before World War II, Latin American governments adopted import substitution policies that licensed government corporations and selective private elites to develop local industries that substituted for imports. Such policies propelled a massive and rapid reallocation of indigenous resources from agriculture to industry, impoverishing rural areas and driving rural populations into overcrowded and slum-infested cities.[19]

Progress was made, to be sure, especially in the early decades.[20] The large Latin American countries grew at rates of 6–8 percent per year from 1940 to 1982, comparable to growth in the Soviet Union, which was pursuing similar policies. But the price was high. The mistake was not government activism; it was government and private-sector monopolies. No or very little competition existed, either internally or externally. Monopolies imposed a high cost on resources and ensured that growth could be sustained only as long as capital and labor remained plentiful and cheap. Forced savings from the countryside, supplemented by generous foreign aid and petrodollar recycling, kept the capital flowing in the 1960s and 1970s. But in the 1980s, the flow abruptly stopped. Mounting debt precipitated financial and then industrial bankruptcy. Once again, the United States and external circumstances were blamed for Latin America's economic dilemma. The real causes, however, were domestic economic policies and institutions that not only reflected but exacerbated political inequalities.[21]

The shift to greater market competition in Latin America was slow and difficult. Chile moved to more competitive policies in the late 1970s, but its military government perpetuated the coercion and favoritism of Latin America's traditional elite politics.[22] The real breakthrough came in Mexico. Abandoning 150 years of autarchic policies, Mexico joined the GATT in 1986 and dismantled the citadel of Mexico's economic nationalism, the Ministry of Commerce and Industry. Technocrats in the Finance Ministry and president's office began to deregulate the economy and allow greater foreign access and competition.[23] Reagan administration policies in the United States supported this trend. Running for office in 1980, Reagan first proposed the idea of a

North American Accord, a free trade area among the United States, Mexico, and Canada. Twelve years later, the North American Free Trade Agreement (NAFTA) was concluded, reducing over a period of 10–15 years all tariff and nontariff barriers in agricultural as well as manufactured goods and further liberalizing trade in services and foreign investment. Along the way, President George H. W. Bush proposed that NAFTA be expanded into an Enterprise for the Americas Initiative. President Clinton convened a summit meeting of thirty-four democratically elected hemispheric leaders in Miami in December 1994 to recast this initiative as the Free Trade Area of the Americas (FTAA), a tariff-free market in the Western Hemisphere to be established by 2005.

NAFTA, despite a serious economic crisis in Mexico in 1995, has been an extraordinary success. But it has also met extraordinary resistance. At the end of the Clinton administration, the United States was refusing to implement key provisions of NAFTA, and the FTAA initiative was dead in the water. The debate reflects both economic issues and, perhaps more important, political ideologies.

In the short run, NAFTA has had negligible consequences for U.S. jobs and wages.[24] Technological change and productivity growth in the United States are far more important in explaining job displacement. The wage disparities between Mexico and the United States (wider than, say, between Canada and the United States) are in fact almost perfectly offset by similar disparities in productivity. U.S. workers, benefiting from better technology, infrastructure, and training, accomplish more in a given period of time than Mexican workers. Hence they get paid more per hour or day.

Opening markets with Mexico, therefore, does not create a giant "sucking sound" (Ross Perot's famous phrase during the debate over NAFTA) as U.S. jobs flee south. What it does create is the opportunity for each country to move resources within its own economy incrementally into enterprises where its productivity is relatively greater. Over time, this move raises productivity and wage levels above that which a nation could achieve without trade. The only way such trade can become inefficient is if productivity is consistently higher than wages in Mexico or consistently lower than wages in the United States. Then trade *would* encourage jobs to move to Mexico because Mexican workers would be more productive compared to their relative wages. That may happen occasionally in the short term, due, for example, to a sharp devaluation of the currency (see later discussion). Over time, however, wages and productivity do not stay out of line for very long.[25]

In economic terms, therefore, NAFTA or any free trade arrangement is unchallengeable as long as wages and productivity track one another within individual countries. Politics, however, distorts the economic benefits in three ways. First, jobs are lost in the relatively low-productivity sectors in each country. The least efficient workers need to be retrained and reemployed in higher-productivity sectors. Because any change may be unwelcomed, even change for the better, workers and unions often resist and prefer restrictions on trade.

Second, in the context of open markets, countries, particularly poorer ones like Mexico, may be tempted to devalue as a way to force wages below productivity, stimulate export production, and raise long-term productivity. Devaluation, however, is a painful remedy, leading to recession and domestic unemployment. It is usually forced on a country that has distorted its economy by other means. NAFTA, for example, did not cause the Mexican devaluation of 1994–95. That devaluation resulted from a loss of confidence in the Mexican economy due to government policies that overstimulated demand and imports. When devaluation occurred, Mexico benefited from NAFTA. Although U.S. exports to Mexico declined sharply, Mexican exports to the United States expanded briskly. That pushed Mexico's recovery in the right direction, shifting resources into higher productivity and hence more efficient sectors. Mexico rebounded quickly and paid off early the emergency loans provided by both the United States and the IMF. What is more, U.S. exports recovered; by the first half of 1996, they exceeded precrisis levels.[26] If NAFTA had not been there, Mexico would still have had to devalue, but protectionist restrictions would have pushed resources into less efficient sectors and made recovery slower and more costly.

Third, politics distorts arrangements such as NAFTA by excluding other countries. Mexico may be relatively more efficient than the United States in producing textiles, but Chile or Peru may be even more efficient than Mexico. Why should the United States buy textiles from Mexico and not from Chile or Peru? This is the economic logic behind expanding NAFTA to include further countries until the free trade area embraces all of the Americas. Politics, however, argues against this logic. South America is less politically or economically oriented toward the United States than Mexico, Central America, and the Caribbean.[27] Consequently, in 1991, Brazil and Argentina formed a free trade community of their own, known as Mercosur. Mercosur has trade agreements with the European Union and competes with NAFTA to include Chile and other countries. In April 2001, Brazil opposed efforts by President George W. Bush to revitalize NAFTA and accelerate the completion of the FTAA by 2003.

Ultimately, economic arrangements require a closer sense of political community. Until Brazil and other South American countries draw closer to the United States, trade and monetary integration will be contentious. The NAFTA arrangement with Mexico was unthinkable as long as Mexico was a one-party regime with no prospects for more open political and economic activities. Similarly, the expansion of NAFTA into an FTAA depends on the further democratization of other Latin American societies and wider global trade liberalization that reduces competition among regional blocs such as the EU, NAFTA, and Mercosur.

Nevertheless, at the turn of the millennium, NAFTA and its potential expansion are in trouble. In the United States ideologies and self-images of various groups block progress. Labor and environmental groups want to raise Mexican labor and environmental standards immediately to U.S. levels, in effect robbing Mexico of any chance to compete and develop. More extreme groups see a corporate conspiracy to oppress labor and deface the environment, even though only rich countries have high labor and environmental standards and all of them have become rich in good part through corporate development, entrepreneurial initiative, and freer trade. Groups on the right, which strongly resist immigration from Mexico, also oppose open markets, which offer the best chance to create jobs in Mexico and keep the immigrants at home. Even supporters of NAFTA make their case too cynically. The United States and Mexico (as well as other Latin American countries) care about other things besides jobs and material self-advancement. They care too about the prospects of democracy and individual freedom.

The opportunity for wider freedom comes at a time when Hispanics are becoming the largest U.S. ethnic minority. The coincidence of these two developments—a fragile but nevertheless real democratic movement across all of Latin America and a more involved, Hispanic-oriented U.S. citizenry—is unprecedented. It would be tragic to lose the opportunity because the United States has set its sights too low.

The Middle East

The Middle East here refers to the states of North Africa (Morocco, Algeria, Tunisia, Libya, Egypt, and Sudan), the Levant (Israel, Jordan, Syria, and Lebanon), the Persian Gulf (Iraq, Iran, Saudi Arabia, Kuwait, Bahrain, Qatar, United Arab Emirates, and Oman), Yemen, Turkey, and the nonstate entity of Palestine. During the Cold War, three factors defined U.S. interests in this region: the Soviet Union, oil, and Israel. U.S. policy in the region was aimed at keeping the Soviet Union out, the oil flowing, and Israel safe.

The end of the Cold War seemed to eliminate two of the three reasons for U.S. involvement in the Middle East. The Soviet Union was gone, and without Soviet meddling Israel was much safer and could negotiate its own peace. Oil remained a concern, but with the Reagan-era policies of strategic petroleum reserves and energy deregulation, oil prices declined and temporary disruptions seemed less threatening. U.S. dependence on Middle East imports shrank significantly.[28]

Yet the United States intervened militarily in the Middle East after the Cold War in a bigger way than it ever had before. In 1991, the largest U.S. military operation since World War II expelled Iraqi invaders from Kuwait. U.S. policy makers then followed up with deeper diplomatic and security commitments. Was this engagement simply a misguided Cold War reflex?[29]

It was not. Structural distributions of power and identity suggest that the United States still has sufficient incentives to intervene in the Middle East. But these incentives are no longer self-evident. They do not derive from great-power rivalries outside the region, as they did during the Cold War; nor do they derive after the Cold War from a convergence of national identities with countries in the region, as post–Cold War U.S. interests in Latin America do. Rather, U.S. interests stem from a set of direct and indirect moral and material stakes that are relatively balanced. The material stake is oil, and because oil is fungible, a relatively decreasing level of U.S. direct dependence on Persian Gulf supplies does not diminish this stake. The moral stakes are twofold: to reassure Europe and Japan, which are more directly dependent on Middle East oil, that the United States will defend Persian Gulf supplies and to help Israel maintain a democratic and independent Jewish homeland. These material and moral stakes are roughly equal in weight and thus ensure that the United States will probably sustain a strong presence in the Middle East even after the Cold War.

The Middle East was a part of European and western identity and interests long before oil was discovered. The eastern Mediterranean is the cradle of western civilization, and Palestine the birthplace of both Judaism and Christianity. The Middle East is also the home of Islam. From the seventh century on, Islam and the West have been inextricably linked, not only in terms of conquest—the Muslim push into Europe from roughly the eighth through the sixteenth centuries, the Christian crusades into the Holy Land in the eleventh and twelfth centuries, western colonialism in Africa and the Middle East in the eighteenth through twentieth centuries—but also in terms of self-images.[30] In various enduring and changing ways, these self-images conflict. They cause entanglement, even when no hard interest such as oil is involved (as, for example, in the contemporary conflict in Bosnia). Indeed, self-images create hard interests. A clear example is the historical quest of both Jews and Palestinians for independent homelands in Palestine.

The Middle East today lies at the crossroads of entangled identities, between democratic, democratizing, and nondemocratic countries. Do these crossroads define new fault lines of clashing civilizations?[31] Or is lasting peace just around the corner, achievable if Israel and the Palestinian Authority sign a final peace accord? From the perspective of this book, the conflicts are neither so unalterable that the crossroads are doomed to be the "bloody borders" of a new world division nor so malleable that a small dose of permanent borders and secular modernization will ensure peace. The Arab-Israeli peace talks, important as they may be, are not enough. They suffer from the lack of broader military, economic, and social arrangements in the region that could tip the balance between suspicion and tolerance. U.S. efforts to reach an Israeli-Palestinian agreement in the 1990s did not fail for lack of talks; they failed because the United States did not maintain the balance of power against Iran, Iraq, and other rejectionist states and create the sense of confidence that might ignite economic and social progress in the region.

Identities diverge more sharply in the Middle East than in any other developing region, and economic ties focus too narrowly on oil and arms sales to generate wider prosperity. These structural features of political animosity and economic vulnerability require a more predictable balance of military power and substantial domestic economic reforms before the belligerents can achieve the self-confidence to make a lasting peace.

Since the early 1970s, U.S. policy has concentrated primarily on the Arab-Israeli negotiating process, based on the formula of swapping land for peace implicit in UN Resolutions 242 and 338—the shuttle diplomacy after the 1973 war, the Camp David Accords in 1979, and the Madrid peace process since 1991.[32] This focus was probably the only option in the earlier period of the Arab-Israeli conflict, and it remains necessary today. But it was never sufficient. Today four broader elements need to be emphasized: a clear understanding with Israel, after the end of the Cold War, of the underlying rationale for U.S. support; a realistic assessment of both the possibilities and limitations for the evolution of Arab and Muslim societies toward political liberalization and economic development; a more fixed and predictable set of diplomatic and military alignments in the region; and a serious and sustained program of multilateral economic cooperation, especially with Arab entities that have accepted the prospect of peaceful co-existence with Israel.

ALLIED PARTNERSHIP IN THE MIDDLE EAST

The Middle East is not contiguous with the United States in the same way that Europe and Japan are positioned directly across the oceans from the United States. There is no piece of territory in the Middle East that the United States absolutely must defend because its loss would directly jeopardize American security. Nevertheless, the Middle East is contiguous to Europe, and, as noted earlier, Europe and Japan are far more dependent on Middle East oil than is the United States. Hence, America's stake in the Middle East derives in part from its stake in Europe and Japan and calls for the kind of partnership among the United States, Europe, and Japan that currently characterizes U.S.-European policies in the Balkans.

During the Cold War, the United States exercised undisputed (indeed, after the Suez crisis of 1956, often unilateral) leadership in the Middle East. It did so both because the United States was the only western nuclear power that could deter Soviet intrusions and because Europe and Japan had no united or coherent Middle East diplomacy. After the Cold War, neither of these reasons apply to the same degree. Russia still exerts influence in the region, but less in the Arab-Israeli dispute than in the Balkans and in the northern Persian Gulf, the Caucasus region, and central Asia. In addition, Russia no longer challenges the status quo either in the Middle East or in Europe. And the European allies today are moving haltingly, although perceptibly, toward more coherence in foreign policy, especially since the NATO experience in Kosovo, where EU members recognized that they depended too heavily on U.S. defense capabilities. If these trends persist, America's direct material stake in the Middle East will decline, whereas its indirect stake through a permanent political partnership with a democratic Europe and Japan will increase.

From a perspective that takes into account both identity and power, allied policies do not aim solely at preserving geostrategic real estate in the eastern Mediterranean but also at preserving a type of society in the region that is open, democratic, and nonviolent. Israel, as long as it remains such a society, is a starting point for peaceful allied ties in the Middle East. Without at least one mature democracy in the area, the allies, especially the United States, are less likely to pursue policies that can bring about a wider peace. If it is only territory or oil that the allies seek to secure, they can do this best by the cynical manipulation and fluid balance-of-power politics advocated by realists. But such a strategy is hard to sustain in mature democracies, especially America, because public support usually insists on goals that go beyond the balance of power.

DEMOCRACY AND ISRAEL

Given this logic, both the possibilities and the limits of U.S. policy in the Middle East depend on the evolution of democratic identities there. Table 7.2 provides power and identity indicators for the region. Israel is a solid democracy, ranking only slightly below its peers in Europe and Japan. It has experienced repeated and hotly contested elections and a regular rotation of opposing parties in power. It has divided and accountable political institutions, although its military and intelligence services enjoy wider latitude for covert activities than would be the case in democracies not involved in a perpetual state of wartime mobilization. And it has a civic tradition, based on western, Judeo-Christian values of individualism, voluntarism, private property, and capitalism, which limits the authority of government in the society as a whole.

At the beginning of the millennium, however, Israel may be poised on the knife's edge of a major identity struggle between its secular political system and its sectarian religious soul. Increasingly divided, a good part of Israeli society has accepted the idea of a secular Jewish state that makes no fundamentalist religious or nationalist claims on the West Bank (Judea and Samaria) and Gaza. Another part, however, holds out for a Greater Israel, demanding annexation of the West Bank and Gaza, and a sectarian society in which religious law plays the dominant role in both public and private life. If the sectarians win this struggle, religious fundamentalism will threaten Israeli democracy no less than Islamic fundamentalism impedes democracy in Arab countries.[33]

211

Table 7.2. Power and Identity Indicators in the Middle East and North Africa

	Population, 1999[a] (millions)	Political				Economic		Military			Social
		Freedom Rating[b]		Polity IV Rating, 1999[c]	Minority (%)[d]	PPP GNI, 1999[e] (billions of dollars)	Economic Freedom, 2001[f]	Budget (% GDP)[g]		Weapons of Mass Destruction and Delivery Systems[h]	Human Development Index, 1998[i]
		PR	CL					1985	1999		
North Africa											
Algeria	30.5	6	5	−2	1	145	3.20	1.7	6.6	B, C, S, M	0.683
Egypt	62.4	6	6	−6	1	217	3.60	7.2	3.4	A, B, C, S, M	0.623
Libya	5.0[b]	7	7	−7	3	NA	4.90	6.2	4.7		NA
Morocco	28.2	5	4	−6	1	94	2.70	5.4	5.0		0.589
Tunisia	9.5	6	5	−3	2	54	2.90	5.0	1.7		0.703
Levant											
Israel	6.1	1	3	10	20	110	2.75	21.2	8.9	A, C, M	0.883
Jordan	4.7	4	5	−2	2	18	2.90	15.9	7.7		0.721
Lebanon	4.3	6	5	NA	5	NA	2.85	9.0	3.4		0.735
Palestine Authority	2.4[j]	5	6	NA	NA	NA	NA	NA	NA		NA
Syria	15.7	7	7	−9	10	54	4.00	16.4	5.6	B, C, S, M	0.660
Persian Gulf											
Bahrain	0.7[b]	7	6	−8	19, 10, 8	NA	1.90	3.5	7.7		0.820
Iran	63.0	6	6	3	24, 8, 7, 10	347	4.70	18.0	6.2	A, B, C, S, M, L	0.709
Iraq	22.5[b]	7	7	−9	20, 5	NA	4.90	37.9	7.6	A, B, C, S	0.583
Kuwait	1.9	5	4	−7	45, 35, 9, 12	NA	2.55	9.1	11.1		0.836
Oman	2.5[b]	6	6	−9	NA	NA	2.70	20.8	10.9		0.730
Qatar	0.5[b]	7	6	10	18, 18, 10, 14	NA	3.15	6.0	15.4		0.819
Saudi Arabia	21.4	7	7	−10	10	223	3.00	19.6	15.5	M	0.747

	Persian Gulf										
United Arab Emirates	2.8[b]	6	5	−8	23, 19, 8	NA	2.05	7.6	6.2	S, M	0.810
Yemen	17.0	5	6	−2	NA	12	3.85	9.9	6.7		0.448
	Northern Tier										
Turkey	64.4	4	5	7	20	415	2.90	4.5	5.5		0.732
TOTAL	365.5					1,708					

Note: NA, not available.

a World Development Report 2000/2001: Attacking Poverty (New York: Oxford University Press, for The World Bank, 2001), 278–79.

b Freedom in the World 1999–2000 (New York: Freedom House, 2000), 596–97. Ratings are based on a scale of 1–7, with 1 signifying the most free in the categories of Political Rights (PR) and Civil Liberties (CL). Population data are taken from respective country page.

c Polity IV: Political Regime Characteristics and Transitions, 1800–1999, Center for International Development and Conflict Management, University of Maryland at College Park, 2000. Rating is based on Democracy Score (scale of 0–10, with 0 signifying low democracy) minus Autocracy Score (scale of 0–10, with 0 signifying low autocracy).

d U.S. Central Intelligence Agency, The World Factbook 2000, http://www.cia.gov/cia/publications/factbook/index.html. Single minority groups with at least 5% of the population are listed separately, with the final number including all minority groups with less than 5%. Minority refers to ethnic origin.

e World Development Indicators 2001 (Washington, D.C.: World Bank, 2001), 12–14. GNI equals GNP plus net receipts of primary income from nonresident sources. Conversions are at Purchasing Power Parity (PPP) exchange rates, not current exchange rates.

f Gerald P. O'Driscoll Jr., Kim R. Holmes, and Melanie Kirkpatrick, 2001 Index of Economic Freedom (Washington, D.C.: The Heritage Foundation, 2001), 8–14. Rankings are based on a scale of 1–5, with 1 signifying the most freedom. The score is based on trade policy, fiscal burden of government, government intervention in the economy, monetary policy (inflation), capital flows and foreign investment, banking, wage and price controls, property rights, business regulations, and black markets.

g The Military Balance, 2000/2001 (London: Oxford University Press, for The International Institute for Strategic Studies, 2000), 297–301.

h Countries proven or suspected to have Atomic, Biological, or Chemical weapons and Short-range, Medium-range, or Long-range military missile capabilities, as cited in the following sources and from interviews with government officials. Federation of American Scientists, http://www.fas.org; Center for Non-Proliferation Studies, Monterey Institute of International Studies, http://www.cns.miis.edu; Henry R. Stimson Center, http://www.stimson.org; Stockholm International Peace Research Institute, http://www.sipri.se; U.S. Department of Defense, Proliferation: Threat and Response (Washington, D.C.: Department of Defense, 1997); U.S. Department of Defense, http://www.defenselink.mil/pubs.

i Human Development Report 2000 (New York: Oxford University Press, for the United Nations Development Programme, 2000), 157–60. Rankings are based on life expectancy, real GDP per capita, and a combination of adult literacy and school enrollment ratios. The highest possible index value (better off) is 1.0, while the lowest possible value is 0.

j Data are for West Bank and Gaza.

In a sense, the settlement question is a proxy for Israel's identity struggle. The settlements in the West Bank and Gaza, which grew substantially under the first Likud government, are now widespread and continue to be built. Altogether, there are approximately 200 settlements and 200,000 Jewish settlers, most of them in the West Bank (including Jerusalem). Sectarians push the settlements as a step toward the annexation of the West Bank and Gaza; secularists oppose them for fear of diluting the Jewish state (annexation would add about 2 million Arabs to the 1.1 million in a current population of 6.2 million Israelis) or, if Jewish prerogatives are preserved, for fear of creating a racist state. Only Israelis can decide this struggle over Israeli identity. But they need to understand the consequences their decision may have for U.S. and allied support. A Greater Israel achieved against the opposition of local Arabs would significantly alter the calculus of western ties with Israel.

DEMOCRACY AND ISLAM

Beyond Israel, the political landscape of the Middle East is depressing.[34] According to table 7.2, there are no other democracies in the Middle East. Hence, there is no prospect in the near or medium term that Israel might look forward to peaceful, nonmilitarized relations with neighboring countries. Turkey and Jordan come closest to being potential democracies, and they rank far down on the Freedom House scale of political rights and civil liberties.

Turkey has regular elections and rotation of governments. But its military is not subordinate to the political process and intervenes periodically, as it did in 1997 to pressure Turkey's first coalition government led by Islamist parties to resign. Turkey's civic culture is still significantly conflicted between a revived Islamic movement and a seventy-five-year-old secular tradition inaugurated by the nationalist leader Kemal Ataturk. Turkey also faces internal and external military conflicts. It battles separatist Kurds in its southeast and in northern Iraq, Syria, and Iran. It competes with Russia and Iran for overland supply routes to transport the potentially huge oil and gas resources from the Caspian Sea, and it conducts historical rivalries with both Armenia on its eastern border and Greece on its western border. Nevertheless, Turkey is also a U.S. and western ally in NATO and recently concluded a military agreement with Israel that calls for joint training and planning activities. It is potentially a key link between western Europe and the Middle East, as well as between western Europe and central Asia.

Egypt and Jordan have elected parliaments and multiple parties, although religious movements such as the Muslim Brotherhood are banned in Egypt. But press and judicial freedoms are limited, and the president in Egypt and the Hashemite monarch in Jordan exercise power in a largely uncontested manner. Syria is an authoritarian state run by a military socialist government dominated by members of a minority Islamic sect known as Alawites (considered heretics by the main Sunni and Shia branches). Lebanon, its once-preeminent Maronite Christian community severely weakened by civil war, is for all practical purposes dominated by Syria.

Among the North African states, Morocco has a reformist monarch who confers limited powers on a parliament, which in 2000 was led by an opposition prime minister. Algeria elected an opposition Islamic party in 1991, but a military coup prevented it from coming to power. Today, Algeria has a civilian government backed by the military, which is fighting an ongoing war against Muslim fundamentalists. Tunisian authorities, although secularized under the earlier one-party rule of Habib Bourguiba, permit only restricted elections and parliamentary opposition. Libya is run by an ideological autocrat, Muammar al Qaddafi; and Sudan is governed in the north by a radical Islamic regime waging a civil war against the largely Christian and animist populations in the south.

In the Persian Gulf, Kuwait stakes a marginal claim to democracy, on a par perhaps with that of Jordan. It has a full and freely elected parliament, which was suspended twice before and then revived after the Persian Gulf War and in which opposition groups dominate. But the Sabah, or ruling family, still controls all important matters. The other states of the Gulf Cooperation Council—Saudi Arabia, Bahrain, United Arab Emirates (UAE), Qatar, and Oman—are conservative monarchies. Iran is a Shiite theocracy. It holds regular elections for the parliament and presidency, which moderates have won since 1997, but unelected clerics continue to exercise supreme power, controlling the military, police, judicial, and intelligence agencies. Iraq is a fascist state, and Yemen (united in 1990) is still a largely feudal society divided between traditional clans in the north and a socialist-oriented urban population in the south. The transition Palestinian Authority, created by the Israeli–Palestine Liberation Organization (PLO) peace talks in 1993, is effectively a satrapy of Yasser Arafat and his dominant Al-Fatah wing of the PLO.

Is democracy compatible with Islam? Bernard Lewis, the highly respected historian of Islam, doubts it.[35] The two civilizations—the West and Islam—are too exclusionary, he argues. Both insist on certain inalienable universal rights—in the West, the right of individual human beings to life, liberty, and the pursuit of happiness, including freedom of religion; in Islam, the right to live under the law of God or sharia, not just in private life but in the public life of the state as well. According to Lewis, these rights diametrically conflict. A democracy that establishes law on the basis of open debate and decision making among pluralist groups is hardly a reliable administrator of God's law. And a theocracy that insists on the pervasive application of God's law can hardly permit the secularization of politics. Muslims may participate in pluralist politics, as, for example, in Jordan. But if they gain power, can they give it up? As Michael Field points out, "in the eyes of most [Islamic] jurists, it would be wrong for an Islamic government to allow the people to vote it out of office."[36] The people would be voting against God's law.

Lewis may be too pessimistic. Conflicts between Islam and democracy are real, to be sure. Fundamentalist Islam of the sort advocated by the militant Islamic Salvation Front (FIS) in Algeria or the Muslim Brotherhood in Egypt is incompatible with democracy. But so are neo-Nazi fundamentalism in Germany, Jewish ultra-orthodoxy in Israel, and militant Christian fanaticism in the United States. All democracies are vulnerable to internal nondemocratic forces. The difference is how they cope with these forces. Mature democracies rely on strong civil societies to debate and isolate extremist elements. Weaker democracies use legal bans or outright force. At some point, of course, the use of force negates democracy, whether it is being employed to preserve democracy or to overthrow it. At this stage, democracy in the Middle East is threatened from both ends—secular governments that limit free parties, press, and courts because they fear Islamic fundamentalists, and fundamentalist movements that use free parties, press, and courts to gain power with the intent to overthrow democracy.

What would it take to strengthen rationalist factors in Islamic life? Modernization would help, but modernization itself lacks legitimation. Islam has had no equivalent of the Reformation or Enlightenment to validate religious freedom and material progress.[37] Without such validation, modernization looks like an attempt "to weaken and remove Islamic norms, laws, and values and replace them with pagan norms and laws and values imported from the West—to desacrilize, to de-Islamize, in a word, to Westernize the divinely established and divinely guided Muslim polity."[38] Islam's confrontation with the West is itself an obstacle. Christianity reformed without being under siege, but Islam feels besieged, and lacks, as Fouad Ajami writes, "the self-confidence and imagination societies need if they are to reinvent themselves."[39]

Not surprisingly, Muslim societies with the greatest historical self-confidence have made the most progress in trying to integrate modernization and Islam. Egypt and Turkey are both ancient, pre-Islamic cultures that are still relatively homogenous, despite Islamic and, in the case of Egypt, Arab schisms. At the beginning of the twentieth century, both countries underwent secularizing reforms. Since the 1970s, however, both have been buffeted by the revival of fundamentalism. Can these two countries hold off the new assault against secularism? To succeed completely, secular leaders have to demonstrate that the separation of religion and politics does not diminish religion in society but anchors it in individual choice, rather than in state power.

Egypt's and Turkey's experience suggests two points about convergence and peace in the Middle East. First, national and cultural self-confidence are prerequisites of political change. It is not surprising that Egypt was the first Muslim and Arab state to make peace with Israel. Because it was the most self-confident and politically modern state in the Middle East, only Egypt could have weathered the storm of abuse that followed the Camp David Accords. As it was, the storm swept away Egypt's leader, Anwar Sadat, but the state and his peace policy did not collapse. In less secure states—Syria, Iraq, and even Jordan—peace threatens not only leaders but also national unity. This first point suggests that Israel can best build convergence in the Middle East with stronger, not weaker, Arab neighbors. The problem in the current negotiations is that Israel is now dealing with countries—Lebanon, Syria, and the Palestinian Authority—that are all considerably weaker than Egypt. One of them, the Palestinian Authority, is not a coherent entity at all.

The second point to draw from the experience of Egypt and Turkey is that any convergence of political identities between Israel and further Muslim states is going to take a very long time. Even Egypt, according to its own Nobel Prize–winning author Naguib Mahfouz, "may still be a hundred years away from being able to cope with real democracy."[40] Jordan is no doubt still farther away. Lebanon has moved backward since its civil war, and Syria, like Iraq, is held back less by Islam than by brutal personalist and clan-based politics. The new Palestinian Authority in the West Bank and Gaza is unstable. It has an elected council, but Arafat acts autocratically and faces growing opposition from within this council as well as from more militant groups that reject the Israeli-Arab agreements—the principal groups being Hamas, located in the West Bank and Gaza, and Hezbollah, operating out of southern and eastern Lebanon.

MILITARY ALIGNMENTS AND TERRORISM

If Israel has few stable partners to work with and convergence is at best a long-term proposition, the Middle East needs more certain and fixed military alignments. Military expenditures are higher in this part of the world than in any other part, and no fewer than four states have or are on their way to acquiring nuclear weapons (table 7.2). When identities diverge, balancing power is not only necessary, but helpful. Formal alliances are not in the cards, not even between Israel and the United States. But the Middle East needs what Shimon Peres called in another context "Good Fences"—clear military alignments to contain rejectionist states and terrorism, but also growing social and economic contacts to reduce suspicions.[41]

Good Fences draws clear lines between the core countries that support the peace process and those that do not. Israel, Egypt, and Jordan (and indirectly Turkey, Morocco, and perhaps Tunisia) are the core countries. These countries are currently trying to pull the Palestinian Authority toward reconciliation. Pulling on the Palestinian Authority from the other side are Syria, Lebanon, and the rejectionist states of Iraq, Iran, Libya, and Sudan. (Algeria is consumed by its own civil war.) The conservative monarchies in the Persian Gulf are sitting on the fence; they accept the peace process, but shy away from any line-drawing for fear of antagonizing dissident fundamentalists in their own societies.

The core states need to be associated more closely with an evolving Arab-Israeli peace settlement. Along with the United States and Europe, they can help to monitor security functions in the West Bank and Gaza. In 2001, the United States was training Palestinian police units and providing intelligence services to adjudicate disputes between Israeli and Palestinian security forces. The European Union was supplying aid and monitoring human rights. Over the longer run, the core states might also be involved in these activities.

A second alignment would gradually build a bridge between the core states and the Persian Gulf monarchies. The Persian Gulf War convinced the Gulf monarchies that they could not safeguard their security without direct U.S. military assistance. Six of the Gulf states—Kuwait, Bahrain, United Arab Emirates, Saudi Arabia, Qatar, and Oman—now have defense ties (not treaties) with the United States.[42] Unfortunately, the Gulf states cooperate only marginally with one another (e.g., through the Gulf Cooperation Council) and resist any visible defense association with Arab states outside the Gulf, such as Egypt and Syria.[43] In the past, the Gulf states relied mostly on maneuver and bribes to keep their radical neighbors at bay, but these policies have failed, and they are too expensive and dangerous for the future. If the United States keeps forces in the Persian Gulf, it must look for ways to enhance multilateral cooperation among the Gulf states and to associate them more directly with the core states.

The final axis of military alignment in the Middle East is balancing power against the rejectionist states—dual containment of Iran and Iraq (and indirectly Libya and Sudan) and a firm hand toward Syria and Lebanon.[44] There are many critics of dual containment, a policy initiated by the George H. W. Bush administration after the Gulf War to sequester and, if necessary, sanction Iran and Iraq for supporting terrorism and developing weapons of mass destruction.[45] Some criticized this policy for doing too little to overthrow Saddam Hussein in Iraq; others criticized it for doing too much and discouraging a more moderate government in Iran.[46] Neither argument is persuasive. Rollback in Iraq drags the United States deeper into the morass of domestic politics in the Persian Gulf; rapprochement with Iran sanctions Teheran's efforts to disrupt the peace process and destabilize the Gulf. It also does less than a solid partnership with Turkey to counter Russian influence in the Caucasus region or develop oil resources with Turkey's friend, Azerbaijan, in the Caspian Sea. Containing both Iraq and Iran, albeit in different ways, is still a more sensible strategy than either rapprochement with Iran or rollback in Iraq.

The United States might usefully try a different tack. It might share more influence with Europe, which now gets a free ride in the Middle East.[47] Europe maneuvers to restrain American power in peacetime, but benefits from American power in wartime. What if the United States included the allies more directly in the peace talks? One option is to create a negotiating contact group for the Arab-Israeli peace process, similar to the contact group that exists for Bosnia. The United States would continue to exercise leadership, which Europe would probably concede as it eventually did in Bosnia, but the European presence, which Israel has opposed and moderate Arabs have supported, might bring more balance to the negotiating process. A more explicit U.S.-European partnership might also strengthen broader western diplomacy, allowing more common positions across the entire front of North African and Middle East states from Algeria (where France is concerned) to Turkey (where the EU plays a key role) to Iran (where U.S. interests are paramount). Moreover, despite all protests to the contrary, the exclusive U.S. role in the Middle East negotiations has never been that critical, except to start these negotiations and from time to time to salvage them.[48] With the end of the Cold War, the U.S. role becomes more critical in strengthening the broader pillars of peace in the Middle East. In addition to military balancing, this role now requires much more energetic economic and social programs to develop the region.

ECONOMIC AND SOCIAL COOPERATION

A strategy of Good Fences involves cooperation to ameliorate the economic and social conditions caused by diverging political identities. In the Middle East, unfortunately, there has been very little such cooperation. When identities diverge sharply, they not only preclude significant economic interactions, but turn economics into an instrument of war. From the late 1940s on, the Arab states implemented an economic embargo against Israel as well as third-country firms that traded or invested in Israel. Israel, in turn, subordinated economic development in the West Bank and Gaza to security needs, restricting trade and shutting the border in response to terrorist attacks. This policy reduced a large chunk of Palestinian employment and GNP; one-third of the Palestinian workforce depends on jobs in Israel, accounting for one-quarter of Palestinian GNP. There are pockets of growth. Israel itself is an advanced economy, and the oil-rich Persian Gulf states are wealthy. But the economy of the entire Arab world is smaller than Canada's, and Israel's economy groans under the weight of its military machine, direct defense expenditures absorbing 8.9 percent of GDP in 1999 (see table 7.2) and indirect costs totaling much more. The Middle East, as a whole, is a basket case.

North African and front-line Arab states, such as Egypt and Syria, suffer from the legacy of socialist policies implemented under the pan-Arab nationalist movements of the 1950s and 1960s. The Persian Gulf monarchies and Iran labor under the centralizing policies encouraged by authoritarianism and Islam. The governments in all of these countries dominate the economies. In the more secular states, Egypt, Syria, and Iraq, governments are the main employers. In the Gulf monarchies (Saudi Arabia, Kuwait, etc.), governments control the principal resource, oil, and allocate contracts and subsidies to balance competing family elites and to pamper the ordinary citizen with free education, health, and other social services. In the radical states—Iran and Sudan—governments formally denounce western capitalism (significantly limiting interest on bank loans and corporate profits) and operate their economies almost entirely on a patronage basis. Many of these economies survive largely on the basis of extortion. Egypt and Jordan, for example, obtain large amounts of aid from the West for their peace efforts. With the end of the Cold War, however, aid is declining. The largesse is drying up. Even the oil-rich states face a financial squeeze. Oil revenues are down from their peak in the early 1980s; oil income in the Gulf monarchies, adjusted for inflation, was less in 1995 than it was in 1980.[49] Income rose with oil price increases in 1999–2000, but costs also rose. The Gulf War and arms expenditures caused military budgets to skyrocket;[50] population growth has sharply increased social and economic subsidies. As government budgets are squeezed, elites and ordinary citizens alike fight that much harder for handouts from the government.

Peace is obviously a prerequisite for economic growth. But peace has existed between Egypt and Israel for more than twenty years, and no signifi-cant economic cooperation has taken place. Something else is needed—politi-cal confidence. Middle Eastern governments have little confidence, not only toward one another but toward their own people. Fearing political instability, they are unwilling to encourage economic liberalization or even social con-tacts among states in the region. Astonishingly, fewer than 5,000 Egyptian tourists have visited Israel since the Camp David Accords. A half million Israelis have been to Egypt, reflecting perhaps the greater wealth of Israel. Altogether, the spigot of human interaction is barely dripping, and the Middle East remains a desert of unconnected human life and society.

Where should the process begin? The Madrid peace conference in 1991 launched a multilateral process to foster more human and economic contacts, on the assumption that such contacts might reinforce the peace process,[51] and some progress has been achieved. The Regional Economic Development Working Group (REDWG), created at Madrid, held a series of intergovern-mental meetings and developed a list of projects to be funded by donor coun-tries and carried out by regional governments. But the donor countries, par-ticularly the United States and the European Union, disagreed over who would lead and fund these projects.

In addition, the United States initiated parallel conferences—most important were the Middle East and North African (MENA) summits—to stimulate interest and investment from the private sector. Private-sector investment was limited, however, by the paucity of nongovernment busi-ness partners in Middle East countries and depended more directly than government projects on the peace talks and political confidence. Once the peace talks flagged in 1996, the MENA process stalled. Key countries such as Saudi Arabia and Egypt boycotted the fourth summit in Doha,

Qatar, in November 1997. For all practical purposes, economic cooperation did not reinforce peace but rather fell victim to the deteriorating peace process.

Is it possible to develop more substantial economic alignments in the region, even without a final peace settlement? It is, but not without a major recasting of U.S. diplomatic strategy. Much more effort will have to focus on the long-term transformation of individual Arab economies, independent of the peace talks. Even if peace exists, as it has between Egypt and Israel and now between Jordan and Israel, economic cooperation does not follow because growth-oriented economic policies and institutions are lacking.

An economic strategy to address these realities has two parts. The first is a long-term program to transform and integrate individual Arab economies into European and other global markets. Donor assistance would no longer be pegged to the peace process (i.e., more aid for more peace). It would be geared, rather, to domestic economic reforms. World trends are readying more of the Arab countries for such reforms. The international financial institutions could lead multiyear programs to privatize, liberalize, and stabilize domestic economic policies. Because of domestic divisions, the peace process would still exert an indirect constraint on reform, but each country's program would stand on its own legs, so to speak. There would be no multilateral process, such as the REDWG or MENA, that countries could manipulate for political purposes.

The second part of a new economic strategy focuses multilateral efforts on the occupied territories. The West Bank and Gaza, together with Jordan and Israel, constitute the one market in the area where significant economic activity exists and growth is possible in the short to medium term even without a final peace. Despite Israeli preeminence in this market and the absence of peace in the 1970s and 1980s, output in the occupied territories grew from 13.8 percent of Israel's GNP in 1970 to 22.7 percent in 1986. Per capita income in 1987 was over $1,700, higher than that in the contiguous Arab states of Jordan and Syria.[52] Ironically, after the 1993 Oslo accords, per capita income fell by 17 percent in 1994–96. And despite some growth in 1998–99, Israeli closures in 2000 plunged the occupied territories once again into sharp recession.[53] Clearly prospects for revived growth await the cessation of new hostilities. But in the aftermath of a future cease-fire, the allies and the parties to the conflict might give more emphasis to practical economic cooperation and increased multilateral assistance than to a final peace settlement, the foundations for which do not yet exist.

As Israel makes clear, there will be no peace without security. But it is equally clear that there will be no peace without economic hope. Both military and economic alignments are needed. Politics leads in both cases, building trust to provide safety and wider markets. But politics cannot go very far if military and economic commitments lag behind. In the Middle East, broader U.S. policies need to catch up with the peace talks, providing clearer military alignments to encourage moderate states and to isolate rejectionist ones and providing more focused economic programs to benefit the people of the occupied territories and front-line states such as Jordan.

Sub-Saharan Africa

Materially, America has few interests at stake in Africa (the forty-eight nations that lie south of the Sahara Desert; Egypt, Tunisia, Algeria, Libya, Sudan, and Morocco are dealt with in the Middle East section of this chapter). Unlike the Middle East, Africa commands no essential resource, even though it is rich in practically all resources, including oil. And it is the poorest continent—in 2000 nineteen of the twenty poorest countries in the world, and thirty of the forty poorest, were in Africa.[54] Further, except for the Horn of Africa, Africa is not central strategically. Soviet intervention in Africa (Angola, Mozambique, and Somalia) in the 1970s caused alarm, but it did so largely because it reflected a new Soviet capacity to project power beyond the periphery of the former Soviet Union and thus intensified the Cold War in Europe. America has no history of repeated intervention or imperialism in Africa, as it has in Latin America and Asia, and America has fought no major wars in Africa, as it has in the Middle East and Asia. In classic power terms, Africa does not matter much in American or world affairs.

Yet Africa does matter in U.S. and international diplomacy. In the midst of the Cold War, the United Nations mobilized, eventually with full U.S. support, one of the most aggressive, coherent, and persistent international efforts ever undertaken to end apartheid and white rule in South Africa. This action, particularly the near-total boycott of apartheid South Africa by both government and business communities, was not only unprecedented—it was successful. In spring 1994, South Africa passed peacefully to government control by the black majority. What accounts for this kind of diplomacy in a world in which, according to realists, only power matters?

Identity, as this book argues, also matters, even or especially when power does not. Apartheid was something that became utterly repugnant to most of the world, not because it was a material threat but because it was a moral outrage. As Africa emerged in the mid-twentieth century from almost complete colonization (only Liberia and Ethiopia escaped foreign rule), apartheid was the last remnant of one of the ugliest chapters in the history of human oppression. The enslavement, colonization, and white rule of an entire continent deprived black Africans not only of liberty and often of life, but also, and more devastatingly, of a sense of identity.[55] In the mid-twentieth century, the West finally confronted this horrific legacy, and the struggle against apartheid marked both the end of the repression of black identity and the beginning of the long march toward full liberty and equality for black peoples in Africa and around the world.

America deals with this legacy more directly than any other western or European country. Black Americans constitute approximately 12 percent of the U.S. population, three or four times more than that in any other industrial democracy. The great majority of these Americans descended from slaves. Their ancestors did not come to the promised land; they came to the American gulag. They were not freed legally until 1863, long after many European countries had abolished slavery. They did not gain true legal and political equality until after World War II, and they have made meaningful social and economic progress only in recent decades. Emancipated black Americans are the new driving force shaping American policies toward Africa.

In foreign policy, as in domestic policy, there are two ways to make up for racial discrimination: public aid and economic preferences (affirmative actions), and private reforms and market opportunity (individual and nongovernmental initiatives). For much of the postwar period, the United States and Europe tried the aid and preference approach—the decolonization of Africa and much of Asia in the 1950s and 1960s was followed by three decades of massive foreign aid and preference programs. International institutions set up soft-loan windows (subsidized loans) and poured billions of dollars into the developing world, particularly Africa. Trade was organized on the basis of reverse discrimination. The UN Conference on Trade and Development (UNCTAD), established in 1964, created special tariff preferences for manufactured exports from developing countries and, in the wake of the oil crisis, proposed a massive Commodity Import Program (CIP) to fix higher prices and create market cartels for all major raw material exports. Numerous other preference schemes involving subsidies, price-fixing, and discrimination were launched for the benefit of developing countries, including codes of conduct to regulate multinational corporations, technology transfer, shipping, fishing, and ocean seabed resources.

As the poorest of the poor, Africa was a primary beneficiary of much of this foreign aid, receiving about 30 percent of the total aid from industrial countries. It cannot be said that none of this aid did any good. Basic human needs were addressed in many countries; life expectancy, literacy, and primary education increased. Still, the results, particularly in Africa, were astoundingly meager. From 1965 to 1990, Africa's per capita income rose only 0.2 percent per year.[56]

The aid approach failed, not because it was insufficient or ill intentioned, but because it ignored domestic policies that make the largest contribution to success or failure.[57] African countries that made the most progress—Botswana, Kenya, Ivory Coast, Mauritius, and South Africa—did so on the basis of domestic policies that used educated elites (often white or Asian citizens), encouraged domestic and foreign competition, and maintained reasonable economic policies and political stability. Countries that failed used domestic institutions and resources to wage ethnic warfare and build personal fortunes—Guinea, Angola, and Zimbabwe—or implemented Marxist statist policies that snuffed out economic incentives and political freedom—Tanzania and Uganda. In general, except in South Africa, foreign aid donors ignored domestic repression. Some of the countries most favored by aid, such as Tanzania, proved to be among the worst offenders in denying their citizens basic freedom.[58]

Developing countries in Asia that escaped poverty in the 1970s and 1980s did so mostly on the basis of sound domestic policies and open international trade and investment. Their approach focused on domestic reforms in agriculture, education, health, and macroeconomic policies and encouraged private capital formation, both foreign and domestic, to exploit export opportunities. Less ethnic diversity in Asia facilitated development, but also encouraged corporatist industrial and financial institutions and authoritarian governments. In this context, Africa's greater ethnic diversity is both an obstacle and an asset. It is an obstacle because it threatens political stability; it is an asset because it facilitates a domestic system of checks and balances and competitive markets. In the short run, Africa has to master division and political instability. Over the long run, it has to master inclusion and economic growth.

POLITICAL STABILITY AND MILITARY INTERVENTION
A common perception sees Africa as a continent lost in tendentious tribalism. National boundaries, drawn up by colonial masters (mostly at the Congress of Berlin in 1878), bear little if any relationship to the sources of identity for most African people. Sub-Saharan Africa has 600 million people and 48 nations. It has more than 2,000 tribes or ethnic groups. Most have their own languages and dialects—750 separate languages altogether. Only four countries are ethnically homogeneous—Botswana, Lesotho, Somalia, and Swaziland. The rest are carved up in a mind-numbing kaleidoscope of crossing and crisscrossing ethnic, tribal, and national boundaries. Congo (the former Zaire) alone has 75 distinct languages.[59]

How does one build a nation in this context? Early postindependence leaders in Africa tried to build nations through the state as a central institution that controlled and dispensed all political and economic patronage. One-party or military regimes dominated. Great leaders such as Kwame Nkrumah in Ghana, Mobutu Sese Seko in Zaire (now Congo), Jomo Kenyatta in Kenya, and Julius Nyerere in Tanzania governed in the autocratic and imperial manner of tribal kings. Many ruled by playing off one ethnic group against another. The colonial powers showed little respect for ethnic differences; African leaders followed their example. Ethnic tensions erupted all over Africa. In 2001, civil and interstate conflicts raged between militant groups in Liberia, Sierra Leone, and surrounding countries in west Africa, between the Congo and neighboring states in central Africa, and between belligerents in the Sudan and bordering countries in east Africa.[60] The butchery played out on western television. Can anything be done to stop it? What can America do?

U.S. foreign policy traditions offer little help. Realists counsel doing nothing because American power is not at stake. Internationalists, on the other hand, are too eager to make every conflict an occasion for intervention. Doing nothing damages America's psyche, particularly with regard to its own racial makeup and problems. Doing too much perpetuates historical paternalism, if not colonialism. Credible and sustainable American intervention requires a balance of moral and material interests—at the moment, U.S. material stakes are too modest and U.S. moral stakes too erratic to support sustained commitments. To achieve a better balance, structural constraints dictate that U.S. policies aim, over time, to increase material stakes through trade and investment and to temper moral impulses by intervening only when there is substantial local and regional support.

Outside nations have to help, and to help in a major way. But when the power of outside nations is so overwhelming and political identities are so different, Africans have to decide if they want international help.[61] If they do not, outside peacekeeping or humanitarian forces should not go in. Feeding people in the middle of a tribal or civil war is not a humanitarian mission. It does not save lives; it merely keeps people alive today to die in the fighting tomorrow. And protecting people in these circumstances, in addition to feeding them, puts the humanitarian mission right in the middle of the tribal and civil war. There is no such thing as a purely humanitarian mission in an ongoing conflict. The United States learned this lesson painfully in Somalia.

If the participants do not or are not in a position to ask for help, the best the world community can do is to set up refugee and relief activities as close to the borders of the conflict as possible. Innocent civilians who make it on their own to the relief centers can be cared for and protected, presumably without the need for protective forces because the camps are safely beyond the conflict. If the fighting spreads, the international relief effort has no choice but to pack up its wards and wagons and retreat still further from the conflict.

This is the scenario played out in Rwanda in 1994, when UN and nongovernmental aid organizations set up refugee camps on the current border between Rwanda and the Congo. It was not a pretty spectacle. It did little to help the victims, and it did nothing to stop the cameras or to address the psychic wounds to the countries watching a devaluation of human life (for which President Clinton apologized during his brief visit to Rwanda in 1998). But the alternative is not pretty either. Military intervention to restore peace is not a surgical operation.[62] It requires the insertion of large fighting forces by the international community, and it inevitably involves casualties. Worst of all, it involves a replay of imperial rule. Force has to be applied decisively and probably kept in place for a considerable period of time. Suggestions that Rwanda could have been helped with small and temporary forces are not convincing.[63] The participants have to be cajoled or coerced into cooperating with one another and with the international peacekeeping operation. NATO, with UN legitimation, is playing precisely this role in Bosnia and Kosovo. Why not in Africa as well?

The difference between the Balkans and Africa is twofold. U.S. moral commitments in the two areas are the same, but the U.S. material stake in Africa is less; and the United States gets regional support in the Balkans (where the Europeans carry 80 percent of the military and financial burden). Intervention in Africa may still be warranted, but it will require the development of stronger African institutions and a multilateral consensus in the United Nations. It is not a task for the United States alone or for the industrial nations alone, although Europeans might be more heavily involved than the United States in Africa, just as they are in the Balkans.

The United Nations and the Organization of African Unity (OAU) bear the primary responsibility. In 1993, the OAU approved a new mechanism for preventing, managing, and resolving conflicts in Africa.[64] This mechanism recognized the need to consider and potentially intervene in situations that were previously believed to constitute exclusively domestic affairs. But the OAU has shown little willingness or ability to implement this mandate. To date, peacekeeping activities in Africa have been either ad hoc, local African undertakings[65] or UN operations (Sierra Leone, Liberia, Angola, Mozambique, Namibia, etc.). When the UN failed to put such a force together in Rwanda, in part because the belligerents rejected the idea and said they would attack UN troops if they intervened,[66] the United States proposed an African Crisis Response Force (ACRF), to be paid for half by the United States and half by Europe.[67] France swiftly objected, seeing it as an attempt by the United States to bolster its influence in the region.

Until African nations take the lead, there is likely to be little systematic development of crisis peacekeeping forces for Africa. Africa needs a viable regional organization that has the diplomatic and monitoring capabilities of an institution like the OSCE in Europe and a standing military force that is preferably part of the United Nations. How such a UN force might be constituted and commanded is a serious issue. Weakness in command led not only to American losses in Somalia, but to Indian and Jordanian losses in Sierra Leone. If effective command structures are established and UN forces exercise and train regularly, as NATO forces do, U.S. personnel could be part of UN operations in Africa.[68]

Africa will not shed its ethnic divisions quickly. What matters is how it handles these divisions. Some border adjustments may be possible. Eritrea's separation and independence from Ethiopia suggests that old borders are not necessarily sacrosanct. (Europe teaches the same lesson in Czechoslovakia's

Velvet Revolution.) Ethnic separation, where it does not involve widescale ethnic cleansing, may be possible, although it is no panacea for conflict. On the other hand, African states show a powerful capacity to reconcile as well as perpetrate ethnic strife. Nigeria healed the wounds of its civil war rather quickly, although other divisions plague that country. The nation-state is still a viable unit in most of Africa;[69] smaller ethnic units are simply not compatible with economic and technological realities. If anything, African states need to strengthen subregional cooperation, both as a way to soften polarized ethnic conflicts and to create larger economic units.[70]

DEMOCRACY IN AFRICA

The first requirement in much of Africa is stability and nation-building. But the postindependence experience suggests that stability by nondemocratic means, one-party and patronal rule, is ephemeral and costly. It leads to unacceptable human rights abuses and unnecessary nationalist and mercantilist conflicts with industrial countries. Hence, democracy in Africa is also a first-order priority.

Compared to the Middle East and Asia, Africa has a political culture that is not, in the abstract, hostile to democracy.[71] Half of Africa is Christian and hence open to individualism. Although village life is communal, it is also participatory.

Table 7.3 shows identity and power indicators for the sub-Saharan African countries. Some countries—South Africa, Mauritius, São Tomé and Príncipe, and Cape Verde—have democracy rankings that compare favorably with western countries. A number of others fall closely behind—Benin, Botswana, Madagascar, and Namibia. Overall, in terms of democratic credentials, the region looks much better than the Middle East and just as good as Asia. Compared to Latin America, however, Africa is clearly less democratic.

Africa also has had little prior experience with democracy, even in terms of multiparty elections. Before 1990, only five countries had held free elections with competing parties—Botswana, Gambia, Mauritius, Senegal, and Zimbabwe. (South Africa did not qualify because of its restricted franchise.) Only one of these, Mauritius, had ever witnessed a peaceful change of government through elections. Political institutions of all sorts—party mechanisms, legislative procedures, and executive bureaucracies—are weak in Africa. Thus, Africa starts well behind Latin America in cumulative democratic experience, but ahead of the Middle East and many Asian states in terms of a more democratically friendly political culture.

After 1989, Africa experienced a virtual explosion in democratic activity. By the end of 1997, only four of the forty-eight sub-Saharan African countries had not held a competitive multiparty election—Nigeria, Somalia, Swaziland, and Zaire (now Congo). (Nigeria did hold an election in 1993, but the results were immediately annulled by the military.) From 1990 to 1994, fifty-four elec-

Table 7.3. Power and Identity Indicators in Sub-Saharan Africa

		Political				Economic		Military			Social
	Population, 1999[a] (millions)	Freedom Rating[b]		Polity IV Rating, 1999[c]	Minority (%)[d]	PPP GNI, 1999[e] (billions of dollars)	Economic Freedom, 2001[f]	Budget (% GDP)[g]		Weapons of Mass Destruction and Delivery Systems[h]	Human Development Index, 1998[i]
		PR	CL					1985	1999		
Angola	12.4	6	6	−3	37, 25, 13, 25	14	4.50[l]	15.1	16.5		0.405
Benin	6.1	2	3	6	1	6	2.90	1.1	1.4		0.411
Botswana	1.6	2	2	9	5	10	2.95	1.1	5.2		0.593
Burkina Faso	11.0	4	4	−1	40, 60	11	3.30	1.1	2.1		0.303
Burundi	6.7	6	6	−2	14, 1	4	4.00[l]	3.0	6.4		0.321
Cameroon	14.7	7	6	−4	31, 19, 11, 10, 8, 7	22	3.20	1.4	1.5		0.528
Cape Verde	0.4[b]	1	2	NA	28, 1	NA	3.35	0.9	2.7		0.688
Central African Republic	3.5	3	4	6	34, 27, 21, 8	4	NA	1.4	4.0		0.371
Chad	4.5	6	5	−2	NA	6	3.60	2.9	2.9		0.367
Comoros	0.6[b]	6	4	−2	NA	NA	NA	NA	NA		0.510
Republic of the Congo	2.9	6	5	−6	48, 20, 17, 12	NA	3.70	1.9	3.4		0.507
Congo (formerly Zaire)	49.8	7	6	NA	200+ groups	2	4.70[l]	1.5	7.8		0.430
Djibouti	0.4	4	6	3	35, 5	NA	3.35	7.9	5.0		0.447
Equatorial Guinea	0.4	7	7	−5	NA	NA	3.90	2.0	1.8		0.555
Eritrea	4.0	7	4	−6	40, 7	4	NA	5.7[k]	44.4		0.408
Ethiopia	62.8	5	5	NA	32, 9, 6, 6, 7	39	3.65	17.9	7.1		0.309

Gabon	1.2^b	5	5	−4	NA	6	3.25	1.8	2.1	0.592
Gambia	1.3^b	7	5	−5	1	2	3.35	1.5	3.5	0.396
Ghana	18.9	3	3	2	0	35	3.10	1.0	1.2	0.556
Guinea	7.2	6	5	−1	40, 30, 20, 10	14	3.10	1.8	1.7	0.394
Guinea-Bissau	1.2^b	3	5	6^j	1	1	4.00	5.7	1.9	0.331
Ivory Coast	14.7	6	4	4^j	23, 18, 15, 11	NA	3.00	0.8	1.0	0.420
Kenya	30.0	6	5	−2	22, 14, 13, 12 11, 6, 6, 15, 1	30	3.15	3.1	3.1	0.508
Lesotho	2.1	4	4	NA	0	5	3.40	4.6	4.2	0.569
Liberia	2.9^b	4	5	0	3,3	NA	NA	2.4	5.6	NA
Madagascar	15.1	2	4	6	NA	12	3.10	2.0	0.8	0.483
Malawi	10.8	3	3	7	NA	6	3.55	1.0	1.8	0.385
Mali	10.9	3	3	4	5	8	2.95	1.4	1.2	0.380
Mauritania	2.6	6	5	−6	40, 30, 30	4	3.70	NA	NA	0.451
Mauritius	1.2^b	1	2	10	27, 5	11	2.95	0.3	2.0	0.761
Mozambique	17.3	3	4	6	2	14	3.35	8.5	4.1	0.341
Namibia	1.7	2	3	6	6, 7	9	2.95	2.7^k	4.4	0.632
Niger	10.5	5	5	4	22, 9, 8, 5	8	3.50	0.5	1.7	0.293
Nigeria	123.9	4	3	4	250 groups	95	3.35	3.4	4.4	0.439
Rwanda	8.0	7	6	−5	15, 1	7	3.60	1.9	6.2	0.382
São Tomé and Príncipe	.2^b	1	2	NA	NA	NA	NA	NA	NA	NA
Senegal	9.3	4	4	−1	43, 24, 15, 18	13	3.05	1.1	1.6	0.416
Seychelles	0.1^b	3	3	NA	NA	NA	NA	2.1	1.8	0.786
Sierra Leone	4.9	3	5	NA	10	2	3.80^l	1.0	1.5	0.252
Somalia	7.1	7	7	NA	15	NA	4.80^l	6.2	4.6	NA
South Africa	42.1	1	2	9	14, 9, 3	367	3.05	2.7	1.3	0.697
Swaziland	1.0^b	6	5	−9	3	NA	3.00	NA	NA	0.655
Sudan	28.0	7	7	−7	39, 6, 3	NA	3.85^l	NA	NA	0.477
Tanzania	32.9	4	4	−6	100 groups	16	3.50	4.4	1.7	0.415
Togo	4.6	5	5	−2	37 groups	6	3.75	1.3	2.3	0.471
Uganda	21.5	5	5	−1	17, 12, 8, 8, 6, 6, 5, 38	25	3.00	1.8	2.5	0.409

Table 7.3. (Continued)

		Political			Economic		Military			Social
	Population, 1999[a] (millions)	Freedom Rating[b]		Polity IV Rating, 1999[c]	PPP GNI, 1999[e] (billions of dollars)	Economic Freedom, 2001[f]	Budget (% GDP)[g]		Weapons of Mass Destruction and Delivery Systems[h]	Human Development Index, 1998[i]
		PR	CL		Minority (%)[d]			1985	1999		
Zambia	9.9	5	4	1	1	7	3.15	1.1	2.5		0.420
Zimbabwe	11.9	6	4	−6	2	32	4.25	5.6	6.1		0.555
TOTAL	636.6					857					

Note: NA, not available.

[a]*World Development Report 2000/2001: Attacking Poverty* (New York: Oxford University Press, for The World Bank, 2001), 278–79.

[b]*Freedom in the World 1999–2000* (New York: Freedom House, 2000), 596–97. Ratings are based on a scale of 1–7, with 1 signifying the most free in the categories of Political Rights (PR) and Civil Liberties (CL). Population data are taken from respective country page.

[c]*Polity IV: Political Regime Characteristics and Transitions, 1800–1999,* Center for International Development and Conflict Management, University of Maryland at College Park, 2000. Rating is based on Democracy Score (scale of 0–10, with 0 signifying low democracy) minus Autocracy Score (scale of 0–10, with 0 signifying low autocracy).

[d]U.S. Central Intelligence Agency, *The World Factbook 2000,* http://www.cia.gov/cia/publications/factbook/index.html. Single minority groups with at least 5% of the population are listed separately, with the final number including all minority groups with less than 5%. Minority refers to ethnic origin.

[e]*World Development Indicators 2001* (Washington, D.C.: World Bank, 2001), 12–14. GNI equals GNP plus net receipts of primary income from nonresident sources. Conversions are at Purchasing Power Parity (PPP) exchange rates, not current exchange rates.

[f]Gerald P. O'Driscoll Jr., Kim R. Holmes, and Melanie Kirkpatrick, *2001 Index of Economic Freedom* (Washington, D.C.: The Heritage Foundation, 2001), 8–14. Rankings are based on a scale of 1–5, with 1 signifying the most freedom. The score is based on trade policy, fiscal burden of government, government intervention in the economy, monetary policy (inflation), capital flows and foreign investment, banking, wage and price controls, property rights, business regulations, and black markets.

[g]*The Military Balance, 2000/2001* (London: Oxford University Press, for The International Institute for Strategic Studies, 2000), 297–301.

[h]Countries proven or suspected to have Atomic, Biological, or Chemical weapons and Short-range, Medium-range, or Long-range military missile capabilities, as cited in the following sources and from interviews with government officials. Federation of American Scientists, http://www.fas.org; Center for Nonproliferation Studies, Monterey Institute of International Studies, http://www.cns.miis.edu; Henry R. Stimson Center, http://www.stimson.org; Stockholm International Peace Research Institute, http://www.sipri.se; U.S. Department of Defense, *Proliferation: Threat and Response* (Washington, D.C.: Department of Defense, 1997); U.S. Department of Defense, http://www.defenselink.mil/pubs.

[i]United Nations, *Human Development Report 2000* (New York: Oxford University Press, for the United Nations Development Programme, 2000), 157–60. Rankings are based on life expectancy, real GDP per capita, and a combination of adult literacy and school enrollment ratios. The highest possible index value (better off) is 1.0, while the lowest possible value is 0.

[j]Data are for 2000 (1999 data unavailable).

[k]Data are for 1995 (1985 data unavailable).

[l]Data are for 2000 (2001 data unavailable).

tions (including separate parliamentary and presidential elections in some countries) took place in twenty-nine countries. Thirty elections passed muster by international election observers as free and fair. Eleven involved a peaceful transfer of power from an incumbent party to an opposition candidate, something quite unprecedented in African leadership successions. The most important transfer took place in South Africa, but others included Benin, Burundi, Cape Verde, the Central African Republic, the Republic of Congo, Madagascar, Malawi, Niger, São Tomé and Príncipe, and Zambia. Three other countries—Lesotho, Mali and Namibia—installed new governments in elections in which incumbents declined to run.[72]

Very quickly, however, the bloom came off the rose. Of the initial elections in fifteen additional countries between 1994 and 1997, none met international standards of being free and fair. In eleven cases, opposition parties boycotted the elections, and a peaceful transfer of power (with no incumbent running) occurred in only one, Sierra Leone in 1996. In all of those countries except Tanzania, military leaders, who had seized power earlier, ran in civilian elections to bolster their international standing. That they felt the need to do so said something about the new pressure to conform to democratic standards. But in four countries—Burundi, Sierra Leone, Republic of Congo, and Niger—democratic elections were reversed by military coup before second elections could be held. And in two others, military coups either ended multiparty regimes (Gambia) or perpetuated authoritarian rule (Congo, formerly Zaire).

Thirteen of the seventeen new democracies in Africa held second elections between 1995 and 1997, but half of these elections (eleven out of twenty-three cases) resulted in deteriorating performances compared to the initial elections. In only two cases—Madagascar and Benin—did power change hands from one party to an opposing party. In the Ivory Coast, Zambia, Mali, and Comoros, incumbents manipulated election rules and tolerated or even encouraged violence in the election process. Local government elections fared even worse. African democracy is not anchored in grassroots constituencies.

By the end of the millennium, one-party rule persisted in such key African countries as Kenya and Uganda. And although Nigeria, the most populous state in Africa, ended direct military rule in 1999 and transferred power to an elected civilian government, that government was headed by a former general who had led a military regime in the 1970s. Sectarian differences continued to divide Nigeria between the Muslim north and Christian south.

The major drawback in Africa is weak institutions. Democracy is at best thin and does not penetrate much beyond elections.[73] Legislatures in Africa have little experience with real power, and civil society is fractured by ethnic divisions and weak traditions for protecting property, safety, and contractual rights. Nevertheless, democracy begins somewhere, and African states have begun the long trek. Ghana and Senegal ended one-party rule in 1999–2000, and

South Africa held second elections transferring power within the dominant African Congress Party. Reversion to widespread one-party rule is unlikely. More likely is multiparty fragmentation, stalemate, and, regrettably, in some cases civil war. Our conclusion is not to knock multiparty elections but to focus on building institutions that hold elected officials and military leaders accountable and create a civil and economic society that relies less on government to achieve citizen goals.

MARKETS AND CIVIL SOCIETY

How can Africa develop with weak institutions? Will not democracy, which encourages rather than constrains diversity and pluralism, simply make development more difficult? These are the questions that have justified authoritarian rule and statist economic policies since Africa's independence. But they are the wrong questions. African countries do not need strong states to develop—they need strong *societies,* that is, a strong sense of community and common purpose, which a state may symbolize but cannot create. Africa's postindependence authoritarian leaders used the state to create personal fiefdoms. As Kofi Annan, the UN secretary-general, noted, they created "an acute form of 'winner-takes-all' politics, where victory at the ballot box has translated into total control over a nation's wealth and resources."[74]

Democracy could do much better. Indeed, the only country in Africa that has achieved Asian-type growth (8 percent per year during 1965–90), Botswana, is a democracy, albeit one in which the same party has won every election since independence.[75] Democracy is a formula for accommodating diversity, unleashing economic incentives, and creating a sense of common worth. Democracy in Africa, although it may be a long time coming, should not be delayed because it is thought to complicate development. Elites and the state apparatus they construct and control, not ethnic pluralism, are the chief obstacles to development in Africa.[76]

Africa needs better indigenous political leadership, but not a stronger or bigger state. It needs leaders who can rise above ethnic origins and create a sense of fair play and rules that apply to all ethnic and socioeconomic groups. Democratic processes contribute directly to the creation of this sense of fairness. South Africa may be an example. Elections in 1994, considered by all to be free and fair, produced a unity government that included the white minority and struggled to marginalize extremists. This government produced a new constitution. The white-dominated National Party then withdrew from the government and now plays the role of the loyal opposition. The transition still has a long way to go. Crime is rising, and whites continue to dominate economic life. The government has yet to prove its capacity to provide safety and opportunity for all its citizens. But the country is moving in the right direction.

The old debate between aid and markets paid little attention to civil society, yet the protection of minorities and the promotion of nongovernmental institutions are the best defenses against the abuses of both governments and markets. Human rights are now a recognized area of international, not just domestic, concern. Aid should focus on protecting basic human rights, such as habeas corpus, and on promoting participatory rights, both to obtain access to politics and to achieve higher incomes in the economic and social system. This new type of aid is called "democracy promotion," understood in the fullest sense of not only facilitating free and fair elections, but building up the capacities of individual citizens to participate in the life of the nation.[77]

In Africa, most of the citizens are still rural inhabitants. Two-thirds of the African economy is agricultural; by comparison, the same proportion of the Latin American economy is industrial. Because Africa is still feudal, traditional approaches to promoting civil society—for example, working with labor and professional groups in urban areas—are less relevant. The target has to be the agricultural society.

Three policies are key to promoting civil society in Africa—agricultural development, privatization and small-industry investment, and export orientation. Agriculture must lead. Based on arable land, Africa could produce 130 times more food than it does today.[78] It has 2 billion acres of arable land that are not being cultivated. The surplus generated by agriculture could then be plowed back into education, health, and housing for the still largely agricultural population. Some of this population may migrate to cities, but much of it may have to be accommodated in the countryside. Cottage industries—textiles, toys, and plastics—should be encouraged. Some labor can be absorbed in the construction of rural infrastructure, such as roads, storage facilities, and communication lines. The objective, however, is not to keep the poor on the farm indefinitely, as some of the anti-city ideologies of the 1970s prescribed (e.g., the "small is beautiful" movement) and as some nostalgic environmental movements do today. The objective is to move people gradually, as the human and social situation permits, into the industrial economy and the nationally, regionally, and internationally oriented urban communities.

Once we understand that the old Marxist-capitalist debate is over, development policy can draw from a more critical assessment of the Asian development experience. Competitive industries do not spring full-grown from the ground. They are cultivated and, yes, for a time, protected. Depending only on foreign investment and export-oriented industries is not enough. Too often, enclave economies develop that do not automatically spill over into the domestic market. Firms, both foreign and domestic, need to be nurtured to develop the local market and then expand into exports.

How should industries be selected for development? Here the Asian model needs serious correction. Government bureaucracies, state-directed banks, and their monopolist counterparts in the corporate sector are not efficient allocators of capital. They tend to overinvest based on personal ties, not corporate performance. A competitive banking system and commercial markets for equity and investment capital are essential. Laws that privatize existing state property and promote greater private entrepreneurship are then needed to ensure a vigorous competition for labor and capital.

Government policy, in short, has a critical role to play. But the international community should finally get it right as to what that role is. Government invests in education and health to populate the civil society with independent and activist citizens. It provides safety and an impartial judicial system to protect private property and contracts. It creates the rules for private competition and mobility in all sectors—labor, capital, and trade. It opens markets for countries that are too small to develop on their own. And it maintains stable macroeconomic policies and financial markets.[79] To illustrate, since the mid-1990s over two-thirds of sub-Saharan African countries have been implementing government policies along these lines, and in 1995–96 these countries averaged growth rates of 5 percent per annum. Countries implementing IMF programs grew fastest.

IMF programs are not the problem. The problem is how these programs are implemented by local governments. IMF programs provide currency support for developing countries if these countries meet certain targets for reducing budget deficits, money supply, and inflation. But IMF programs cannot work if local politicians cut budget deficits by reducing education and health expenditures for the poor rather than cutting subsidies for elite urban hospitals or raising taxes on the rich. Nor can they work if central banks are corrupt or incompetent to manage the money supply. The IMF becomes a convenient scapegoat for bad policies by elitist governments, but it is not the cause of these policies.

If the critics want to put pressure on the IMF and other international institutions where it really counts, let them insist on greater cooperation and accountability among the various international agencies. The real scam in the IMF and World Bank is not the substance of their programs but the secrecy, rivalry, and lack of public accountability of their bureaucracies. The IMF and the World Bank carry out interdependent economic functions. The IMF is responsible for sound economic policies (e.g., fiscal and monetary policies), and the World Bank is responsible for structural development (e.g., human and physical infrastructure). The two functions go hand in hand, yet the two institutions often duplicate or ignore one another. They operate, for all practical purposes, in a political vacuum. There is no world parliament or presidency to impose accountability. The only available source of accountability is stronger international economic policy coordination among the major industrial nations. As I note in chapter 4, such coordination is the central role of the G-7 summit process. In tandem with the broader G-20 process (established in 1999 and including the G-7 countries plus key developing nations such as China, Mexico, India, and Brazil), the G-7 countries need to exert stronger management of the IMF and World Bank and restrict their activities to more limited but coordinated goals.

The international trade regime is also critical for African countries. With more and smaller countries than any other continent, Africa needs healthy regional and global markets to promote the development of its national markets. In 1991 the OAU set a target of economic integration of Africa by 2025. But little progress has been made. Frustrated, the OAU recreated itself in 2001 as the African Union, modeled after the European Union. But this effort, inspired and financed by Libyan strongman Muammar al-Qaddafi, is more politics than substance. Africa is too diverse to unify economically. Subregional common market efforts may be more feasible; some already exist, such as the Common Market for Eastern and Southern Africa, the Southern African Development Community, and the Economic Community of West African States. Quantitative barriers to trade have fallen and exchange rate regimes have been liberalized. These trends are minimal and not yet locked in, but they move in the right direction and should be complemented by broader global trade liberalization efforts.

Unfortunately, the United States is providing only grudging support. After three years of pusillanimous debate, the U.S. Congress finally passed a bill in 2000 to lower tariffs and quotas on imports from African, Caribbean, and Central American countries, including limited quantities of apparel and textile imports. But the bill contains labor standards and other conditions that restrict eligibility and may do little more than divert imports from some poor countries to others.[80] Africa needs much more. Its share of world trade is minuscule and actually fell from the 1950s to mid-1990s.[81] Yet, eventually, trade is the continent's best hope because foreign capital will not come into the continent without more open markets and lower costs of production. And without private capital, Africa remains dependent on permanent aid and periodic debt relief, which is the same thing as aid. Africa and other developing countries should be the focus of a major new, U.S.-led, global trade round that sharply raises the prospects of bringing these countries into the globalization process.

* * *

During the Cold War, America felt besieged in the developing world. Proxy wars and Organization of Petroleum Exporting Countries (OPEC) oil crises challenged America's will to contain the Soviet Union and protect old and new democracies in western Europe and Japan. Today, the United States and other industrial democracies have unparalleled influence in the developing world. Democratic values and institutions are spreading, particularly in Latin America and parts of Asia. And market reforms in manufacturing staged a decisive breakthrough in Asia and are now doing the same in parts of Latin America.

This process of political and economic liberalization is still in its infancy. Africa and the Middle East remain largely excluded, and Asia and Latin America face stiff challenges in the financial and service sectors, which are now as important as manufacturing. But the opportunities have never been greater. The United States can seize these opportunities by expanding markets and market assistance, prodding local leaders to accept more responsibility, and working cooperatively with regional and international institutions to stabilize religious and ethnic conflicts. Military power is a continuing fact in much of the developing world, but nowhere is it a threat to U.S. interests. The fear of threats from the developing world—terrorism, drugs, and pollution—is not the right starting point for American foreign policy. The opportunity to increase the political and economic well-being of these countries and thereby enhance America's moral and material stake in the developing world is.

American Foreign Policy in the Twenty-first Century

U.S. foreign policy in the twenty-first century depends as much on identity change in the United States and other countries as it does on external geopolitical circumstances. Indeed, domestic change is often the primary source of external power shifts. Power in the information age is generated by internal economic and technological development more than by external acquisition of foreign markets or resources. Domestic policies create and destroy wealth, not foreign conquests. In the 1980s, the United States rebuilt its economic might by focusing on the transformation of its domestic market. Japan, by contrast, lost ground by focusing on external markets and neglecting internal reforms. In the new information economy, wealth and power derive from domestic innovation and productivity, not from export market share and patient capital that ignore profitability.

The pundits of the late 1980s were wrong. Great powers do not rise and fall because they exhaust their resources in external military adventures.[1] The United States stretched its military resources extensively and still won the Cold War. Similarly, the Soviet Union lost no external wars. And considering that the United States spent heavily on both military and economic investments, the Soviet Union did not face an inexorable trade-off between its military and domestic investments. The Soviet Union lost because it failed to inspire and unleash the talents of its own people. It lost because none of its citizens supported the use of its vast military power and none had the incentive to work, save, and invest to expand the Soviet economy.

Traditional studies ignore these motivational and ideological factors.[2] In the 1970s, they focused on the decline of U.S. external power, a redistribution of wealth to the oil-producing states and a loss of military prestige to North Vietnam and its patron, the Soviet Union. These studies predicted the rise of new powers. "The global productive balances," Paul Kennedy wrote in 1987, "have already begun to tilt in certain directions: away from Russia and the United States, away also from the EEC to Japan and China."[3] "The rise of the Pacific region is likely to continue," he concluded.[4] The United States was going to have to get used to a new multipolar world in which it was only one of several opposing great powers.[5]

On almost every count, the traditional studies have not been borne out. Russia did indeed decline, but not for reasons given by traditional studies. Russia kept sinking even after it shed the burdens of Soviet empire in central Europe and Afghanistan. The western powers did not decline at all. The United States experienced a spectacular rebirth, not only "winning" the Cold War but becoming once again the dominant economic power in the world.[6] The EU also surged ahead to create a single market and common currency and, despite an initially weak euro, experienced slow but steady growth into the late 1990s. By contrast, the Pacific region floundered. Japan hit a big pothole in the early 1990s and was still struggling at the beginning of the new millennium to crawl out of a decade-long slump. China slowed to 3–4 percent annual growth (after subtracting excess inventories) from a previous level of 10–12 percent growth and faced potentially crippling problems of unemployment, corruption, and social unrest. The rest of Asia suffered a severe financial crisis in 1997–98 and began a long process of restructuring from export-led manufacturing growth to information-oriented service sectors, including in particular a more competitive banking and financial industry. The "Asian Miracle," in short, aborted; and "the rise of the Pacific region" unexpectedly turned into a trouble-laden stall.

What did the traditional studies miss? They missed domestic developments. The U.S. decline in the 1970s was more the consequence of domestic policies than external power shifts.[7] Profligate economic policies ignited inflation and slowed growth, well before the oil crisis began. Poisonous political scandals immobilized the federal government, and civil rights and feminist issues divided the nation into warring cultural and racial camps. But in the 1980s America reversed course. The nation found a new consensus to adopt more productive economic policies and to strengthen America's self-confidence in the strategic struggle with the Soviet Union. After a serious recession in 1981–82, U.S. GDP grew from 1983–89 at an average annual rate of 4.3 percent, and, after a mild recession in 1990–91, grew again from 1992–99 at an average annual rate of 3.6 percent. In less than two decades, the United States powered ahead once again to the top of the pyramid, while the Soviet Union collapsed and Japan stalled.

Figure C.1 tells the story graphically. In the 1980s, pundits predicted the decline of American power (measured in the figure as share of world GDP), and based on what they saw since 1950, they were right. Even during the heyday of American productivity growth and postwar boom in the 1950s and 1960s, American power steadily declined relative to other countries. But that decline was not significant. In fact, it is exactly what American policy makers wanted. They sought to rebuild World War II adversaries—principally Germany and Japan—to strengthen the West in the Cold War struggle with the Soviet Union. They understood what the pundits did not understand: relative power is used to narrow differences in relative national purpose and identity.

Figure C.1. U.S. Relative Power and Identity

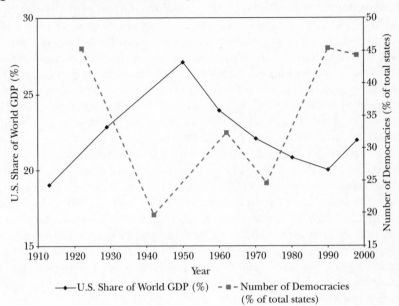

—◆—U.S. Share of World GDP (%)   - ■ - Number of Democracies
(% of total states)

Sources: For data entries from 1910–90, democracy measures from Samuel P. Huntington, *The Third Wave: Democratization in the Late Twentieth Century* (Norman: University of Oklahoma Press, 1993), 26; and GDP measures from Angus Maddison, *Monitoring the World Economy 1820–1992* (Paris: OECD Development Centre, 1995), 182–83, 227 (tables C-16a, G-2). For comparable data entires for 1998, democracy measure from *Freedom in the World 1999–2000* (New York: Freedom House, 2000), 5; and GDP measure from Angus Maddison, *The World Economy: A Millennial Perspective* (Paris: OECD Development Centre, 2001), 175, 184.

As Europe and Japan rebuilt, they drew closer politically and economically to the United States. Democracy consolidated among these countries, and relative military power mattered less as these countries set aside the balance of power and developed peaceful, law-governed commercial relations that outlived the struggle with the Soviet Union.

After the 1970s, America's relative decline slowed, and in the 1990s America's relative power sharply rebounded. At the same time, America's democratic identity spread still wider. By 2000, 44.3 percent of all countries in the world were free and another 31.3 percent were partly free. This convergence of political identities around more liberal domestic institutions changes profoundly the context in which American power operates.

America's relative military power is largely irrelevant for day-to-day relations among the mature democracies. These countries do not threaten one another militarily and coordinate their use of military power toward third countries through NATO. Because domestic identities have converged, the

United States needs far less relative power to achieve its objectives with these countries or, if it acts collectively, with nondemocratic countries as well.

This book offers a framework for considering simultaneously both traditional power factors and domestic identity changes. From this perspective, what does American foreign policy look like as we enter the twenty-first century? Power relationships will certainly shift in the future, as they have in the past. But domestic changes will drive these shifts, not exogenous forces such as "uneven rates of economic growth" or "technological breakthroughs."[8]

Technological change paints a broad canvas in which policy choices are framed. No country will gain power in the twenty-first century if it does not accommodate the profound technological transformations taking place in the new information society. The relative shift of capital and labor to high-skilled services, as opposed to labor-intensive manufacturing, construction, and agricultural production, is inexorable. Each country will navigate this shift through its own unique domestic institutions and cultural values, as we note in chapter 4. But no country is going to avoid this transformation and remain a significant player in the world of the twenty-first century—not Russia, not China, not Japan, and not the European Union, all of whom currently lag behind the information technology front-runner, the United States.

Within the broad canvas of technological change, however, domestic policies and institutions in individual countries will decide who wins and who loses the international sweepstakes of relative power. Some domestic institutions will work better than others, either because they are relatively efficient, or because they motivate maximum effort on the part of their people even though they are relatively inefficient, or because they do both. Political parties, media pundits, and scholars will argue which set of domestic policies or institutions is best. Capitalism, freed of its old nemesis of Marxism, will face new ideological adversaries—third way, communitarian, environmentalist, and postmodern alternatives. Liberalism, freed of its most recent enemy, communist totalitarianism, will face new challenges from multicultural and nonwestern ideologies, such as radical Islam. The debates are necessary and healthy. History, as much as we might wish otherwise, has no end. Still, we would hope, there are lessons to be learned from the past.

Traditional studies draw lessons from historical patterns in the evolution of relative power. Are there comparable lessons to be drawn from historical patterns in the evolution of relative identities? Two general lessons suggest themselves. First, all political institutions motivate people by some combination of appeal to individual development and self-interest, on the one hand, and community development and collective interest, on the other. These appeals motivate the acquisition and use of power and influence not just *if* an entity survives but, more important, *what kind* of entity survives. The major sources of identity relevant to national behavior, as we discuss in chapter 1, include rational (ideological), traditional (cultural, historical, etc.), and charismatic sources. In the twentieth century, rational sources, such as liberalism and communism, dominated. In the twenty-first century, ethnic and cultural divisions may reassert themselves.[9] But these divisions (as we observe in Bosnia, Kosovo, and other parts of the world) are now contending against the widespread forces of democratic rationalism and secular modernization.

What separates the equilibrium-oriented world of pre-industrial Europe from the progress-oriented world of the twenty-first century is precisely the belief that people can improve their circumstances—human and material—by rational procedures and institutions.[10] For the past two centuries, various procedures and institutions (fascism, socialism, communism, and liberalism) have contended against one another to set performance standards for the world. At the beginning of the twenty-first century, liberalism holds the high ground. Liberal institutions and markets seem to work best to liberate individual expression and creativity, and this mobilization of individuals of all genders, races, and religions unleashes enormous physical capacity to increase military and economic power. Liberalism's ascent may be temporary. Nationalism may be on its way back; the end of history is probably not at hand. But the bar of success has been set by liberal societies. Whatever new political appeal does better by way of motivating and unifying the people to increase power will have to clear this bar, or the liberal societies themselves will have to lower it by failing to perform.

This fact, it would seem, is one lesson of the Cold War. The United States and other free societies prevailed in the Cold War because, despite their many faults, they inspired their people to greater sacrifice and achievement than communist societies did. Thus, if nations or regional actors wish to succeed in the struggle for power in the future, they may have to succeed to some extent in the struggle for liberty as well. In the twenty-first century, can anyone imagine a nation becoming a dominant power that kills (e.g., the effect of population controls in China) or mutilates (e.g., genital mutilation in parts of Africa) its female citizens, employs only a minuscule fraction of its women after marriage (Japan), or demands that its women remain hidden from public places (fundamentalist Islam)? If Confucian, Muslim, and other nonwestern societies do not overcome these self-imposed handicaps, they may cause unspeakable disruption and damage in the world (especially if they clash militarily with the West), but they will not prevail over the course of time. There is no rolling back the material consequences of the emancipation of individual human beings.

In any society, therefore, a significant degree of individualism may be necessary to achieve the full material potential of that society. In this sense, individualism is indeed universal. But individualism will always come wrapped in a social package, and it will be combined with different kinds of cultural appeal to community and collective self-interest. In fact, this sort of variation is certain.

Liberal democracies already face new challenges. Multiculturalism (which places more emphasis on traditional sources of ethnic, religious, and cultural identity) and nonwestern societies (which insist on greater parental and public authority) seem to some leaders and societies to provide more order and community than do individualistic democracies. To meet this challenge, traditional liberalism will have to rediscover its community roots—roots that lie in the common commitment of liberal societies to the value of each individual human being and to the right of that individual to reach his or her full potential. This commitment is a powerful source of community and derives from some combination of reason and religion—the rational belief that all human beings can reason and thus be educated, and the religious belief (what else can it be?) that, even if they do not possess equal capacities to reason, they are equally worthy, whatever their level of performance. The belief in individual worth is the product of the Reformation; the commitment to individual reason and education is a product of the Enlightenment. Neither commitment alone can suffice to produce both the equality and the excellence (performance) that characterize liberal socie-ties. But together, these commitments constitute substantial grounds for successful community and drive the traditional liberal quest to secure political and civil rights for all individuals, whatever their race, religion, gender, class, or occupation, and to worry continuously about the acceptable range of inequality consistent with both excellence and social justice.

The second lesson we can draw from the past is that economic policy choices matter. Material growth is not primarily an exogenous phenomenon; markets are shaped by politics and by the laws of scarcity and competition. The way a nation organizes itself politically circumscribes, to a considerable extent, the way that nation organizes itself economically. Liberal societies generally do not choose statist economic systems, and centralized governments generally do not choose liberal market economies. China is trying to be an exception, and the jury is still out as to whether it will wind up like prewar Germany and Japan, threatening other nations, or like postwar Chile, South Korea and Taiwan, eventually democratizing. But there is another source of limits on economic choices that does not exist in politics: physical and economic scarcity. Resources are always limited at some price, and some, such as fossil fuels and petroleum, may be limited physically. Just as history suggests that a struggle for power, at least in the information age, is also a struggle for liberty, it further suggests that the struggle for wealth is, in good part, a struggle to encourage significant economic competition. Because resources (labor, capital, raw materials, and even imagination) are limited at some price, competition ensures a more efficient use of those resources that are available and thus a greater output for the same relative input. It is a point that economic debate often obscures because, without perfect competition, economic analysis also suggests that second-best solutions may be more efficient in practice. The real choice, however, is not between perfect markets (which exist only theoretically) and second-best solutions; it is between less imperfect and more imperfect markets. History offers powerful evidence that more competition works better than less, at least across the broad middle range of options that most countries face. This may be the reason that all advanced societies are capitalist economies, even though some poor societies are also capitalist, at least in name (e.g., India); no advanced society has a statist economy that centralizes production and marginalizes competition.

In *broad* terms, economic science has progressed to the point that we know the basic determinants of growth. No economy since 1900 has increased wealth over a sustained period of time by means of chronic fiscal deficits, runaway inflation, protectionist trade policies, or severe restrictions on foreign investment, capital flows, and exchange rates. Because most countries start their development from a baseline of agricultural subsistence and relative isolation from foreign markets, the general direction of economic policy to achieve growth has been, since the industrial revolution, toward more open and competitive markets. Certainly, the G-7 countries and the international financial institutions should not lose sight of this important lesson of history when they recommend policies for emerging nations around the world, even as they recognize and work with the political factors that limit social tolerance for monetary and fiscal discipline, trade liberalization, foreign workers and direct investment, and market-based exchange rates.

These two lessons from history are crucial. They suggest the things that public policy can most directly affect to move countries around in the various configurations of identity and power that this study has elaborated (see figure 1.2). As I argue in the introduction and chapter 1, U.S. national interest, defined in the broadest terms of both identity and power, is best served by helping to move countries, when possible, toward the configuration of democratic hierarchy (union, as in the case of the EU) or democratic security community (as in the case of the G-7). The objective here is not union or community for its own sake, as it was perhaps for traditional internationalists who saw just about any arms control agreement or international organization as necessarily good for American national interests. The objective is *democratic* union or community. The United States does not want to see a European Union emerge that is not democratic or less democratic than the existing, separate nation-states.

Similarly, it is not globalization or integrated markets per se that the United States seeks through closer trade and investment relations with the EU, Japan, emerging nations, and the democratizing states in the formerly communist parts of Europe. Integrated markets might bring the United States closer to the continental model of social welfare economics, or they might bring Europe closer to the U.S. model of entrepreneurial economics. The latter is obviously more in the U.S. national interest. Nevertheless, neither U.S. nor

European interests would be well served by homogenizing the two models and eliminating the tension and interplay between them. As I argue in chapter 4, global markets do not require a level playing field to foster freer trade, if level means a single set of internal rules for all countries. What global markets do require is a certain minimum level of social safety provisions for the poorest countries and poorest groups within each country. Beyond that, global markets also require vigorous competition of public policies and private companies to use resources more efficiently. That is the reason this study opts for an inward-oriented or competitive model of international economic policy coordination. Countries need the flexibility to try different policies in different situations and to test those policies against the rigors of international competition and resource scarcity. This competitive approach differs from what has been called embedded liberalism, which suggests deeper and deeper layers of social protection (continental Europe's model); it represents instead *enlightened liberalism,* which suggests self-reliant, competitive capitalism on a base of progressive programs to educate and emancipate the disadvantaged (the Anglo-Saxon model).

Viewed from this perspective, the success of U.S. foreign policy in the twenty-first century will be determined by domestic developments in U.S. relations with four principal sets of countries or regions. Figure C.2 illustrates these relationships in terms of their centrality to American interests, defined in terms of identity and power. In contrast to the traditional billiard ball or balance-of-power model of interstate relations, figure C.2 shows countries in terms of their political affinity to one another. The particular country being analyzed (in this study the United States, but it could be any country) sits at the center of the diagram. Other countries then align themselves in concentric circles around that country depending on the convergence or divergence of their identities with the center country. If countries with disproportionate power line up close to the center country, as the EU and Japan do with the United States today, the diagram depicts an interstate system in which conflict is minimized. If powerful countries lie farther away from the center country, as the Soviet Union did from the United States during the Cold War, the diagram resembles a more traditional bipolar or multipolar model of interstate relations, which will involve more conflict.

The first and most important relationship for the United States is that between the United States and other mature democracies in Europe (circle 2 in fig. C.2; relations with Japan are dealt with below). This relationship is not only closest to the core of America's own national identity (circle 1 in fig. C.2), it represents over half of the military capability of the entire world. This relationship is thus the anchor in the world for both U.S. identity and U.S. relative economic and military power. If circle 2, U.S.-EU, drifts away from circle 1, seismic shock waves will once again divide the world's richest and most pow-

Figure C.2. Conceptual Map for American Foreign Policy in the Twenty-First Century

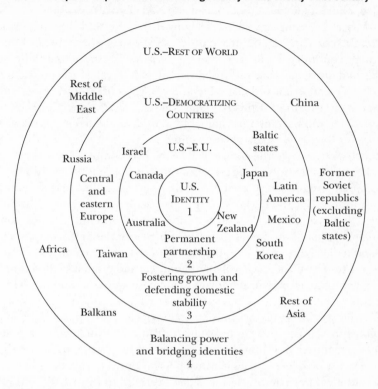

erful nations. America's position in the world will dramatically weaken, and threats to America's national interests will exponentially increase.

What could produce such a devastating reversal of U.S. fortunes in the twenty-first century? Two developments might contribute to this outcome. One would be the breakup of the European Union, precipitated most likely by a stronger Germany, weaker France, indecisive Great Britain, or some combination thereof. The other and related development would be the withdrawal of the American presence in Europe, precipitated most likely by an escalation of economic quarrels with Europe. The United States would then revert to an offshore rather than a forward balancing role. Neither development seems likely at the moment. American leadership is not about to abandon Europe (witness the expansion of NATO); and the European Union, despite the debut of a weak euro and often to the surprise of American officials, continues to march forward, including now perhaps in the area of security as well after Europe's unhappiness with its meager contribution to the NATO air campaign against Kosovo. Individual European allies participate in the U.S.-led military operations against terrorism in Afghanistan, and this new out-of-area terrorist threat may both expedite Europe's plan to deploy a separable European defense force (see chapter 4) and provide the geopolitical glue to keep European and NATO forces united.

Still there are some signs of a damaging drift in EU and U.S.-EU relations. Economic restructuring in Europe proceeds at a snail's pace. In 2001, unemployment continued to average above 8 percent. To compensate, the newly established European Central Bank lowered interest rates, accepted a weaker euro (stronger dollar), and may be tempted to relax fiscal guidelines if unemployment rises further. If this happens, the U.S. trade deficit, already large and growing, will become unsustainable. A trade and currency crisis may be in store for the new U.S.-EU relationship.

If such a crisis arises, the choices will be relatively simple. The United States will have to maintain low interest rates to prevent the rise of the dollar, risking eventual inflation in its own economy, or accept a slowdown of domestic growth induced by the higher dollar and widening current account deficit. The latter course will test the political consensus in the United States to maintain open markets. Europe will either incur higher domestic prices from monetary and fiscal laxity, weakening the euro and reducing incentives for further domestic restructuring, or it will maintain fiscal and monetary discipline and rely on accelerated structural reforms to increase domestic demand. This second course will test Europe's, especially Germany's, political consensus to reduce the tax and regulatory burden on European industries. The economic relationship between the United States and the EU will become a political tug-of-war between how long America can accept a growing trade deficit and how soon European countries can reach a consensus to restructure.

Sound economics may give way again, as it did in the 1970s, to political expediency. Stalled restructuring will further delay the expansion of the EU to include democratizing countries in the East, sour global trade liberalization talks, and consume the fiscal resources that Europe needs to adopt a more self-reliant security policy. Unless Europe increases defense spending, the United States will not be inclined (and rightly so) to share responsibility for military missions in NATO, the Balkans, or the Middle East and Persian Gulf. Tensions will recur, and future Bosnias or Kosovos may divide the alliance again. A traditional scramble may follow for bilateral and national measures to safeguard military and economic security. The traditional balance-of-power and equilibrium politics will reemerge.

Realists expect this scenario. It could happen, but it is not inevitable. Making the right choices could avoid it, the most important being an American commitment to Europe for the long term, the permanent partnership advocated in this study. Such a commitment would encourage America to ride out and shape the slow restructuring of Europe. America accepts a wider trade deficit, at least for a time, if Europe accelerates restructuring and moves more decisively to expand the EU, both internally and externally. In effect, America underwrites a deeper and wider EU (just as it underwrote the original EC).

What does America get in return? It gets a growing and more self-confident European partner that moves faster toward security and foreign policy union and accepts greater defense burdens in western affairs (a European pillar in NATO). And what if Europe still does not move ahead, even with American support? (It might not because, as this study has emphasized, critical choices are mostly a matter of domestic politics and policies, not of international trade or financial concessions.) In this worst case, America may not gain immediately, but what does it lose? Perhaps in helping Europe, America delays an adjustment of its current account and forfeits a small amount of growth (from fewer exports and larger imports). But this loss can be offset by sound domestic policies, which propelled U.S. growth in the 1990s despite slow or no growth in Europe (and Japan). On the other hand, if America does not stick with Europe over the long run, it risks a lot more. It will face the world alone—its foreign obligations will multiply rapidly as it gears up to manage a balance of power, including now military as well as economic power, with the most powerful industrial nations of Europe.

Just as the western half of Europe may fail whatever the United States does, the eastern half of Europe may fail whatever the G-7 does. But the international environment counts for something, and the West's failure sharply increases the chances of setbacks and violence in the former Soviet bloc. It is often argued that conflicts in the East (e.g., how to deal with Russia) may divide the West, but it is equally true that divisions in the West may provide opportunities for conflicts in the East (e.g., paralysis in NATO encouraging Russian meddling in unstable areas such as Kosovo). The second set of domestic relationships crucial to the future of U.S. foreign policy, therefore, is the relationship between the U.S. and EU, on the one hand, and the democratizing states along the gradient from Poland to Russia, on the other (circles 2, 3, and 4 in fig. C.2).

The critical domestic variable in this set of relationships is Russia. In figure C.2, Russia lies on the circle between the democratizing countries of central and eastern Europe and the nondemocratic countries of the Caucasus region and central Asia. Its chances of successfully democratizing are somewhat greater than those of China, but substantially less than those of the central and eastern European countries or the Baltic states. In that sense, the expansion of NATO and the EU cannot wait for Russia to democratize. These institutions must reach out to consolidate democracy and markets where they are most advanced. The purpose of alliance, in this case, is not to deal with actual threats (military aggression) but to defuse potential threats (domestic instability). Although western expansion fuels the xenophobia of nondemocratic groups in Russia in the short run, it marginalizes these groups over the longer run. They will have fewer and fewer options as the world around them stabilizes along democratic lines.

Contrary to the arguments heard during the NATO debate, therefore, NATO expansion helps democracy in Russia, just as NATO expansion to

Poland, Hungary, and the Czech Republic marginalizes nondemocratic forces in Lithuania, Slovenia, Romania, and Bulgaria—potentially the next formerly communist states to join western institutions. The expansion of NATO and the EU, preferably in tandem, is the only way to shape a meaningful security community in the whole of Europe. Anything short of that perpetuates the risks of instability along the democratizing gradient between Poland and Russia. And unless this instability evaporates on its own, failing to expand western institutions does not avoid drawing new lines in Europe; it simply postpones it.

Having clarified this point, I must stress, however, that western institutions have their limits. They cannot have a significant impact on the consolidation of democracy in Russia or the former Soviet republics, with the exception of the Baltic states and possibly Ukraine and Moldova. Russia is simply too big and too robust historically and culturally to be influenced much by the West. It will change, if it changes at all, largely on its own. The international environment may affect the timing and consequences of these changes beyond Russia's borders, but it cannot make anything happen inside Russia. And it is what happens inside Russia that will largely decide what happens in Belarus, the Caucasus region, and the central Asian republics.

Russia's domestic situation has been complicated by the war against terrorism in Afghanistan. In this war, Russia and the United States back antidemocratic governments in central and southwest Asia, which also fight against Muslim extremists in their own societies. While unavoidable (there are no democratic alternatives in these countries), this alliance with authoritarian governments hardens Russian domestic politics and facilitates repression in Chechnya and other Russian breakaway provinces. It also complicates U.S. relations with democratic countries, such as India. The price of these alignments over time may be reduced credibility for America's democratic leadership, less democracy in Russia, and more opportunities for renewed Russian imperialism in central Asia and the Caucasus.

Ukraine and Moldova are most vulnerable to a backsliding of democracy in Russia. Like Poland and Romania, they have identities partially shaped by historical inclusion in the West. Unlike Russia, they are smaller and less robust or unified historically and culturally. NATO expansion and Russian evolution meet at the crossroads of these two countries. If Russia becomes more open, NATO and the EU may expand to include Ukraine and Moldova, helping perhaps to tip the balance of forces inside Russia itself. If, on the other hand, Russia becomes more closed, NATO and EU expansion becomes a potential casus belli. Under these circumstances, NATO expansion into Estonia and Latvia would also provoke conflict, especially if Europe is unable to develop a relevant military pillar in NATO that could provide security arrangements in the Baltic states more acceptable to Russia.

Because the situation in Russia and other former Soviet republics is uncertain, the United States needs an alternative to NATO. NATO is not likely to be able to stabilize democratization processes (however feeble) in many of the former Soviet republics. For this purpose, the United States needs the United Nations and its European counterpart, the OSCE. If the war in Afghanistan succeeds, the United States should use the opportunity to develop a UN peacekeeping force in Afghanistan and perhaps in neighboring central Asian states, jointly administered with Russia under chapter VII provisions of the UN charter. Such a UN peacekeeping activity in this unstable and terrorist-infested region would serve two purposes: it would enhance transparency in that part of the former Soviet Union where Russian imperialism is most likely to reassert itself, and it would safeguard against the possibility that Russia and the United States would come into conflict in this area. The United Nations already plays this role diplomatically in southeastern Europe and the Balkan conflict. There it legitimizes NATO's presence and facilitates the inclusion of Russian forces. In the near abroad, where NATO is unlikely to play a military role, the United Nations would provide both the military and diplomatic presence to ensure international accountability.

A third set of domestic relationships crucial for American foreign policy in the twenty-first century is that between the United States and Japan, followed by China and the rest of Asia (circles 2 and 4 in fig. C.2). Japan sits on the border of circle 2 in figure C.2. It is there deliberately to suggest that Japanese democracy benefits neither from the proximity of other mature democracies in Asia nor from the long and settled liberal traditions of democracy in Europe. Japanese democracy is, in a sense, the outpost of western liberalism, the test case of whether enduring democracy that contributes to the democratic peace is possible outside the North Atlantic area. What is clear from figure C.2, however, and where the identity and power approach in this study differs decisively from most traditional analysis, is that Japan is much closer to the United States than is China.

The American public senses this fact, but American leaders are dangerously purblind on the U.S.-Japan relationship.[11] Both Republican (Nixon) and Democratic (Clinton) presidents have given China priority and alienated Japan (Nixon with his surprise opening to China, and Clinton with his geo-economic rivalry with Japan). Realists, such as Henry Kissinger, openly advocate an evenhanded triangulation of U.S. policy in Asia.[12] Along with economic nationalists, they fixate on the "painfully" and "maddeningly" different cultural practices in Japan,[13] while admiring China's proud culture that is offended by American prescriptions for human rights and the rule of law.

If the United States continues to move in this direction, it will be out of Asia within the next decade. U.S.-Chinese relations will be contentious for some time to come. China is not even contemplating democratic reforms (village elections are marginal—see chapter 6), and China's trade deficit with the United States is already larger than that of Japan. Realists reach for some sort of grand strategic relationship to tie the United States and China together. But against whom is this new strategic partnership directed—Japan, Russia,

India? Realist partnerships depend on antagonisms. Unfortunately, if antagonisms do not exist, realists risk creating them. That is what an Asian policy premised on China will do. It will create profound antagonisms with Japan, fail to reconcile the inevitable tensions with China, and eventually force America to leave the region. No American public will long support a policy that pays an economic price to save an authoritarian regime in China or perpetuates a military commitment to defend an increasingly alienated Japan.

This book suggests another approach. Concentric multilateralism builds a core foundation for American policy in Asia on stronger relations among the Asian democracies. It anchors this foundation in Japan, drawing Japan over time further into the inner circle of mature western democracies (circle 2 of fig. C.2). It then stabilizes the Japanese democracy in a wider regional association with other long-standing democracies in the region, such as Australia, New Zealand, and India, and with newly democratizing countries such as South Korea, Taiwan, the Philippines, Thailand, and, potentially, other ASEAN states. These widening circles, anchored by the trilateralization of military planning and operations among Japan, South Korea, and the United States, simultaneously reach out to include China through economic engagement in APEC and the WTO and through confidence-building security initiatives in ARF. In the more contentious political environment of Asia (as compared to Europe), the United States needs to pursue both power balancing and diplomatic confidence-building.

The situation in Asia at the moment is far less contentious than anything the United States had to deal with in Europe during the Cold War. Concentric multilateralism, therefore, is not containment. But it is also not détente, an anchorless pursuit of economic engagement with China that leaves Japan and aspiring democratizing states in Asia exposed to opaque and unpredictable Chinese intentions. North Korea is a threat in Asia unlike anything that exists today in Europe, including the ethnic instability in the former Yugoslavia. Taiwan is also becoming an increasingly delicate problem. As it democratizes, its identity inevitably becomes more independent of mainland China. That does not sanction a formal declaration of independence by Taiwan, but it also raises the imperative for the United States to defend Taiwan against unprovoked Chinese threats or attacks. Asia illustrates the value of a perspective that includes both identity and power. In relations with China, the United States needs to balance power and pursue converging identities simultaneously, not cycle back and forth between hawkish and dovish initiatives toward China.[14]

The fourth and final set of domestic relationships crucial to U.S. foreign policy in the twenty-first century is U.S. relations with emerging nations (circles 3 and 4 in fig. C.2). The most promising set of relationships in this category is with Latin America. Democracy is on a roll in the Western Hemisphere, and the opportunity for better U.S. ties with these countries, especially Mexico, has never been greater. It would be an historic omission of unprecedented magnitude if U.S. foreign policy missed this opportunity. In Latin America's case, U.S. size and proximity are such that the external environment matters a great deal. In the past, U.S. weight in the hemisphere has been a hindrance as well as a potential help. The hindrance was due mostly to the tendency to treat Latin America largely in terms of great-power conflicts in Europe (colonial competition and then the Cold War). These conflicts are now gone. The United States is free to use its full weight to facilitate market and democratic transitions in Latin America.

Instead, just as Latin America abandons communist-inspired insurgencies and statist-oriented economic policies, the United States has gone to sleep at the wheel of world trade and economic leadership. Failure to implement existing NAFTA provisions (e.g., lifting restrictions on Mexican trucks), let alone expanding NAFTA, betrays a barely concealed contempt, perhaps even chauvinism, toward Mexican and other Latin American societies. The United States can do better. In 2001, the George W. Bush administration put the expansion of NAFTA and the realization of the Free Trade Area for the Americas (FTAA) at the top of its international economic agenda, using this regional initiative to drive Europe and Japan toward wider global trade negotiations in the WTO. Mexico, Brazil, and Argentina (the latter two cooperating in Mercosur) are the key countries. If they grow and progressively democratize, the United States faces not only a more prosperous future because of booming emerging markets in the south, but it realizes a political identification with Latin America (and its own Hispanic American citizens) that finally transcends colonialism and cultural contempt.

Just as the United States has special opportunities in Latin America, Europe and Japan have larger obligations in Africa and the Middle East. Here, partnership with other democracies promises dividends for American foreign policy. Historically, America has resented European colonial ties in Africa and the Middle East. Now, sometimes, Europe resents America's special (colonial-like?) relationship with Israel, and America and France, in particular, perpetuate a petty bureaucratic rivalry for influence in west, east, and central Africa. In the process, American and western values suffer. Genocide goes unattended in Rwanda, and the Arab-Israeli conflict perpetuates serious injustices on both sides of the dividing line.

Just as Europe expects America to earn its seat at the table of wider and deeper European integration, Europe has to earn its seat at the table of larger influence in the Middle East and Africa. At the moment, the price is economic, a stronger European role in mobilizing the resources that will be needed to rebuild an embattled Middle East and an impoverished central Africa. But, over the longer run, the price is strategic. Europe has to pay for more of the security costs of stability in these regions.

For the moment, America sets the policies. It contains Iraq and Iran despite persistent European objections; it leads the Middle East peace negotiations despite an obvious bias toward Israel; and it isolates rogue states such as Libya and Sudan despite African and European skepticism. But the United States can only do so much, even if Europe were to help more. Neither Africa nor the Middle East can make real progress without stronger local contributions. Africa needs its own leader and model—the best, but still distant, prospect is South Africa. The Middle East needs a local community for peace, preferably much closer political and economic relations among Israel, the moderate Arab states (Jordan and Egypt), and the conservative gulf monarchies—followed perhaps, someday, by reconciliation with Syria, Lebanon, and the rejectionist states of Iraq and Iran.

Democracy is not likely to help much in either region. Israel and South Africa are footholds. But Israel is too conflicted between religious fundamentalists and secular democrats and too embattled with its own Arab citizens to inspire much respect or imitation in the Middle East, especially in a Muslim environment not generally hospitable to western-style democracy. And South Africa may never grow much beyond the one-party model of democracy that falls short of regular transfers of power among parties with significant differences. As unpalatable as it may be, American values and power may not be that engaged in Africa. They remain engaged in the Middle East largely because of oil (a stake of diminishing significance during the course of the twenty-first century) and because of a flickering common interest with Europe to prevent the reigniting of great-power rivalries in the Balkans, Middle East, and Caucasus region—rivalries that could spill over once again and engage U.S. central moral and strategic interests in the heart of Europe.

* * *

The map of U.S. foreign policy interests portrayed by figure C.2 is quite different from the traditional maps of nationalism, internationalism, and realism. Nationalists and neoisolationists advocate policies that blow the circles of figure C.2 apart into separate entities engaged with one another in a traditional billiard-ball style of international politics. Internationalists interpret figure C.2 as an American solar system with the sun (the United States) at the center and the various satellites hovering around it, drawing their nurturance and eventually democratic identity from the center power. Realists take the billiard-ball map of neoisolationists and rack the balls into various fluctuating alliances to balance power among rising (China) and falling (Russia) states, preserving equilibrium. None of these maps offers an escape from the historical tendency of American foreign policy to prefer the nationalist or reformist maps unless or until a central threat reemerges.

Terrorist attacks on September 11, 2001, did not resolve the basic dilemma in American foreign policy. They simply ushered in a new realist phase of American foreign policy in which, for the moment, internationalist coalitions serve the most basic nationalist cause, namely to defend a country's citizens and property. If and when the cause is won, the internationalist and nationalist propensities will part ways once again, the former building nations and chasing a broad globalist agenda of reducing poverty, pollution, proliferation, and political polarization around the world, the other reassessing America's involvement in foreign feuds (which make it a target of terrorism) and husbanding resources for homeland defense.

Meanwhile, the world never stays the same. The potential threats and opportunities of the next phase of international history are already percolating on world maps. They are just not visible to traditional foreign policy analysts. They are occurring inside countries, in Islam's struggle with modernization and in the uncertain transition of formerly communist and authoritarian states toward market economies and more liberal governments. These changes will crystallize the surface of world politics into new families and fault lines of ethnic, national, and regional identities. The United States can wait until the new divisions—clash of civilizations, multipolar balance of power, and so on—are evident and threatening. Or it could influence now what is going on beneath the surface of world politics if it had a conceptual map to guide it.

This book provides that conceptual map. At the beginning of the twenty-first century, the United States inhabits a world that is closer to its ideals than it has ever been before. At the center of this world are the United States and all the major industrialized nations of the world. These countries not only control most of the world's wealth, military power, and future technological potential, they discipline this power with similar domestic standards of democratic institutions and market economics. Together, these countries dominate the rest of the world. If America can learn to share power and responsibility with the mature democracies in Europe and Asia, its core interests are essentially unassailable in the twenty-first century, and its prospects of dealing with the rest of the world in a measured and respectful way are greatly enhanced. Its partnership with Europe and Japan builds on the same principles of divided powers, aggressive debate, and competitive initiatives that test political ideas and shape consensus at home. This partnership ensures that ideas are persuasive within the democratic family, or that they are not adopted. And if these ideas are persuasive among democracies, they are also more likely to be fair and just to those countries outside the democratic family and more likely, perhaps, to influence them at the margins to develop more liberal political and economic societies of their own.

If America cannot feel comfortable in such a world, even if it increasingly accepts limits on its sovereignty by shaping decisions collectively with other democracies, it is surely not the country it set out to be or still thinks it is. America carved itself out of an Old World of despotisms and pre–industrial-age deprivation; it now has the chance to lead a New World of industrialized democracies and information-age prosperity. Surely, going abroad, at least among these mature democracies, is like coming home. America can be, at last, at home abroad.

Notes

CHAPTER ONE: IDENTITY AND POWER

1. In this study, I assume that mentality (ideas) and reality (power) are independent, albeit interactive, variables affecting human and state behavior. Ideas interpret and influence all reality, but they do not determine it. Some ideas are false and get slapped down by reality. Early Mexicans thought the conquering Spanish were gods. They treated them as such, and they were enslaved. How do we know when ideas are false? The only sure guide to valid ideas, that is, ideas that stand the test of time and experience, is free and open debate. Thomas Jefferson said it best in 1800, speaking to potential separatists in the new American republic, "If there be any among us who wish to dissolve this union or change its republican form, let them stand undisturbed as monuments of the safety with which error of opinion may be tolerated where reason is left free to combat it." Quoted in Merrill D. Peterson, *Adams and Jefferson: A Revolutionary Dialogue* (Athens: University of Georgia Press, 1976), 92.
2. Washington, quoted in Charles Beard, *The Idea of National Interest: An Analytical Study of American Foreign Policy with the Collaboration of G.H.E. Smith,* ed. Alfred Vagts and William Beard (Chicago: Quadrangle Books, 1966), 40.
3. Palmerston, quoted in Asa Briggs, *The Age of Improvement* 1783–1867 (London: Longmans, 1959), 352.
4. Hans J. Morgenthau, *Politics among Nations: The Struggle for Power and Peace,* 6th ed., ed. Kenneth W. Thompson (New York: Alfred A. Knopf, 1985), 5.
5. Hans J. Morgenthau, *In Defense of the National Interest* (New York: Alfred A. Knopf, 1952), 32–33.
6. Morgenthau, *Politics among Nations,* 12.
7. Morgenthau, *In Defense of the National Interest,* 39.
8. On the rise and consolidation of the sovereign state, see Hendrik Spruyt, *The Sovereign State and Its Competitors* (Princeton: Princeton University Press, 1994); Daniel Philpott, *Revolutions in Sovereignty: How Ideas Shaped Modern International Relations* (Princeton: Princeton University Press, 2001).
9. On the role of these factors, see, respectively, Bruce Bueno de Mesquita, *The War Trap* (New Haven: Yale University Press, 1981), 40–46; Dale C. Copeland, *The Origins of Major War* (Ithaca: Cornell University Press, 2000); Fareed Zakaria, *From Wealth to Power: The Unusual Origins of America's World Role* (Princeton: Princeton University Press, 1998); Stephen Van Evera, *Causes of War: Power and the Roots of Conflict* (Ithaca: Cornell University Press, 1999); Charles L. Glaser and Chaim Kaufmann, "What Is the Offense-Defense Balance and Can We Measure It?" *International Security* 22, no. 4 (1998): 44–83.
10. See Stephen M. Walt, *The Origins of Alliances* (Ithaca: Cornell University Press, 1987). Formal theorists have shown how intentions matter even in the most basic realist circumstances of the security dilemma. See Charles L. Glaser, "Political Consequences of Military Strategy: Expanding and Refining the Spiral and Deterrence Models," *World Politics* 44, no. 4 (1992): 497–539. For useful critiques of recent realist research, see articles by John H. Vasquez and others in the Forum section of *American Political Science Review* 91, no. 4 (1997): 899–937; Jeffrey W. Legro and Andrew Moravcsik, "Is Anybody Still a Realist?" *International Security* 24, no. 2 (1999): 5–56.

11. See Thomas J. Christensen, "Perceptions and Alliances in Europe, 1865–1940," *International Organization* 51, no. 1 (1997): 65–99; William Curti Wohlforth, *The Elusive Balance: Power and Perceptions during the Cold War* (Ithaca: Cornell University Press, 1993); Aaron Friedberg, *The Weary Titan: Britain and the Experience of Relative Decline, 1895–1905* (Princeton: Princeton University Press, 1988). For a comprehensive review of the impact of psychological factors on state behavior, see J. M. Goldgeier and P. E. Tetlock, "Psychology and International Relations Theory," *Annual Review of Political Science* 22, no. 4 (2001): 67–92.

12. See Jack Snyder, *Myths of Empire: Domestic Politics and International Ambition* (Ithaca: Cornell University Press, 1991); James Goldgeier, *Leadership Style and Soviet Foreign Policy: Stalin, Khrushchev, Brezhnev and Gorbachev* (Baltimore: Johns Hopkins University Press, 1994).

13. See Elizabeth Kier, *Imagining War: French Military Doctrine between the Wars* (Princeton: Princeton University Press, 1997); Deborah D. Avant, *Political Institutions and Military Change* (Ithaca: Cornell University Press, 1994); Michael C. Desch, "Culture Clash: Assessing the Importance of Ideas in Security Studies," *International Security* 23, no. 1 (1998): 141–70.

14. See Randall L. Schweller, *Deadly Imbalances: Tripolarity and Hitler's Strategy of World Conquest* (New York: Columbia University Press, 1998).

15. See Samuel P. Huntington, "The Erosion of American National Interests," *Foreign Affairs* 76, no. 5 (1997): 28.

16. See Robert O. Keohane and Helen Milner, eds., *Internationalization and Domestic Politics* (New York: Cambridge University Press, 1996); Robert D. Putnam, "Diplomacy and Domestic Politics: The Logic of Two-Level Games," *International Organization* 42, no. 3 (1988): 427–61.

17. See Peter J. Katzenstein, ed., *The Culture of National Security: Norms and Identity in World Politics* (New York: Columbia University Press, 1996); Alexander Wendt, *Social Theory of International Politics* (New York: Cambridge University Press, 1999); Martha Finnemore, *National Interest in International Society* (Ithaca: Cornell University Press, 1996).

18. Recent constructivist scholarship recognizes the need for an individualistic as well as a collectivist dimension of state identity. Wendt, for example, acknowledges the need for what he calls "rump individualism." An autonomous identity of states exists, but in his scheme of things social identity matters more. See Wendt, *Social Theory of International Politics,* 178–84. Other constructivist scholars see a larger role for independent or reflective processes by which actors argue against and alter the prevailing social structure. See Thomas Risse, " 'Let's Argue!': Communicative Action in World Politics," *International Organization* 54, no. 1 (2000): 1–39; Paul Kowert and Jeffrey Legro, "Norms, Identity and Their Limits: A Theoretical Reprise," in *The Culture of National Security: Norms and Identity in World Politics,* ed. Peter J. Katzenstein (New York: Columbia University Press, 1996), 451–98.

19. For the Gorbachev story, see Risse, "Let's Argue!" 23–28.

20. On the crucial role of the option to use force in distinguishing between cooperative (domestic) and anarchic (international) politics, see Robert Powell, "Absolute and Relative Gains in International Relations Theory," *American Political Science Review* 85, no. 4 (1991): 1303–21; for the later development of Powell's work, see *In the Shadow of Power: States and Strategies in International Politics* (Princeton: Princeton University Press, 1999).

21. For the best comparative discussion I have found of the nature of identity formation at the personal, national, and international levels, see William Bloom, *Personal Identity, National Identity and International Relations* (Cambridge, U.K.: Cambridge University Press, 1990). See also Anthony D. Smith, *National Identity* (Reno: University of Nevada Press, 1991).

22. As Samuel Huntington notes, "faith and family, blood and belief, are what people identify with and what they fight and die for." "If Not Civilization, What?" *Foreign Affairs* 72, no. 6 (1993): 194.

23. Max Weber talks about all three sources of political identity or legitimacy: traditional, rational (or ideological), and charismatic. See Max Weber, *From Max Weber: Essays in Sociology,* trans. and ed. H. H. Gerth and C. Wright Mills (New York: Oxford University Press, 1946), 78–79.

24. The internal dimension of national identity draws more from the liberal than the social theory of international politics. In liberal theory, national identity is constructed from the bottom up, starting with individual citizens. Domestic or internal identity "is defined as

the set of preferences shared by individuals concerning the proper scope and nature of public goods provision [geographical borders, political decision-making processes, and socioeconomic regulations], which in turn specifies the nature of legitimate domestic order by stipulating which social actors belong to the polity and what is owed them." Andrew Moravcsik, "Taking Preferences Seriously: A Liberal Theory of International Politics," *International Organizations* 51, no. 4 (1997): 525.

25. See Jonathan Mercer, "Anarchy and Identity," *International Organization* 49, no. 2 (1995): 229–53.

26. Kenneth N. Waltz, *The Theory of International Politics* (New York: Random House, 1979), 103–4. Here I use the term *legitimacy* in the same sense as Waltz. I am not making a judgment that the rules of any specific nation are legitimate or illegitimate; I am simply identifying empirically the basis on which governments and societies empower public agents to counter private force. I address the crucial role of legitimacy in Waltz's definition of the state in "Power and Legitimacy" (unpublished manuscript, July 1995). See also Helen Milner, "The Assumption of Anarchy in International Relations Theory," in *Neorealism and Neoliberalism: The Contemporary Debate,* ed. David A. Baldwin (New York: Columbia University Press, 1993), 152.

27. John Ruggie criticizes Waltz on this point. See John Ruggie, "Continuity and Transformation in the World Polity: Toward a Neorealist Synthesis," in *Neorealism and Its Critics,* ed. Robert O. Keohane (New York: Columbia University Press, 1986), 131–58.

28. Used in subsequent chapters, these two data sets track the institutional and normative rules by which countries legitimate the internal use of force. The first set, the Polity IV data set, available through the University Consortium for Political and Social Research at the University of Michigan, tracks institutional features of regimes (autocracy, democracy, and eight indicators of political authority). The second set, the index of political freedom available through Freedom House in New York, tracks both institutional and normative features of regimes, such as the protection of civil liberties.

29. For such a debate, see Lawrence E. Harrison and Samuel P. Huntington, eds., *Culture Matters: How Values Shape Human Progress* (New York: Basic Books, 2000). In an earlier study, Huntington uses cultural or civilization measures of identity to distinguish among states and examine their relationships. See Samuel P. Huntington, *The Clash of Civilizations and the Remaking of World Order* (New York: Simon and Schuster, 1996). Marxists and neo-Marxists use class measures to define capitalist and noncapitalist states, and realists traditionally emphasize a combination of geographic and cultural factors (geopolitics).

30. I draw these features from the broad literature on democracy. For excellent coverage of the issues involved in the contemporary spread and evolution of democracy, see the *Journal of Democracy,* especially volumes 8–11 (1997–2000).

31. Thomas Risse-Kappen, "Collective Identity in a Democratic Community: The Case of NATO," in *The Culture of National Security: Norms and Identity in World Politics,* ed. Peter J. Katzenstein (New York: Columbia University Press, 1996), 367.

32. More studies recognize the separate existence of internal and external identities. For example, see Peter Katzenstein, *Cultural Norms and National Security: Police and Military in Postwar Japan* (Ithaca: Cornell University Press, 1996), 7–11, and also chap. 7; Dana P. Eyre and Mark C. Suchman, "States, Norms, and the Proliferation of Conventional Weapons: An Institutional Theory Approach," in *The Culture of National Security: Norms and Identity in World Politics,* ed. Peter J. Katzenstein (New York: Columbia University Press, 1996), 98; Michael N. Barnett, "Identity and Alliances in the Middle East," in *The Culture of National Security: Norms and Identity in World Politics,* ed. Peter J. Katzenstein (New York: Columbia University Press, 1996), 412; Kowert and Legro, "Norms, Identities, and Their Limits," 474–83. See also Jefrey W. Legro, "Culture and Preferences in the International Cooperation Two Step," *American Political Science Review* 90, no. 1 (1996): 118–38.

33. This element of external or social identity is also present in neorealism, but it is weak. Waltz argues that anarchy socializes states into roles depending on their size, but this socialization is minimal. It does not entail any stable relationships because anarchy requires that states remain flexible and capable of aligning with anyone to preserve the balance of power. On this aspect of Waltz, see Wendt, *Social Theory of International Politics,* 16.

34. See Joseph M. Grieco, *Cooperation among Nations: Europe, America, and Non-Tariff Barriers to Trade* (Ithaca: Cornell University Press, 1990); Joseph M. Grieco, "Realist International Theory and the Study of World Politics," in *New Directions in International Relations Theory,* ed. Michael Doyle and G. John Ikenberry (Boulder: Westview Press, 1997), 163–201.

35. There are well-known difficulties in making distinctions among offensive, accommodationist, and defensive attitudes toward the use of force. Nevertheless, these distinctions are made and form the basis of substantial theorizing in the literature about the causes of war. See Glaser and Kaufmann, "What Is the Offense-Defense Balance?" 44–83. For a theory of realism based on aggressive states, see John Mearsheimer, *The Tragedy of Great Power Politics* (New York: W. W. Norton, 2001).

36. The three levels of nonmaterial relations correspond to the type, role, and collective kinds of identity that Wendt discusses in *Social Theory of International Politics,* 224–33.

37. See Zbigniew Brzezinski, "A Geostrategy for Eurasia," *Foreign Affairs* 76, no. 5 (1997): 56; Henry Kissinger, *Diplomacy* (New York: Simon and Schuster, 1994), 533. Kissinger defines the state in terms of both autonomous identity and relative international power: "a state is by definition the expression of some concept of justice that legitimates its internal arrangements and of a projection of power that determines its ability to fulfill its minimum functions. . . ." *Does America Need a Foreign Policy? American Foreign Policy in the Twenty-First Century* (New York: Simon and Schuster, 2001), 20.

38. See John Lewis Gaddis, "The Tragedy of Cold War History: Reflections on Revisionism," *Foreign Affairs* 73, no. 1 (1994): 145. Gaddis's conclusion is at odds with neorealist views. As Waltz argues, the Cold War resulted from a power struggle, not opposing domestic systems: "the world was never bipolar because two blocs opposed each other but because of the preeminence of bloc leaders." *Theory of International Politics,* 130.

39. Morgenthau, *Politics among Nations,* 236, 238.

40. Kissinger, *Diplomacy,* 79, 84. In an earlier book, Kissinger writes about international politics in terms that come very close to the notions of power and identity I employ. "What is considered just depends on the domestic structure of [the statesman's] state; what is possible depends on [that state's] resources, geographic position and determination, and on the resources, determination and domestic structure of other states." Henry Kissinger, *A World Restored: Metternich, Castlereagh and the Problems of Peace 1812–1822* (Boston: Houghton Mifflin, 1973), 5. In short, international behavior depends on both relative domestic identity and relative geopolitical power. Nevertheless, when dealing with aristocratic monarchies in nineteenth-century Europe, Kissinger ascribes much more influence to the manipulation of statesmen, such as Metternich and Bismarck, than to the constraints of domestic politics (chaps. 2, 3, 17).

41. Samuel P. Huntington, "The Clash of Civilizations?" *Foreign Affairs* 72, no. 3 (1993): 25. Huntington elaborates this argument in *Clash of Civilizations.*

42. Earlier studies hint at the possibility of juxtaposing the identities and power capabilities of various states. The contribution of this book is to define the two variables of identity and power independently of one another and make the juxtaposition explicit. See Robert O. Keohane and Joseph S. Nye, *Power and Interdependence: World Politics in Transition* (Boston: Little, Brown and Company, 1977), especially the diagram on p. 217; Ruggie, "Continuity and Transformation in the World Polity," 200.

43. Some analysts are explicit about this limitation. David Lake examines U.S. foreign policy from a strategic interaction perspective. But he selects his case studies, or "defining moments" when the United States had to decide whether to cooperate with other countries for security purposes, assuming a constant level of threat at the structural level and explores only how the United States chose to meet this level of threat by unilateral action, alliance, or integrative means. See David A. Lake, *Entangling Relations: American Foreign Policy in Its Century* (Princeton: Princeton University Press, 1999), chap. 1. Arthur Stein identifies the more generic problem that strategic choice analysis confronts because it ignores structure or "decontextualizes the role of domain." "The Limits of Strategic Choice: Constrained Rationality and Incomplete Explanations," in *Strategic Choice and International Relations,* ed. David A. Lake and Robert Powell (Princeton: Princeton University Press, 1999), 223.

44. See Thomas Risse-Kappen, *Cooperation among Democracies: The European Influence on American Foreign Policy* (Princeton: Princeton University Press, 1995); Alexander Wendt and Daniel Friedheim, "Hierarchy under Anarchy," *International Organization* 49, no. 4 (1995): 689–723.

45. For a study of how states behave differently under hegemony than anarchy, see William C. Wohlforth, "The Stability of a Unipolar World," *International Security* 24, no. 1 (1999): 5–42.

46. On the differences between security communities and anarchy, see Karl W. Deutsch, *Political Community in the North Atlantic Community* (Princeton: Princeton University Press, 1957); Emmanuel Adler and Michael Barnett, eds., *Security Communities* (Cambridge: Cambridge University Press, 1998).

47. For critiques of the democratic peace, see Joanne S. Gowa, *Ballots and Bullets: The Elusive Democratic Peace* (Princeton: Princeton University Press, 1999); Miriam Fendius Elman, ed., *Paths to Peace: Is Democracy the Answer?* (Cambridge, Mass.: MIT Press, 1997).

48. For studies emphasizing these features, see Bruce Russett, *Grasping the Democratic Peace: Principles for a Post-Cold War World* (Princeton: Princeton University Press, 1993), 119; James Lee Ray, *Democracy and International Conflicts: An Evaluation of the Democratic Peace Proposition* (Columbia: University of South Carolina Press, 1996); Bruce Russett and John R. Oneal, *Triangulating Peace: Democracy, Interdependence, and International Organizations* (New York: W. W. Norton, 2001). For a comprehensive review of this research, see Steve Chan, "In Search of Democratic Peace: Problems and Promise," *Mershon International Studies Review* 41, no. 1 (1997): 59–92.

49. The logic behind such a development is presented by Edward D. Mansfield and Jack Snyder, "Democratization and the Danger of War," *International Security* 20, no. 1 (1995): 5–39; Jack Snyder, *From Voting to Violence: Democratization and Nationalist Conflict* (New York: W. W. Norton, 2000). Spencer Weart also looks at differences in stages of democratic development as a source of conflict among democracies. See Spencer Weart, *Never at War: Why Democracies Will Not Fight One Another* (New Haven: Yale University Press, 1997).

50. For a skeptical view of the possibility and permanence of a democratic peace, see Randall Schweller, "U.S. Democracy Promotion: Realist Reflections," in *American Democracy Promotion: Impulses, Strategies, and Impacts,* ed. Michael Cox, G. John Ikenberry, and Takashi Inoguchi (New York: Oxford University Press, 2000), 41–63. On the possible collapse of the democratic peace, see John Owen, *Liberal Peace, Liberal War: American Politics and International Security* (Ithaca: Cornell University Press, 1997).

51. On the rise and fall of hegemons from a realist perspective, see Robert Gilpin, *War and Change in World Politics* (Cambridge, U.K.: Cambridge University Press, 1981); Paul Kennedy, *The Rise and Fall of the Great Powers: Economic Change and Military Conflict from 1500 to 2000* (New York: Random House, 1987).

52. See Michael W. Doyle, *Empires* (Ithaca: Cornell University Press, 1986).

53. Scholars increasingly recognize the two tracks of anarchy, although they have yet to develop a way to treat both material and nonmaterial aspects evenly and explicitly. Joseph S. Nye Jr. writes, "Politics is not merely a struggle for physical power, but also a contest over legitimacy." *Understanding International Conflicts: An Introduction to Theory and History,* 3d ed. (New York: Longman, 2000), 158. See also Barnett, "Identity and Alliances," 446.

54. For example, Arthur M. Schlesinger Jr., the American historian of realpolitik persuasion, writes, "ideology is the curse of public affairs because it converts politics into a branch of theology and sacrifices human beings on the altar of abstractions." "Foreign Policy and the American Character," *Foreign Affairs* 62, no. 1 (1983): 16. We might ask in response, of course, how many millions of people have been sacrificed on the altar of realpolitik.

55. See George F. Kennan, *At a Century's Ending: Reflections, 1982–1995* (New York: W. W. Norton, 1996); Kissinger, *Diplomacy,* especially chaps. 17–20.

56. As Moravcsik points out, "power balancing served throughout [the Cold War] as a static, interim instrument to maintain the status quo, but shifting state preferences explain the outbreak and eventual passing of the conflict." "Taking Preferences Seriously," 546–47.

57. Kissinger wrote in 1976, for example, that the Soviet challenge "will not go away" and "will perhaps never be conclusively 'resolved'." *American Foreign Policy* (New York: W. W.Norton, 1977), 304. He also confessed in the early 1990s to Vladimir Putin, then an aide to the mayor of St. Petersburg and today the president of Russia, that he had no explanation for the Soviet withdrawal from central Europe that ended the Cold War: "Frankly, to this day I don't understand why Gorbachev did that." Putin agreed: "We would have avoided a lot of problems if the Soviets had not made such a hasty exit." Vladimir Putin, *First Person* (New York: Public Affairs, 2000), 81. Ronald Reagan, by contrast, anticipated the end of the Cold War, predicting in 1981 that history "will dismiss [communism] as some bizarre chapter in human history whose last pages are even now being written." Quoted in Tony Smith, *America's Mission: The United States and the Worldwide Struggle for Democracy in the Twentieth Century* (Princeton: Princeton University Press, 1994), 273.

58. See Robert O. Keohane, *After Hegemony: Cooperation and Discord in the World Political Economy* (Princeton: Princeton University Press, 1984).

59. See G. John Ikenberry, *After Victory: Institutions, Strategic Restraint, and the Building of Order after Major Wars* (Princeton: Princeton University Press, 2001).

60. On the role of ideas in changing foreign policy behavior, see Jeffrey W. Legro, "Whence American Internationalism," *International Organization* 54, no. 2 (2000): 253–89.

61. The literature along these lines is immense. For one classic statement, see Susan Strange, *The Retreat of the State: The Diffusion of Power in the World Economy* (New York: Cambridge University Press, 1996).

62. See Waltz, *Theory of International Politics,* 89–91, where he assumes that markets and anarchy are structurally similar. I critique this assumption in "Why Markets and International Politics Differ" (unpublished manuscript, November 1994); see also Barry Buzan, Charles Jones, and Richard Little, *The Logic of Anarchy: Neorealism to Structural Realism* (New York: Columbia University Press, 1993).

63. For a classical realist treatment of markets, see Robert Gilpin, *The Political Economy of International Relations* (Princeton: Princeton University Press, 1987), especially chap. 3.

64. See Adam Smith, *The Theory of Moral Sentiments,* ed. D. D. Raphael and A. L. Macfie (Oxford: Clarendon Press, 1976), 152 (pt. 3, 3.35 of original text).

65. See Adam Smith, *An Inquiry into the Nature and Causes of the Wealth of Nations,* ed. Kathryn Sutherland (New York: Oxford University Press, 1993), 22.

66. This point is demonstrated empirically in Francis Fukuyama, *Trust: The Social Virtues and the Creation of Prosperity* (New York: Free Press, 1995). The same point is made in the context of regional development in Italy by Robert D. Putnam, *Making Democracy Work: Civic Traditions in Modern Italy* (Princeton: Princeton University Press, 1993), chap. 4.

67. On globalization as being out of control or going too far, see William Greider, *One World, Ready or Not: The Manic Logic of Global Capitalism* (New York: Simon and Schuster, 1997); Dani Rodrik, *Has Globalization Gone Too Far?* (Washington, D.C.: Institute for International Economics, 1997).

68. For a similar two-part breakdown of global political and economic processes, see James M. Goldgeier and Michael McFaul, "A Tale of Two Worlds: Core and Periphery in the Post-Cold War Era," *International Organization* 46, no. 2 (1992): 467–91.

69. National parliaments in the EU countries influence and oversee the international commitments of their respective governments, but international executive actions by the EU are still one step removed from the accountability parliaments impose on national executive actions. See Lisa L. Martin, *Democratic Commitments: Legislatures and International Cooperation* (Princeton: Princeton University Press, 2000).

70. Robert Heilbroner, *21st Century Capitalism* (New York: W. W. Norton, 1993), 74. An exception to the second part of Helibroner's generalization may be India. Although its mode of economic organization is capitalist, India is not an advanced capitalist economy. On the other hand, although it is democratic, India is still a young democracy in which democratic processes were suspended in the mid-1970s by government decree and religious nationalism still engenders fear between the Hindu nationalist party and the Muslim minority.

71. For conclusions along these lines, see Michael Mandelbaum, *The Dawn of Peace in Europe* (New York: The Twentieth Century Fund Press, 1996).

CHAPTER TWO: TRADE-OFFS

1. I use the labels neoisolationism, internationalism, and realism to characterize foreign policy attitudes and self-images, not any particular period of American foreign policy. I exclude isolationism per se, which differs from neoisolationism only in the sense that true isolationists reject all government intervention in foreign affairs and accept only private-sector trade and investment initiatives. For helpful discussions of America's foreign policy traditions, see Manfred Jonas, *Isolationism in America, 1935–1941* (Ithaca: Cornell University Press, 1966); Selig Adler, *The Isolationist Impulse: Its Twentieth Century Reaction* (London: Abelard-Schuman, 1957); Felix Gilbert, *To the Farewell Address* (Princeton: Princeton University Press, 1961); Dexter Perkins, *The American Approach to Foreign Policy* (Cambridge, Mass.: Harvard University Press, 1952).
2. For representative neoisolationist and nationalist perspectives, see Jonathan Clarke and James Clad, *After the Crusade: American Foreign Policy for the Post-Superpower Age* (Lanham: Rowman and Littlefield, 1995); Walter A. McDougall, *Promised Land, Crusader State: America's Encounter with the World since 1776* (Boston: Houghton Mifflin, 1997); Ronald Steel, *Temptations of a Superpower* (Cambridge, Mass.: Harvard University Press, 1996); Patrick J. Buchanan, *The Great Betrayal: How American Sovereignty and Social Justice Are Being Sacrificed to the Gods of the Global Economy* (Boston: Little, Brown, 1998); Eric A. Nordlinger, *Isolationism Reconfigured: American Foreign Policy for a New Century* (Princeton: Princeton University Press, 1995).
3. Alan Tonelson, "Clinton's World," *Atlantic Monthly* 271, no. 2 (1993): 72. See also Clarke and Clad, *After the Crusade,* 91.
4. Christopher Layne, "From Preponderance to Offshore Balancing: America's Future Grand Strategy," *International Security* 22, no. 1 (1997): 86–125; Christopher Layne, "The Unipolar Illusion: Why New Great Powers Will Rise," *International Security* 17, no. 4 (1993): 3–52.
5. Nordlinger, *Isolationism Reconfigured,* 6. Nordlinger makes the most effective case for neoisolationism. For earlier books touting U.S. impregnability, see Johnson Hagood, *We Can Defend America* (Garden City: Doubleday, Doran, 1937); George Fielding Eliot, *The Ramparts We Watch: A Study of the Problems of American National Defense* (New York: Reynal and Hitchcock, 1938).
6. John Mearsheimer makes this argument most effectively. See John Mearsheimer, "Back to the Future: Instability in Europe after the Cold War," *International Security* 15, no. 1 (1990): 5–56.
7. Nordlinger, *Isolationism Reconfigured,* 46.
8. Geoeconomic arguments were very popular in the first Clinton administration. For representative arguments, see Edward N. Luttwak, *The Endangered American Dream: How to Stop the United States from Becoming a Third World Country and How to Win the Geo-Economic Struggle for Industrial Supremacy* (New York: Simon and Schuster, 1993); Jeffrey E. Garten, *A Cold Peace: America, Japan, Germany, and the Struggle for Supremacy* (New York: Times Books, 1992); Lester Thurow, *Head to Head: The Coming Economic Battle among Japan, Europe, and America* (New York: William Morrow, 1992); Richard Rosecrance, *The Rise of the Trading State* (New York: Basic Books, 1986).
9. See Thomas Jefferson, "Thomas Jefferson, First Inaugural Address, 1801," in *An American Primer,* ed. Dumas Malone and Daniel J. Boorstin (New York: New American Library, 1966), 234.
10. As Jonas notes, neutrality legislation in the 1930s "gave indirect encouragement to the Axis Powers." *Isolationism in America,* 199. Similarly, Jefferson's embargo hurt France more than England. See Lawrence S. Kaplan, *Entangling Alliances with None* (Kent: Kent State University Press, 1987). A recent example is the UN embargo against Bosnia, which hurt Muslim Bosnians far more than it did Croat or Serb Bosnians.
11. U.S. trade officials warned explicitly that the auto trade dispute could undermine the U.S.-Japanese security alliance. See my *Trade and Security: American Policies at Cross-Purposes* (Washington, D.C.: American Enterprise Institute Press, 1995), 1.
12. This is an ignored question in the revisionist literature on Japan. See Chalmers Johnson, *MITI and the Japanese Miracle* (Stanford: Stanford University Press, 1982); Karl van Wolferen, *The Enigma of Japanese Power: People and Politics in a Stateless Nation* (New York: Knopf, 1989);

Clyde V. Prestowitz Jr., *Trading Places: How We Allowed Japan to Take the Lead* (New York: Basic Books, 1998); Laura D'Andrea Tyson, *Who's Bashing Whom? Trade Conflict in High Technology* (Washington, D.C.: Institute for International Economics, 1992).

13. The CATO Institute often advances the libertarian (and Jeffersonian) view that strategic nationalism need not imply economic nationalism, that commerce can be carried out without alliances or serious political conflict. See Doug Bandow, *The Politics of Envy: Statism and Theology* (New Brunswick, N.J.: Transaction, 1994); Ted Galen Carpenter, "An Independent Course," *National Interest* 21 (1990): 28–31.

14. Josef Joffe, "Doing Well by Doing Good," *National Interest* 50 (1997–98): 78.

15. Patrick Buchanan, "America First—and Second, and Third," *National Interest* 19 (1990): 77.

16. As Owen Harries, who is sympathetic to Buchanan's views, nevertheless points out, "When Buchanan speaks of the American people it is clear that he does not have in mind all of the people who live in America. . . . Rather, he presumes the existence of an essential and elect American people, one that for him represents spiritual authenticity and historical community—a people composed overwhelmingly if not exclusively of Anglo-Saxons and Celts and Christians." "Pat's World," *National Interest* 43 (1996): 111. One ardent but thoughtful nationalist acknowledges that racist undercurrents infect the nationalist outlook. He worries that minorities may be reluctant to join the hard-core nationalist coalition because they fear the cultural conservatism of nationalist elites. See Alan Tonelson, "Beyond Left and Right," *National Interest* 4 (1993–94): 18.

17. Henry Kissinger, *Diplomacy* (New York: Simon and Schuster, 1994), 66–67. Ironically, Kissinger advocates a policy of equilibrium, not primacy, that he doubts, in the end, statesmen can implement.

18. For representative examples of realist perspectives, see Kissinger, *Diplomacy;* George F. Kennan, *At a Century's Ending: Reflections, 1982–1995* (New York: W. W. Norton, 1996); Richard L. Kugler, *Toward a Dangerous World: U.S. National Security for the Coming Turbulence* (Santa Monica: Rand, 1995); Richard M. Haass, *The Reluctant Sheriff: The United States after the Cold War* (New York: Council on Foreign Relations, 1997); Kim R. Holmes, ed., *A Safe and Prosperous America: A U.S. Foreign and Defense Policy Blueprint* (Washington, D.C.: Heritage Foundation, 1993); James Kurth, "America's Grand Strategy: A Pattern of History," *National Interest* 43 (1996): 3–20; James Schlesinger, "New Instabilities, New Priorities," *Foreign Policy* 85 (1991–92): 3–25.

19. "Balance of power theory leads one to predict," says Kenneth Waltz, perhaps the best-known realist in the academic world, "that other countries, alone or in concert, will try to bring American power into balance." "The Emerging Structure of International Politics," *International Security* 18, no. 2 (1993): 53. Similarly Christopher Layne, another realist, declares that "Unipolar moments cause geopolitical backlashes that lead to multipolarity." "Unipolar Illusion," 32.

20. Kissinger, *Diplomacy,* 23. James Schlesinger says that "The world order of the future will revert to that which existed before 1939, and most notably after World War I: It will be marked by power politics, national rivalries and ethnic tensions." "Quest for a Post-Cold War Foreign Policy," *Foreign Policy* 85 (1991–92): 4.

21. See Owen Harries and Michael Lind, "Realism and Its Rivals," *National Interest* 34 (1993–94): 111.

22. See, for example, Kugler: "if democracies are willing to tolerate hierarchy and exploitation within their own borders, why would they be unwilling to practice them outside in the anarchical international system that determines the standing of states?" *Toward a Dangerous World,* 29.

23. See George F. Kennan, *American Diplomacy, 1900–1950* (Chicago: University of Chicago Press, 1951), 65–66; see also the insightful critique of Kennan and realism in Joshua Muravchik, *Exporting Democracy: Fulfilling America's Destiny* (Washington, D.C.: American Enterprise Institute Press, 1991), chap. 3.

24. Quoted in Schlesinger, "Quest for a Post-Cold War Foreign Policy," 27. Another favorite line of de Tocqueville that realists like to quote is: "It is the nature of democracies to have, for the most part, the most confused or erroneous ideas on foreign affairs, and to decide questions of foreign policy on purely domestic considerations." Quoted in Kennan, *At a Century's Ending,* 35.

25. See Schlesinger, "Quest for a Post-Cold War Foreign Policy," 22.
26. See Kissinger, *Diplomacy*, 814, 828–29; Zbigniew Brzezinski, *Out of Control: Global Transition on the Eve of the Twenty-First Century* (New York: Charles Scribners' Sons, 1993), 176. Kissinger concedes that "there is an area of discretion which should be exercised in favor of governments and institutions promoting democratic values...." But then he quickly adds, "American idealism needs the leaven of geopolitical analysis," and notes implausibly that "Great Britain would have gone to war to prevent the occupation of the Channel ports in the Low Countries [Belgium and the Netherlands] even if they had been taken over by a major power governed by saints." *Diplomacy*, 811–12. We might ask what threat saints would have posed.
27. Kissinger seems never to have met an opportunity to negotiate that he did not like. He criticizes Franklin Roosevelt for failing to negotiate a postwar settlement with Stalin in 1942–44 and various other American presidents for failing to negotiate accommodations with the Soviet Union thereafter—in 1945–46 to head off the Cold War, in 1952 to preempt militarization of the Cold War, in 1959 to settle the status of Berlin, and in the late 1960s to initiate détente. Kissinger admits that such negotiations often lead nowhere. "In such a world," he writes, "no clear-cut terminal point beckoned, and the solution to one problem was more likely to turn into an admission ticket to the next one." *Diplomacy*, 742; see also chaps. 16, 17, 20, 23, 29.
28. See George F. Kennan, *Around the Cragged Hill: A Personal and Political Philosophy* (New York: W. W. Norton, 1993), 183.
29. Kissinger sums up Reagan's genius as follows: "Like Wilson, Reagan had a much surer grasp of the workings of the American soul." He "instinctively sandwiched tough Cold War geostrategic policies between an ideological crusade and a utopian evocation of peace that appealed simultaneously to the two major strands of American thought on international affairs—the missionary and the isolationist, the theological and the psychiatric." *Diplomacy*, 764, 767, 784.
30. "The Reagan foreign policy," Kissinger predicts, "was more in the nature of a brilliant sunset than the dawn of a new era." *Diplomacy*, 802.
31. Henry Kissinger, *Does America Need a Foreign Policy? Toward a Diplomacy for the 21st Century* (New York: Simon and Schuster, 2001), 32.
32. Ibid., 25, chap. 2.
33. For primacist perspectives, see Francis Fukuyama, *The End of History and the Last Man* (New York: Avon Books, 1992); Joshua Muravchik, *The Imperative of American Leadership: A Challenge to Neo-Isolationism* (Washington, D.C.: American Enterprise Institute Press, 1991); Charles Krauthammer, "The Unipolar Moment," *Foreign Affairs: America and the World* 70, no. 1 (1990–91): 23–34; Samuel P. Huntington, "Why International Primacy Matters," *International Security* 17, no. 4 (1993): 68–84; Joseph S. Nye Jr., *Bound to the Lead: The Changing Nature of American Power* (New York: Basic Books, 1990); George Weigel, *Idealism without Illusions: U.S. Foreign Policy in the 1990s* (Washington, D.C.: Ethics and Public Policy Center, 1994). See also my *The Myth of America's Decline: Leading the World Economy in the 1990s* (New York: Oxford University Press, 1990). For a European view sympathetic to the primacist America perspective, see Josef Joffe, "How America Does It," *Foreign Affairs* 76, no. 5 (1997): 13–28.
34. William Kristol and Robert Kagan, "Toward a Neo-Reaganite Foreign Policy," *Foreign Affairs* 75, no. 4 (1996): 23.
35. This strategy was also the thrust of a U.S. Defense Department planning document leaked to the press in 1992. It was later disavowed, but it reflected nevertheless the primacist perspective in the recent American foreign policy debate. See Patrick E. Tyler, "U.S. Strategy Plans for Insuring No Rivals Develop," *New York Times*, 8 March 1992, p. A1; "Excerpts from Pentagon's Plan: Prevent the Re-emergence of a New Rival," *New York Times*, 8 March 1992, p. A14.
36. Kristol and Kagan, "Toward a Neo-Reaganite Foreign Policy," 31–32.
37. Muravchik, *Imperative of American Leadership*, 49.
38. Huntington, "Why International Primacy Matters," 83.
39. It may be particularly difficult to draw the line if a country's domestic values are believed to be universal. See Muravchik, *Exporting Democracy*.

40. Walter Lippmann was a perennial critic of the gap between goals and resources in American foreign policy. For a prize-winning account of Lippmann's writings and life, see Ronald Steel, *Walter Lippmann and the American Century* (New York: Random House, 1981). Robert W. Tucker is a more recent Lippmann-like critic of the gap between U.S. global pretensions and its aversion to paying the costs. See Robert W. Tucker, "The Future of a Contradiction," *National Interest* 43 (1996): 20–28; Robert W. Tucker and David C. Hendrickson, *The Imperial Temptation: The New World Order and America's Purpose* (New York: Council on Foreign Relations, 1992).

41. See Paul Kennedy's best-seller, *The Rise and Fall of Great Powers: Economic Change and Military Conflict from 1500 to 2000* (New York: Random House, 1987).

42. Samuel P. Huntington, "The West: Unique, Not Universal," *Foreign Affairs* 75, no. 6 (1996): 28–47. See also Samuel P. Huntington, *The Clash of Civilizations and the Remaking of World Order* (New York: Simon and Schuster, 1996).

43. Huntington, "The West: Unique, Not Universal," 41.

44. Ibid., 44.

45. Huntington, *Clash of Civilizations,* 304.

46. Samuel P. Huntington, "The Erosion of American National Interests," *Foreign Affairs* 76, no. 5 (1997): 35. Paradoxically, Huntington himself contributes to the triumph of multiculturalism by denying the universal applicability of western values—precisely the claim of multiculturalists.

47. Ibid., 32.

48. Ibid., 49. See also Samuel P. Huntington, "The Lonely Superpower," *Foreign Affairs* 78, no. 2 (1999): 35–50, in which he counsels America to accept a diminished role.

49. See Brzezinski, *Out of Control,* 150–51. In a later book Brzezinski reverts to a strict primacist analysis, portraying world politics as a traditional great-power contest for primacy to secure the heartland of Eurasia. See Zbigniew Brzezinski, *The Grand Chessboard: American Primacy and Its Geostrategic Imperatives* (New York: Basic Books, 1997). Brzezinski's ambivalence between power politics and technological globalism is long-standing. See Zbigniew Brzezinski, *Between Two Ages: America's Role in the Technetronic Era* (New York: Viking Press, 1970).

50. Brzezinski, *Out of Control,* 65.

51. Ibid., 92.

52. Ibid., 91–92.

53. Ibid., 92.

54. Ibid., 151.

55. Ibid., 100.

56. On this point see Muravchik, *Imperative of American Leadership,* chap. 5. Brzezinski and Huntington also see American leadership as indispensable and worry about nationalism in Europe and, especially, Japan. See Zbigniew Brzezinski, "A Geostrategy for Eurasia," *Foreign Affairs* 76, no. 5 (1997), especially 52, 63; Huntington, "Why International Primacy Matters," 82.

57. Robert Jervis, "International Primacy: Is the Game Worth the Candle?" *International Security* 17, no. 4 (1993): 59.

58. For internationalist perspectives, see Tony Smith, *America's Mission: The United States and the Worldwide Struggle for Democracy in the Twentieth Century* (Princeton: Princeton University Press, 1994); David Callahan, *Between Two Worlds: Realism, Idealism, and American Foreign Policy after the Cold War* (New York: HarperCollins, 1994); G. John Ikenberry, *After Victory: Institutions, Strategic Restraint, and the Building of Order after Major Wars* (Princeton: Princeton University Press, 2001); James Chace, *The Consequences of the Peace: The New Internationalism and American Foreign Policy* (New York: Oxford University Press, 1992); John Gerard Ruggie, *Winning the Peace: America and World Order in the New Era* (New York: Columbia University Press, 1996).

59. As Charles Beard writes, Wilson saw a "world of democracies founded in the principles of institutional regularity, orderly procedure, popular consent, and respect for persons and property as exemplified in the United States." *The Idea of National Interest: An Analytical Study of American Foreign Policy,* ed. Alfred Vagta and William Beard (Chicago: Quadrangle, 1966), 125. By contrast, Jefferson was a mixture of doubts and hopes about the future of

democracy abroad; see Robert W. Tucker and David C. Hendrickson, "Thomas Jefferson and Foreign Policy," *Foreign Affairs* 69, no. 2 (1990): 154. On John Quincy Adams's views, see McDougall, *Promised Land, Crusader State,* 67.

60. In the end, of course, Wilson was disappointed. His instrument of national self-determination was hijacked by ethnic rather than democratic nationalism. See Smith, *America's Mission,* chap. 4.

61. Theodore C. Sorensen, "Rethinking National Security," *Foreign Affairs* 69, no. 3 (1990): 17. See also G. John Ikenberry, "The Myth of Post-Cold War Chaos," *Foreign Affairs* 75, no. 3 (1996): 79–92.

62. On such global changes, see John Mueller, *Quiet Cataclysm: Reflections on the Recent Transformation of World Politics* (New York: HarperCollins, 1995).

63. As David Hendrickson points out, Clinton's goals of democracy enlargement were much more ambitious than George Bush's goals of a new world order. See David Hendrickson, "Salvaging Clinton's Foreign Policy," *Foreign Affairs* 73, no. 5 (1994): 26–44.

64. For arguments supporting withdrawal from Europe or leaving NATO as it is, see, respectively, Callahan, *Between Two Worlds;* Michael Mandelbaum, *The Dawn of Peace in Europe* (New York: The Twentieth Century Fund Press, 1996). The Clinton administration has been accused of pursuing the third alternative of expanding NATO at minimal cost.

65. For such an argument, see Charles Maynes, "A Workable Clinton Doctrine," *Foreign Policy* 93 (1993–94): 3–22.

66. See Mandelbaum, *Dawn of Peace in Europe,* chaps. 4–6.

67. See Maynes, "Workable Clinton Doctrine," 8–9.

68. Brzezinski, *Out of Control,* 96.

69. See Ruggie, *Winning the Peace,* 25.

70. David Callahan worries, for example, that U.S. dominance introduces a new kind of apartheid in global affairs; see *Between Two Worlds,* 151. John Ruggie frets that globalization exacerbates inequalities, particularly for low-wage workers, and unravels the "embedded liberalism" that linked trade and social commitments under the postwar Bretton Woods system; see *Winning the Peace,* chap. 6. And Brzezinski warns about a culture of materialism and "permissive cornucopia" and calls for a renewal of America's spirit; see *Out of Control,* pt. 2, chap. 2.

71. See, for example, Ruggie, *Winning the Peace,* 165–69.

72. Charles Krauthammer, "The Lonely Superpower: How to Bear America's New World Burden," *New Republic* 205, no. 5 (1991): 24.

CHAPTER THREE: NATIONAL IDENTITY

1. Peter Brimelow, *Alien Nation: Common Sense about America's Immigration Disaster* (New York: Random House, 1995), 10.

2. The phrase "historyless people" is from Arthur M. Schlesinger Jr., *The Cycles of American History* (Boston: Houghton Mifflin, 1986), 17.

3. See Paul Johnson, *A History of the American People* (New York: HarperCollins, 1999), 158. In addition, in the United States, both houses of parliament and the executive were elected (albeit, in the case of the Senate, indirectly until 1913), while in Britain neither the executive (still appointed by the crown) nor the upper house was elected. (Great Britain did lead America in freeing slaves, doing so in 1833.)

4. Henry Steele Commager, *Commager on Tocqueville* (Columbia: University of Missouri Press, 1993), 22.

5. On the Britishness of the founding fathers, see Alexander DeConde, *Ethnicity, Race, and American Foreign Policy: A History* (Boston: Northeastern University Press, 1992); and on the singular advantage conferred by the Constitution, see Schlesinger, *Cycles of American History,* 20–21.

6. Robert Hughes, *Culture of Complaint: The Fraying of America* (New York: Oxford University Press, 1993), 12.

7. See DeConde, *Ethnicity, Race, and America Foreign Policy,* 24–25.

8. Thomas Jefferson, First Inaugural Address, in *Inaugural Addresses of the Presidents of the United States* (Washington, D.C.: Government Printing Office, 1989), 15.

9. Excessive litigation is a problem of domestic and foreign policy in America. It is often a consequence of being unaware of the moral and political context in which problems are framed. As Louis Hartz writes vividly, "law has flourished on the corpse of philosophy in America." *The Liberal Tradition in America* (New York: Harcourt, Brace and World, 1955), 10. See also Walter Olson, *Litigation Explosion: What Happened When America Unleashed the Lawsuit* (New York: Truman Talley Books, 1992).

10. Daniel J. Boorstin, *The Americans: The National Experience* (New York: Vintage Books, 1965), 68. See also the other two books in the trilogy, *The Americans: The Colonial Experience* (New York: Vintage Books, 1964); *The Americans: The Democratic Experience* (New York: Vintage Books, 1974).

11. de Tocqueville describes the participatory character of American democracy as follows: "No sooner do you set foot upon American ground than you are stunned by a kind of tumult; a confused clamor is heard on every side, and a thousand simultaneous voices demand the satisfaction of their social wants." *Democracy in America*, vol. 2 (New York: Vintage Books, 1960), 249.

12. Boorstin, *Americans: The National Experience*, 400.

13. Samuel Eliot Morison, *The Oxford History of the American People*, vol. 1 (New York: New American Library, 1972), 235; see also vol. 2 (1972); vol. 3 (1972).

14. Boorstin, *Americans: The National Experience*, 3. Paul Johnson makes the same point: "A man could stand on Cape Cod with his face to the sea and feel all the immensity of the Atlantic Ocean in front of him, separating him, like a benevolent moat, from the restrictions and conformities of narrow Europe." *History of the American People*, 46.

15. On the continuity of European, especially English, and American political thought, see Samuel H. Beer, *To Make a Nation: The Rediscovery of American Federalism* (Cambridge, Mass.: Belknap Press, 1993); Theodore Draper, *A Struggle for Power: The American Revolution* (New York: Times Books, 1996); Forrest McDonald, *E Pluribus Unum: The Formation of the American Republic, 1776–1790* (Indianapolis: Liberty Press, 1965).

16. For an insightful characterization of the Philadelphia system, see Daniel H. Deudney, "The Philadelphia System: Sovereignty, Arms Control, and the Balance of Power in the American States-Union, circa 1787–1861," *International Organization* 49, no. 1 (1995): 191–228. See also David C. Hendrickson, "Three Governing Systems in American History: Philadelphian, Appomattox, and Washington" (paper prepared for the International Studies Association Convention, Chicago, Ill., February 2001). Hendrickson's distinction between the Appomattox and Washington systems corresponds historically to my distinction between the U.S. identity phases of electoral democracy and social democracy.

17. See Seymour Martin Lipset and Gary Marks, *It Didn't Happen Here: Why Socialism Failed in the United States* (New York: W. W. Norton, 2000).

18. This tendency appears especially among left-of-center journalists in the United States. See Hedrick Smith, *Rethinking America* (New York: Random House, 1995).

19. See Morison, *Oxford History of the American People*, vol. 2, 47. Walter A. McDougall makes a similar point: "Republicans saw the Federalists' pro-British stance as evidence of their favor for a hierarchical society *at home*, and Federalists saw the Democratic Republicans' pro-French stance as indicative of their favor for extreme democracy *at home*." *Promised Land, Crusader State: America's Encounter with the World since 1776* (Boston: Houghton Mifflin, 1997), 30.

20. Morison, *Oxford History of the American People*, 2:51.

21. Ibid.

22. The XYZ Affair took its name from the low-level French bureaucrats (dubbed Messieurs X, Y, and Z) who insulted American peace envoys to France by suggesting that the United States pay the French government to stop seizing American ships.

23. Quoted in Gaddis Smith, *The Last Years of the Monroe Doctrine 1945–1993* (New York: Hill and Wang, 1994), 22, 24.

24. Henry Kissinger, *Diplomacy* (New York: Simon and Schuster, 1994), 30.

25. See Morison, *Oxford History of the American People*, vol. 2, 146.

26. John Adams, quoted in Boorstin, *Americans: The National Experience*, 399.

27. For a biography of Theodore Roosevelt that captures the eruption of the reunited nation, see Edmund Morris, *The Rise of Theodore Roosevelt* (New York: Ballantine, 1979).

28. For an arresting account of Lincoln's struggle to save the Union and the role played by emancipation, see Richard Hofstadter, *The American Political Tradition and the Men Who Made It* (New York: Vintage Books, 1989). In the end, according to Hofstadter, Lincoln saw the struggle "as a war to defend not only Union but the sacred principles of popular rule and opportunity for the common man" (161).

29. Seymour Martin Lipset, *American Exceptionalism: A Double-Edged Sword* (New York: W. W. Norton, 1996), 46; see also page 20 for a similar quotation. Numerous studies document the critical role that liberal ideas of individual freedom played in shaping U.S. national identity. Among others, see Samuel P. Huntington, *American Politics: The Promise of Disharmony* (Cambridge, Mass.: Belknap Press, 1981). To be sure, more communal notions of American identity—ethnic and republican (states' rights)—have contested liberal ones, both before and since the Civil War. Today, as we note later in this chapter, multicultural notions are challenging liberal ones. However, even critics of U.S. liberal identity acknowledge that "liberal ideas have one inestimable value: they can be employed to claim basic rights universally, for every human being, black or white, female or male, alien or citizen . . ."—precisely the role liberal values played after the Civil War in legitimating national government and law in America. Roger M. Smith, "The 'American Creed' and American Identity: The Limits of Liberal Citizenship in the United States," *Western Political Quarterly* 41, no. 2 (1988): 229–30. See also Roger M. Smith, *Civic Ideals: Conflicting Visions of Citizenship in U.S. History* (New Haven: Yale University Press, 1997).

30. For these data through 1995, see OECD, *Historical Statistics 1960–1990* (Paris: OECD, 1990); OECD, *National Accounts* (Paris: OECD, 1998). Japan has an even smaller government than the United States, which reflects the facts that it does not provide completely for its own defense and provides the least social benefits of any industrial government in a society that is already highly homogeneous and egalitarian. See chapters 4 and 6 in this book for further discussion of Japan.

31. For a critical view of the influence of religion in American politics, see Arthur Schlesinger, Jr. *Cycles of American History,* chaps. 1, 3. The exact relationship between private faith and public life is, of course, much disputed and goes back to the nation's origins. As Walter McDougall tells us, the founding fathers did not agree on "whether liberty derived in the first instance from the Cross or from natural law," that is, from religion or from reason. But, McDougall adds, "Puritans, Anglicans, Quakers, Unitarians, and deists were all prepared to name the Deity, not some human agency, as the author of freedom." *Promised Land, Crusader State,* 15. At the very least, we can agree with columnist William Raspberry when he writes, "The constitutional requirement is that government not 'establish' religion, not that it root out religion." "Christmas without Meaning?" *Washington Post,* 24 December 1993, p. A15.

32. In the United States, for example, 57 percent of the population affiliates actively with churches, as opposed to 13 percent in Germany, 22 percent in Great Britain, 4 percent in France, and 7 percent in Italy. Catholic Ireland has the highest figure at 51 percent, still below the U.S. number. See Ben Wattenberg, *The First Universal Nation* (New York: Free Press, 1991), 116. See also Andrew Greeley, "American Exceptionalism Reaffirmed," in *Is America Different? A New Look at American Exceptionalism,* ed. Byron E. Shafer (Oxford: Clarendon Press, 1991), 98; Lipset, *American Exceptionalism,* 60–67. For insightful studies of the role of religion in American life, see Stephen L. Carter, *The Culture of Disbelief* (New York: Basic Books, 1983); Stephen L. Carter, *The Dissent of the Governed: A Meditation on Law, Religion, and Loyalty* (Cambridge, Mass.: Harvard University Press, 1998); Robert William Fogel, *The Fourth Great Awakening and the Future of Egalitarianism* (Chicago: University of Chicago Press, 2000).

33. For *Federalist Paper* No. 10, see *The Federalist Papers by Alexander Hamilton, James Madison, and John Jay,* ed. Garry Wills (New York: Bantam Books, 1982), 42–49.

34. Ibid., 44.

35. Ibid.

36. Ibid., 47.

37. Boorstin, *Americans: The National Experience*, 34.
38. Fareed Zakaria offers a classical realist interpretation of this period, explaining America's rise to world power in terms of strengthened state institutions and growing relative power. But his account says little about America's changing cosmopolitan and capitalist identity, which motivated the strengthening of state institutions and the projection of American power. See Fareed Zakaria, *From Wealth to Power: The Unusual Origins of America's World Role* (Princeton: Princeton University Press, 1998).
39. Tony Smith calls American foreign policy in this period "conservative radicalism"—radical on political and administrative reforms, conservative on social and economic reforms. See Tony Smith, *America's Mission: The United States and the Worldwide Struggle for Democracy in the Twentieth Century* (Princeton: Princeton University Press, 1994), 180.
40. See McDougall, *Promised Land, Crusader State*, 182.
41. See Timothy M. Smeeding, "American Income Inequality in a Cross-National Perspective: Why Are We So Different?" *Luxembourg Income Study Working Papers* No. 157, April 1997. http://www.lissy.ceps.lu/wpapers.htm. These data, of course, must be put in perspective. In several ways, they overstate income inequalities in America. First, average income levels in the United States are higher than in Europe or Japan. Second, income comparisons exclude noncash income, such as food stamps, housing subsidies, and wealth or financial assets. When income data are adjusted for wealth (e.g., homes, which many lower-middle-class and even poor families in America own), the concentration of wealth in the United States drops by half and is not seriously out of line with other industrial nations. Third, income is usually measured by household. In America, the composition of households has changed dramatically in the last thirty years. Many more women work and form households with another wage earner, pushing up the number of higher-income families. At the lower end of the income spectrum, more households consist of a single, unmarried, or divorced wage earner, often unskilled, which pushes up the number of lower-income families. Thus, the income gap widens for social, not economic, reasons. Fourth, studies show that mobility up and down the income ladder is greater in the United States than in other countries. For useful discussions of these problems, see Edward N. Wolff, *Top Heavy: A Study of the Increasing Inequality of Wealth in America* (New York: The Twentieth Century Fund Press, 1995); W. Michael Cox and Richard Alm, *Myths of Rich and Poor* (New York: Basic Books, 1999).
42. As Lipset writes about the United States, "While the country can clearly no longer be described as laissez-faire, it is still less welfare-oriented, less statist and more laissez-faire than almost all the European nations." *American Exceptionalism*, 27.
43. Quoted in Hans Kohn and Daniel Walden, eds., *Readings in American Nationalism* (New York: Van Nostrand Reinhold, 1970), 141.
44. Aaron Wildavsky, "Resolved, That Individualism and Egalitarianism Be Made Compatible in America—Political-Cultural Roots of Exceptionalism," in *Is America Different? A New Look at American Exceptionalism*, ed. Byron E. Shafer (Oxford: Clarendon Press, 1991), 129.
45. *Federalist Paper* No. 10, in *Federalist Papers*, 44.
46. *Federalist Paper* No. 51, in *Federalist Papers*, 261. de Tocqueville makes a similar argument: "Whatever efforts a people may make, they will never succeed in reducing all the conditions of society to a perfect level; and even if they happily attained that absolute and complete equality of position, the inequality of minds would still remain, which, coming directly from the hands of God, will forever escape the laws of man." *Democracy in America*, vol. 2, 138.
47. On the postwar Bretton Woods compromise, see my *The Myth of America's Decline: Leading the World Economy in the 1990s* (New York: Oxford University Press, 1990), especially pt. 2. The academic literature divides on the question how much government intervention the Bretton Woods system condoned. American academics, who are overwhelmingly social democrats (see the survey data in Lipset, *American Exceptionalism*, chap. 6), argue that the commitment to free trade in international markets involved "embedded liberalism"—an extensive commitment to government intervention in domestic markets, which included not only fiscal and monetary policy but also regulatory, employment, and welfare policies. More conservative academics, including me, argue that the data do not support this view. American and some European governments did not go much beyond commitments to an active fiscal policy. Government intervention in Europe in state-owned industries and regulatory

areas actually receded in the 1950s. See the charts in Nau, *Myth of America's Decline,* 41–42. For the most frequently cited social democratic argument, see John Gerard Ruggie, "International Regimes, Transactions, and Change: Embedded Liberalism in the Postwar Economic Order," in *International Regimes,* ed. Stephen D. Krasner (Ithaca: Cornell University Press, 1983), 195–233.

48. See my "Rethinking Economics, Politics, and Security in Europe," in *Reshaping Western Security: The United States Faces a United Europe,* ed. Richard N. Perle (Washington, D.C.: American Enterprise Institute Press, 1991), 11–39.

49. See G. John Ikenberry, *After Victory: Institutions, Strategic Restraint, and the Rebuilding of Order after Major Wars* (Princeton: Princeton University Press, 2001).

50. For example, the more social democratic states of western Europe prefer foreign aid programs in developing countries, whereas the more individualistic United States prefers open trade and investment markets. See David Halloran Lumsdaine, *Moral Vision in International Politics: The Foreign Aid Regime, 1949–1989* (Princeton: Princeton University Press, 1993).

51. See, for example, Peter J. Katzenstein's analysis of consensual politics in Germany, *Party and Politics in West Germany: The Growth of a Semisovereign State* (Philadelphia: Temple University Press, 1987).

52. Quoted in David McCullough, *Truman* (New York: Simon and Schuster, 1992), 445.

53. Ibid., 547.

54. See Ronald Reagan, *An American Life* (New York: Simon and Schuster, 1990), 554.

55. It is useful to recall that the left wing of the Social Democratic Party in West Germany and the Communist Party in East Germany signed a joint declaration as late as 1987 that, for all practical purposes, erased any significant distinctions between social democracy and totalitarian communism. See F. Stephen Larrabee, ed., *The Two German States and European Security* (New York: St. Martin's Press, 1989), 22–23.

56. For systematic data from 1960–94, see OECD, *Historical Statistics* (Paris: OECD, 1996), 42–43.

57. Some initially vocal critics of Reagan budget deficits now take this view; see Lou Cannon, *President Reagan: The Role of a Lifetime* (New York: Public Affairs, 2000), 758–59.

58. Thomas Sowell, *Ethnic America* (New York: Basic Books, 1981), 4.

59. The term "large" rules out Belgium, Canada, and Switzerland, which are culturally more diverse but still white and European.

60. See Brimelow, *Alien Nation,* 132.

61. Arthur Schlesinger, Jr. *The Disuniting of America: Reflections on a Multicultural Society* (New York: W. W. Norton, 1992), 16. Schlesinger is criticizing this definition of multiculturalism.

62. See Michael Lind, *The Next American Nation: The New Nationalism and the Fourth American Revolution* (New York: Free Press, 1996), 5. To distinguish his view from that of liberals and multiculturalists, Lind insists that America as a nation is not an idea at all. "The very notion of a country based on an idea," he says, "is absurd" (4–5). But if nations are facts only, we may wonder why nations have not always existed, like stars. The nation may be a fact but it is a *human* fact, constructed at a point in time by ideas and a common interpretation of history. For a three-part breakdown and discussion of American identity similar to mine, see Jack Citrin, Ernst B. Haas, Christopher Muste, and Beth Reingold, "Is American Nationalism Changing?" *International Studies Quarterly* 38, no. 1 (1994): 1–33.

63. Wattenberg, *First Universal Nation.*

64. John H. Rutherford, *The Moral Foundation of United States Constitutional Democracy* (Pittsburgh: Dorrance Publishing, 1992), 23–24. Other scholars see individualism as corroding rather than constructing community; see Robert D. Putnam, *Bowling Alone: The Collapse and Revival of American Community* (New York: Simon and Schuster, 2000).

65. See John Rawls, *A Theory of Justice* (Cambridge, Mass.: Harvard University Press, 1971); John Rawls, *Political Liberalism* (New York: Columbia University Press, 1993). For a critique of Rawls, see George Klosko, "Rawls's Political Philosophy and American Democracy," *America Political Science Review* 87, no. 2 (1993): 348–60. On the group-oriented views of some black Americans, see Lipset, *American Exceptionalism,* 116.

66. See "The Supreme Court: Excerpts from High Court Ruling in Racial Districting Case," *New York Times,* 30 June 1995, p. A22.

67. For an eye-opening documentation of black progress, see Abigail Thernstrom and Stephan Thernstrom, *America in Black and White: One Nation Indivisible* (New York: Simon and Schuster, 1998). See also Orlando Patterson, *The Ordeal of Integration: Progress and Resentment in America's "Racial" Crises* (Washington, D.C.: Civitas Counterpoint, 1997).

68. See William Greider, *One World, Ready or Not* (New York: Simon and Schuster, 1997); Saskia Sassen, *Losing Control? Sovereignty in the Age of Globalization* (New York: Columbia University Press, 1996); Alan Tonelson, *The Race to the Bottom: Why a Worldwide Worker Surplus and Uncontrolled Free Trade Are Sinking American Living Standards* (Boulder: Westview, 2001).

69. See Samuel P. Huntington, "The Erosion of National Interest," *Foreign Affairs* 76, no. 5 (1997): 28–50. DeConde documents the splintering and debilitating effect of ethnic divisions on American foreign policy throughout American history; see DeConde, *Ethnicity, Race, and American Foreign Policy,* 82.

70. Tony Smith, *Foreign Attachments: The Power of Ethnic Groups in the Making of American Foreign Policy* (Cambridge, Mass.: Harvard University Press, 2000).

CHAPTER FOUR: PERMANENT PARTNERSHIP

1. The United States issued such threats in the context of the auto dispute with Japan in 1995. See my *Trade and Security: U.S. Policies at Cross-Purposes* (Washington, D.C.: American Enterprise Institute Press, 1995), 1. See also implicit U.S. threats to diminish ties with Europe in 1993–94 if economic conflicts persisted, in Sean Kay, *NATO and the Future of European Security* (Lanham: Rowman and Littlefield, 1998), 124.

2. I am not alone in advocating permanent entanglement with other democracies. For similar recommendations, see the Rand Corporation study, David C. Gompert and F. Stephen Larrabee, eds., *America and Europe: A Partnership for a New Era* (Cambridge, U.K.: Cambridge University Press, 1997); David C. Hendrickson, "In Our Own Image: The Sources of American Conduct in World Affairs," *National Interest* 50 (1997–98): 9–22.

3. Clinton policies warned Europe that the United States might turn more to Asia and often bypassed Japan to highlight a new strategic partnership with China. Realists, such as Kissinger, give China at least equal status with Japan in U.S. national interests. See Henry Kissinger, *Diplomacy* (New York: Simon and Schuster, 1994), 811–12, chap. 31.

4. In 1994, for example, Great Britain responded to an increase in crime with legislation that significantly reduced the legal rights of the accused, something that would not be allowed under the written constitutional guarantees in the United States. See Seymour Martin Lipset, *American Exceptionalism: A Double-Edged Sword* (New York: W. W. Norton, 1996), 49.

5. On contemporary German political culture, see Peter J. Katzenstein, ed., *Tamed Power: Germany in Europe* (Ithaca: Cornell University Press, 1997); Ernst B. Haas, *Nationalism, Liberalism, and Progress,* vol. 1 (Ithaca: Cornell University Press, 1996), chap. 6.

6. These laws were softened somewhat in 1999. Foreigners who have lived in Germany for eight years (previously fifteen years) are eligible for citizenship, and their children receive automatic citizenship. But dual citizenship is not permitted. At age 23, children must give up a foreign passport.

7. See John Newhouse, *Europe Adrift* (New York: Pantheon, 1997), chap. 5. See also Hans George Betz, *Radical Right-Wing Populism in Western Europe* (New York: St. Martin's Press, 1994). On the Austrian crisis, see Roger Cohen, "If Democracy Is Not Enough," *New York Times,* 2 February 2000, p. A12.

8. The key bargains were struck in the two years following the collapse of the Berlin Wall—initially the agreement on European Monetary Union and then the parallel agreement on European Political Union, both consummated in the Maastricht Treaty of December 1991. See Philip Zelikow and Condoleezza Rice, *Germany Unified and Europe Transformed: A Study in Statecraft* (Cambridge, Mass.: Harvard University Press, 1995).

9. See, for example, Thomas U. Berger, "Norms, Identity, and National Security in Germany and Japan," in *The Culture of National Security: Norms and Identity in World Politics,* ed. Peter J. Katzenstein (New York: Columbia University Press, 1996), 317–57.

10. For various perspectives, see Bradley Richardson, *Japanese Democracy: Power, Coordination and Performance* (New Haven: Yale University Press, 1997); Masao Miyamoto, *Straightjacket Society: An Insider's Irreverent View of Bureaucratic Japan* (New York: Kodansha International, 1994); Gerald L. Curtis, *The Japanese Way of Politics* (New York: Columbia University Press, 1998).

11. The lack of accountability in Japanese politics is Karel van Wolferen's main argument in his best-selling book, *The Enigma of Japanese Power* (New York: Alfred A. Knopf, 1989). There he calls the Japanese government a pyramid with no leadership at the top. Elsewhere, van Wolferen argues bluntly that "Japanese democracy has not been realized. It exists only in potential." Quoted in Nicholas Kristof, "Dutchman Strikes Chord in a Less Confident Japan," *New York Times*, 4 June 1995, p. 12.

12. These complaints are particularly strong among revisionist students of Japan. In addition to van Wolferen, *Enigma of Japanese Power*, see Chalmers Johnson, *MITI and the Japanese Miracle* (Stanford: Stanford University Press, 1982); Clyde V. Prestowitz Jr., *Trading Places: How We Allowed Japan to Take the Lead* (New York: Basic Books, 1988); James Fallows, *More Like US: Making America Great Again* (Boston: Houghton Mifflin, 1989).

13. For more optimistic assessments of democracy in Japan, see Kent E. Calder, *Crisis and Compensation: Public Policy and Political Stability in Japan, 1949–1986* (Princeton: Princeton University Press, 1988); Kent E. Calder, *Strategic Capitalism: Public Policy and Private Purpose in Japanese Industrial Finance* (Princeton: Princeton University Press, 1993). On the limits of the Japanese economy, see Daniel I. Okimoto, *Between MITI and the Market: Japanese Industrial Policy for High Technology* (Stanford: Stanford University Press, 1989); Scott Callon, *Divided Sun: MITI and the Breakdown of Japanese High-Tech Industrial Policy, 1975–1993* (Stanford: Stanford University Press, 1995); Bill Emmott, *The Sun Also Sets: The Limits to Japan's Economic Power* (New York: Times Books, 1989); Bill Emmott, *Japanophobia: The Myth of the Invincible Japanese* (New York: Times Books, 1992); Christopher Wood, *The End of Japan Inc.* (New York: Simon and Schuster, 1994).

14. Paradoxically, some revisionist scholars who severely criticize the irresponsibility of the Japanese bureaucracy in economic areas remain quite complacent about the prospective responsibility of the Japanese bureaucracy in military areas. They recommend that Japan assume a more independent military role, allowing U.S. forces to be withdrawn from Asia. See Chalmers Johnson and E. B. Keehn, "East Asian Security: The Pentagon's Ossified Strategy," *Foreign Affairs* 74, no. 4 (1995): 103–4. I discuss these security issues further in chap. 6.

15. For example, when the parliament passed legislation in 1992 to permit the deployment of noncombat forces under UN peacekeeping auspices, it insisted that missions could not include roles such as monitoring a cease-fire or collecting weapons and that these restrictions could not be lifted without returning the issue to parliament. See Milton Leitenberg, "The Participation of Japanese Military Forces in U.N. Peacekeeping Operations," Maryland/Tsukuba Papers on U.S.-Japan Relations, University of Maryland and University of Tsukuba, June 1996.

16. Article 9 of the U.S.-drafted Japanese constitution reads in part: "The Japanese people forever renounce war as a sovereign right of the nation and the threat or use of force as means of settling international disputes." "The Constitution of Japan," in *Japan Access* (Tokyo: Kodansha International Ltd., for the Ministry of Foreign Affairs, Government of Japan, 1998), 2. For an in-depth examination of Japanese police and military policy and institutions, see Peter J. Katzenstein, *Cultural Norms and National Security: Police and Military in Postwar Japan* (Ithaca: Cornell University Press, 1996).

17. For a careful assessment of these issues, see Michael J. Green and Patrick M. Cronin, eds., *The U.S.-Japan Alliance: Past, Present, and Future* (New York: Council on Foreign Relations, 1999).

18. I once asked a Japanese friend how the Japanese decide the direction in which they would like to go. He replied: "We start walking." This is obviously not the goal-oriented, rational method of cost-benefit analysis so familiar in the United States.

19. Quoted in Kenneth B. Pyle, "The Burden of Japanese History and the Politics of Burden Sharing," in *Sharing World Leadership? A New Era for America and Japan*, ed. John H. Makin and Donald C. Hellmann (Washington, D.C.: American Enterprise Institute Press, 1989), 56. Ruth Benedict takes a similar view in her seminal study of Japanese culture: "Japan's motivations are situational. She will seek her place within a world at peace if circumstances

permit. If not, within a world organized as an armed camp." *The Chrysanthemum and the Sword: Patterns of Japanese Culture* (Boston: Houghton Mifflin, 1946), 316.

20. Edward J. Lincoln, *Japan's New Global Role* (Washington, D.C.: Brookings Institution, 1993), 14.

21. This is the position taken by Lincoln, *Japan's New Global Role;* Zbigniew Brzezinski, *The Grand Chessboard: American Primacy and Its Geostrategic Imperatives* (New York: Basic Books, 1997), 186. On the other hand, other analysts, even though they recognize the problems of Japanese democracy, insist that Japan take on larger military responsibilities. See Chalmers Johnson's comments, quoted in Leitenberg, "Participation of Japanese Military Forces," 45.

22. See "The North Atlantic Treaty," in *The North Atlantic Treaty Organization: Facts and Figures* (Brussels: The NATO Information Service, 1989), 377.

23. European influence over U.S. national security policy within NATO was not insubstantial. Examining NATO decisions over forty years, Thomas Risse-Kappen concludes that "the European allies influenced American foreign policy routinely and not just in some isolated incidents." *Cooperation among Democracies: The European Influence on U.S. Foreign Policy* (Princeton: Princeton University Press, 1995), 3.

24. Nevertheless, the North Atlantic Assembly is quite active. For an account of Assembly activities in connection with NATO enlargement, see the study by a participant, then U.S. Congressman Gerald B. Solomon, *The NATO Enlargement Debate, 1990–1997* (Westport: Praeger, 1989).

25. The only serious instance in which the allies sharply opposed one another with respect to the use of force was the Suez Crisis in 1956. The United States intervened to stop British and French military actions in the Middle East against Egypt. This incident occurred, however, in the earliest stages of NATO military cooperation and involved lingering colonial issues, which had divided the allies before World War II. The Suez Crisis was always the exception in NATO cooperation, not the rule, and the conditions for such a crisis are simply not as readily conceivable today. See Risse-Kappen, *Cooperation among Democracies,* chap. 4.

26. Quoted in "A Survey of NATO," *The Economist,* 24 April 1999, 10. See also Guido Lenzi, ed., *WEU at Fifty* (Paris: Institute for Security Studies of the Western European Union, 1998).

27. For background on the G-7, see Nicholas Bayne, *Hanging in There: G-7 and G-8 Summits in Maturity and Renewal* (Brookfield, Vt.: Ashgate, 2000); Peter I. Hajnal, *G-7/G-8 System: Evolution, Role and Documentation* (Brookfield, Vt.: Ashgate, 1999).

28. On this point, see Robert E. Hunter, "Maximizing NATO: A Relevant Alliance Knows How to Reach," *Foreign Affairs,* 78, no. 3 (1999): 203.

29. Russia joined the political discussions in the 1990s to create the G-8, and proposals have been made to include China. See Brzezinski, *Grand Chessboard,* 186. German Chancellor Gerhard Schroeder and the late Japanese prime minister Keizo Obuchi floated a proposal to include China in the G-8 summit in Japan in July 2000. See Naoka Nakamae, "China Has No Intention of Attending G-8," *Financial Times,* 23 February 2000, p. 8.

30. A leading proponent of this perspective over the years is C. Fred Bergsten, director of the Institute for International Economics in Washington. See C. Fred Bergsten and C. Randall Henning, *Global Economic Leadership and the Group of Seven* (Washington, D.C.: Institute for International Economics, 1996). For a critique of this view, see my article and debate with Bergsten in *Foreign Policy:* C. Fred Bergsten, "The Cost of Reaganomics," *Foreign Policy* 44 (1981): 12–37; Henry R. Nau, "Where Reaganomics Works," *Foreign Policy* 57 (1984–85): 14–38; C. Fred Bergsten, "The State of the Debate: Reaganomics—the Problem?" *Foreign Policy* 59 (1985): 132–44; Henry R. Nau, "The State of the Debate: Reaganomics—the Solution?" *Foreign Policy* 59 (1985): 144–53.

31. Even premier institutions, such as the World Bank, face problems of administrative corruption and license that in national bureaucracies would normally be exposed by parliamentary oversight committees.

32. For details on the Williamsburg Summit, see my *The Myth of America's Decline: Leading the World Economy in the 1990s* (New York: Oxford University Press, 1990), chap. 8.

33. See Seth Mydans, "Pressed by IMF, Indonesia Accepts Economic Reforms," *New York Times,* 15 January 1998, p. A1.

34. For useful perspectives, see Kevin Featherstone and Roy H. Ginsberg, *The United States and the European Community in the 1990s: Partners in Transition* (New York: St. Martin's Press, 1993); Geir Lundestad, *Empire by Integration: The United States and European Integration, 1945–1997* (New York: Oxford University Press, 1998).

35. The competence of the EU is divided between intergovernmental and integrated institutions. Community institutions, such as the European Council, European Council of Ministers, European Commission, European Court of Justice, and European Parliament, operate under integrated or supranational authority as laid out in the original European Community treaties and more recent Maastricht and Amsterdam treaties. The CSFP and Justice and Home Affairs, on the other hand, are strictly intergovernmental initiatives in which national authorities retain control. On the evolution and future of the EU, see, respectively, Andrew Moravcsik, *The Choice for Europe: Social Purpose and State Power from Messina to Maastricht* (Ithaca: Cornell University Press, 1998); Simon Serfaty, *Europe 2007: From Nation-States to Member States* (Washington, D.C.: Center for Strategic and International Studies, 2000).

36. This combination of disbelief and disparagement was reflected in a series of articles that appeared as Europe prepared for and launched its common currency in 1998–99. See, among others, Martin Feldstein, "EMU and International Conflict," *Foreign Affairs* 76, no. 6 (1997): 60–74; C. Fred Bergsten, "America and Europe: Clash of the Titans," *Foreign Affairs* 78, no. 2 (1999): 20–35. For a European response, bewildered by American stridency, see William Wallace and Jan Zielonka, "Misunderstanding Europe," *Foreign Affairs* 77, no. 6 (1998): 65–80.

37. For an elaboration of this critique, see my *Trade and Security*.

38. On the decision to expand NATO, see James M. Goldgeier, *Not Whether but When: The U.S. Decision to Enlarge NATO* (Washington, D.C.: Brookings Institution, 1999).

39. For an account of this early period in the Clinton administration's policies toward Europe, see Kay, *NATO and the Future*, 124.

40. These initiatives culminated in the issuance of a Trans-Atlantic Trade Agenda during President Clinton's trip to Madrid in December 1995. For details of this agenda and reports of U.S. foot-dragging, see Ellen L. Frost, *Transatlantic Trade: A Strategic Agenda* (Washington, D.C.: Institute for International Economics, 1997); Guy de Jonquieres, "Britain to Seek Closer EU-US Relationship," *Financial Times*, 2 October 1995, p. 6; Kyle Pope and Robert S. Greenberger, "Europe Seeks Trade Pact with U.S. Similar to NAFTA," *Wall Street Journal*, 27 November 1995, p. A14; Nathaniel C. Nash, "Showing Europe that U.S. Still Cares," *New York Times*, 3 December 1995, p. 20.

41. In the automobile dispute in 1995, U.S. negotiators implicitly threatened to cut security ties if trade issues were not satisfactorily resolved. See comments at the time by Jeffrey Garten, undersecretary of commerce for international trade, quoted in David E. Sanger, "The Corrosion at the Core of Day Pacifica," *New York Times*, 14 May 1995, sec. 4, p. 1; Michael McCurry, press secretary to the president, quoted in David E. Sanger, "100% Tariffs Set on 13 Top Models of Japanese Cars," *New York Times*, 17 May 1995, p. A1.

42. For a discussion of these behind-the-border policies and their impact on trade, see various publications of the Brookings Institution Project on Integrating National Economies, particularly F. M. Scherer, *Competition Policies for an Integrated World Economy* (Washington, D.C.: Brookings Institution, 1994); Richard R. Nelson and Sylvia Ostry, *Techno-Nationalism and Techno-Globalism: 'High Tech' Industrial Policies—Conflict and Cooperation* (Washington, D.C.: Brookings Institution, 1995); Robert Z. Lawrence, *Regionalism, Multilateralism, and Deeper Integration* (Washington, D.C.: Brookings Institution, 1996). See also Susan Berger and Ronald Dore, eds., *National Diversity and Global Capitalism* (Ithaca: Cornell University Press, 1996); Laura D'Andrea Tyson and John Zysman, eds., *American Industry in International Competition: Government Policies and Corporate Change* (Ithaca: Cornell University Press, 1983); Jeffrey A. Hart, *Rival Capitalists: International Competitiveness in the United States, Japan, and Western Europe* (Ithaca: Cornell University Press, 1992).

43. On the impact of culture and business activities on efficiency, see Francis Fukuyama, *Trust: The Social Virtues and the Creation of Prosperity* (New York: Free Press, 1995).

44. Paul Krugman, a well-known economist, identifies and critiques this obsession in "Competitiveness: A Dangerous Obsession," *Foreign Affairs* 73, no. 2 (1994): 28–45.

45. See I. M. Destler, *The National Economic Council: A Work in Progress* (Washington, D.C.: Institute for International Economics, 1996).

46. Key exponents of this strategy populated high offices in the first Clinton administration. Laura D'Andrea Tyson was head of the President's Council of Economic Advisers and the chair of the National Economic Council. See Laura D'Andrea Tyson, *Who's Bashing Whom? Trade Conflict in High Technology Industry* (Washington, D.C.: Institute for International Economics, 1992). Jeffrey E. Garten was undersecretary of commerce for international trade. See Jeffrey E. Garten, *A Cold Peace: America, Japan, Germany, and the Struggle for Supremacy* (New York: Basic Books, 1992); Jeffrey E. Garten, *The Big Ten: The Big Emerging Markets and How They Will Change Our Lives* (New York: Basic Books, 1997). Lawrence H. Summers was assistant, deputy, and then secretary of the Treasury. See his highly critical views of Japan before he came into office, Lawrence H. Summers, "The Ishihara-Morita Brouhaha," *International Economy* 3, no. 6 (1998–99): 49–55.

47. For an exposition of this model, see Robert Wade, *Governing the Market: Economic Theory and the Role of Government* (Princeton: Princeton University Press, 1990); James Fallows, *Looking at the Sun: The Rise of the New East Asian Economic and Political System* (New York: Pantheon Book, 1994).

48. Lawrence, *Regionalism, Multilateralism, and Deeper Integration*, xix. The U.S. automobile industry is a case in point. The U.S. industry rebounded in the 1990s because of the domestic competition it faced from Japan in the 1980s. By contrast, Japan's industry, protected at home, built up massive excess capacity and was no longer the dominant leader by the end of the 1990s.

49. For example, from 1993 to 1999, 81 percent of the new jobs created in the United States were in industry and occupation categories paying above-median wages, and 65 percent were in the highest paying third of these categories. See Council of Economic Advisers and U.S. Department of Labor, Office of the Chief Economist, "20 Million Jobs: January 1993–November 1999," Washington, D.C., December 1999, 50.

50. Paul Krugman, *Pop Internationalism* (Cambridge, Mass.: MIT Press, 1996), 9.

51. Ibid.

52. In this discussion I draw liberally from Miles Kahler, *International Institutions and the Political Economy of Integration* (Washington, D.C.: Brookings Institution, 1995).

53. On the dispute-settlement procedures of the WTO and NAFTA, see Sylvia Ostry, *The Post–Cold War Trading System: Who's on First?* (Chicago: University of Chicago Press, 1997), chaps. 6–7; Claude E. Barfield, *Free Trade, Sovereignty, Democracy: The Future of the World Trade Organization* (Washington, D.C.: American Enterprise Institute Press, 2001); John H. Jackson, *The World Trade Organization: Constitution and Jurisprudence* (London: Royal Institute of International Affairs, 1998).

54. For the distinction between outward-first and inward-first styles of U.S. foreign economic diplomacy developed in this section, see Robert L. Paarlberg, *Leadership Abroad Begins at Home: U.S. Foreign Economic Policy after the Cold War* (Washington, D.C.: Brookings Institution, 1995).

55. For the primary intellectual justification for this outward-first approach, see Bergsten and Henning, *Global Economic Leadership;* Richard N. Cooper et al., *Can Nations Agree? Issues in International Economic Cooperation* (Washington, D.C.: Brookings Institution, 1989); Ralph C. Bryant, *International Coordination of National Stabilization Policies* (Washington, D.C.: Brookings Institution, 1996). For a history of summitry, largely from this perspective, see Robert D. Putnam and Nicholas Bayne, *Hanging Together: Cooperation and Conflict in Seven-Power Summits*, rev. ed. (Cambridge, Mass.: Harvard University Press, 1987).

56. For a development of the inward-first style of leadership and an analysis of the Reagan administration's first-term international economic policies, see my *Myth of America's Decline.*

57. For a debate and sharpened contrast between the inward-first and outward-first approaches, see Bergsten, "Cost of Reaganomics"; Nau, "Where Reaganomics Works"; and responses to this debate by Bergsten, "State of the Debate"; Nau, "State of the Debate." Bergsten participated in summits such as Bonn in 1978, which he evaluates highly. I participated in summits such as Williamsburg in 1983, which I evaluate highly. Both of us may be accused of

bias. Viewing the two approaches as alternatives is probably the balanced way to proceed. For such a balanced treatment, see Paarlberg, *Leadership Abroad Begins at Home.*

58. The United States, for example, never met fiscal policy commitments made in the famous Louvre Agreement in 1987. See Nau, *Myth of America's Decline,* chap. 9. See also Yoichi Funabashi, *Managing the Dollar: From the Plaza to the Louvre* (Washington, D.C.: Institute for International Economics, 1988); Wendy Dobson, *Economic Policy Coordination: Requiem or Prologue?* (Washington, D.C.: Institute for International Economics, 1991).

59. For more balanced views of U.S. unilateralism as negotiating leverage, see John R. Bolton, "Unilateralism Is Not Isolationism," in *Understanding Unilateralism in American Foreign Relations,* ed. Gwyn Prins (London: Royal Institute of International Affairs, 2000), 50–83; Michael J. Glennon, "There's a Point to Going It Alone: Unilateralism Has Often Served Us Well," *Washington Post,* Outlook Section, 12 August 2001, p. B2.

60. The war chest includes anti-dumping laws against unfair import prices, countervailing duties against subsidized foreign exports, section 301 authority against unfair trade practices of all sorts, bilateral agreements to curb foreign imports (called voluntary export restraint agreements) and to increase American exports (called voluntary import expansion agreements), and discriminatory regional free trade areas such as NAFTA, the Free Trade Area for the Americas (FTAA), and APEC.

61. The shift of U.S. official opinion was particularly visible to U.S. trade partners. As Sylvia Ostry, Canadian analyst and participant in the Uruguay Round, laments, the attitude of U.S. officials "is a deeply disturbing trend, however understandable." *Post-Cold War Trading System,* 237.

62. Tyson, *Who's Bashing Whom?* 45.

63. See Jeffrey Garten quoted in George Melloan, "Trade Isn't War; Repeat, Trade Isn't War," *Wall Street Journal,* 1 May 1995, p. A15. Clyde Prestowitz, a former Reagan trade official but an outspoken critic of traditional multilateral trade negotiations, argues that because it "will take much time ... to plug the hole in the WTO rules," the WTO Charter should be amended "stating clearly that where the WTO has no rules, it also cannot block unilateral action." Clyde V. Prestowitz Jr., "The Looking-Glass Deal," *Washington Post,* 2 July 1995, p. C4.

64. See my "Clinton's Legacy Fades: U.S. Trade Leadership Languishes," in *The World Trade Organization Millennium Round: Freer Trade in the 21st Century,* ed. Klaus Guenther Deutsch and Bernhard Speyer (London: Routledge, 2001): 245–62.

65. See Claude E. Barfield, ed., *Expanding U.S.-Asian Trade and Investment* (Washington, D.C.: American Enterprise Institute Press, 1996).

66. Also, in imperfect markets, some regional trade arrangements may actually increase efficiency. See Lawrence, *Regionalism, Multilateralism and Deeper Integration.*

67. On the strategy and agenda for a new round, see Jeffrey J. Schott, *The WTO after Seattle* (Washington, D.C.: Institute for International Economics, July 2000); Ernest H. Preeg, "From Here to Free Trade: The Quest for a Multilateral/Regional Synthesis," in *Trade Strategies for a New Era,* ed. Geza Feketekuty (New York: Council on Foreign Relations, 1997).

68. See Paul Volcker's conclusions, for example, in Paul Volcker and Toyoo Gyohten, *Changing Fortunes: The World's Money and the Threat to American Leadership* (New York: Random House, 1992), 294. Volcker and Gyohten headed the U.S. and Japanese central banks in the 1980s. Barry Eichengreen, an academic economist, reaches similar conclusions in *International Monetary Arrangements for the 21st Century* (Washington, D.C.: Brookings Institution, 1994). For an alternative view supporting fixed rates, see Judy Shelton, *Money Meltdown* (New York: Free Press, 1994).

69. Martin Feldstein, chairman of the Council of Economic Advisers in Ronald Reagan's first-term administration, is sympathetic to the inward-first style of leadership and critical of EMU policies: "The shift of policy decisions from national governments to the European level would eliminate the ability to learn from the experiences of individual countries that try different policies and to benefit from the competitive pressures to adopt national policies that succeed." "EMU and International Conflict," 67–68.

70. This is the recommendation, for example, of Bergsten and Henning, *Global Economic Leadership,* 29. The Clinton administration advocated stimulus for both Europe and Japan in 1996 and continued to do so for Japan in 1999–2000.

71. Feldstein, for example, just assumes that the EMU will reinforce structural rigidity: "A politically more unified Europe would make it easier to enforce policies that prevent changes in national labor laws or national transfer payments that would reduce structural unemployment and increase national competitiveness." "EMU and International Conflict," 68.

72. The historical record suggests that outward-first summits, such as Bonn in 1978 and Tokyo in 1986, encourage stimulative policies, while inward-first summits, such as Williamsburg in 1983, encourage policies of restraint. See my *Myth of America's Decline*, conclusion, 349.

73. For a similar recommendation to initiate a Single Market Exercise, see the report by the Carnegie Endowment Study Group on US-EC Relations, *Atlantic Frontiers: A New Agenda for US-EC Relations* (Washington, D.C.: Carnegie Endowment for International Peace, 1993). Robert B. Zoellick (chairman of the Carnegie Endowment Study Group) became the U.S. trade representative under the new Republican administration in 2001.

74. For excellent reviews of the European SME, see Michael Calingaert, *European Integration Revisited: Progress, Prospects, and U.S. Interests* (Boulder: Westview, 1996); Michael Calingaert, *The 1992 Challenge from Europe: Development of the European Community's Internal Market* (Washington, D.C.: National Security Planning Association, 1988).

CHAPTER FIVE: WINNING THE PEACE

1. This was not expected to happen. In a famous article in 1979, Jeane Kirkpatrick argued that no communist country had ever become more liberal on its own, whereas authoritarian states had evolved in certain cases toward greater democracy. Now we know that both types of states can become more liberal. See Jeane Kirkpatrick, "Dictatorships and Double Standards," *Commentary* 68 (1979): 34–45.

2. Realists argue that Clinton's policies were misfocused because they put domestic and arms control concerns above great-power issues. Commenting on the president's visit to Moscow in June 2000, Henry Kissinger writes, "the administration policy toward Russia has focused on Russia's domestic redemption. The Moscow visit can make progress if it begins the process of treating Russia as a serious power. It will fail if it becomes the occasion for disquisitions on Russia's domestic structure or for arms control schemes doomed to failure in America." "Mission to Moscow," *Washington Post*, 15 May 2000, p. A23.

3. See Zbigniew Brzezinski, "The Premature Partnership," *Foreign Affairs* 73, no. 2 (1994): 67–83; Henry Kissinger, "The Question of Aid," *Washington Post*, 31 March 1992, p. 17A.

4. This is the position taken by the Clinton administration and its leading official on Russian affairs, Deputy Secretary of State Strobe Talbott. See Strobe Talbott, "Democracy and the National Interest," *Foreign Affairs* 75, no. 6 (1996): 47–64.

5. For a study that demonstrates the importance of proximity to the mature democracies of the West as an explanation of successful consolidation of democracy and markets in the East, see Jeffrey S. Kopstein and David A. Reilly, "Geographic Diffusion and the Transformation of the Postcommunist World," *World Politics* 53, no. 1 (2000): 1–38.

6. See Edward Mansfield and Jack Snyder, "Democratization and War," *Foreign Affairs* 74, no. 3 (1995): 79–98; Jack Snyder and Karen Ballentine, "Nationalism and the Marketplace of Ideas," *International Security* 21, no. 2 (1996): 5–41.

7. Amy Knight, *Spies without Cloaks: The KGB's Successors* (Princeton: Princeton University Press, 1996), 133; for extensive analysis, see chaps. 5–7.

8. Quoted in Fred Hiatt, "Shevardnadze's Second Act," *Washington Post*, 2 May 1999, p. B7. See also "Russia's Imperial Yearning," *The Economist*, 24 June 2000, p. 57.

9. For various scenarios of conflict in this region, see Richard L. Kugler, *Enlarging NATO: The Russia Factor* (Santa Monica: Rand, 1996).

10. For this history, see Catherine Kelleher, *The Future of European Security* (Washington, D.C.: Brookings Institution, 1995); Richard H. Ullman, ed., *The World and Yugoslavia's Wars* (New York: Council on Foreign Relations, 1996).

11. As Mikhail Gorbachev, the father of liberal reforms in the former Soviet Union, explains, "Expanding NATO's umbrella, including its nuclear weapons, to cover Poland, the Czech

Republic, Slovakia, and Hungary—moving NATO's frontiers some 400 miles closer to Moscow and the Russian heartland—is seen as a fundamental violation of Western guarantees after Russia dissolved the Warsaw Pact and agreed to German reunification." Mikhail S. Gorbachev, "NATO's Plans Threaten Start II," *New York Times,* 10 February 1996, p. 23. See also an article by then Foreign Minister Andrei Kozyrev, "Partnership or Cold War?" *Foreign Policy* 99 (1995): 3–15. American officials deny that expanding NATO violated U.S.-Soviet understandings; see Robert B. Zoellick, "Two Plus Four: The Lessons of German Unification," *National Interest* 61 (2000): 22.

12. This issue divides the policy community right down the middle. Take two prominent realists: Zbigniew Brzezinski advocates Russian membership; Henry Kissinger emphatically rejects it. The difference lies in assessments of the prospects for democratic reform in Russia. Brzezinski thinks Russian democracy may be consolidated at some point; Kissinger considers that outcome remote and improbable. See Zbigniew Brzezinski, "Living with Russia," *National Interest* 61 (2000): 5–17; Henry Kissinger, "The Dilution of NATO," *Washington Post,* 8 June 1997, p. C9.

13. Russia maintains an official liaison at NATO. In 1998, some thirty-eight high-ranking military representatives from partner countries worked at NATO headquarters. See William Drozdiak, "NATO Ponders Future Effectiveness," *Washington Post,* 30 May 1998, p. A16.

14. This special status gives Russia a security role equivalent to that of the United States. Both countries have veto power on the Security Council and both are called on in article 43 of chapter VII of the UN Charter to set up a Military Staff Committee to organize and command UN peacekeeping forces. Because of the Cold War, the Military Staff Committee was never established, but it still offers a means to staff and deploy UN forces under joint U.S.-Russian control.

15. For a discussion of the various conditions under which the WEU might act independently of the United States, see Dieter Mahncke, *Parameters of European Security,* Chaillot Paper 10 (Paris: Western European Union, Institute for Security Studies, 1993), 31–37. Whether a western European defense pillar will add to or subtract from NATO depends on the assessment of how widely U.S. and European strategic interests differ. Mahncke sees relatively narrow differences, as does Josef Joffe, "How America Does It," *Foreign Affairs* 76, no. 5 (1997): 13–28. Michael Howard, on the other hand, concludes that "if the members of an enlarged European Union were to ever develop a single coherent defense and foreign policy, it would be as likely to itself in opposition to that of the United States as in support of it." "An Unhappy Successful Marriage," *Foreign Affairs* 78, no. 3 (1999): 175.

16. See, for example, Michael Mandelbaum, *The Dawn of Peace in Europe* (New York: The Twentieth Century Fund Press, 1996).

17. NATO does have plans to inject forces temporarily in case of an emergency (e.g., if Serbia attacks ethnic Hungarians on the border of Hungary). Russia objects to such plans, reflecting again one of the drawbacks of including Russia in NATO discussions. On force-planning disputes in the NATO-Russia Joint Council, see Michael R. Gordon, "Russia Remains Uneasy over NATO Expansion," *New York Times,* 14 March 1999, p. 1.

18. See Andrew Jack and Vijai Maheshwari, "Russia Accused of Driving Wedges between Baltics," *Financial Times,* 5 May 2000, p. 3. For the ethnic Russian problem in Latvia, Estonia, Kazakhstan, and Ukraine, see David D. Laitin, *Identity in Formation: The Russian-Speaking Populations in the Near Abroad* (Ithaca: Cornell University Press, 1998).

19. On Baltic security issues, see Olav F. Knudsen, *Cooperative Security in the Baltic Region,* Chaillot Paper 33 (Paris: Institute for Security Studies, Western European Union, 1998); Hans Binnendijk and Jeffrey Simon, "Baltic Security and NATO Enlargement," *National Defense University Strategic Forum* no. 57 (1995); Peter van Ham, ed., *The Baltic States: Security and Defense after Independence,* Chaillot Paper 19 (Paris: Western European Union, Institute for Security Studies, 1995).

20. For recommendations to include Lithuania in the next phase of NATO expansion, see Zbigniew Brzezinski, "NATO: The Dilemmas of Expansion," *National Interest* 53 (1998): 13–17. See also a Council on Foreign Relations Task Force report (chaired by Brzezinski), *U.S. Policy toward Northeastern Europe* (New York: Council on Foreign Relations, 1999).

21. Finland and Sweden, after debating the NATO issue in 1997, stated that NATO membership was not their current aim, but that they "stand by their freedom to choose the contents and form of their connection with the political and military cooperation emerging in Europe." Knudsen, *Cooperative Security*, 38.

22. On the Yugoslavian civil wars, see Ivo H. Daalder, *Getting to Dayton: The Making of America's Bosnia Policy* (Washington, D.C.: Brookings Institution, 2000); Susan L. Woodward, *Balkan Tragedy: Chaos and Dissolution after the Cold War* (Washington, D.C.: Brookings Institution, 1995).

23. For background, see the discussion in chapter 4 and in Kelleher, *Future of European Security.*

24. For a suggestion from a conservative think tank along these lines, see John C. Hulsman, "A Grand Bargain with Europe," Background #1360, Heritage Foundation, Washington, D.C., April 17, 2000.

25. On the CIS, see Kugler, *Enlarging NATO,* chap. 3. See also Mark Webber, *CIS Integration Trends: Russia and the Former Soviet South* (London: Royal Institute of International Affairs, 1997); Roy Allison and Christopher Bluth, eds., *Security Dilemmas in Russia and Eurasia* (London: Royal Institute of International Affairs, 1998).

26. See Serge Schmemann, "Yeltsin Suggests a Role for Russia to Keep Peace in Ex-Soviet Lands," *New York Times,* 1 March 1993, p. A1; Daniel Williams, "Russia Asserts Role in Ex-Soviet Republics," *Washington Post,* 29 September 1993, p. A25.

27. Michael Specter, "Russian Parliament Denounces Soviet Union's Breakup," *New York Times,* 16 March 1996, p. 3. For background at the time on Yeltsin's "war" with the Duma, see Peter Reddaway and Dmitri Glinski, *The Tragedy of Russia's Reforms: Market Bolshevism against Democracy* (Washington, D.C.: United States Institute of Peace Press, 2001), 512–13.

28. These agreements have been long on symbols and short on substance—Russia is particularly reluctant to assume the economic costs of annexing Belarus. Nevertheless, the symbolism of Yeltsin and later Putin embracing Belarus dictator Alexander Lukashenko is not necessarily reassuring. See Charles Clover, "Russia and Belarus in New Treaty on Reunification," *Financial Times,* 9 December 1999, p. 3.

29. See Anatol Lieven, *Ukraine and Russia: A Fraternal Rivalry* (Washington, D.C.: United States Institute of Peace Press, 1999).

30. For background, see Dale F. Eickelman, *Russia's Muslim Frontiers* (Bloomington: Indiana University Press, 1993); Martha Brill Olcott, *Central Asia's New States: Independence, Foreign Policy, and Regional Security* (Washington, D.C.: United States Institute of Peace Press, 1996); M. E. Ahrari, *The Great Game in Muslim Central Asia* (Washington, D.C.: Institute for National Security Studies, National Defense University, 1996). As of August 2000, Russia had ground forces and equipment in Armenia, Georgia, Moldova, Tajikistan, and Ukraine. Russian forces also served in peacekeeping operations in Bosnia, Georgia/Abkhazia, Georgia/Ossetia, Moldova/Trans-Dniester, and Yugoslavia. See International Institute for Strategic Studies, *The Military Balance 2000–2001* (London: Oxford University Press, 2000), 125–26.

31. In spring and summer 1993, Russian officials called for UN (CSCE) intervention in the Caucasus region, but the United States showed no interest and, after the UN failure in Somalia in fall 1993, rejected further peacekeeping cooperation with the UN. See John Lloyd, "Yeltsin Seeks Peace-Keeping Role on Borders," *Financial Times,* 1 March 1993, p. 16; and the complaint by Andrei Kozyrev, then Russian foreign minister, that a timely arrival of UN forces in Georgia might have avoided a civil war in that country, quoted in Celestine Bohlen, "Moscow Sidesteps a Role in Georgia," *New York Times,* 24 September 1993, p. A6. See also coverage of these events in Sean Kay, *NATO and the Future of European Security* (Lanham: Rowman and Littlefield, 1998), 77–79.

32. The following discussion draws freely from Adrian Karatnycky, Alexander Motyl, and Aili Piano, eds., *Nations in Transit 1999–2000* (New Brunswick: Transaction, 2001).

33. As of 1999, Poland, Hungary, Estonia, Lithuania, and Latvia have had two such transitions; and Slovenia, Slovakia, and the Czech Republic one.

34. Anatol Lieven, *The Baltic Revolution: Estonia, Latvia, Lithuania and the Path to Independence* (New Haven: Yale University Press, 1993), 71–72.

35. Leonid Kuchma, the former prime minister, supported largely by Russophile sections of Ukraine, defeated Leonid Kravchuk, a longtime communist official supported by the western-

leaning areas in Ukraine. Kuchma was reelected in 1999, but the OSCE called the elections fraudulent. See Charles Clover, "OSCE Finds Ballot Rigging in Ukraine Poll," *Financial Times,* 18 November 1999, p. 2. See also Sharon Wolchik and Volodymyr Zviglyanich, eds., *Ukraine: The Search for a National Identity* (Lanham: Rowman and Littlefield, 1999); Alexander Motyl, *Dilemmas of Independence: Ukraine after Totalitarianism* (New York: Council on Foreign Relations, 1993). For helpful background, see Karen Dawisha and Bruce Parrott, *Russia and the New States of Eurasia* (Cambridge, U.K.: Cambridge University Press, 1994).

36. Even the most optimistic Clinton officials conceded the point. As Deputy Secretary of State Strobe Talbott, the lead U.S. official for Russian relations, says, "It is too early to proclaim Russian democratization irreversible." Quoted in Thomas W. Lippman, "U.S. Narrows Its Partnership with Russia," *Washington Post,* 22 November 1998, p. A33. For assessments of Russian political prospects, see Dimitri K. Simes, *After the Collapse: Russia Seeks Its Place as a Great Power* (New York: Simon and Schuster, 1999); Michael McFaul, *Russia's 1996 Presidential Election: The End of Polarized Politics* (Stanford: Hoover Institution Press, 1997); David Remnick, *Resurrection: The Struggle for a New Russia* (New York: Vintage, 1998); Anders Åslund and Martha Brill Olcott, eds., *Russia after Communism* (Washington, D.C.: Carnegie Endowment for International Peace, 2000); Reddaway and Glinski, *Tragedy of Russia's Reforms.*

37. For an assessment of Putin's early policies, see Peter Reddaway, "Will Putin Be Able to Consolidate Power?" *Post-Soviet Affairs* 17, no. 1 (2001): 24–44.

38. For an analysis of America's democracy-promotion efforts, see Michael Cox, G. John Ikenberry, and Takashi Inoguchi, eds., *American Democracy Promotion: Impulses, Strategies, and Impacts* (New York: Oxford University Press, 2000); Constantine C. Menges, "The United States and the Encouragement of Democracy Abroad," Program on Transitions in Democracy, Elliott School of International Affairs, George Washington University, Washington, D.C., October 1999.

39. See my "America's Identity, Democracy Promotion and National Interests: Beyond Realism, Beyond Idealism," in *American Democracy Promotion: Impulses, Strategies, and Impacts,* ed. Michael Cox, G. John Ikenberry, and Takashi Inoguchi (New York: Oxford University Press, 2000), 127–51.

40. The estimate, made by Michael McFaul, is quoted in David Hoffman, "Proliferation of Parties Gives Russia a Fractured Democratic System," *Washington Post,* 1 October 1995, p. A27. See also Maxim Boycko, Andrei Shleifer, and Robert Vishny, *Privatizing Russia* (Cambridge, Mass.: MIT Press, 1995); Joseph R. Blasi, Maya Kroumova, and Douglas Kruse, *Kremlin Capitalism: The Privatization of the Russian Economy* (Ithaca: Cornell University Press, 1997).

41. Reddaway and Glinski, *Tragedy of Russia's Reforms.*

42. For early Russian policies to reform the economy, see two sharply contrasting accounts: Marshall Goldman, *Lost Opportunity: Why Economic Reforms in Russia Have Not Worked* (New York: Norton, 1994); Anders Åslund, *How Russia Became a Market Economy* (Washington, D.C.: Brookings Institution, 1995). On the continuing microeconomic distortions in the Russian economy, see Harry Broadman and Francesca Recanatini, "Is Russia Restructuring? New Evidence on Job Creation and Destruction," World Bank Paper, Washington, D.C., 16 February 2001.

43. See James A. Leach, "The New Russian Menace," *New York Times,* 10 September 1999, p. A27.

44. On these early events in Poland and other former communist states, see Shafiqul Islam and Michael Mandelbaum, eds., *Making Markets: Economic Transformation in Eastern Europe and the Post-Soviet States* (New York: Council on Foreign Relations, 1993); Richard Porter, ed., *Economic Transformation in Central Europe: A Progress Report* (London: Centre for Economic Policy Research, 1994). For a more recent assessment by a participant in Poland's government, see Grzegorz W. Kolodko, *From Shock to Therapy: The Political Economy of Postsocialist Transformation* (New York: Oxford University Press, 2001).

45. See Stephan Wagstyl, "Economic Hurdles Threaten to Thwart Romania's High Ambitions," *Financial Times,* 9 March 2001, p. 3.

46. John Tagliabue, "On Top in Bulgaria: New Premier Is the Old King," *New York Times,* 13 July 2001, p. A4.

47. Some analysts fault American policy for not making aid available on the scale of the Marshall Plan after World War II. But, as Jack F. Matlock Jr., former U.S. ambassador in Moscow,

notes, "a version of the Marshall Plan for the USSR would not have worked in 1989." See Jack F. Matlock Jr., *Autopsy of an Empire* (New York: Random House, 1995). For a critique of aid policy in central and eastern Europe, see Janine Wedel, *Collision and Collusion: The Strange Case of Assistance to Central and Eastern Europe* (New York: St. Martin's Press, 1999).

48. In the mid-1990s, for example, Hungary spent more than 30 percent of its GDP on welfare, more than any other country in Europe other than Sweden. See Virginia Marsh, "Hungarian Coalition Left Exposed," *Financial Times,* 21 September 1995, p. 3.

49. Jeane Kirkpatrick, "Cheaper than Another War," *Washington Post,* 9 September 1991, p. 15A.

CHAPTER SIX: FROM BILATERALISM TO MULTILATERALISM

1. Secretary of State James A. Baker III explicitly recognized the hub-and-spoke pattern of U.S. relations with Asia in 1991. See James A. Baker, "America in Asia: Emerging Architecture for a Pacific Community," *Foreign Affairs* 70, no. 5 (1991–92): 1–19. See also his memoirs, James A. Baker with Thomas M. Defrank, *The Politics of Diplomacy: Revolution, War and Peace, 1989–1992* (New York: G. P. Putnam's Sons, 1995). The Southeast Asian Treaty Organization (SEATO) was a multilateral exception to the bilateral pattern, but it did not include Japan or South Korea and was quickly superseded by U.S. bilateral treaties with those two countries.

2. Yoichi Funabashi, *Asia Pacific Fusion: Japan's Role in APEC* (Washington, D.C.: Institute for International Economics, 1995), 174.

3. See Edwin O. Reischauer, *The Japanese Today: Change and Continuity* (Cambridge, Mass.: Belknap Press, 1988), 33.

4. Henry Kissinger, *Diplomacy* (New York: Simon and Schuster, 1994), 828. On a Bismarckian strategy for balancing power through bilateral alliances, see Josef Joffe, "How America Does It," *Foreign Affairs* 76, no. 5 (1997): 13–28.

5. See, for example, Richard J. Samuels, *Rich Nation, Strong Army: National Security and the Technological Transformation of Japan* (Ithaca: Cornell University Press, 1994). Samuels argues that Japan has a long-standing historical predisposition toward national autonomy and in the long run will reassert its military independence and influence.

6. See Selig S. Harrison, ed., *Japan's Nuclear Future: The Plutonium Debate and East Asian Security* (Washington, D.C.: Carnegie Endowment for International Peace, 1996), 3–4. Polls show that only 11 percent of the Japanese people say they like Koreans, and only 6 percent of Koreans say they like the Japanese. See Kent E. Calder, *Pacific Defense: Arms, Energy, and America's Future in Asia* (New York: William Morrow, 1996), 100–101. In popularity polls, as Reischauer notes, Japanese consistently rank western democracies above their closest neighbors, the two Koreas and Russia; see Reischauser, *Japanese Today,* 404.

7. On China's intense distrust of Japan, see Thomas J. Christensen, "China, the U.S.-Japan Alliance, and the Security Dilemma in Asia," *International Security* 23, no. 4 (1999): 49–80.

8. In southeast Asia, as John Bresnan observes, "political parties of the kind familiar to Americans are notable for their absence." *From Dominoes to Dynamos: The Transformation of Southeast Asia* (New York: Council on Foreign Relations, 1994), 55.

9. That is the view of Zbigniew Brzezinski, *The Grand Failure: The Birth and Death of Communism in the Twentieth Century* (New York: Charles Scribner's Sons, 1989), 147.

10. See Barry Gills, "The Hegemonic Tradition in East Asia: A Historical Perspective," in *Gramsci, Historical Materialism and International Relations,* ed. Stephen Gill (Cambridge, U.K.: Cambridge University Press, 1993).

11. The classic study on Japan's self-image is Ruth Benedict, *The Chrysanthemum and the Sword: Patterns of Japanese Culture* (Boston: Houghton Mifflin, 1946).

12. These different structures of power may account for different levels of violence. By some accounts, Asia experienced fewer wars than Europe because it had longer periods of imperial rule. See Dave Kang, "Asian Nations Bandwagon," in *The Emerging International Relations of the Asia-Pacific Region,* ed. G. John Ikenberry and Michael Mastanduno (New York: Columbia University Press, forthcoming). The different structures of power may also help explain the great difficulty Asian countries have in reconciling long-standing historical differences with one

another. The Japanese have only grudgingly acknowledged their responsibility for World War II. China has never acknowledged the atrocities of Mao (as the Soviet Union did those of Stalin in the 1950s). Because identity is rooted in hierarchical relationships rather than individual or group equality, the need to save face takes precedence over the need to atone.

13. For helpful discussions of human rights and democracy in Asia, see William Theodore de Bary, *Asian Values and Human Rights: A Confucian Communitarian Perspective* (Cambridge, Mass.: Harvard University Press, 1998); Larry Diamond and Marc F. Plattner, eds., *Democracy in East Asia* (Baltimore: Johns Hopkins University Press, 1998).

14. Quoted in Fareed Zakaria, "A Conversation with Lee Kuan Yew," *Foreign Affairs* 73, no. 2 (1994): 111.

15. Quoted in Bresnan, *From Dominoes to Dynamos,* 61.

16. Quoted in Kazuo Ogura, "A Call for a New Concept of Asia," *Japan Echo* 20, no. 2 (1992): 40.

17. Kenneth Lieberthal, *Governing China: From Revolution through Reform* (New York: W. W. Norton, 1995), 12.

18. Lowell Dittmer, *China under Reform* (Boulder: Westview, 1994), 158.

19. Brzezinski, *Grand Failure,* 250.

20. Lieberthal, *Governing China,* 302.

21. Andrew J. Nathan, *China's Crisis: Dilemmas of Reform and Prospects for Democracy* (New York: Columbia University Press, 1990), 175.

22. See John Pomfret, "In Rural China, Democracy Not All It Seems," *Washington Post,* 26 August 2000, p. 1; Merle Goldman, "In Rural China, A Brief Swell of Electoral Waters," *Washington Post,* 21 February 1999, Outlook Section, p. B2; Michael Laris, "China Praises Sichuan Election," *Washington Post,* 27 February 1999, p. A17.

23. See "The Tiananmen Papers," intro. Andrew J. Nathan, *Foreign Affairs* 80, no. 1 (2001).

24. Quoted in ibid., 32.

25. Quoted in Seth Faison, "China's Leader Announces Sell-Off of State Enterprises," *New York Times,* 13 September 1997, p. 7.

26. See Rahul Jacob, "Frustration Grows with Hong Kong Leaders and Opposition Alike," *Financial Times,* 25 May 2000, p. 4; Rahul Jacob, "WTO Accession: The Role of Hong Kong," *Financial Times Survey: China,* 13 November 2000, p. IV.

27. Alastair Iain Johnston, "Cultural Realism and Strategy in Maoist China," in *The Culture of National Security: Norms and Identity in World Politics,* ed. Peter Katzenstein (New York: Columbia University Press, 1996), 216–27. See also Alastair Iain Johnston, *Cultural Realism: Strategic Culture and Strategy in Chinese History* (Princeton: Princeton University Press, 1995). For a balanced and comprehensive review of China's outlook, see David Shambaugh, "Facing Reality in China Policy," *Foreign Affairs* 80, no. 1 (2001): 50–64.

28. See World Bank, *The Chinese Economy: Fighting Inflation, Deepening Reforms* (Washington, D.C.: World Bank, 1996).

29. A select committee of Congress chaired by Christopher Cox investigated the extent of Chinese espionage in American nuclear weapons laboratories. For the overview of the Cox Report, see the text in *New York Times,* 26 May 1999, pp. A17–A18.

30. Quoted in Barton Gellman, "U.S. and China Nearly Came to Blows in 1996," *Washington Post,* 21 June 1998, p. A20. Paul Bracken concludes that "China appears to be set to field a regional force of missiles that will change the military-technical balance of power in Asia [and] make any outside country think twice about moving forces there in a crisis." "How the West Was One-Upped," *Washington Post,* 3 June 1999, p. A27. See also Paul Bracken, *Fire in the East: The Rise of Asian Military Power and the Second Nuclear Age* (New York: Harper-Collins, 1999). Peter Rodman makes the same point: "China's new weaponry will be sufficient in the near term to raise the risks and inhibitions to an American President who contemplates intervening in a future crisis in the Taiwan Strait or South China Sea." *Between Friendship and Rivalry: China and America in the 21st Century* (Washington D.C.: Nixon Center, 1998), v.

31. From 1991 to 1999, China bought approximately $8 billion worth of Russian weapons, including seventy-two Sukhoi-27 fighters with a license to coproduce two hundred more, sixty Sukhoi-30 fighters, fifteen Ilyushin-72 transport aircraft, twenty-four Mi-17 transport

helicopters, one hundred RD-33 turbofan engines for China's J-10 fighter, the SA-10 "Grumble" air-defense missile system with one hundred missiles, four kilo-class diesel submarines, two Sovremennyi-class guided missile destroyers, fifty T-72 main battle tanks, and seventy armored personnel carriers. China has also bought advanced military weaponry from France and other western countries. For summaries, see Paul H. B. Godwin, "Force Projection and China's National Military Threat" (paper prepared for the 6th Staunton Hill Conference on the Chinese People's Liberation Army, American Enterprise Institute, *Coolfont* Conference Center, Berkeley Springs, W. Va., June 1995); David Shambaugh, "China's Military Views the World: Ambivalent Security," *International Security* 24, no. 3 (1999–2000): 52–80.

32. China has constructed a long runway (which can accommodate SU-27s) and port facility on Woody Island, the largest of the Paracel Islands, and an early warning radar system on Fiery Cross Reef, an island in the Spratlys. The latter facility is more than 1,000 kilometers from Hainan, the nearest Chinese territory. China used force in January 1995 to evict Philippine fishermen from Mischief Reef and fortified this outcropping in the Spratly archipelago. China is also pressing Myanmar to allow a listening post on Victoria Point, an island within 300 kilometers of the Malacca Straits. For background, see Bob Catley and Makmur Keliat, *Spratlys: The Dispute in the South China Sea* (Aldershot: Ashgate, 1997).

33. Some less conservative estimates place the total Chinese military budget close to $100 billion. See Nicholas D. Kristof, "The Real Chinese Threat," *New York Times Magazine,* 27 August 1995, pp. 50–51; National Security Planning Associates, *Security Perspectives and Defense Priorities in the Asia-Pacific* (Washington, D.C.: U.S. Department of Defense, 1995).

34. Chas W. Freeman, "Preventing War in the Taiwan Strait," *Foreign Affairs* 77, no. 4 (1998): 7. Kurt Campbell, a key defense department official in the Clinton administration, and Derek Mitchell concluded in 2001 that "the military systems that Beijing has fielded over the past five years look less like heavily armored bargaining chips and more like true military capabilities that could be used on the battlefield." "Crisis in the Taiwan Strait?" *Foreign Affairs* 80, no. 4 (2001): 18.

35. See Thomas W. Lippman, "Chinese Missile Buildup Is Threat to Taiwan, Report Says," *Washington Post,* 26 February 1999, A20. For a skeptical analysis of China's ability to invade Taiwan, see Michael O'Hanlon, "Why China Cannot Conquer Taiwan," *International Security* 25, no. 2 (2000): 51–87.

36. The arms race in Asia is evident in table 6.1. Military expenditures are considerably higher in Asia than in Latin America and Africa and on a par with expenditures in the Middle East. China's explosion of a nuclear weapon in 1964 provoked Japan to examine for the first time broader nuclear options and to declare that tactical nuclear weapons would not be inconsistent with Japan's self-defense-oriented constitution. In 1994, Prime Minister Tsutomu Hata said, "Japan has the capability to possess nuclear weapons but has not made them"; the government later retracted his statements. Quoted in David Sanger, "In Face-Saving Turn, Japan Denies Nuclear Know-How," *New York Times,* 22 June 1994, p. A10.

37. The costs are estimated to be, depending on the scenario, from $40 billion to $2.2 trillion. See Soogil Yong, Chang-Jae Lee, and Hyoungsoo Zang, "Preparing for the Economic Integration of Two Koreas: Policy Challenges to South Korea," in *Economic Integration of the Korean Peninsula,* ed. Marcus Noland (Washington, D.C.: Institute for International Economics, 1998), 266.

38. Quoted in Nayan Chanda, "U.S. Policy in Northeast Asia: An Asian Perspective," in *Brookings Northeast Asia Survey 2000–01,* ed. Catharin Dalpino and Bates Gill (Washington, D.C.: Brookings Institution, 2001), 19.

39. For helpful histories of the volatile Taiwan issue in U.S.-Chinese relations, see Harry Harding, *The United States and China since 1972: A Fragile Relationship* (Washington, D.C.: Brookings Institution, 1992); James Mann, *About Face: A History of America's Curious Relationship with China, from Nixon to Clinton* (New York: Alfred A. Knopf, 1999); Patrick Tyler, *A Great Wall: Six Presidents and China: An Investigative History* (New York: The Century Foundation Press, 1999); David M. Lampton, *Same Bed, Different Dreams: Managing U.S.-China Relations, 1989–2000* (Berkeley: University of California Press, 2001).

40. Kent E. Calder, "Japan's Energy Angst and the Caspian Great Game," *National Bureau of Asian Research Analysis* 12, no. 1 (2001): 90.

41. See Sheldon W. Simon, "Security, Economic Liberalism, and Democracy," *National Bureau of Asian Research Analysis*, 7, no. 2 (1996): 24.
42. On the Chinese-Russian military relationship and other aspects of China's military policy, see Shambaugh, "China's Military Views of the World: Ambivalent Security." For a more concerned view of Russian-Chinese cooperation, see Constantine C. Menges, "Russia, China and What's Really on the Table," *Washington Post*, 29 July 2001, Outlook Section, p. B2.
43. A bipartisan study group headed by Richard Armitage and Joseph Nye, defense officials in the George H. W. Bush and Clinton administrations respectively (Armitage later became deputy secretary of state in the George W. Bush administration), proposed in October 2000 that the United States and Japan accelerate defense cooperation by, among other things, greater jointness in training and facilities, strengthened intelligence collaboration, and broadened missile defense programs. See *The United States and Japan: Advancing toward a Mature Partnership* (Washington, D.C.: Institute for National Strategic Studies, National Defense University, 2000).
44. For a review of Japan's use of its Self-Defense Forces in UN peacekeeping activities, see Milton Leitenberg, "The Participation of Japanese Military Forces in U.N. Peacekeeping Operations," Maryland/Tsukuba Papers on U.S.-Japan Relations, University of Maryland, and University of Tsukuba, June 1996. In 2001, Japan also sent medical and logistical support to U.S. and other allied forces in Afghanistan.
45. For a comprehensive study of missile defense issues and reactions in Asia, see Michael J. Green and Toby F. Dalton, "Asian Reactions to U.S. Missile Defense," *National Bureau of Asian Research Analysis* 11, no. 3 (2000).
46. David Ibison, "S. Korea Halts Military Link with Japan," *Financial Times*, 13 July 2001, p. 6.
47. See Richard Armitage, "A Comprehensive Approach to North Korea," *National Defense University Strategic Forum*, no. 159 (1999). For background on U.S.-Japan-South Korean military relations, see Ralph A. Cossa, ed., *US-Korea-Japan Relations: Building toward a "Virtual Alliance"* (Washington, D.C.: Center for Strategic and International Studies Press, 1999); Victor D. Cha, *Alignment despite Antagonism: The United States-Korea-Japan Security Triangle* (Stanford: Stanford University Press, 1999); Michael Green, "U.S.-Japan-ROK Trilateral Security Cooperation: Prospects and Pitfalls" (paper presented at annual meeting of the American Political Science Association, Washington, D.C., August 1997).
48. Singapore, Malaysia, and Hong Kong allow U.S. warships to make port calls, although China suspended the privileges in Hong Kong for one year after the NATO bombing of the Chinese embassy in Belgrade in March 1999. Singapore also provides some maintenance services. After expelling U.S. bases in 1992, the Philippine parliament agreed in 1999 to reopen its territory for joint exercises with U.S. forces. For an assessment of how these countries view security issues in the region, see Koong Paiching, "Southeast Asian Countries' Perceptions of China's Military Modernization," Sigur Center for Asian Studies, Elliott School of International Affairs, George Washington University, May 1999.
49. ARF exercises have yielded modest results, such as the issuing of defense white papers and encouraging nongovernmental dialogues on security issues. The Council for Security Cooperation in the Asia Pacific (CSCAP) involves participants from fourteen countries including North Korea, Russia, and Mongolia, but not Taiwan or China. The Northeast Asia Cooperation Dialogue (NEACD) includes the two Koreas plus the four great powers—China, Russia, Japan, and the United States. For a good summary of these organizations see Sheldon W. Simon and Donald K. Emmerson, "Security, Democracy, and Economic Liberalization: Competing Priorities in U.S. Asia Policy," *National Bureau of Asian Research Analysis*, 7, no. 2 (1996).
50. See Harrison, *Japan's Nuclear Future.*
51. Policy makers hesitate to recommend the multilateral approach for fear it will weaken bilateral ties and provoke perceptions of American withdrawal. When Japan revised its defense plan in fall 1994, U.S. officials objected that it placed too much emphasis on multilateral and autonomous capabilities and ignored bilateral obligations. In response, Defense Department officials issued a new U.S. strategy paper for Asia that reaffirmed bilateral commitments and became the basis for the guideline revisions under the U.S.-Japan Security Treaty. See Office of International Security Affairs, *United States Security Strategy for the East Asia Pacific Region* (Washington, D.C.: Department of Defense, 1995);

Joseph S. Nye Jr., "East Asian Security: The Case for Deep Engagement," *Foreign Affairs* 74, no. 4 (1995): 90–103; Patrick M. Cronin, "Japan's Emergent Security Policy," *Joint Forces Quarterly,* no. 7 (1995): 20–23; Michael J. Green, *Arming Japan: Defense Production, Alliance Politics, and the Postwar Search for Autonomy* (New York: Columbia University Press, 1995); Mike M. Mochizuki, ed., *Toward a True Alliance: Restructuring U.S.-Japan Security Relations* (Washington, D.C.: Brookings Institution, 1997); and Daniel I. Okimoto et al., eds., *A United States Policy for the Changing Realities of Asia* (Stanford: Asia Pacific Research Center, 1996).

52. See Selig S. Harrison and Clyde V. Prestowitz Jr., eds., *Asia after the "Miracle": Redefining U.S. Economic and Security Policies* (Washington, D.C.: Economic Strategy Institute, 1998), p. 10. See also Jeffrey E. Garten, *A Cold Peace: America, Japan, Germany, and the Struggle for Supremacy* (New York: Times Books, 1992); Clyde V. Prestowitz, Jr., *Trading Places* (New York: Basic Books, 1988); and James Fallows, *Looking at the Sun: The Rise of the New East Asian Economic and Political System* (New York: Pantheon, 1994).

53. See Dennis Encarnation, *Rivals beyond Trade: America versus Japan in Global Competition* (Ithaca: Cornell University Press, 1992).

54. See James C. Abegglen, *Sea Change: Pacific Asia as the New World Industrial Center* (New York: Free Press, 1994); Kozo Yamamura and Walter Hatch, "A Looming Entry Barrier: Japan's Production Networks in Asia," *National Bureau of Asian Research Analysis* 8, no. 1 (1997).

55. Edward J. Lincoln, *Japan's New Global Role* (Washington, D.C.: Brookings Institution, 1993), 199.

56. See Richard Katz, *Japan, the System that Soured: The Rise and Fall of the Japanese Economic Miracle* (New York: M. E. Sharpe, 1998), especially his update of chapter 3 at http://www.mesharpe.com/katz_chap_3.htm.

57. Edward J. Lincoln, *Troubled Times: U.S.-Japan Trade Relations in the 1990s* (Washington, D.C.: Brookings Institution, 1999), 106.

58. See Lester Thurow, *Head to Head: The Coming Economic Battle among Japan, Europe, and America* (New York: William Morrow, 1992), 126. See also Fallows, *Looking at the Sun,* 368, 412.

59. Some attribute the model's success primarily to government intervention. See Chalmers Johnson, *MITI and the Japanese Miracle* (Stanford: Stanford University Press, 1982); Robert Wade, *Governing the Market: Economic Theory and the Role of Government* (Princeton: Princeton University Press, 1990). Others attribute it to corporate or private sector initiatives, not operating independently of the state as in pluralist societies but working closely with government in a kind of corporate-led strategic capitalism. See Kent E. Calder, *Strategic Capitalism: Private Business and Public Purpose in Japanese Industrial Finance* (Princeton: Princeton University Press, 1994); Kent E. Calder, *Crisis and Compensation: Public Policy and Political Stability in Japan 1949–1986* (Princeton: Princeton University Press, 1988); Daniel I. Okimoto, *Between MITI and the Market* (Stanford: Stanford University Press, 1989). Still others stress the process of dialogue between government and business in Japan and other Asian countries, which often blurs the whole question of which sector takes the initiative. See Richard J. Samuels, *The Business of the Japanese State: Energy Markets in Comparative and Historical Perspective* (Ithaca: Cornell University Press, 1987). Finally, some studies attribute Japan's success, unconvincingly, to its greatest weakness, namely its financial system. See Daniel Burstein, *Yen! Japan's New Financial Empire and Its Threat to America* (New York: Simon and Schuster, 1988). For a more realistic assessment of Japan's financial sector, see Eugene R. Dattel, *The Sun That Never Rose: The Inside Story of Japan's Failed Attempt at Global Financial Dominance* (Chicago: Probus, 1994).

60. Abegglen, *Sea Change,* 206. The view that Japan's approach was superior was popularized by Chalmers Johnson's quip: "The Cold War is over, and Japan won." *Japan: Who Governs?* (New York: W. W. Norton, 1995), 8. Clyde Prestowitz also argued that Japan's system was more balanced between producer and consumer interests (the U.S. system being too consumer oriented), provided more long-term and patient investment capital (the U.S. system being too oriented toward equity markets and quarterly earning reports), and did not carry individualism to excess (which, Prestowitz argued, was America's "fatal flaw"). See Prestowitz, *Trading Places,* especially 14, 24, 332.

61. See Scott Callon, *Divided Sun: MITI and the Breakdown of Japanese High-Tech Industrial Policy 1975–1993* (Stanford: Stanford University Press, 1995), 170. Callon chronicles the failure of many programs of Japan's Ministry of International Trade and Industry, the super-bureaucracy that led Japan's earlier industrialization and became a legend in studies that attribute Japan's success to government intervention (e.g., Johnson, *MITI and the Japanese Miracle*).

62. See Edward J. Lincoln, "Japan's Financial Mess," *Foreign Affairs* 77, no. 3 (1998): 57–67. For other critical studies of Japan's economy, see Katz, *Japan, the System that Soured*; Peter Hartcher, *The Ministry: How Japan's Most Powerful Institution Endangers World Markets* (Boston: Harvard Business School Press, 1998).

63. McKinsey and Co., *Capital Productivity* (Washington, D.C.: McKinsey Global Institute, June 1996).

64. Paul Krugman, "The Myth of Asia's Miracle," *Foreign Affairs* 73, no. 6 (1994): 70. Krugman's conclusions are not uncontroversial, but no one has turned up evidence that the Asian model uses capital or labor more efficiently than the American model. See World Bank, *The East Asian Miracle: A World Bank Research Report* (New York: Oxford University Press, 1993).

65. The Japanese, for example, repatriated many of their investments in American real estate at a considerable loss. These were the same investments that had generated in the 1980s sensational charges of a Japanese takeover of America's key resources. See Martin Tolchin and Susan Tolchin, *Buying into America: How Foreign Money Is Changing the Face of Our Nation* (New York: Times Books, 1988).

66. For a similar view of Japan's situation, see Sebastian Mallaby, "In Asia's Mirror," *National Interest*, no. 52 (1998): 13–22. In eleven fiscal stimulus packages from 1992–2000, Japan spent $1.2 trillion to achieve an annual growth rate of less than 1 percent. The fiscal deficit was running approximately 8 percent of GDP, and total national debt exceeded 200 percent of GDP, if off-budget lending is included. Bad loans are estimated to equal as much as 50–60 percent of GDP. Meanwhile, short-term interest rates were barely above zero, reflecting the end of the string on monetary stimulus as well. See David Asher and Robert H. Dugger, "Could Japan's Financial Mount Fuji Blow Its Top?" MIT-Japan Program, Massachusetts Institute of Technology, Cambridge, Mass., May 2000.

67. For this view, see Steven Radalet and Jeffrey Sachs, "Asia's Reemergence," *Foreign Affairs* 76, no. 6 (1998): 44–60; Robert Wade, "The Coming Fight over Capital Flows," *Foreign Policy*, no. 113 (1998–99): 41–55.

68. For this view, see Sebastian Edwards, "A Capital Idea? Reconsidering a Financial Quick Fix," *Foreign Affairs* 78, no. 3 (1999): 18–22; David Hale, "The IMF, Now More than Ever," *Foreign Affairs* 77, no. 6 (1998): 7–14; Michael E. Porter and Hirotaka Takeuchi, "Fixing What Really Ails Japan," *Foreign Affairs* 78, no. 3 (1999): 66–82.

69. Michael Armacost, former U.S. ambassador in Tokyo, notes how focusing bilaterally on Japan allows Japan to outflank the United States by neutralizing natural allies. See Michael Armacost, *Friends or Rivals? The Insider's Account of U.S.-Japan Relations* (New York: Columbia University Press, 1996), 184. For a similar critique, see Robert A. Manning and Paula Stern, "The Myth of the Pacific Community," *Foreign Affairs* 73, no. 6 (1994): 79–94.

70. See Guy de Jonquieres, "Asian Ambition," *Financial Times*, 28 November 2000, p. 14.

71. Australia initiated the APEC forum in 1989. The United States initially reacted with considerable doubt, if not concern. See Funabashi, *Asia Pacific Fusion*.

72. Nicholas Lardy, a longtime student of the Chinese economy, makes this prediction. See James Kynge, "Against All Odds: China May Struggle to Save Distressed Assets," *Financial Times*, 24 May 2001, p. 4. See also Nicholas R. Lardy, *China's Unfinished Economic Revolution* (Washington, D.C.: Brookings Institution, 1998). On China's lumbering state sector, see Edward S. Steinfeld, *Forging Reform in China: The Fate of State-Owned Industry* (Cambridge, U.K.: Cambridge University Press, 1998).

73. See Neil A. Martin, "China Boosts Exports with Stealth Devaluation," *Barron's Market Week*, 18 December 2000, 10.

CHAPTER SEVEN: BEYOND INDIFFERENCE

1. Reflecting the realist view of American interests in the developing world, Owen Harries, editor of the *National Review,* writes, "Now that the United States is not engaged in a global struggle against a serious enemy, huge tracts of the world that used to be regarded as important may be viewed with geo-political indifference...." "Fourteen Points for Realists," *National Interest,* no. 30 (1992–93): 110.

2. John Quincy Adams remarked in 1821, "I have not seen and do not now see any prospect that the [Latins] will establish free and liberal institutions of government.... There is no community of interests or of principles between North and South America." Quoted in Walter A. McDougall, *Promised Land, Crusader State: The American Encounter with the World since 1770* (Boston: Houghton Mifflin, 1997), 67. As Peter H. Smith writes, "the fundamental determinants of United States–Latin American relations have been the role and activity of *extrahemispheric* actors, not the United States or Latin America itself." *Talons of the Eagle: Dynamics of US–Latin American Relations* (New York: Oxford University Press, 1996), 7. See also Lester D. Langley, *The Americas in the Age of Revolution, 1750–1850* (New Haven: Yale University Press, 1996); Howard J. Wiarda, *Democracy and Its Discontents: Development, Independence, and U.S. Policy in Latin America* (Lanham: Rowman and Littlefield, 1995).

3. In reference to the Dominican Republic, John Kennedy formulated the dilemma best: "There are three possibilities, in descending order of preference: a decent democratic regime, a continuation of the Trujillo [authoritarian] regime, or a Castro [communist] regime. We ought to aim at the first, but we can't really renounce the second until we are sure we can avoid the third." Quoted in Arthur M. Schlesinger Jr., *A Thousand Days: John F. Kennedy in the White House* (Boston: Houghton Mifflin, 1965), 769. See also Abraham F. Lowenthal, ed., *Exporting Democracy: The United States and Latin America* (Baltimore: Johns Hopkins University Press, 1991).

4. In a comprehensive study of U.S. involvement in Nicaragua from 1977–90, Robert Kagan catalogues how the Sandinista government repeatedly formulated policies to oppose the United States rather than to serve its own best interests. See Robert Kagan, *A Twilight Struggle: American Power and Nicaragua, 1977–1990* (New York: Free Press, 1996). Robert A. Pastor agrees and points out that Panama and Costa Rica exerted considerable influence because they did not oppose but altered U.S. aims. See Robert A. Pastor, *Whirlpool: U.S. Foreign Policy toward Latin America and the Caribbean* (Princeton: Princeton University Press, 1992), 16–17. Cuba also bases its foreign policies on little more than opposition to the United States. See Jorge I. Dominguez, "Cuba in the International Community in the 1990s: Sovereignty, Human Rights, and Democracy," in *Beyond Sovereignty: Collectively Defending Democracy in the Americas,* ed. Tom Farer (Baltimore: Johns Hopkins University Press, 1996), 297–316. Latin American opposition to the United States is understandable, to be sure. As Peter H. Smith writes, "for weaker participants in an unequal world, nationalism may be one of the few options available." *Talons of the Eagle,* 8–9. But there is a difference between understanding the roots of anti-U.S. nationalism in Latin America and endorsing it as a viable policy option that has some chance of liberating Latin American from the psychological yoke of the United States.

5. Samuel P. Huntington notes the importance of changes in the declarations of the Catholic Church for democratic openings in southern Europe and Latin America. See Samuel P. Huntington, *The Third Wave: Democratization in the Late Twentieth Century* (Norman: University of Oklahoma Press, 1991).

6. On the similarities and links between democratic transitions in Europe and Latin America, see Juan J. Linz and Alfred Stepan, *Problems of Democratic Transition and Consolidation: Southern Europe, South America, and Post-Communist Europe* (Baltimore: Johns Hopkins University Press, 1996); Jorge G. Casteneda, *Utopia Unarmed: The Latin American Left after the Cold War* (New York: Alfred A. Knopf, 1993).

7. As Abraham F. Lowenthal and Jorge I. Dominguez conclude, "effective democratic governance—the daily practice of constitutional rule under law with stable political institutions that mediate among power contenders, restrain the dominant, and protect the weak—is far from consolidated; in many countries it is not even gaining strength. In fact, effective

democratic governance has yet to be constructed in most countries of the region." "Introduction: Constructing Democratic Governance," in *Constructing Democratic Governance: Latin America and the Caribbean in the 1990s*, ed. Jorge I. Dominguez and Abraham F. Lowenthal (Baltimore: Johns Hopkins University Press, 1996), 3.

8. This discussion of Latin American democracy draws on, among others, two excellent books commissioned by the Inter-American Dialogue: Jorge I. Dominguez and Abraham F. Lowenthal, eds., *Constructing Democratic Governance: Latin America and the Caribbean in the 1990s* (Baltimore: Johns Hopkins University Press, 1996); Tom Farer, ed., *Beyond Sovereignty: Collectively Defending Democracy in the Americas* (Baltimore: Johns Hopkins University Press, 1996). See also Larry Diamond, Juan J. Linz, and Seymour Martin Lipset, eds., *Democracy in Developing Countries: Latin America* (Boulder: Lynne Rienner, 1989); Guillermo O'Donnell, "Delegative Democracy?" *Journal of Democracy* 5, no. 1 (1994): 55–69; Larry Diamond, "Is the Third Wave Over?" *Journal of Democracy* 7, no. 3 (1996): 20–38.

9. See Tom Farer, "Collectively Defending Democracy in the Western Hemisphere," in *Beyond Sovereignty: Collectively Defending Democracy in the Americas*, ed. Tom Farer (Baltimore: Johns Hopkins University Press, 1996), 2.

10. For an assessment of democracy in Latin America in early 2001, see Peter Hakim, "The Uneasy Americas," *Foreign Affairs* 80, no. 2 (2001):46–62.

11. Latin American legislatures also suffer from severe malapportionment. A wide discrepancy exists between the share of legislative seats and the share of population in individual electoral districts. See Richard Snyder and David Samuels, "Devaluing the Vote in Latin America," *Journal of Democracy* 12, no. 1 (2001): 146–60.

12. See Diamond, "Is the Third Wave Over?" 29.

13. See article 5(d) of the OAS charter in Ann Van Wynen Thomas and A. J. Thomas Jr., *The Organization of American States* (Dallas: Southern Methodist University Press, 1963), 414.

14. See Viron L. Vaky and Heraldo Muñoz, *The Future of the Organization of American States* (New York: The Twentieth Century Fund Press, 1993), app. 2, 108; Dominigo E. Acevedo and Claudia Grossman, "The Organization of American States and the Promotion of Democracy," in *Beyond Sovereignty: Collectively Defending Democracy in the Americas*, ed. Tom Farer (Baltimore: Johns Hopkins University Press, 1996), 132–50.

15. Passed in 1995, the Helms-Burton Act mandates sanctions on non-U.S. firms that invest in expropriated U.S. property in Cuba.

16. For recommendations to pursue a more multilateral approach in Colombia, see Council on Foreign Relations and Inter-American Dialogue, *Toward Greater Peace and Security in Colombia: Forging a Constructive U.S. Policy* (New York: Council on Foreign Relations Press, 2000). This is the report of an independent task force, Bob Graham and Brent Scowcroft, co-chairs; Michael Shifter, project director.

17. See Vaky and Muñoz, *Future of the Organization of American States*, 20–22. The Inter-American Defense Board exists separately from the OAS. Established in 1942, it brings together the military leadership of the United States and Latin America, but it reports directly to national defense ministries, not the OAS, and is chaired and seen to be dominated by the United States.

18. See Jorge G. Casteneda, "Democracy and Inequality in Latin America: A Tension for the Times," in *Constructing Democratic Governance: Latin America and the Caribbean in the 1990s*, ed. Jorge I. Dominguez and Abraham F. Lowenthal (Baltimore: Johns Hopkins University Press, 1996), 42–64.

19. The adoption of import substitution policies was a choice, not a necessity. Asian countries from the beginning were less inclined to adopt such policies, preferring rural-based agricultural reforms and more export-oriented industrial strategies. See Joan M. Nelson, ed., *Economic Crisis and Policy Adjustment: The Politics of Adjustment in the Third World* (Princeton: Princeton University Press, 1990), 38.

20. Within a half century, Latin America's population went from 70 percent rural and illiterate to 70 percent urban and literate. See Wiarda, *Democracy and Its Discontents*, 263.

21. Hernando de Soto exposes the pernicious effects of local restrictions on entrepreneurial and business activities that drove the urban masses into an encapsulated, albeit highly dynamic, informal sector operating without the protection of law. See Hernando de Soto, *The Mystery of Capital* (New York: Basic Books, 2000).

22. For a helpful account, see Paul E. Sigmund, *The United States and Democracy in Chile* (Baltimore: Johns Hopkins University Press, 1993).

23. For an informative account of Mexico's transformation, see Pedro Aspe, *Economic Transformation the Mexican Way* (Cambridge, Mass.: MIT Press, 1993). Aspe is a former finance minister in Mexico who was involved in the transformation.

24. As Sidney Weintraub notes, "just about all the arguments about the trade balance and job loss and creation [during the NAFTA debate] are rubbish." *NAFTA at Three: A Progress Report* (Washington, D.C.: Center for Strategic and International Studies, 1997), 5.

25. For one of the most detailed studies, see Stephen S. Golub, *Labor Costs and International Trade* (Washington, D.C.: American Enterprise Institute, 1999).

26. See Ellen L. Frost, "Gaining Support for Trade from the American Public," in *Trade Strategies for a New Era: Ensuring U.S. Leadership in a Global Economy,* ed. Geza Feketekuty and Bruce Stokes (New York: Council on Foreign Relations and Monterey Institute of International Studies, 1998), 66.

27. In 1999, Argentina and Brazil exported 11.3 and 22.5 percent of their exports to the United States, respectively, while Mexico and Canada exported 88.3 and 87.6 percent, respectively. See *Direction of Trade Statistics Yearbook 1999* (Washington, D.C.: International Monetary Fund, 2000).

28. Three of the top four oil suppliers to the United States in 2000 were Mexico, Canada, and Venezuela. In 2000, the United States imported 26.5 percent of total crude oil imports from the Persian Gulf; in 1977, it imported 36.5 percent.

29. For a critique of U.S. intervention along these lines, see Robert W. Tucker and David Hendrickson, *The Imperial Temptation* (New York: Council on Foreign Relations Press, 1992).

30. Bernard Lewis, *Islam and the West* (New York: Oxford University Press, 1993).

31. See Samuel P. Huntington, "The Clash of Civilizations?" *Foreign Affairs* 72, no. 3 (1993): 22–50; Samuel P. Huntington, *The Clash of Civilizations and the Remaking of World Order* (New York: Simon and Schuster, 1996).

32. For a review of the earlier diplomacy, see William B. Quandt, *Peace Process: American Diplomacy and the Arab-Israeli Conflict since 1967,* rev. ed. (Washington, D.C.: Brookings Institution, 2001).

33. Key to this struggle in Israel is immigration patterns. In the late 1950s and 1960s, immigrants to Israel were largely Ashkenazi Jews from western states, who are more secular. After 1970, the majority were Sephardic Jews from North Africa and the Middle East, who are more fundamentalist. (Israeli immigration in the 1990s was massive, about 400,000 immigrants per year in a country of 6.2 million people, the equivalent of 20 million immigrants per year in the United States.) Today, the two forces are almost perfectly balanced in Israeli politics, as evidenced by the repeated swings in the 1990s between Likud governments with more sectarian supporters and Labor governments with more secular groups.

34. For an eclectic mix of views on the politics of various countries in the Middle East, see Michael Field, *Inside the Arab World* (Cambridge, Mass.: Harvard University Press, 1995); William R. Polk, *The Arab World Today* (Cambridge, Mass.: Harvard University Press, 1991); Milton Viorst, *Sandcastles: The Arab in Search of the Modern World* (New York: Alfred A. Knopf, 1994); Fouad Ajami, *The Vanished Imam: Musa al Sadr and the Shia of Lebanon* (Ithaca: Cornell University Press, 1986); F. Gregory Gause III, *Oil Monarchies: Domestic and Security Challenges in the Arab Gulf States* (New York: Council on Foreign Relations Press, 1994); Emmanuel Sivan, "Constraints and Opportunities in the Arab World," *Journal of Democracy* 8, no. 2 (1997): 103–14; Iliya Harik, "Pluralism in the Arab World," *Journal of Democracy* 5, no. 3 (1994): 43–57.

35. Lewis, *Islam and the West,* 186. Lewis's view is controversial. For other opinions, see Dale F. Eichelman and James Piscatori, *Muslim Politics* (Princeton: Princeton University Press, 1996); John L. Esposito and John O. Voll, *Islam and Democracy* (New York: Oxford University Press, 1997); John L. Esposito, *The Islamic Threat: Myth or Reality?* (New York: Oxford University Press, 1993).

36. Field, *Inside the Arab World,* 256.

37. The same may also be true of orthodox fundamentalism in the Jewish tradition. See Amors Elon, "Israel and the End of Zionism," *New York Times Magazine,* 19 December 1996, pp. 22–30.

For an intriguing study of one Islamic cleric who some believe may fulfill the role of Martin Luther in Islam, see Valla Vakil, *Debating Religion and Politics in Iran: The Political Thought of Abdolkarim Sorousch,* Occasional Paper Series no. 2 (New York: Council on Foreign Relations Press, 1996).

38. Lewis, *Islam and the West,* 31.

39. Fouad Ajami, *The Arab Predicament: Arab Political Thought and Practice since 1967,* rev. ed., (Cambridge, U.K.: Cambridge University Press, 1992), 26.

40. Quoted in ibid.

41. "Good Fences" was a 1976 project on the Lebanese border that ensured Israeli defense positions while opening up border clinics to help the people of southern Lebanon. See Shimon Peres, *Battling for Peace: A Memoir* (New York: Random House, 1995), 193. On identity and military balances in the Middle East, see Michael N. Barnett, "Identity and Alliances in the Middle East," in *The Culture of National Security: Norms and Identity in World Politics,* ed. Peter Katzenstein (New York: Columbia University Press, 1996), 400–447.

42. A U.S. Navy arrangement with Bahrain dates back to the late 1940s. The United States pre-positions planes and other equipment in Kuwait and Saudi Arabia and has port access and facilities in Qatar, the United Arab Emirates, and Oman. U.S. warships patrol the Persian Gulf.

43. The six Arab Gulf states created the Gulf Cooperation Council in 1981 in response to the Iran-Iraq war. Some of the Gulf states have border disputes with one another, and the smaller ones resent Saudi hegemony. After the Gulf War, Egypt and Syria, both of whom supported the U.S. attack against Iraq, volunteered to station military forces in the Persian Gulf, but neither the United States nor the Gulf states pressed to have this Damascus Plan realized.

44. For arguments supporting dual containment, see Anthony Lake, "Confronting Backlash States," *Foreign Affairs* 73, no. 2 (1994): 45–46; Daniel Byman, Kenneth Pollack, and Gideon Rose, "The Rollback Fantasy," *Foreign Affairs* 78, no. 1 (1999): 24–42.

45. See various contributions in Geoffrey Kemp and Janice Gross Stein, eds., *Powder Keg in the Middle East: The Struggle for Gulf Security* (Lanham: Rowman and Littlefield, 1995). See also F. Gregory Gause III, "The Illogic of Dual Containment," *Foreign Affairs* 73, no. 2 (1994): 56–57.

46. For the hard-line view against Iraq, see William Kristol and Robert Kagan, "Bombing Iraq Isn't Enough," *New York Times,* 30 January 1998, p. A21. For the soft-line view against Iran, see Zbigniew Brzezinski, Brent Scowcroft, and Richard Murphy, "Differentiated Containment," *Foreign Affairs* 76, no. 3 (1997): 20–31.

47. On Europe's role in the Middle East, see Roy H. Ginsberg, *The European Union in International Politics: Baptism by Fire* (Lanham: Rowman and Littlefield, 2001).

48. The biggest U.S. contribution came with victory in the Cold War and then the Gulf War, which initiated the multilateral peace process in Madrid in 1991. The United States had virtually no direct role in the Oslo peace accords between Israel and the Palestinians in 1993 or the Israeli-Jordan peace treaty in 1994. The United States was more significant in salvaging the talks at various points, such as in 1997–98, and in pressing toward a final settlement in 1999–2000. But talks stalled in part because U.S. proposals went beyond what the parties were ready or able to accept.

49. Patrick Clawson, "US-GCC Security Relations, II: Growing Domestic Economic and Political Problems," *National Defense University Strategic Forum* no. 40 (1995).

50. Phebe Marr, "US-GCC Security Relations, I: Differing Threat Perceptions," *National Defense University Strategic Forum,* no. 39 (1995). Most arms purchases came in the early 1990s, with deliveries taking place in the late 1990s. See Anthony H. Cordesman, "The New Balance of Gulf Arms," *Middle East Policy* 6, no. 4 (1999): 80–104.

51. Some countries, particularly Syria and Lebanon, boycotted these talks. The discussion here relies heavily on Dalia Dassa Kaye, *Beyond the Handshake: Multilateral Cooperation in the Arab-Israeli Peace Process, 1991–1996* (New York: Columbia University Press, 2001). See also Bruce Jentleson, "The Middle East Arms Control and Regional Security Talks: Progress, Problems and Prospects," Institute on Global Conflict and Cooperation Policy Paper 26, University of California at San Diego, 1996.

52. See Dassa Kaye, *Beyond the Handshake,* 38.

53. Leila Farsakh, "Under Siege: Closure, Separation and the Palestinian Economy," *Middle East Report* 30, no. 4 (2000): 22–25.

54. World Bank, *World Development Indicators 2001* (Washington, D.C.: World Bank, 2001).

55. Basil Davidson, *The Search for Africa: History, Culture, Politics* (New York: Times Books, 1994). The number of black slaves transported to the Western Hemisphere is disputed, but conservative estimates range from 10 to 15 million. The vast majority (90 percent) went to the West Indies and South America. (Brazil today has a population that is 45 percent black.) On the eve of the Civil War, blacks numbered about 4 million out of a population of 37 million in the United States. See Peter Duignan and L. H. Gann, *The United States and Africa: A History* (Cambridge, U.K.: Cambridge University Press, 1984).

56. The income growth calculation is made on the basis of purchasing power parity rates of currency exchange. See World Bank, *World Development Report 1992: Development and the Environment* (Oxford: Oxford University Press, 1992).

57. Recent research demonstrates how foreign aid in many instances encouraged bad domestic policies (such as increased government spending and deficits) and generally poor economic performance. See World Bank, *Assessing Aid: What Works, What Doesn't and Why?* (New York: Oxford University Press, 1998); Michael O'Hanlon and Carol Graham, *A Half Penny on the Federal Dollar: The Future of Development Aid* (Washington, D.C.: Brookings Institution, 1997); David Dollar and Craig Burnside, "Aid, Policies, and Growth," Policy Research Paper 1777, World Bank, Washington, D.C., 1997.

58. As Stephen McCarthy comments on the Tanzanian experience and its leader, Julius Nyerere, "the forced movement of people and the authoritarian top-down imposition of a particular mode of production, which the government-sponsored Ujamaa villages came to be, was clearly a development disaster, the very antithesis of the people-centered development philosophy which Nyerere liked to proclaim." *Africa: The Challenge of Transformation* (London: I. B. Tauris, 1994), xiv.

59. David Lamb, *The Africans* (New York: Vintage, 1987), 9. Tribe is not the same as kin or clan. Historically the basic unit of identity in Africa has been kinship. A clan might embrace a somewhat wider circle. The tribe or ethnic group is a still larger social grouping based on common language and customs. All three of these groupings remain important in contemporary Africa. See McCarthy, *Africa*, 196–98.

60. In 1998, sixteen African nations were involved in some form of internal conflict, spawning an estimated 6–7 million refugees. On the pervasive role of the military, see John W. Harbeson, ed., *The Military in African Politics* (New York: Praeger, 1987).

61. See Francis M. Deng, Sadikiel Kimaro, Terrence Lyons, Donald Rothchild, and I. William Zartman, *Sovereignty as Responsibility: Conflict Management in Africa* (Washington, D.C.: Brookings Institution, 1996).

62. See William E. Odom, "Intervention for the Long Run: Rethinking the Definition of War," *Harvard International Review* 22, no. 4 (2001): 48–53.

63. See Alan J. Kuperman, *The Limits of Humanitarian Intervention: Genocide in Rwanda* (Washington, D.C.: Brookings Institution, 2001).

64. See David R. Smock and Chester A. Crocker, eds., *African Conflict Resolution: The U.S. Role in Peacemaking* (Washington, D.C.: United States Institute of Peace Press, 1995). See also Yassin El-Ayouty, ed., *The Organization of African Unity after Thirty Years* (Westport: Praeger, 1994).

65. Several subregional organizations are active in various African conflicts. The Economic Community of Western African States (ECOWAS) has provided diplomatic mediation and troops (principally from Nigeria and Ghana) in the conflict in Liberia. An ECOWAS force led by Nigeria intervened in Sierra Leone in 1998 to restore the democratically elected government. The Intergovernmental Authority on Drought and Development (IGADD) in east Africa has facilitated negotiations between the warring parties in Sudan. The Southern Africa Development Community (SADC) brings together the ten states of southern Africa to focus on political reconciliation and economic development in the postapartheid era.

66. See Donald G. McNeil Jr., "Burundi Army Stages Coup, and New Fighting Is Feared," *New York Times*, 26 July 1996, p. A3.

67. Thomas W. Lippman, "U.S. Presses for All-Africa Crisis Force," *Washington Post*, 28 September 1996, p. 1. African leaders had proposed a similar force in 1991, calling for a Con-

ference on Security, Stability, Development and Cooperation in Africa (CSSDCA) to organize continental peacekeeping initiatives. See Smock and Crocker, *African Conflict Resolution,* 7, 97, 109–10.

68. In 2001, the United States provided transport, communication, and other logistical support for Nigerian forces in Sierra Leone, and it trained peacekeeping troops in Senegal, Malawi, and Uganda.

69. Stephen McCarthy reaches a similar conclusion. See McCarthy, *Africa,* 196–200.

70. One suggestion for the Rwanda-Burundi conflicts, after stability is restored, is to encourage closer cooperation among Rwanda, Burundi, Tanzania, and Uganda, allowing Hutu-Tutsi rivalries to play out in a more pluralistic environment. See Ali A. Mazrui, "The African State as a Political Refugee," *International Journal of Refugee Law* 7, special issue (1995): 21–36.

71. See Claude Ake, "Rethinking African Democracy," in *The Global Resurgence of Democracy,* ed. Larry Diamond and Mark F. Plattner (Baltimore: Johns Hopkins University Press, 1993), 70–83.

72. For a list and analysis of the elections discussed here and in subsequent paragraphs, see John A. Wiseman, *The New Struggle for Democracy in Africa* (Brookfield: Ashgate, 1996), 107–42; Larry Diamond and Marc F. Plattner, eds., *Democratization in Africa* (Baltimore: Johns Hopkins University Press, 1999), especially chaps. 1 and 2.

73. See Fareed Zakaria, "The Rise of Illiberal Democracy," *Foreign Affairs* 76, no. 6 (1997): 22–44.

74. Kofi Annan, "An Africa Responsible for Itself," *Washington Post,* 29 April 1998, p. A21.

75. See "Botswana," in *Freedom in the World 1999–2000* (New York: Freedom House, 2000), 93–95.

76. This is also the conclusion of a study by the World Bank, *Can Africa Claim the 21st Century?* (Washington, D.C.: World Bank, 2000), especially chap. 2.

77. Michael Cox, G. John Ikenberry, and Takashi Inoguchi, eds., *American Democracy Promotion: Impulses, Strategies, and Impacts* (New York: Oxford University Press, 2000).

78. Lamb, *Africans,* xiv.

79. See Anupam Basu, Evangelos A. Calamitsis, and Dhaneshwar Ghura, *Promoting Growth in Sub-Saharan Africa* (Washington, D.C.: International Monetary Fund, 2000); Council on Foreign Relations, *Promoting U.S. Economic Relations with Africa,* Task Force Report (New York: Council on Foreign Relations, 1998). For a balanced assessment of the role of government in development, see Deepak Lal and H. Myint, *The Political Economy of Poverty, Equity and Growth* (Oxford: Clarendon Press, 1997).

80. See Jagdish Bhagwati and Arvind Panagariya, "A Trojan Horse for Africa," *Financial Times,* 20 June 2000, p. 13. This judgment by Bhagwati and Panagariya may be too harsh. Despite continuing restrictions and slower U.S. growth, U.S. imports from African countries covered by the bill rose 24 percent in the first quarter of 2001 compared to the same period in 2000. See Robert B. Zoellick, "Trade Helps Africans Help Themselves," *Wall Street Journal,* 23 May 2001, p. A26.

81. See World Bank, *Can Africa Claim the 21st Century?* 20.

CONCLUSION: AMERICAN FOREIGN POLICY IN THE
TWENTY-FIRST CENTURY

1. The best-known argument along these lines is Paul Kennedy, *The Rise and Fall of the Great Powers* (New York: Random House, 1987). See also Robert Gilpin, *The Political Economy of International Relations* (Princeton: Princeton University Press, 1987); Robert Gilpin, *War and Change in World Politics* (Cambridge, U.K. Cambridge University Press, 1981).

2. Paul Kennedy, for example, dismisses motivational and ideological factors: "if these features are hardly mentioned here, it is because many societies in their time have thrown up individuals and groups willing to dare all and do anything in order to make the world their oyster. What distinguished the captains, crews, and explorers of Europe was that they possessed the ships and the firepower with which to achieve their ambitions, and that they

came from a political environment in which competition, risk, and entrepreneurship were prevalent." What counted, in other words, were capabilities, not intentions, motivations, purposes, ideologies, and so on. And, although these capabilities came out of a political environment of competition, risk and entrepreneurship, Kennedy does not study this non-material source of power. Kennedy, *Rise and Fall*, 27–28.

3. Ibid., 538.

4. Ibid., 441.

5. See Henry Kissinger, *Diplomacy* (New York: Simon and Schuster, 1994).

6. See Henry R. Nau, *The Myth of America's Decline: Leading the World Economy into the 1990s* (New York: Oxford University Press, 1990); Joseph S. Nye Jr., *Bound to Lead: The Changing Nature of American Power* (New York: Basic Books, 1990).

7. This is the argument I lay out in my *Myth of America's Decline*.

8. Exogenous forces explain change in traditional studies. See Kennedy, *Rise and Fall*, xv; Gilpin, *Political Economy of International Relations*, chap. 3.

9. As we note in chapter 2, Henry Kissinger argues that, after a century of ideological struggle, the world is returning to the traditional, historically grounded, culturally motivated, equilibrium-based world of the nineteenth century. See Kissinger, *Diplomacy*, chaps. 1, 31.

10. Here I agree with my colleague Ernst B. Haas, who expresses an unshakable faith in human progress. He and I disagree, however, on the relative role of market versus government initiatives to achieve such progress. See Ernst B. Haas, *Nationalism, Liberalism, and Progress* 2 vols. (Ithaca: Cornell University Press, 1997). See also a volume dedicated to Haas, Emmanuel Adler and Beverly Crawford, eds., *Progress in Postwar International Relations* (New York: Columbia University Press, 1991).

11. The public views Japan as more important to the United States than China (47 vs. 28 percent). Elites in the United States, on the other hand, consider Japan and China to be equally important (48 vs. 47 percent). See John E. Rielly, ed., *American Public Opinion and U.S. Foreign Policy 1999* (Chicago: Chicago Council on Foreign Relations, 1999), 5.

12. Kissinger puts good U.S.-Chinese relations at the top of this triangle: "Good American relations with China are therefore the prerequisite for good long-term relations with Japan, as well as for good Sino-Japanese relations." *Diplomacy*, 829. I reverse these priorities and argue that good U.S.-Japanese relations are the prerequisite for good U.S.-Chinese and Chinese-Japanese relations.

13. The terms in quotations are from ibid., 828. In a later book, in which Kissinger recognizes that relations among democracies are different, he excludes Japan entirely from the democratic world and argues that "any resemblance between Japanese and Western political institutions is usually largely superficial." *Does America Need a Foreign Policy? Diplomacy in the 21st Century* (New York: Simon and Schuster, 2001), 120.

14. Admittedly, interest group politics accounts for some of this cycling. But in the case of U.S. policies toward China, elites, not interest groups, may be the stronger cause. Elite analysis could benefit from a more comprehensive and consistent identity and power approach.

Index

Note: Page numbers followed by letters *f*, *n*, and *t* refer to figures, notes, and tables, respectively.

Cornell Studies in Political Economy

A series edited by Peter J. Katzenstein

Monetary Sovereignty: The Politics of Central Banking in Western Europe
by John B. Goodman

Politics in Hard Times: Comparative Responses to International Economic Crises
by Peter Gourevitch

Cooperation among Nations: Europe, America, and Non-Tariff Barriers to Trade
by Joseph M. Grieco

Nationalism, Liberalism, and Progress, Volume I: The Rise and Decline of Nationalism
Volume II: The Dismal Fate of New Nations
by Ernst B. Haas

Pathways from the Periphery: The Politics of Growth in the Newly Industrializing Countries
by Stephan Haggard

The Politics of Finance in Developing Countries
edited by Stephan Haggard, Chung H. Lee, and Sylvia Maxfield

Rival Capitalists: International Competitiveness in the United States, Japan, and
Western Europe
by Jeffrey A. Hart

Reasons of State: Oil Politics and the Capacities of American Government
by G. John Ikenberry

The State and American Foreign Economic Policy
edited by G. John Ikenberry, David A. Lake, and Michael Mastanduno

The Nordic States and European Unity
by Christine Ingebritsen

The Paradox of Continental Production: National Investment Policies in North America
by Barbara Jenkins

The Government of Money: Monetarism in Germany and the United States
by Peter A. Johnson

Corporatism and Change: Austria, Switzerland, and the Politics of Industry
by Peter J. Katzenstein

Cultural Norms and National Security: Police and Military in Postwar Japan
by Peter J. Katzenstein

Small States in World Markets: Industrial Policy in Europe
by Peter J. Katzenstein

Industry and Politics in West Germany: Toward the Third Republic
edited by Peter J. Katzenstein

Norms in International Relations: The Struggle against Apartheid
by Audie Jeanne Klotz

International Regimes
edited by Stephen D. Krasner

Disparaged Success: Labor Politics in Postwar Japan
by Ikuo Kume

Business and Banking: Political Change and Economic Integration in Western Europe
by Paulette Kurzer

"Rich Nation, Strong Army": National Security and the Technological Transformation of Japan
    by Richard J. Samuels
Crisis and Choice in European Social Democracy
    by Fritz W. Scharpf, translated by Ruth Crowley and Fred Thompson
Winners and Losers: How Sectors Shape the Developmental Prospects of States
    by D. Michael Shafer
Ideas and Institutions: Developmentalism in Brazil and Argentina
    by Kathryn Sikkink
The Cooperative Edge: The Internal Politics of International Cartels
    by Debora L. Spar
The Hidden Hand of American Hegemony: Petrodollar Recycling and International Markets
    by David E. Spiro
The Origins of Nonliberal Capitalism: Germany and Japan in Comparison
    edited by Wolfgang Streeck and Kozo Yamamura
Fair Shares: Unions, Pay, and Politics in Sweden and West Germany
    by Peter Swenson
Union of Parts: Labor Politics in Postwar Germany
    by Kathleen Thelen
Democracy at Work: Changing World Markets and the Future of Labor Unions
    by Lowell Turner
Fighting for Partnership: Labor and Politics in Unified Germany
    by Lowell Turner
Troubled Industries: Confronting Economic Change in Japan
    by Robert M. Uriu
National Styles of Regulation: Environmental Policy in Great Britain and the United States
    by David Vogel
Freer Markets, More Rules: Regulatory Reform in Advanced Industrial Countries
    by Steven K. Vogel
The Political Economy of Policy Coordination: International Adjustment since 1945
    by Michael C. Webb
The Myth of the Powerless State
    by Linda Weiss
The Developmental State
    edited by Meredith Woo-Cumings
International Cooperation: Building Regimes for Natural Resources and the Environment
    by Oran R. Young
International Governance: Protecting the Environment in a Stateless Society
    by Oran R. Young
Polar Politics: Creating International Environmental Regimes
    edited by Oran R. Young and Gail Osherenko
Governments, Markets, and Growth: Financial Systems and the Politics of Industrial Change
    by John Zysman
American Industry in International Competition: Government Policies and Corporate Strategies
    edited by John Zysman and Laura Tyson